The Haynes General Motors Automatic Transmission Overhaul Manual

by Eric Godfrey and John H Haynes

Member of the Guild of Motoring Writers

Models covered:

THM200-4R, THM350, THM400 and THM700-R4 - Rear Wheel Drive Transmissions

THM 125/125C, THM 3T40, THM 440-T4 and THM 4T60 Front Wheel Drive Transaxles

Does not include the electronic THM700-R4 (4L60-E) or the THM 440-T4 (4T60-E)

(9U6 - 10360)

ABCDE
FGHIJ
KLMNO
PQR
2

Haynes Publishing Group
Sparkford Nr Yeovil
Somerset BA22 7JJ England

Haynes North America, Inc
859 Lawrence Drive
Newbury Park
California 91320 USA
www.haynes.com

Acknowledgements

We are grateful to B&M Racing and Performance Products for allowing us to photograph some of the transmission overhaul procedures at their facility. Thanks to Automotive Transmission Parts Inc. for providing us with some of the parts used in the repair and modifications chapters.

Special thanks to Brian Applegate, Randy Cannon and Jim Rose of B&M Racing and Performance Products for their help, cooperation and technical expertise provided in producing this manual.

Special thanks to Craig Calkins and Todd Otis of CRC Performance Transmissions in Thousand Oaks, CA and to Jeff Watson and Jim Rose of Champion Transmissions of Thousand Oaks, CA for their help, cooperation and technical expertise in producing this manual.

Also contributing to this manual were Mike Forsythe, Jeff Killingsworth, Bob Henderson and Jeff Kibler

---

A book in the Haynes Automotive Repair Manual Series

Printed in Malaysia

ISBN 1 56392 423 4

Library of Congress Catalog Card Number 95-80972

Contents

Notes

Chapter 1   Introduction

How to use this repair manual

The manual is divided into Chapters. Each Chapter is sub-divided into Sections, some of which consist of consecutively numbered Paragraphs (usually referred to as "Steps", since they're normally part of a procedure). If the material is basically informative in nature, rather than a step-by-step procedure, the Paragraphs aren't numbered.

The first six Chapters contain material on tools and equipment, identification, theory and fundamentals of automatic transmissions, as well as troubleshooting and in-vehicle repairs. Chapters 7 and 8 cover the specifics of the overhaul procedure, beginning with removing the transmission from the vehicle. Chapter 9 discusses simple transmission modifications you can perform at home.

The term "**see illustration**" (in parentheses), is used in the text to indicate that a photo or drawing has been included to make the information easier to understand (the old cliché "a picture is worth a thousand words" is especially true when it comes to how-to procedures). Also, every attempt is made to position illustrations directly opposite the corresponding text to minimize confusion. The two types of illustrations used (photographs and line drawings) are referenced by a number preceding the caption. Illustration numbers denote Chapter and numerical sequence within the Chapter (i.e., 3.4 means Chapter 3, illustration number four in order).

The terms "**Note**", "**Caution**", and "**Warning**" are used throughout the text with a specific purpose in mind - to attract the reader's attention. A "**Note**" simply provides information required to properly complete a procedure or information which will make the procedure easier to understand. A "**Caution**" outlines a special procedure or special steps which must be taken when completing the procedure where the "**Caution**" is found. Failure to pay attention to a "**Caution**" can result in damage to the component being repaired or the tools being used. A "**Warning**" is included where personal injury can result if the instructions aren't followed exactly as described.

Even though extreme care has been taken during the preparation of this manual, neither the publisher nor the author can accept responsibility for any errors in, or omissions from, the information given.

What is an overhaul?

A transmission overhaul involves restoring the internal parts to the specifications of a new transmission. During an overhaul, the clutches, bands, bushings, seals and gaskets are routinely replaced. The parts needed for a typical overhaul are generally included in overhaul kits available from transmission parts manufacturers. Additionally, all other parts in the transmission are carefully inspected for damage and excessive wear. Any marginal parts must be replaced. Generally, the torque converter is replaced as well, since it's usually in less-than-perfect condition at this point.

It's not always easy to determine when, or if, a transmission should be completely overhauled, as a number of factors must be considered.

High mileage is not necessarily an indication that an overhaul is needed, while low mileage doesn't preclude the need for an overhaul. Frequency of servicing is probably the most important consideration. A transmission in a vehicle that's been driven normally and had frequent fluid and filter changes, as well as other required maintenance, will most likely give many thousands of miles of reliable service. Conversely, a neglected and abused transmission may require an overhaul very early in its life. Slippage and noises often indicate serious transmission problems, but could also have simple remedies. A low fluid level can often give symptoms just like those of a failing transmission. Before determining your transmission needs an overhaul, refer to the troubleshooting information in Chapter 5.

Before beginning the transmission overhaul, read through this entire manual to familiarize yourself with the scope and requirements of the job. Overhauling a transmission isn't particularly difficult if you have the correct equipment; however, it is time consuming. Plan on the vehicle being tied up for a minimum of two weeks, especially if parts must be ordered or reconditioned. Check on availability of parts and make sure that any necessary special tools and equipment are obtained in advance. Most work can be done with typical hand tools, although precision measuring tools are required for inspecting parts to determine if they must be replaced. Also, special tools such as those for compressing clutch packs are usually required. Chapter 2 contains information on special tools.

Buying parts

Commonly replaced transmission parts such as clutches, bands, seals and bushings are produced by aftermarket manufacturers and stocked by retail auto parts stores and mail order houses, usually at a savings over dealer parts department prices. Many auto parts stores and mail order houses offer complete transmission overhaul kits, often at a considerable savings over individual parts. Don't buy gaskets separately. A good-quality complete gasket set will save you money and the needless hassle of buying individual gaskets.

Less-commonly replaced items such as planetary gearsets, drums and transmission cases may not be available through these same sources and a dealer parts department may be your only option. Keep in mind that some parts will probably have to be ordered, and it may take several days to get your parts; order early.

Wrecking yards are a good source for major parts that would otherwise only be available through a dealer service department (where the price would likely be high). Transmission cases, planetary gearsets, etc. are commonly available for reasonable prices. Although, you must be very careful when selecting used parts. Running changes are often made during the model year and a newly designed component from a transmission of the same type may not be compatible with your transmission. To insure the used part will be an exact match, select a used transmission for your parts source with the same identification code as the one you're rebuilding. Then as a final precaution, visually compare the replacement part with the damaged component to make sure they are identical. The parts people at wrecking yards have parts interchange books they can use to quickly identify parts from other models and years that are the same as the ones on your transmission.

Chapter 2
Tools and equipment

A place to work

Establish a place to work. A special work area is essential. It doesn't have to be particularly large, but it should be clean, safe, well-lit, organized and adequately equipped for the job. True, without a good workshop or garage, you can still service and repair transmissions, even if you have to work outside. But an overhaul or major repairs should be carried out in a sheltered area with a roof. The procedures in this book require an environment totally free of dirt, which will cause wear or failure if it finds its way into the transmission.

The workshop

The size, shape and location of a shop building is usually dictated by circumstance rather than personal choice. Every do-it-yourselfer dreams of having a spacious, clean, well-lit building specially designed and equipped for working on everything from small engines on lawn and garden equipment to cars and other vehicles. In reality, however, most of us must content ourselves with a garage, basement or shed in the backyard.

Spend some time considering the potential - and drawbacks - of your current facility. Even a well-established workshop can benefit from intelligent design. Lack of space is the most common problem,

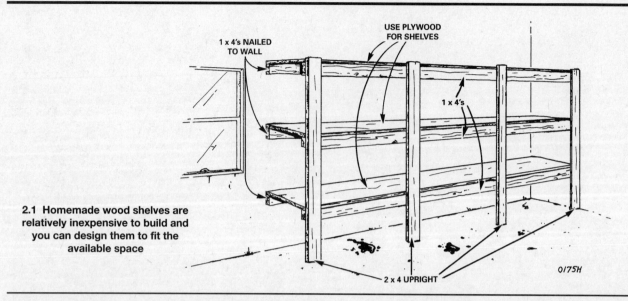

2.1 Homemade wood shelves are relatively inexpensive to build and you can design them to fit the available space

but you can significantly increase usable space by carefully planning the locations of work and storage areas. One strategy is to look at how others do it. Ask local repair shop owners if you can see their shops. Note how they've arranged their work areas, storage and lighting, then try to scale down their solutions to fit your own shop space, finances and needs.

General workshop requirements

A solid concrete floor is the best surface for a shop area. The floor should be even, smooth and dry. A coat of paint or sealant formulated for concrete surfaces will make oil spills and dirt easier to remove and help cut down on dust - always a problem with concrete.

Paint the walls and ceiling white for maximum reflection. Use gloss or semi-gloss enamel. It's washable and reflective. If your shop has windows, situate workbenches to take advantage of them. Skylights are even better. You can't have too much natural light. Artificial light is also good, but you'll need a lot of it to equal ordinary daylight.

Make sure the building is adequately ventilated. This is critical during the winter months, to prevent condensation problems. It's also a vital safety consideration where solvents, gasoline and other volatile liquids are being used. You should be able to open one or more windows for ventilation. In addition, opening vents in the walls are desirable.

Storage and shelves

Once disassembled, a transmission occupies more space than you might think. Set up an organized storage area to avoid losing parts. You'll also need storage space for hardware, lubricants, solvent, rags, tools and equipment.

If space and finances allow, install metal shelves along the walls. Arrange the shelves so they're widely spaced near the bottom to take large or heavy items. Metal shelf units are costly, but they make the best use of available space. And the shelf height is adjustable on most units.

Wood shelves **(see illustration)** are sometimes a cheaper storage solution. But they must be built - not just assembled. They must be much heftier than metal shelves to carry the same weight, the shelves can't be adjusted vertically and you can't just disassemble them and take them with you if you move. Wood also absorbs oil and other liquids and is obviously a much greater fire hazard.

Store small parts in plastic drawers or bins mounted on metal racks attached to the wall. They're available from most hardware, home and lumber stores. Bins come in various sizes and usually have slots for labels.

All kinds of containers are useful in a shop. Glass jars are handy for storing fasteners, but they're easily broken. Cardboard boxes are adequate for temporary use, but if they become damp, the bottoms

eventually weaken and fall apart if you store oily or heavy parts in them. Plastic containers come in a variety of sizes and colors for easy identification. Egg cartons are excellent organizers for small parts like bolts, springs and O-rings. Old metal cake pans, bread pans and muffin tins also make good storage containers for small parts.

Workbenches

A workbench is essential - it provides a place to lay out parts and tools during repair procedures, and it's a lot more comfortable than working on a floor or the driveway. The workbench should be as large and sturdy as space and finances allow. If cost is no object, buy industrial steel benches. They're more expensive than home-built benches, but they're very strong, they're easy to assemble, and - if you move - they can be disassembled quickly and you can take them with you. They're also available in various lengths, so you can buy the exact size to fill the space along a wall.

If steel benches aren't in the budget, fabricate a bench frame from slotted angle-iron or Douglas fir (use 2 x 6's rather than 2 x 4's) **(see illustration)**. Cut the pieces of the frame to the required size and bolt them together with carriage bolts. A 30 or 36 by 80-inch, solid-core door with hardboard surfaces makes a good bench top. And you can flip it over when one side is worn out.

An even cheaper - and quicker - solution? Assemble a bench by attaching the bench top frame pieces to the wall with angled braces and use the wall studs as part of the framework.

Regardless of the type of frame you decide to use for the workbench, be sure to position the bench top at a comfortable working height and make sure everything is level. Shelves installed below the bench will make it more rigid and provide useful storage space.

Tools and equipment

For some home mechanics, the idea of using the correct tool is completely foreign. They'll cheerfully tackle the most complex overhaul procedures with only a set of cheap open-end wrenches of the wrong type, a single screwdriver with a worn tip, a large hammer and an adjustable wrench. Though they often get away with it, this cavalier approach is foolish and dangerous. It can result in relatively minor annoyances like stripped fasteners, or cause catastrophic consequences. It can also result in serious injury.

A complete assortment of good tools is a given for anyone who plans to overhaul transmissions. If you don't already have most of the tools listed below, the initial investment may seem high, but compared to the spiraling costs of routine maintenance and repairs, it's a deal. Besides, you can use a lot of the tools around the house for other types of mechanical repairs. We've included a list of the tools you'll

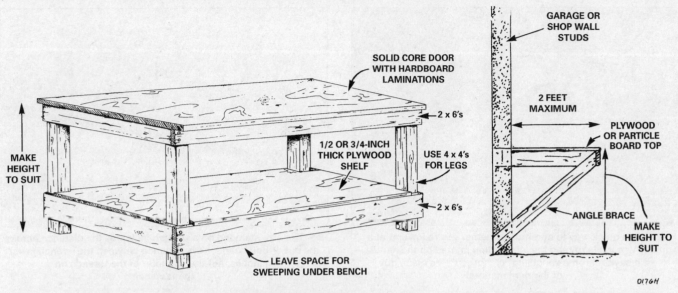

2.2 You can build a sturdy, inexpensive workbench with 4 X 4s, 2 X 6s and a solid-core door with hardboard laminations - or build a bench using the wall as an integral member as shown

2.3 Only a few hand tools are necessary to overhaul automatic transmissions. The tools shown here, along with the special tools discussed later in this Chapter, are all we needed for the overhauls themselves

available from mechanics' tool companies such as Snap-On, Mac, Matco, Kent-Moore, Hayden, OTC, etc. These companies also supply the other tools you need, but they'll probably be more expensive.

Also consider buying second-hand tools from garage sales or used tool outlets. You may have limited choice in sizes, but you can usually determine from the condition of the tools if they're worth buying. You can end up with a number of unwanted or duplicate tools, but it's a cheap way of putting a basic tool kit together, and you can always sell off any surplus tools later.

Until you're a good judge of the quality levels of tools, avoid mail order firms (excepting Sears and other name-brand suppliers), flea markets and swap meets. Some of them offer good value for the money, but many sell cheap, imported tools of dubious quality. Like other consumer products counterfeited in the Far East, these tools run the gamut from acceptable to unusable.

In summary, try to avoid cheap tools, especially when you're purchasing high-use items like screwdrivers, wrenches and sockets. Cheap tools don't last long. Their initial cost plus the additional expense of replacing them will exceed the initial cost of better-quality tools.

Hand tools

A list of general-purpose hand tools

Adjustable wrench - 10-inch
Allen wrench set (1/8 to 3/8-inch or 4 mm to 10 mm)
Ball peen hammer - 12 oz (any steel hammer will do)
Box-end wrenches
Brass hammer
Brushes (various sizes, for cleaning small passages)
Bushing remover and installer
Combination (slip-joint) pliers - 6-inch
Center punch
Cold chisels - 1/4 and 1/2-inch
Cape chisel - 1/2-inch
Combination wrench set (1/4 to 1-inch)
Dial indicator
Extensions - 1-, 6-, 10- and 12-inch
E-Z out (screw extractor) set
Feeler gauge set
Files (assorted)
Floor jack
Gasket scraper
Hacksaw and assortment of blades
Impact screwdriver and bits

need and a detailed description of what to look for when shopping for tools and how to use them correctly. We've also included a list of the special factory tools you'll need for transmission rebuilding.

Buying tools

There are two ways to buy tools. The easiest and quickest way is to simply buy an entire set. Tool sets are often priced substantially below the cost of the same individually priced tools - and sometimes they even come with a tool box. When purchasing such sets, you often wind up with some tools you don't need or want. But if low price and convenience are your concerns, this might be the way to go. Keep in mind that you're going to keep a quality set of tools a long time (maybe the rest of your life), so check the tools carefully; don't skimp too much on price, either. Buying tools individually is usually a more expensive and time-consuming way to go, but you're more likely to wind up with the tools you need and want **(see illustration)**. You can also select each tool on its relative merits for the way you use it.

You can get most of the hand tools on our list from the tool department of any large department store or hardware store chain that sells hand tools. Blackhawk, Cornwall, Craftsman, Lisle, KD, Proto and SK are fairly inexpensive, good-quality choices. Specialty tools are

2.4 One quick way to determine whether you're looking at a quality wrench is to read the information printed on the handle - if it says "chrome vanadium" or "forged", it's made out of the right material

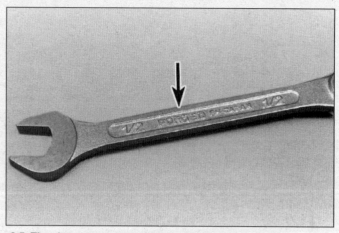

2.5 The size stamped on a wrench indicates the distance across the nut or bolt head (or the distance between the wrench jaws) in inches, not the diameter of the threads on the fastener

Locking pliers
Micrometer(s) (one-inch)
Phillips screwdriver (no. 2 x 6-inch)
Phillips screwdriver (no. 3 x 8-inch)
Phillips screwdriver (stubby - no. 2)
Pin punches (1/16, 1/8, 3/16-inch)
Pliers - lineman's
Pliers - needle-nose
Pliers - snap-ring (internal and external)
Pliers - vise-grip
Pliers - diagonal cutters
Ratchet (reversible)
Scribe
Socket set (6-point)
Soft-face hammer (plastic/rubber)
Standard screwdriver (1/4-inch x 6-inch)
Standard screwdriver (5/16-inch x 6-inch)
Standard screwdriver (3/8-inch x 10-inch)
Standard screwdriver (5/16-inch - stubby)
Steel ruler - 6-inch
Straightedge - 12-inch
Tap and die set
Thread gauge
Torque wrench (capable of reading in-lbs)
Torx socket(s)
Universal joint
Wire brush (large)

What to look for when buying hand tools and general purpose tools

Wrenches and sockets

Wrenches vary widely in quality. One indication of their quality is their cost: The more they cost, the better they are. Buy the best wrenches you can afford. You'll use them a lot.

Start with a set containing wrenches from 1/4 to 1-inch in size. The size, stamped on the wrench **(see illustration)**, indicates the distance across the nut or bolt head, or the distance between the wrench jaws - not the diameter of the threads on the fastener - in inches. For example, a 1/4-inch bolt usually has a 7/16-inch hex head - the size of the wrench required to loosen or tighten it. However, the relationship between thread diameter and hex size doesn't always hold true. In some instances, an unusually small hex may be used to discourage over-tightening or because space around the fastener head is limited. Conversely, some fasteners have a disproportionately large hex-head.

Wrenches are similar in appearance, so their quality level can be difficult to judge just by looking at them. There are bargains to be had, just as there are overpriced tools with well-known brand names. On the other hand, you may buy what looks like a reasonable value set of wrenches only to find they fit badly or are made from poor-quality steel.

With a little experience, it's possible to judge the quality of a tool by looking at it. Often, you may have come across the brand name before and have a good idea of the quality. Close examination of the tool can often reveal some hints as to its quality. Prestige tools are usually polished and chrome-plated over their entire surface, with the working faces ground to size. The polished finish is largely cosmetic, but it does make them easy to keep clean. Ground jaws normally indicate the tool will fit well on fasteners.

A side-by-side comparison of a high-quality wrench with a cheap equivalent is an eye opener. The better tool will be made from a good-quality material, often a forged/chrome-vanadium steel alloy **(see illustration)**. This, together with careful design, allows the tool to be kept as small and compact as possible. If, by comparison, the cheap tool is thicker and heavier, especially around the jaws, it's usually because the extra material is needed to compensate for its lower quality. If the tool fits properly, this isn't necessarily bad - it is, after all, cheaper - but in situations where it's necessary to work in a confined area, the cheaper tool may be too bulky to fit.

Open-end wrenches

Because of its versatility, the open-end wrench is the most common type of wrench. It has a jaw on either end, connected by a flat handle section. The jaws either vary by a size, or overlap sizes between consecutive wrenches in a set. This allows one wrench to be used to hold a bolt head while a similar-size nut is removed. A typical fractional size wrench set might have the following jaw sizes: 1/4 x 5/16, 3/8 x 7/16, 1/2 x 9/16, 9/16 x 5/8 and so on.

Typically, the jaw end is set at an angle to the handle, a feature which makes them very useful in confined spaces; by turning the nut or bolt as far as the obstruction allows, then turning the wrench over so the jaw faces in the other direction, it's possible to move the fastener a fraction of a turn at a time **(see illustration)**. The handle length is generally determined by the size of the jaw and is calculated to allow a nut or bolt to be tightened sufficiently by hand with minimal risk of breakage or thread damage (though this doesn't apply to soft materials like brass or aluminum).

Common open-end wrenches are usually sold in sets and it's rarely worth buying them individually unless it's to replace a lost or broken tool from a set. Single tools invariably cost more, so check the sizes you're most likely to need regularly and buy the best set of wrenches you can afford in that range of sizes. If money is limited, remember that you'll use open-end wrenches more than any other type - it's a good idea to buy a good set and cut corners elsewhere.

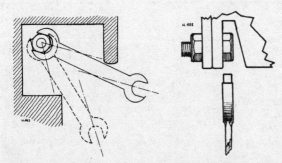

2.6 Open-end wrenches can do several things other wrenches can't - for example, they can be used on bolt heads with limited clearance (above) and they can be used in tight spots where there's little room to turn a wrench by flipping the offset jaw over every few degrees of rotation

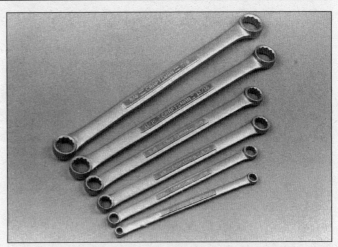

2.7 Box-end wrenches have a ring-shaped "box" at each end - when space permits, they offer the best combination of "grip" and strength

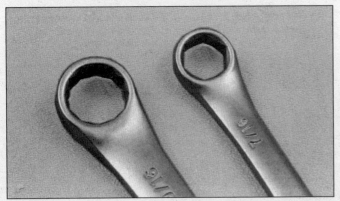

2.8 Box-end wrenches are available in 12 (left) and 6-point (right) openings; even though the 12-point design offers twice as many wrench positions, buy the 6-point first - it's less likely to strip off the corners of a nut or bolt head

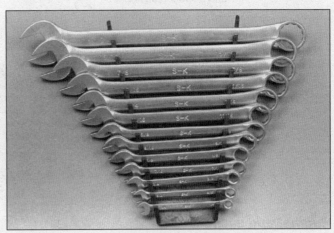

2.9a Buy a set of combination wrenches from 1/4 to 1-inch or from 8 to 22-mm

Box-end wrenches

Box-end wrenches (see illustration) have ring-shaped ends with a 6-point (hex) or 12-point (double hex) opening (see illustration). This allows the tool to fit on the fastener hex at 15 (12-point) or 30-degree (6-point) intervals. Normally, each tool has two ends of different sizes, allowing an overlapping range of sizes in a set, as described for open-end wrenches.

Although available as flat tools, the handle is usually offset at each end to allow it to clear obstructions near the fastener, which is normally an advantage. In addition to normal length wrenches, it's also possible to buy long handle types to allow more leverage (very useful when trying to loosen rusted or seized nuts). It is, however, easy to shear off fasteners if you're not careful, and sometimes the extra length impairs access.

As with open-end wrenches, box-ends are available in varying quality, again often indicated by finish and the amount of metal around the ring ends. While the same criteria should be applied when selecting a set of box-end wrenches, if your budget is limited, go for better-quality open-end wrenches and a slightly cheaper set of box-ends.

Combination wrenches

These wrenches (see illustration) combine a box-end and open-end of the same size in one tool and offer many of the advantages of both. Like the others, they're widely available in sets and as such are probably a better choice than box-ends only. They're generally compact, short-handled tools and are well suited for tight spaces where access is limited.

Flare-nut wrench

A flare-nut wrench (see illustration) is used to remove flared

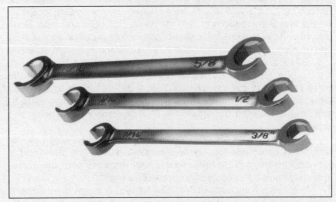

2.9b You will need a set of flare-nut wrenches; they are available in standard SAE and metric sizes

tubing fittings. It is sort of a boxed-end wrench with a section cut away. The cut-out allows you to slip the wrench over the tubing, then on to the nut. The box end is necessary to keep from damaging the soft flare-nut fitting, which would surely be rounded-off by an open-end wrench.

You'll use your flare-nut wrench to remove the oil cooler lines from the transmission fittings. It may be necessary to use a back-up wrench to keep the transmission fittings from turning.

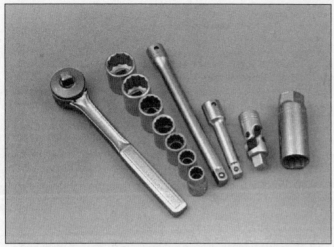

2.10 A typical ratchet and socket set includes a ratchet, a set of sockets, a long and a short extension, a universal joint and a spark plug socket

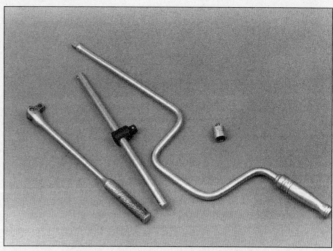

2.11 Lots of other accessories are available for ratchets; From left to right, a breaker bar, a sliding T-handle, a speed handle and a 3/8-to-1/4-inch adapter

2.12 Deep sockets enable you to loosen or tighten an elongated fastener, or to get at a nut with a long bolt protruding from it

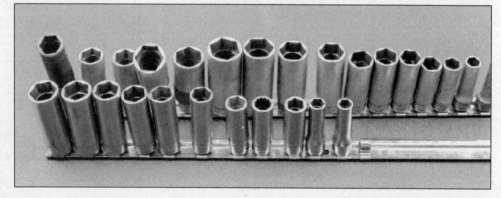

Ratchet and socket sets

Ratcheting socket wrenches (see illustration) are highly versatile. Besides the sockets themselves, many other interchangeable accessories - extensions, U-drives, step-down adapters, screwdriver bits, Allen bits, crow's feet, etc. - are available. Buy six-point sockets - they're less likely to slip and strip the corners off bolts and nuts. Don't buy sockets with extra-thick walls - they might be stronger but they can be hard to use on recessed fasteners or fasteners in tight quarters.

Buy a 1/2-inch drive for work on the outside of the transmission. It's the one you'll use for removing the transmission and most of the parts attached to the transmission. Get a 3/8-inch drive for overhaul work. It's less bulky and its easier to use. Later, you may want to consider a 1/4-inch drive for little stuff like valve body bolts and screws.

Interchangeable sockets consist of a forged-steel alloy cylinder with a hex or double-hex formed inside one end. The other end is formed into the square drive recess that engages over the corresponding square end of various socket drive tools.

Sockets are available in 1/4, 3/8, 1/2 and 3/4-inch drive sizes. A 3/8-inch drive set is most useful for transmission repairs, although 1/4-inch drive sockets and accessories may occasionally be needed.

The most economical way to buy sockets is in a set. As always, quality will govern the cost of the tools. Once again, the "buy the best" approach is usually advised when selecting sockets. While this is a good idea, since the end result is a set of quality tools that should last a lifetime, the cost is so high it's difficult to justify the expense for home use.

As far as accessories go, you'll need a ratchet, at least one extension (buy a three or six-inch size) and maybe a T-handle or breaker bar. Other desirable, though less essential items, are a speeder handle, a U-joint, extensions of various other lengths and

adapters from one drive size to another (see illustration). Some of the sets you find may combine drive sizes; they're well worth having if you find the right set at a good price, but avoid being dazzled by the number of pieces.

Above all, be sure to completely ignore any label that reads "86-piece Socket Set," which refers to the number of pieces, not to the number of sockets (sometimes even the metal box and plastic insert are counted in the total!).

Apart from well-known and respected brand names, you'll have to take a chance on the quality of the set you buy. If you know someone who has a set that has held up well, try to find the same brand, if possible. Take a pocketful of nuts and bolts with you and check the fit in some of the sockets. Check the operation of the ratchet. Good ones operate smoothly and crisply in small steps; cheap ones are coarse and stiff - a good basis for guessing the quality of the rest of the pieces.

One of the best things about a socket set is the built-in facility for expansion. Once you have a basic set, you can purchase extra sockets when necessary and replace worn or damaged tools. There are special deep sockets for reaching recessed fasteners or to allow the socket to fit over a projecting bolt or stud (see illustration). You can also buy screwdriver, Allen and Torx bits to fit various drive tools (they can be very handy in some applications) (see illustration).

Torque wrenches

Torque wrenches (see illustration) are essential for tightening critical fasteners like valve body bolts, oil pump bolts, case bolts, etc. Attempting a transmission overhaul without a torque wrench is an invitation to oil leaks, distortion of the case, damaged or stripped threads or worse.

There are several different types of torque wrenches on the

2.13 Standard and Phillips bits, Allen-head and Torx drivers will expand the versatility of your ratchet and extensions even further

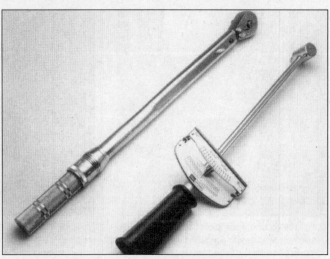

2.14 Torque wrenches (click-type on left, beam-type on right) are the only way to accurately tighten critical fasteners like valve-body bolts, oil pump bolts, etc.

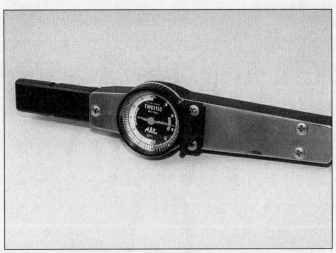

2.15 The 1/4-inch dial-type torque wrench is the most accurate for inch-pound settings - just tighten the fastener until the pointer points to the specified torque setting

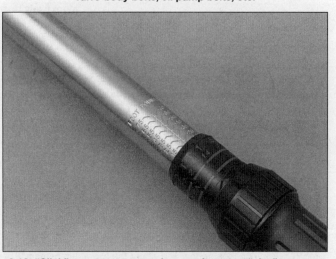

2.16 "Click" type torque wrenches can be set to "give" at a pre-set torque, which makes them very accurate and easy to use

2.17 The impact driver converts a sharp blow into a twisting motion - this is a handy addition to your socket arsenal for those fasteners that won't let go - you can use it with any bit that fits a 3/8-inch drive ratchet

market. The most common are; the "beam" type, which indicates torque loads by deflecting a flexible shaft and the "click" type **(see illustrations)**, which emits an audible click when the torque resistance reaches the specified resistance. Another type is the "dial" type; torque is indicated by a needle on a dial, similar to a dial indicator. Dial types are very accurate down to the inch-pound range.

Torque wrenches are available in a variety of drive sizes, including 1/4, 3/8 and 1/2 inch. Torque ranges vary for particular applications, for transmission rebuilding, you will need two types. You'll need an inch-pound torque wrench, such as the "beam" type or "dial type", for tightening small fasteners like valve body bolts and a 0 to 150 ft-lbs "click" type torque wrench for larger fasteners. Keep in mind that "click" types are usually more accurate than the "beam" type (and more expensive).

Impact drivers

The impact driver **(see illustration)** belongs with the screwdrivers, but it's mentioned here since it can also be used with sockets (impact drivers normally are 3/8-inch square drive). As explained later, an impact driver works by converting a hammer blow on the end of its handle into a sharp twisting movement. While this is a great way to jar a seized fastener loose, the loads imposed on the socket are excessive. Use sockets only with discretion and expect to have to replace damaged ones on occasion.

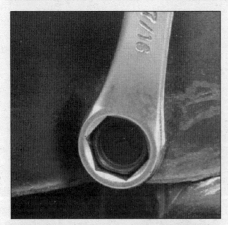

2.18 Try to use a six-point box wrench (or socket) whenever possible - it's shape matches that of the fastener, which means maximum grip and minimum slip

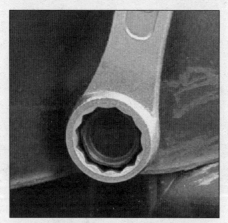

2.19 Sometimes a six-point tool just doesn't offer you any grip when you get the wrench at the angle it needs to be in to loosen or tighten a fastener - when this happens, pull out the 12-point sockets or wrenches - but remember; they're much more likely to strip the corners off a fastener

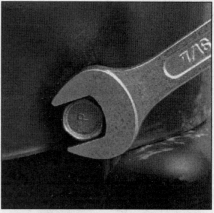

2.20 Open-end wrenches contact only two sides of the fastener and the jaws tend to open up when you put some muscle on the wrench handle - that's why they should only be used as a last resort

Using wrenches and sockets

Although you may think the proper use of tools is self-evident, it's worth some thought. After all, when did you last see instructions for use supplied with a set of wrenches?

Which wrench?

Before you start tearing a transmission apart, figure out the best tool for the job; in this instance the best wrench for a hex-head fastener. Sit down with a few nuts and bolts and look at how various tools fit the bolt heads.

A golden rule is to choose a tool that contacts the largest area of the hex-head. This distributes the load as evenly as possible and lessens the risk of damage. The shape most closely resembling the bolt head or nut is another hex, so a 6-point socket or box-end wrench is usually the best choice **(see illustration)**. Many sockets and box-end wrenches have double hex (12-point) openings. If you slip a 12-point box-end wrench over a nut, look at how and where the two are in contact. The corners of the nut engage in every other point of the wrench. When the wrench is turned, pressure is applied evenly on each of the six corners **(see illustration)**. This is fine unless the fastener head was previously rounded off. If so, the corners will be damaged and the wrench will slip. If you encounter a damaged bolt head or nut, always use a 6-point wrench or socket if possible. If you don't have one of the right size, choose a wrench that fits securely and proceed with care.

If you slip an open-end wrench over a hex-head fastener, you'll see the tool is in contact on two faces only **(see illustration)**. This is acceptable provided the tool and fastener are both in good condition. The need for a snug fit between the wrench and nut or bolt explains the recommendation to buy good-quality open-end wrenches. If the wrench jaws, the bolt head or both are damaged, the wrench will probably slip, rounding off and distorting the head. In some applications, an open-end wrench is the only possible choice due to limited access, but always check the fit of the wrench on the fastener before attempting to loosen it; if it's hard to get at with a wrench, think how hard it will be to remove after the head is damaged.

Using sockets to remove hex-head fasteners is less likely to result in damage than if a wrench is used. Make sure the socket fits snugly over the fastener head, then attach an extension, if needed, and the ratchet or breaker bar. Theoretically, a ratchet shouldn't be used for loosening a fastener or for final tightening because the ratchet mechanism may be overloaded and could slip. In some instances, the location of the fastener may mean you have no choice but to use a ratchet, in which case you'll have to be extra careful.

Never use extensions where they aren't needed. Whether or not

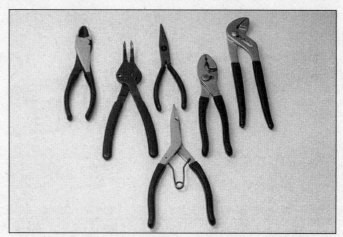

2.21 A typical assortment of the types of pliers you'll need for transmission work - from the left; diagonal side cutters, internal snap-ring pliers, needle-nose pliers, slip-joint pliers, groove-joint pliers and at the bottom, external snap-ring pliers

an extension is used, always support the drive end of the breaker bar with one hand while turning it with the other. Once the fastener is loose, the ratchet can be used to speed up removal.

Pliers

Some tool manufacturers make 25 or 30 different types of pliers. You only need a fraction of this selection **(see illustration)**. Get a good pair of slip-joint pliers for general use. A pair of needle-nose models is handy for reaching into hard-to-get-at places. A set of diagonal wire cutters (dikes) is essential for electrical work and pulling out cotter pins. Vise-Grips are adjustable, locking pliers that grip a fastener firmly - and won't let go - when locked into place. A full set of snap-ring pliers are also essential to any transmission overhaul.

Internal snap-ring pliers have extended tips that lock into the snap rings, allowing you to expand or contract the snap ring for removal **(see illustration)**. This type of snap-ring pliers can be purchased with removable tips and reversible handles.

External snap-ring pliers remove snap-rings by expanding them away from the piece they are recessed in **(see illustration)**. Typically they are heavy-duty as compared to the internal type. A good pair of external snap-ring pliers will have a notch in each end to hold the

2.22 Snap-ring pliers lock into the holes of the snap-ring

2.23 External snap-ring pliers have flat, notched blades - they expand external rings, like the one shown here

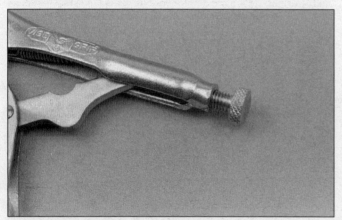

2.24 To adjust the jaws on a pair of locking pliers, grasp the part you want to hold with the jaws, tighten them down by turning the knurled knob on the end of one handle and snap the handles together - if you tightened the knob all the way down, you'll probably have to open it up (back it off) a little before you can close the handles

2.25 If you're persistent and careful, damaged fasteners can be removed with locking pliers

snap-ring in place. When buying any type of snap-ring pliers, make sure the jaws can't twist. If they can, you will have a tough time removing strong snap-rings.

Locking pliers, such as Vise-Grips (a brand name), come in various sizes; the medium size with curved jaws is best for all-around

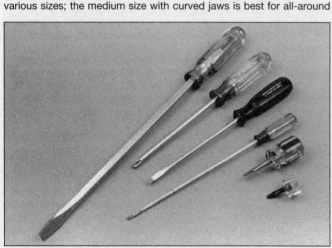

2.26 Screwdrivers come in myriad lengths, sizes and styles

work. However, buy a large and small one if possible, since they're often used in pairs. Although this tool falls somewhere between an adjustable wrench, a pair of pliers and a portable vise, it can be invaluable for loosening and tightening fasteners - it's the only pliers that should be used for this purpose.

The locking pliers jaw opening is set by turning a knurled knob at the end of one handle. The jaws are placed over the head of the fastener and the handles are squeezed together, locking the tool onto the fastener (see illustration). The design of the tool allows extreme pressure to be applied at the jaws and a variety of jaw designs enable the tool to grip firmly even on damaged heads (see illustration). Locking pliers are great for removing fasteners that have been rounded off by badly-fitting wrenches.

As the name suggests, needle-nose pliers have long, thin jaws designed for reaching into holes and other restricted areas. Most needle-nose, or long-nose, pliers also have wire cutters at the base of the jaws.

Look for these qualities when buying pliers: Smooth operating handles and jaws, jaws that match up and grip evenly when the handles are closed, a nice finish and the word "forged" somewhere on the tool.

Screwdrivers

Screwdrivers (see illustration) come in a wide variety of sizes and price ranges. Reasonably priced brands of good quality are available at department stores, auto parts stores and specialty tool stores, but don't buy "bargain-priced" low-quality screwdriver sets at discount tool stores. Even if they look exactly like more expensive brands, the metal tips and shafts are made with inferior alloys and aren't properly heat treated. They usually bend the first time you apply some serious torque.

2.27 Pocket screwdrivers are very handy when removing small parts

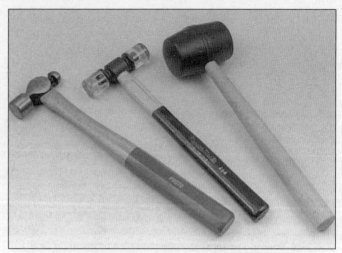

2.28 A ball-peen hammer, soft-face hammer and rubber mallet (left-to-right) will be needed for various tasks (any steel hammer can be used in place of the ball peen hammer)

A screwdriver consists of a steel blade or shank with a drive tip formed at one end. The most common tips are standard (also called straight slot and flat-blade) and Phillips. You will use the standard blade screwdriver the most in an overhaul **(see illustration)**. The other end has a handle attached to it. Traditionally, handles were made from wood and secured to the shank, which had raised tangs to prevent it from turning in the handle. Most screwdrivers now come with plastic handles, which are generally more durable than wood.

The design and size of handles and blades vary considerably. Some handles are specially shaped to fit the human hand and provide a better grip. The shank may be either round or square and some have a hex-shaped bolster under the handle to accept a wrench to provide more leverage when trying to turn a stubborn screw. The shank diameter, tip size and overall length vary too. As a general rule, it's a good idea to use the longest screwdriver possible, which allows the greatest possible leverage.

If access is restricted, a number of special screwdrivers are designed to fit into confined spaces. The "stubby" screwdriver has a specially shortened handle and blade. There are also offset screwdrivers and special screwdriver bits that attach to a ratchet or extension.

The important thing to remember when buying screwdrivers is that they really do come in sizes designed to fit different size fasteners. The slot in any screw has definite dimensions - length, width and depth. Like a bolt head or a nut, the screw slot must be driven by a tool that uses all of the available bearing surface and doesn't slip. Don't use a big wide blade on a small screw and don't try to turn a large screw slot with a tiny, narrow blade. The same principles apply to Allen heads, Phillips heads, Torx heads, etc. Don't even think of using a slotted screwdriver on one of these heads! And don't use your screwdrivers as levers, chisels or punches! This kind of abuse turns them into bad screwdrivers quickly.

Hammers

Resorting to a hammer should always be the last resort. When nothing else will do the job, a medium-size ball peen hammer, a heavy rubber mallet and a heavy soft-brass hammer **(see illustration)** are often the only way to loosen or install a part.

A ball-peen hammer has a head with a conventional cylindrical face at one end and a rounded ball end at the other and is a general-purpose tool found in almost any type of shop. It has a shorter neck than a claw hammer and the face is tempered for striking punches and chisels. A fairly large hammer is preferable to a small one. Although it's possible to find small ones, you won't need them very often and it's much easier to control the blows from a heavier head. As a general rule, a single 12 or 16-ounce hammer will work for most jobs, though occasionally larger or smaller ones may be useful.

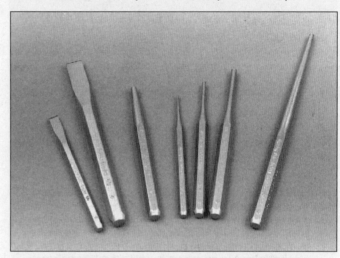

2.29 Cold chisels, center-punches, pin punches and line-up punches (left-to-right) will be needed sooner or later for many jobs

A soft-face hammer is used where a steel hammer could cause damage to the component or other tools being used. A steel hammer head might crack an aluminum part, but a rubber or plastic hammer can be used with more confidence. Soft-face hammers are available with interchangeable heads (usually one made of rubber and another made of relatively hard plastic). When the heads are worn out, new ones can be installed.

Check the condition of your hammers on a regular basis. The danger of a loose head coming off is self-evident, but check the head for chips and cracks too. If damage is noted, buy a new hammer - the head may chip in use and the resulting fragments can be extremely dangerous. It goes without saying that eye protection is essential whenever a hammer is used.

Punches and chisels

Punches and chisels **(see illustration)** are used along with a hammer for various purposes in the shop. Drift punches are often simply a length of round steel bar used to drive a component out of a bore or the equipment it's mounted on. A typical use would be for removing or installing a bearing or bushing. A drift of the same diameter as the bearing outer race is placed against the bearing and tapped with a hammer to knock it in or out of the bore. Most manufacturers offer special installers for the various bushings and bearings in a

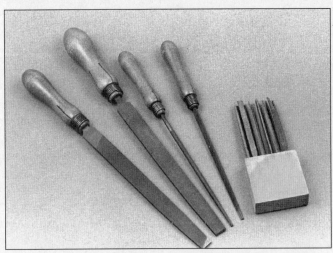

2.30 Get a good assortment of files - they're handy for deburring, marking parts, removing rust, filing the heads off rivets, restoring threads and fabricating small parts

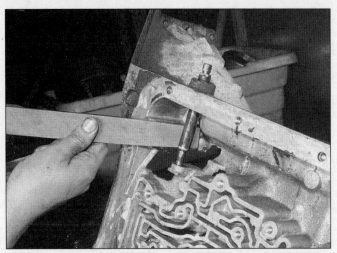

2.31 Using a flat file to deburr a manual shaft prevents possible damage to the case on removal

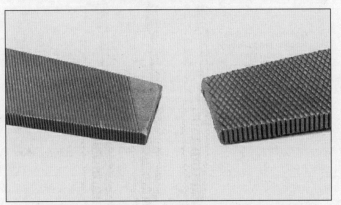

2.32 Files are either single-cut (left) or double-cut (right) - generally speaking, use a single-cut file to produce a very smooth surface; use a double-cut file to remove large amounts of material quickly

particular transmission. For bushing removal and installation, it's best to buy a universal bushing driver kit containing assorted size bushing removers and installers. If nothing else is available it's possible to use a socket of the appropriate diameter to tap the bushing or bearing in or out; an unorthodox use for a socket, but it works.

Smaller diameter drift punches can be purchased or fabricated from steel bar stock. In some cases, you'll need to drive out items like corroded transmission mounting bolts. Here, it's essential to avoid damaging the threaded end of the bolt, so the drift must be a softer material than the bolt. Brass or copper is the usual choice for such jobs; the drift may be damaged in use, but the thread will be protected.

Punches are available in various shapes and sizes and a set of assorted types will be very useful. One of the most basic is the center punch, a small cylindrical punch with the end ground to a point. It'll be needed whenever a hole is drilled. The center of the hole is located first and the punch is used to make a small indentation at the intended point. The indentation acts as a guide for the drill bit so the hole ends up in the right place. Without a punch mark the drill bit will wander and you'll find it impossible to drill with any real accuracy. You can also buy automatic center punches. They're spring loaded and are pressed against the surface to be marked, without the need to use a hammer.

Pin punches are intended for removing items like roll pins (semi-hard, hollow pins that fit tightly in their holes). You'll need a small pin punch to remove the roll pins retaining the valves in the valve body. Pin punches have other uses, however. You may occasionally have to remove rivets or bolts retaining the crossmember by cutting off the

heads and driving out the shanks with a pin punch. They're also very handy for aligning holes in components while bolts or screws are inserted.

The primary use of the cold chisel is rough metal cutting - this can be anything from sheet metal work (uncommon on transmissions) to cutting off the heads of seized or rusted bolts or splitting nuts. A cold chisel is also useful for turning out screws or bolts with damaged heads.

All of the tools described in this section should be good quality items. They're not particularly expensive, so it's not really worth trying to save money on them. More significantly, there's a risk that with cheap tools, fragments may break off in use - a potentially dangerous situation.

Even with good-quality tools, the heads and working ends will inevitably get worn or damaged, so it's a good idea to maintain all such tools on a regular basis. Using a file or bench grinder, remove all burrs and mushroomed edges from around the head. This is an important task because the build-up of material around the head can fly off when it's struck with a hammer and is potentially dangerous. Make sure the tool retains its original profile at the working end, again, filing or grinding off all burrs. In the case of cold chisels, the cutting edge will usually have to be reground quite often because the material in the tool isn't usually much harder than materials typically being cut. Make sure the edge is reasonably sharp, but don't make the tip angle greater than it was originally; it'll just wear down faster if you do.

The techniques for using these tools vary according to the job to be done and are best learned by experience. The one common denominator is the fact they're all normally struck with a hammer. It follows that eye protection should be worn. Always make sure the working end of the tool is in contact with the part being punched or cut. If it isn't, the tool will bounce off the surface and damage may result.

Files

Files (see illustration) come in a wide variety of sizes and types for specific jobs, but all of them are used for the same basic function of removing small amounts of metal in a controlled fashion. Files are used mainly for deburring, marking parts, removing rust, filing the heads off rivets, restoring threads and fabricating small parts. You'll occasionally need a flat file for removing nicks and burrs (see illustration).

File shapes commonly available include flat, half-round, round, square and triangular. Each shape comes in a range of sizes (lengths) and cuts ranging from rough to smooth. The file face is covered with rows of diagonal ridges which form the cutting teeth. They may be aligned in one direction only (single cut) or in two directions to form a diamond-shaped pattern (double-cut) (see illustration). The spacing of the teeth determines the file coarseness, again, ranging from rough to smooth in five basic grades: Rough, coarse, bastard, second-cut and smooth.

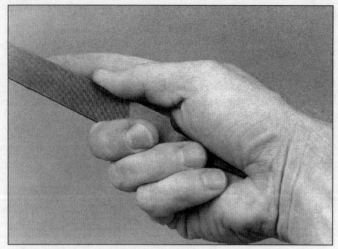

2.33 Never use a file without a handle - the tang is sharp and could puncture your hand

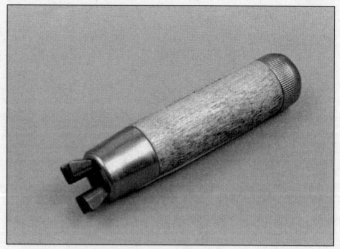

2.34 Adjustable handles that will work with many different size files are also available

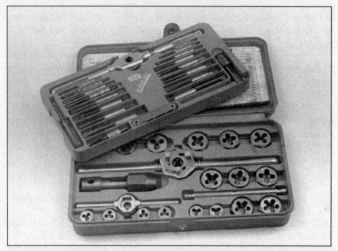

2.35 Tap and die sets are available in inch and metric sizes - taps are used for cutting internal threads and cleaning and restoring damaged threads; dies are used for cutting, cleaning and restoring external threads

Note how the tapered section progressively decreases acrossthe ridge. Plug taps are normally needed for finishing tapped holes in blind bores.

driving square

flute

cutting edge

2.36 Taper, plug and bottoming taps (left-to-right)

You'll want to build up a set of files by purchasing tools of the required shape and cut as they're needed. A good starting point would be flat, half-round, round and triangular files (at least one each - bastard or second-cut types). In addition, you'll have to buy one or more file handles (files are usually sold without handles, which are purchased separately and pushed over the tapered tang of the file when in use) **(see illustration).** You may need to buy more than one size handle to fit the various files in your tool box, but don't attempt to get by without them. A file tang is fairly sharp and you almost certainly will end up stabbing yourself in the palm of the hand if you use a file without a handle and it catches in the work-piece during use. Adjustable handles are also available for use with files of various sizes, eliminating the need for several handles **(see illustration).**

Exceptions to the need for a handle are fine Swiss pattern files, which have a rounded handle instead of a tang. These small files are usually sold in sets with a number of different shapes. Originally intended for very fine work, they can be very useful for use in inaccessible areas. Swiss files are normally the best choice if you need to try and clean or deburr a valve from the valve body in the transmission.

The correct procedure for using files is fairly easy to master. Hold the file by the handle, using your free hand at the file end to guide it and keep it flat in relation to the surface being filed. Use smooth cutting strokes and be careful not to rock the file as it passes over the

surface. Also, don't slide it diagonally across the surface or the teeth will make grooves in the work-piece. Don't drag a file back across the work-piece at the end of the stroke - lift it slightly and pull it back to prevent damage to the teeth.

Files don't require maintenance in the usual sense, but they should be kept clean and free of metal filings. Steel is a reasonably easy material to work with, but softer metals like aluminum tend to clog the file teeth very quickly, which will result in scratches in the work-piece. This can be avoided by rubbing the file face with chalk before using it. General cleaning is carried out with a file card or a fine wire brush. If kept clean, files will last a long time - when they do eventually dull, they must be replaced; there is no satisfactory way of sharpening a worn file.

Taps and Dies

Taps

Tap and die sets **(see illustration)** are available in inch and metric sizes. Taps are used to cut internal threads and clean or restore damaged threads. A tap consists of a fluted shank with a drive square at one end. It's threaded along part of its length - the cutting edges are formed where the flutes intersect the threads **(see illustration).** Taps are made from hardened steel so they will cut threads in materials softer than what they're made of.

Taps come in three different types: Taper, plug and bottoming. The only real difference is the length of the chamfer on the cutting end of the tap. Taper taps are chamfered for the first 6 or 8 threads, which makes them easy to start but prevents them from cutting threads close

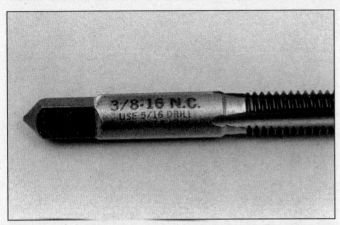

2.37 If you need to drill and tap a hole, the drill bit size to use for a given bolt (tap) size is marked on the tap

2.39 Hex-shaped dies are especially handy for mechanic's work because they can be turned with a wrench

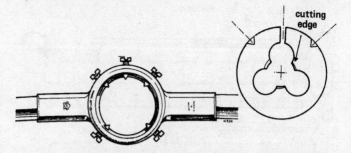

2.38 A die (right) is used for cutting external threads (this one is a split-type/adjustable die) and is held in a tool called a die stock (left)

2.40 A two or three-jaw puller will come in handy for many tasks in the shop and can also be used for working on other types of equipment

to the bottom of a hole. Plug taps are chamfered up about 3 to 5 threads, which makes them a good all around tap because they're relatively easy to start and will cut nearly to the bottom of a hole. Bottoming taps, as the name implies, have a very short chamfer (1-1/2 to 3 threads) and will cut as close to the bottom of a blind hole as practical. However, to do this, the threads should be started with a plug or taper tap.

Although cheap tap and die sets are available, the quality is usually very low and they can actually do more harm than good when used on threaded holes in aluminum transmissions. The alternative is to buy high-quality taps if and when you need them, even though they aren't cheap, especially if you need to buy two or more thread pitches in a given size. Despite this, it's the best option - you'll probably only need taps on rare occasions, so a full set isn't absolutely necessary.

Taps are normally used by hand (they can be used in machine tools, but not when doing transmission repairs). The square drive end of the tap is held in a tap wrench (an adjustable T-handle). For smaller sizes, a T-handled chuck can be used. The tapping process starts by drilling a hole of the correct diameter. For each tap size, there's a corresponding twist drill that will produce a hole of the correct size. Note how the tapered section progressively decreases across the ridge. Plug taps are normally needed for finishing tapped holes in blind bores.

This is important; too large a hole will leave the finished thread with the tops missing, producing a weak and unreliable grip. Conversely, too small a hole will place excessive loads on the hard and brittle shank of the tap, which can break it off in the hole. Removing a broken off tap from a hole is no fun! The correct tap drill size is normally marked on the tap itself or the container it comes in **(see illustration)**.

Dies

Dies are used to cut, clean or restore external threads. Most dies are made from a hex-shaped or cylindrical piece of hardened steel with a threaded hole in the center. The threaded hole is overlapped by three or four cutouts, which equate to the flutes on taps and allow metal waste to escape during the threading process. Dies are held in a T-handled holder (called a die stock) **(see illustration)**. Some dies are split at one point, allowing them to be adjusted slightly (opened and closed) for fine control of thread clearances.

Dies aren't needed as often as taps, for the simple reason it's normally easier to install a new bolt than to salvage one. However, it's often helpful to be able to extend the threads of a bolt or clean up damaged threads with a die. Hex-shaped dies are particularly useful for mechanic's work, since they can be turned with a wrench **(see illustration)** and are usually less expensive than adjustable ones.

The procedure for cutting threads with a die is broadly similar to that described above for taps. When using an adjustable die, the initial cut is made with the die fully opened, the adjustment screw being used to reduce the diameter of successive cuts until the finished size is reached. As with taps, a cutting lubricant should be used, and the die must be backed off every few turns to clear swarf from the cutouts.

Pullers

You'll need a general-purpose puller for transmission rebuilding. Pullers can removed seized or corroded parts, bad bushings or bearings etc. Universal two- and three-legged pullers are widely available in numerous designs and sizes.

The typical puller consists of a central boss with two or three pivoting arms attached. The outer ends of the arms are hooked jaws which grab the part you want to pull off **(see illustration)**. You can

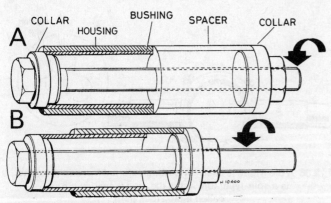

2.41 Typical drawbolt uses - in A, the nut is tightened to pull the collar and bushing into the large spacer; in B, the spacer is left out and the drawbolt is repositioned to install the new bushing

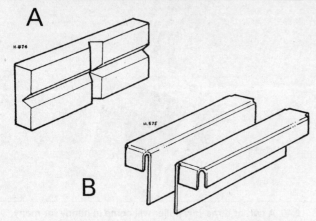

2.43 Sometimes, the parts you have to jig up in the vise are delicate, or made of soft materials - to avoid damaging them, get a pair of fiberglass or plastic "soft jaws" (A) or fabricate your own with 1/8-inch thick aluminum sheet (B)

2.42 A bench vise is one of the most useful pieces of equipment you can have in the shop - bigger is usually better with vises, so get a vise with jaws that open at least four inches

2.44 Although it's not absolutely necessary, an air compressor can make many jobs easier and produce better results, especially when air powered tools are available to use with it

reverse the arms on most pullers to use the puller on internal openings when necessary. The central boss is threaded to accept a puller bolt, which does the work. You can also get hydraulic versions of these tools which are capable of more pressure, but they're expensive.

You can adapt pullers by purchasing, or fabricating, special jaws for specific jobs. If you decide to make your own jaws, keep in mind that the pulling force should be concentrated as close to the center of the component as possible to avoid damaging it.

If all reasonable attempts to remove a part fail, don't be afraid to give up. It's cheaper to quit now than to repair a badly damaged transmission. Either buy or borrow the correct tool, or take the transmission to a dealer or repair shop and ask him to remove the part for you.

Drawbolt extractors

The simple drawbolt extractor is easy to make up and invaluable in every workshop. There are no commercially available tools of this type; you simply make a tool to suit a particular application. You can use a drawbolt extractor to remove bearings and bushings.

To make a drawbolt extractor, you'll need an assortment of threaded rods in various sizes (available at hardware stores), and nuts to fit them. You'll also need assorted washers, spacers and tubing.

Some typical drawbolt uses are shown in the accompanying illustration **(see illustration)**. They also reveal the order of assembly of the various pieces. The same arrangement, minus the tubular spacer section, can usually be used to install a new bushing. Using the tool is quite simple. Just make sure you get the bushing square to the bore when you install it. Lubricate the part being pressed into place, where appropriate.

Bench vise

The bench vise **(see illustration)** is an essential tool in a shop. Buy the best quality vise you can afford. A good vise is expensive, but the quality of its materials and workmanship are worth the extra money. Size is also important - bigger vises are usually more versatile. Make sure the jaws open at least four inches. Get a set of soft jaws to fit the vise as well - you'll need them to grip transmission parts that could be damaged by the hardened vise jaws **(see illustration)**.

Power tools

Really, you don't need any power tools to overhaul an automatic transmission. But if you have an air compressor and electricity, there's a wide range of pneumatic and electric hand tools to make all sorts of jobs easier and faster.

Air compressor

An air compressor **(see illustration)** makes most jobs easier and faster. Drying off parts after cleaning them with solvent, blowing out passages in a case or valve body, running power tools - the list is endless. Once you buy a compressor, you'll wonder how you ever got along without it. Air tools really speed up tedious procedures like removing and installing pan bolts, valve body bolts or case bolts.

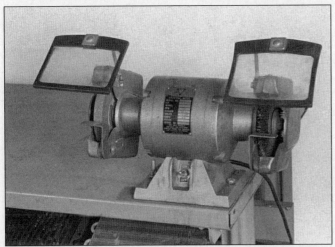

2.45 Another indispensable piece of equipment is the bench grinder (with a wire wheel mounted on one arbor) - make sure it's securely bolted down and never use it with the rests or eye shields removed

2.46 Electric drills can be cordless (above) or 115-volt, AC-powered (below)

2.47 Get a set of good quality drill bits for drilling holes and wire brushes of various sizes for cleaning up metal parts - make sure the bits are designed for drilling in metal!

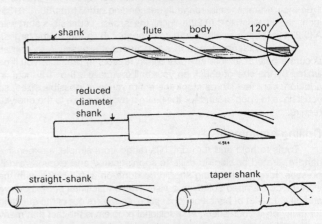

2.48 A typical drill bit (top), a reduced shank bit (center), and a tapered shank bit (bottom right)

Bench-mounted grinder

A bench grinder (see illustration) is also handy. With a wire wheel on one end and a grinding wheel on the other, it's great for cleaning up fasteners, sharpening tools and removing rust. Make sure the grinder is fastened securely to the bench or stand, always wear eye protection when operating it and never grind aluminum parts on the grinding wheel.

Electric drills

Countersinking bolt holes, enlarging oil passages, removing rusted or broken off fasteners, enlarging holes and fabricating small parts - electric drills (see illustration) are indispensable for transmission modification work. A 3/8-inch chuck (drill bit holder) will handle most jobs. Collect several different wire brushes to use in the drill and make sure you have a complete set of sharp metal drill bits (see illustration). Cordless drills are extremely versatile because they don't force you to work near an outlet. They're also handy to have around for a variety of non-mechanical jobs.

Twist drills and drilling equipment

Drilling operations are done with twist drills, either in a hand drill or a drill press. Twist drills (or drill bits, as they're often called) consist of a round shank with spiral flutes formed into the upper two-thirds to

clear the waste produced while drilling, keep the drill centered in the hole and finish the sides of the hole.

The lower portion of the shank is left plain and used to hold the drill in the chuck. In this section, we will discuss only normal parallel shank drills (see illustration). There is another type of bit with the plain end formed into a special size taper designed to fit directly into a corresponding socket in a heavy-duty drill press. These drills are known as Morse Taper drills and are used primarily in machine shops.

At the cutting end of the drill, two edges are ground to form a conical point. They're generally angled at about 60-degrees from the drill axis, but they can be reground to other angles for specific applications. For general use the standard angle is correct - this is how the drills are supplied.

When buying drills, purchase a good-quality set (sizes 1/16 to 3/8-inch). Make sure the drills are marked -High Speed Steel" or "HSS". This indicates they're hard enough to withstand continual use in metal; many cheaper, unmarked drills are suitable only for use in wood or other soft materials. Buying a set ensures the right size bit will be available when it's needed.

2.49 Drill bits in the range most commonly used are available in fractional sizes (left) and number sizes (right) so almost any size hole can be drilled

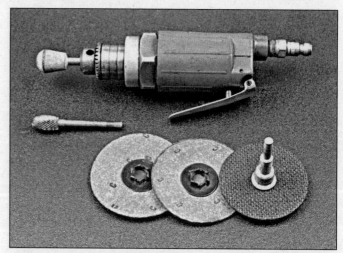

2.50 A good die grinder will deburr, cut, grind, chamfer oil holes and do a lot of other little jobs what would be tedious if done manually

Twist drill sizes

Twist drills are available in a vast array of sizes, most of which you'll never need. There are three basic drill sizing systems: Fractional, number and letter **(see illustration)** (we won't get involved with the fourth system, which is metric sizes).

Fractional sizes start at 1/64-inch and increase in increments of 1/64-inch. Number drills range in descending order from 80 (0.0135-inch), the smallest, to 1 (0.2280-inch), the largest. Letter sizes start with A (0.234-inch), the smallest, and go through Z (0.413-inch), the largest.

This bewildering range of sizes means it's possible to drill an accurate hole of almost any size within reason. In practice, you'll be limited by the size of chuck on your drill (normally 3/8 or 1/2-inch). In addition, very few stores stock the entire range of possible sizes, so you'll have to shop around for the nearest available size to the one you require.

Drilling equipment

Tools to hold and turn drill bits range from simple, inexpensive hand-operated or electric drills to sophisticated and expensive drill presses. Ideally, all drilling should be done on a drill press with the work-piece clamped solidly in a vise. These machines are expensive and take up a lot of bench or floor space, so they're out of the question for many do-it-yourselfers. An additional problem is the fact that many of the drilling jobs you end up doing will be on the transmission itself or the equipment it's mounted on, in which case the tool has to be taken to the work.

The best tool for the home shop is an electric drill with a 3/8-inch chuck. Both cordless and AC drills (that run off household current) are available. If you're purchasing one for the first time, look for a well-known, reputable brand name and variable speed as minimum requirements. A 1/4-inch chuck, single-speed drill will work, but it's worth paying a little more for the larger, variable speed type.

All drills require a key to lock the bit in the chuck. When removing or installing a bit, make sure the cord is unplugged to avoid accidents. Initially, tighten the chuck by hand, checking to see if the bit is centered correctly. This is especially important when using small drill bits which can get caught between the jaws. Once the chuck is hand tight, use the key to tighten it securely - remember to remove the key afterwards!

High-speed grinders

A good die grinder **(see illustration)** will deburr, cut and grind as well as chamfer oil holes - it will do these jobs ten times faster than you can do them by hand. But be very careful when using a high-speed grinder - they remove allot of material very fast.

Safety items that should be in every shop

Fire extinguishers

You should have at least one fire extinguisher in your shop before doing any maintenance or repair procedures **(see illustration)**. Make sure it's rated for flammable liquid fires. Familiarize yourself with its use as soon as you buy it - don't wait until you need it to figure out how to use it. And be sure to have it checked and recharged at regular intervals. Refer to the safety tips at the end of this chapter for more information about the hazards of gasoline and other flammable liquids.

2.51 Buy at least one fire extinguisher before you open shop - make sure it's rated for flammable liquid fires and KNOW HOW TO USE IT!

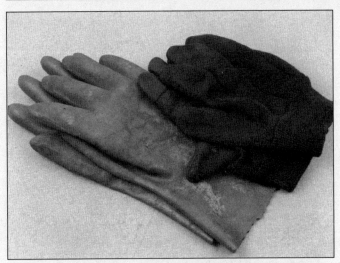

2.52 Get a pair of heavy work gloves for handling hot or sharp-edged objects and a pair of rubber gloves for washing parts with solvent

2.53 One of the most important items you'll need in the shop is a face shield or safety goggles, especially when you're hitting metal parts with a hammer, washing parts in solvent or grinding something on the bench grinder

Gloves

If you're handling hot parts or metal parts with sharp edges, wear a pair of industrial work gloves to protect yourself from burns, cuts and splinters **(see illustration)**. Wear a pair of heavy duty rubber gloves (to protect your hands when you wash parts in solvent.

Safety glasses or goggles

Never work on a bench or high-speed grinder without safety glasses **(see illustration)**. Don't take a chance on getting a metal sliver in your eye. It's also a good idea to wear safety glasses when you're washing parts in solvent.

Diagnostic tools

These tools perform special diagnostic tasks. They're indispensable for determining the condition of your transmission. Using these simple tools will help you determine the difference between an engine problem and a transmission problem. You will also be able to test the working components before you disassemble or remove the transmission from the vehicle. There are only a few basic tools you need to use for diagnosis of the transmission.

Hydraulic pressure gauge

The pressure gauge **(see illustration)** is used to perform an oil pressure test (see Chapter 5). The oil pressure test indicates the hydraulic pressure being generated by the oil pump and actually being used in a specific hydraulic circuit. The transmission oil pressure gauge must read up to 300 psi and have long heavy-duty hose with a 1/8-27 NPT (National Pipe Thread) fitting attached to one end.

Vacuum gauge

The vacuum gauge **(see illustration)** indicates the amount of intake manifold vacuum generated by the engine, in inches of mercury (in-Hg). You'll need a vacuum gauge to correctly diagnose the vacuum modulator system found in certain transmissions.

Tachometer

The tachometer is used in conjunction with the oil pressure gauge to perform an oil pressure test. It's also needed to indicate torque converter stall speed and engine rpm at shift points. Basically, the tool indicates the speed at which the engine crankshaft is turning, in revolutions per minute (rpm) **(see illustration)**.

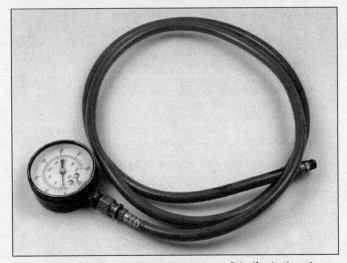

2.54 The hydraulic pressure gauge screws into the test ports on the transmission - it measures the pressure at that port

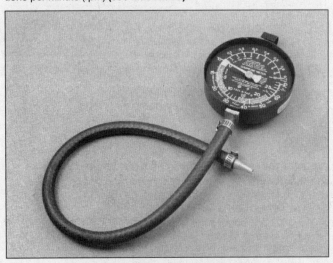

2.55 The vacuum gauge indicates vacuum, in inches of mercury (in-Hg)

Stethoscope

The stethoscope **(see illustration)** amplifies sounds, allowing you to pinpoint possible sources of pending trouble, such as a bad bearing, pump, or excessive play in the transmission.

Vacuum pump

The hand-operated vacuum pump **(see illustration)** is useful in testing the vacuum modulator and it's circuit.

Special transmission overhaul tools

General Motors requires their dealers to maintain trained personnel and purchase the special tools necessary to repair their transmissions. Since these tools are designed for use in a dealership service department, they are designed to aid the dealer technician in completing the job as quickly as possible in this environment. Many of these tools are not necessary for overhaul - they are simply aids to quicker overhauls. For this reason, we don't recommend you buy all the manufacturer's special tools unless you plan to do frequent overhauls. We have found substitute tools and methods for most of the manufacturer's special tools, and have illustrated this in the overhaul chapters. We realize the special tools are sometimes expensive and the home mechanic doesn't have easy access to the tools, so he generally tries to buy as few special tools as possible.

Provided in the lists below are all the special tools General Motors suggests for overhauling the transmissions covered by this manual. The tools are made by Kent-Moore for General Motors and are available to the public **(see illustrations)**. Tools that perform the same function are sometimes available from other tool manufacturers as well. For the tool companies address see the Source List at the end of this manual.

The first two lists are common tools General Motors recommends for use on rear wheel drive and front wheel drive transmissions. The subsequent lists are tools General Motors recommends for each specific transmission. To reiterate: only the tools illustrated in this section and discussed earlier in this Chapter are absolutely required for overhaul. The complete lists are included here as a reference for the advanced transmission specialist.

General Motors special tools

Special tool list common to all rear wheel drive transmissions covered in this manual

J-3289-20 Transmission holding fixture base
J-6125-B Slide hammer
J-8001 Dial indicator set
J-8059 Snap-ring pliers
J-8092 Driver handle
J-8763-02 Transmission holding fixture
J-21369-E Converter leak test fixture
J-21867 Universal pressure gauge set
J-25025-B Oil pump and valve body alignment pin and dial indicator post set
J-26744-A Universal seal installer
J-29369 Universal bushing remover set
J-35138 Universal converter end play measuring tool
J-36850 Transjel assembly lubricant
J-38119 Rear extension housing remover and installer

Special tool list common to all front wheel drive transaxles covered in this manual

J-3289-20 Transmission holding fixture base
J-7079-2 Driver handle
J-8001 Dial indicator set
J-8092 Driver handle
J-21369-D Converter leak test fixture
J-21867 Universal pressure gauge set
J-23327-1 Forward clutch spring compressor
J-23456 Clutch spring compressor frame

2.56 The tach/dwell meter combines the functions of a tachometer and dwell meter into one package - for transmission work, you'll be using the tach function, which indicates the speed - in rpm - at which the engine crankshaft is turning. This tool is essential for checking converter stall speed

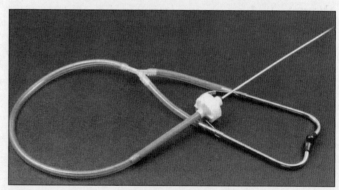

2.57 The stethoscope amplifies sounds, allowing you to pinpoint possible sources of trouble

J-23907 Universal slide hammer
J-25025-A Oil pump and valve body alignment pin and dial indicator post set
J-25359-5 #40 Torx drive bit
J-26744-A Universal seal installer
J-26958 Output shaft alignment and loading tool
J-26958-10 Adapter plug
J-28540 Torque converter seal installer
J-28664-B Transmission holding fixture
J-28667 Drive sprocket bearing installer
J-29130 Axle seal installer
J-29369 Universal bushing remover and installer set
J-29569 Turbine shaft seal installer
J-29829 Turbine shaft seal installer
J-33381 Final drive/clutch assembly remover and installer
J-34757 Output shaft C-clip remover and installer

Special tool list specific to the THM200-4R transmission

J-7057 Dial indicator extension
J-8433 Speedometer gear puller
J-21366 Converter holding strap
J-21426 Rear oil seal installer
J-21427-01 Speedometer gear puller adapter
J-22269-01 Clutch accumulator piston remover and installer
J-23062-14 Case bushing remover and installer
J-23129 Converter housing seal remover

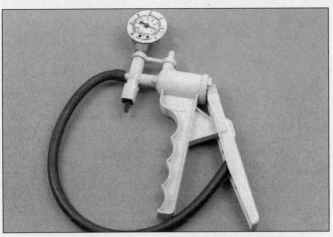

2.58 The vacuum/pressure pump can create a vacuum in a circuit, or pressurize it, to simulate the actual operating conditions

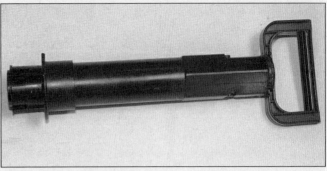

2.59 The Reverse clutch housing remover/installer is needed to overhaul the THM200-4R and THM 125C - its GM tool no. is J-28542-A

J-23327 Clutch spring compressor
J-24036 Pump cover stator shaft and overrun clutch housing bushing remover
J-24684 Pressure regulator valve spring compressor
J-24773-A Pump remover and endplay checking tool
J-25010 Direct clutch seal protector
J-25011 Low-reverse clutch seal protector
J-25013-A Output shaft and rear unit support fixture
J-25014 Intermediate band apply pin gauge
J-25015 Oil pump body and cover alignment band
J-25016 Front oil pump seal and speedometer gear installer
J-25018-A Forward clutch spring compressor adapter
J-25019-20 Front pump bushing remover and installer
J-25022 End play fixture adapter
J-25024-A Forward clutch spring compressor
J-25359-2 #27 Torx drive bit
J-25359-8 #27 Torx drive bit holder
J-28542-A Reverse clutch housing installer and remover
J-29334 Fourth clutch compressor and center support remover
J-29332-A Output shaft support fixture
J-29335 Inner overrun clutch piston seal protector
J-29337 Forward and direct clutch endplay checking tool, shaft bushing remover
J-29696 Turbine shaft seal installer
J-29714-A Servo cover depressor
J-29796 Overdrive unit end play adapter
J-34008 Low-reverse clutch unit remover and installer
J-34725 End play fixture adapter

Special tool list specific to the THM350 transmission

J-3387-2 Pump alignment pin
J-8059 Low-reverse and forward clutch snap ring pliers (Parallel opening jaws)
J-21359-A Pump seal installer
J-21366 Converter holding strap
J-21368 Oil pump body and cover alignment band
J-21426 Rear oil seal installer
J-22269-01 Intermediate servo piston and direct clutch, 2-3 accumulator piston compressor
J-22976 Governor bore bushing service tool set
J-23062-01 Bushing service set
J-23069 Intermediate clutch 1-2 accumulator piston compressor
J-23129 Converter housing seal remover
J-23327 Forward and low-reverse clutch piston spring compressor
J-24466 Modulator checking tool
J-24675 Direct clutch 2-3 accumulator piston compressor
J-26507 Low-reverse clutch support remover
J-38119 Rear extension bushing remover and installer

Special tool list specific to the THM400 transmission

J-4670-01 Forward clutch spring compressor
J-5403 Pressure regulator valve snap ring pliers
J-5586-A Clutch assembly snap ring pliers
J-5590 Speedometer gear installer
J-6116-01 Rear gear assembly holding fixture
J-6133-01 rear oil pump bearing and speedometer gear installer
J-8059 Clutch assembly snap ring pliers (parallel opening jaws)
J-8433 Speedometer gear puller
J-21359-A Extension housing seal and oil pump seal installer
J-21362 Forward and direct clutch inner seal protector
J-21363 Intermediate clutch inner seal protector
J-21364-A Rear gear assembly holding fixture adapter
J-21366 Converter holding strap
J-21368 Pump body and cover alignment band
J-21370-A Band apply pin gauge
J-21409 Forward and direct clutch outer seal protector
J-21426 Extension housing oil seal installer
J-21427-01 Speedometer gear puller adapter
J-21465-01 Bushing service set
J-21664 Forward clutch compressor adapter
J-21795-02 Rear gear assembly remover and installer
J-22269-01 Accumulator piston remover
J-22976 Governor bore bushing service tool set
J-23129 Converter housing seal remover
J-23738-A Modulator vacuum leak tester
J-24396 Intermediate clutch pack alignment tool
J-24466 Modulator checking tool
J-24675 Accumulator piston adapter
J-24684 Pressure regulator valve remover and installer
J-24773-A Oil pump end remover and end play checking tool
J-36352 Speed sensor rotor installation tubes

Special tool list specific to the THM700-R4 transmission

J-21366 Converter holding strap
J-21368 Oil pump body and cover alignment band
J-21426 Output shaft sleeve and case extension oil seal installer
J-21427-01 Speedometer gear puller
J-2269-01 Servo piston compressor
J-23129 Converter housing seal remover
J-23327 Low and reverse clutch spring compressor
J-23456 Clutch spring compressor press
J-24773-A Oil pump remover and end play tool
J-25016 Oil pump seal installer
J-25018-A Input clutch spring compressor adapter
J-25022 End play fixture adapter
J-29714-A Servo cover depressor
J-29837 Output shaft support fixture
J-29882 Overrun clutch inner seal protector
J-29883 Forward clutch inner seal protector
J-33037 Intermediate band apply pin gauge

2.60 The oil pump removal tool (GM tool no. J-24773-A) is needed to remove the oil pump on the THM200-4R and the THM700-R4

J-34196-A Bushing service set
J-34627 Snap ring pliers
J-36352 Speed sensor rotor installer
J-36418-A Turbine shaft seal installer
J-37789-A Oil pump remover and installer for (91 and later models)
J-38119 Rear extension bushing remover and installer
J-38417 Speed sensor remover for trucks
J-39119 Oil pump remover and installer adapter (91 and later)

Special tool list specific to the THM125/125C and 3T40 transaxles

J-25018-A Forward clutch spring compressor adapter
J-26958-11 Adapter bracket
J-28535 Intermediate band apply pin gauge
J-28538 Torque converter end play checking fixture
J-28542 Lo-reverse clutch housing remover and installer
J-28544 Input shaft puller
J-28588 Sun gear snap ring and reverse clutch lower race thrust washer end play checking tool
J-29023 Thermostatic element height gauge
J-34008 Lo-reverse clutch housing remover and installer
J-35914 Pump bearing remover and installer

Special tool list specific to the THM440-T4/4T60 transaxles

J-25359-4 #30 Torx drive bit
J-29830 Torque converter end play checking fixture
J-36619 Anaroid modulator checking tool
J-25019-6 Bushing installer

2.61 The spring compressor assembly (GM tool no. J-21420 and J-23327) can be used to remove the clutch pistons on the THM200-4R, THM350 and THM700-R4 - On THM 125/125C and THM 440-T4 FWD transaxles, the GM tool no. J-23327 is used in conjunction with GM tool no. J-23456 tool to compress the forward clutch assembly

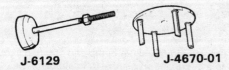

J-6129   **J-4670-01**

2.62 The forward clutch spring compressor assembly (GM tool no. J-6129 and J-4670-01) is used to overhaul the THM400

J-28698 Pump bearing remover and installer
J-33382 1st and 2nd gear/reverse band apply pin gauge
J-33386 Input shaft end play checking tool
J-34091 Input Clutch piston seal protector
J-34092 Third roller clutch piston seal protector
J-34094-A Thermostatic element height gauge
J-34095 Output shaft loading tool adapter
J-34115 Left side axle seal installer
J-34741 Input shaft seal installer
J-34126 Driven sprocket support bearing remover
J-34129 Driven sprocket support bearing installer

Miscellaneous special tools

The following tools are universal and can be used on a variety of transmissions.

Universal clutch spring compressor

A clutch spring compressor is essential for removing the clutch piston and seals in most transmissions. You can use the individual GM special tools or the universal type. The universal type can be used on a wide variety of transmissions for compressing many types of clutch springs. It is available in several different styles from heavy duty full-stand with foot pedal used primarily in professional shops to the bench mount type which can be easily moved and is the most practical for the home mechanic **(see illustration)**.

2.63 The rear gear assembly holding tool (GM tool no. J-21795-02 and J-6125-A) is needed to overhaul the THM400

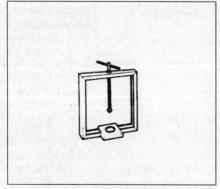

2.64 This is a clutch spring compressor tool (GM tool no. J-23456) - it is used for the THM700-R4, THM 125/125C and the THM 440-T4

2.65 This low-reverse clutch spring compressor for the THM350 and THM700-R4 fits into the case and allows for easy removal of the snap-ring (Hayden tool no. T-0151)

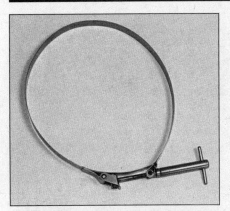

2.66 This is an oil pump body and cover alignment band (GM tool no. J-25015 for the THM200-4R and J-21368 for all other rear wheel drive transmissions)

2.67a Outer seal protectors are plastic covers or domes that compress and protect piston seals as the clutch piston is installed

2.67b Inner seal protectors slide over the outside diameter of a shaft to keep an inner seal from being damaged while it's installed

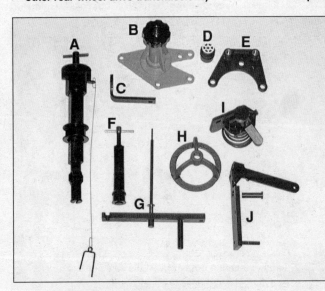

2.68 Special tools required specifically for front wheel drive transaxles

A   Clutch and final drive tool – GM tool No. J-33381 (125C and 440-T4)
B   Output shaft aligning and loading tool – GM tool No. J-26958 (125C and 440-T4)
C   Adapter bracket – GM tool No. J-26958-11 (125C)
D   Adapter plug – GM tool No. J-26958-10 (125C and 440-T4)
E   Output shaft loading tool adapter – GM tool No. J-34095 (440-T4)
F   Input shaft lifting tool – GM tool No. J-28544 (125C)
G   Sun gear/reaction carrier washer selection tool – GM tool No. J-28588 (125C)
H   Forward clutch spring compressor – GM tool No. J-23327-1 (125C and 440-T4)
I   1-2 and reverse band apply pin gauge GM tool No. J-33382 (440-T4)
J   Intermediate apply pin gauge – GM tool No. J-28535 (125C)

Universal bushing removal tool

A universal bushing removal tool makes it easy to remove most of the bushings found in the transmission. The sharp chisel point cuts and lifts the bushing away from the component in the same motion. **(see illustration)**

Bushing driver kit

You can't do without bushing installers when replacing bushings; they are a wise investment. Bushing replacement is an essential part of any overhaul and, without these tools, it is difficult to install a bushing and be sure it won't be damaged or cocked in the bore **(see illustration)**.

2.69 This universal clutch spring compressor will work on many different transmissions - we recommend the use of a clutch spring compressor for all the transmissions covered by this manual

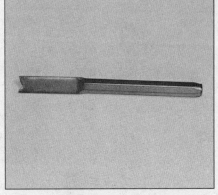

2.70 A general purpose bushing cutter is easy to use and works on most bushings - this one is Hayden tool no. T-0280-C

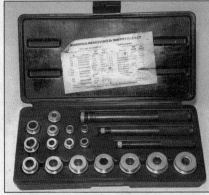

2.71 A special bushing service set is needed to install bushings to the correct depths in their bores

2.72 Check the bushing for alignment and depth before
you remove it

2.73 Use a bushing removal tool to drive out the old bushing

How to remove and install bushings

Before you remove a bushing, you need to check the installed depth of the bushing in the component. Measure how far the bushing is recessed in the bore and check to see if there are any oil holes or alignment marks that the new bushing needs to be aligned with **(see illustration)**. It's helpful to mark the location of the original bushing with a permanent marker before you remove the bushing - this provides a reference point for the installation of the new bushing.

Remove the old bushing with a bushing removal tool **(see illustration)**. Using a bushing removal tool prevents the possibility of damage to the bushing bore or surface it rides on by lifting and cutting the old bushing in the same motion. Other styles of chisels or punches can very easily damage the component you're removing the bushing from.

With the old bushing removed, check the bushing seating surface on the component for cracks or marks indicating a bushing that may have spun. Also look for bluing (a sign of overheating) or deep grooves indicating component damage.

After inspecting the component, select a bushing driver head that fits inside the bushing without play **(see illustration)**. Screw the head on the driver handle and place both the bushing and the installer squarely in the bore **(see illustration)**. Strike

2.74 Bushing installers come in various sizes and styles to
accommodate most bushings

the driver lightly with a hammer until the bushing is seated properly and to the correct depth. Inspect the bushing to be sure it is installed squarely and not cocked in the bore **(see illustration)**.

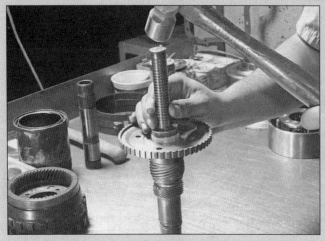

2.75 Use the proper-size bushing installer to drive the
bushing into the bore

2.76 Check that the bushing is properly seated and not
cocked in the bore

Universal seal installation tools

Seal installers are extremely helpful when overhauling an automatic transmission. Close tolerances between pistons and drums with sharp edges can cause seals to be cut or the seal lip will double-over during assembly. Cut (or otherwise damaged) seals are the most common cause of failed overhauls.

Seal installers are hand-held tools that you move around the seal as you install a piston into a clutch housing. The installers come in two basic types: a feeler gauge or "blade" type and a wire loop type. Both types work great for preventing the seals from folding or doubling over **(see illustration)**.

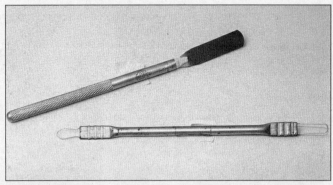

2.77 Blade type and wire loop type lip seal installation tools

How to install a clutch piston seal

Install the seal on the piston and make sure it is properly seated into the piston groove **(see illustration)**. The seal lip always faces the pressure, so make sure the lip faces down into the drum when installed. Properly lubricate the seal with a thin coat of clean automatic transmission fluid **(see illustration)**. Its

important that no foreign particles such as hair, lint or dirt get on the seal after you lubricate it. If the piston has an outer seal that could be cut or folded, place a seal protector over it **(see illustration)**.

Some piston/drum combinations have the inner seal on the drum and not on the piston **(see illustration)**. Place the piston

2.78 Install the seal on the piston; make sure the seal is seated in the groove and the lip is facing the proper direction

2.79 A brush is helpful when applying clean lubricant to the seals

2.80 Install the seal protector over the piston and seal. Once the outer seal protector is installed, it's impossible to damage the seal

2.81 Install the inner seal protector over the hub (if necessary) - it prevents seal damage from the snap-ring groove or splines

2.82 Install the piston squarely in the drum, push down while turning the piston until it's fully seated

2.83 Pull the seal protectors out when the piston is seated. When the piston is properly installed, you should be able to rotate the piston in the bore

2.84 Carefully slide the seal tool around the piston and work the seal lip into the bore - be very careful and do not cut the seal

with the seal protector in the drum and slowly press down on the piston while twisting to allow the piston to seat (**see illustration**). Once the piston is fully seated simply pull the protectors out (**see illustration**).

When installing a piston into a drum and the seal protectors are not available, a seal installation tool is needed. As the piston is being installed, insert the tool between the piston and drum and slowly depress the lip of the seal (**see illustration**). Move the tool around the seal and slowly push the piston down until it is seated. If you feel the tool bind while you are moving it around the circumference of the piston, it may be necessary to remove the piston and check the seal again. Using the seal installation tool method, it may take several tries to properly seat the piston.

2.85 Slide hammers are used to remove the front pump on THM350 and THM400 transmissions. Note that the lower slide hammer is a homemade unit

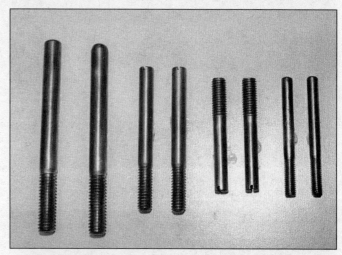

2.86 Alignment studs are a necessary when installing the oil pump and valve body. Note that all of these are homemade

Slide hammers

To remove the front pump on either a THM350 or THM400, a pair of slide hammers are needed. Screw the threaded ends on the slide hammers into the threaded holes on the pump body and tighten securely, then operate the slide hammers in unison (**see illustration**). Slide hammers are also used with certain types of bushing removal tools.

Pump and valve body alignment pin set

These tools are homemade and simple to make. Basically, they are 2-1/2 to 3-1/2 inch bolts of the correct diameter and thread pitch with the heads cut off and slots cut in the ends so they can be removed and installed with a flat-blade screwdriver. When screwed into the case, these pins help keep gaskets and parts aligned properly as they are installed (**see illustration**).

Precision measuring tools

Think of the tools in the following list as the final additions to your tool collection. If you're planning to rebuild a transmission, you've probably already accumulated all the screwdrivers, wrenches, sockets, pliers and other everyday hand tools that you need. Now it's time to round up the stuff you'll need to do your own measurements when you rebuild that transmission.

The tool pool strategy

If you're reading this book, you may be a motorhead, but transmission rebuilding isn't your life - it's an avocation. You may just want to save some money, have a little fun and learn something about

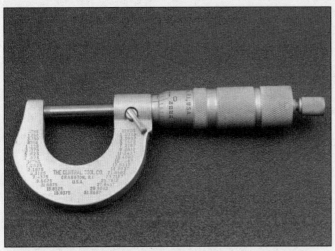

2.87 The one-inch micrometer is helpful when you need to measure the thickness of selective-fit snap-rings, clutch plates, etc.

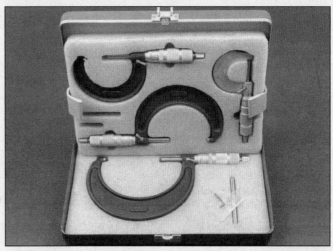

2.88 Get a good-quality micrometer set if you can afford it - this set has four micrometers ranging in size from one to four inches

2.89 Mechanical readout micrometers are easier to read than conventional micrometers, but they're a bit more expensive

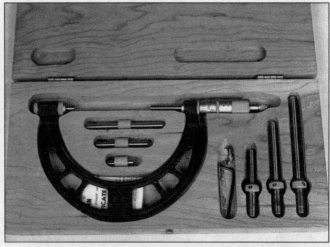

2.90 Avoid micrometer "sets" with interchangeable anvils - they're awkward to use when measuring little parts and changing the anvils is a hassle

transmission rebuilding. If that description fits your level of involvement, think about forming a "tool pool" with a friend or neighbor who wants to get into transmission rebuilding, but doesn't want to spend a lot of money. For example, you can buy a set of micrometers and the other guy can buy a dial indicator and a set of pressure gauges.

Start with the basics

It would be great to own every precision measuring tool listed here, but you don't really need a machinist's chest crammed with exotic calipers and micrometers. You can often get by just fine with nothing more than feeler gauges and a dial indicator. Even most professional transmission builders use only three precision measuring tools 95-percent of the time: a one-inch outside micrometer, a dial indicator and a good feeler gauge set. So start your collection with these three items.

Micrometers

When you're rebuilding a transmission , you need to know the exact thickness of a number of pieces. Whether you're measuring the

diameter of an apply piston or the thickness of a selective washer or a snap-ring, your tool of choice should be the trusty one-inch outside micrometer **(see illustration)**.

Insist on accuracy to within one ten-thousandths of an inch (0.0001-inch) when you shop for a micrometer. You'll probably never need that kind of precision, but the extra decimal place will help you decide which way to round off a close measurement.

To rebuild most transmissions you only need a 0 to 1-inch micrometer. In very rare cases you could use a 1 to 2-inch micrometer. Eventually you may want a set that spans four or even five ranges **(see illustration)**.

Digital and mechanical readout micrometers **(see illustration)** are easier to read than conventional micrometers, but they're a bit more expensive. If you're uncomfortable reading a conventional micrometer, then get a digital or mechanical readout type.

Unless you're not going to use them very often, stay away from micrometers with interchangeable anvils **(see illustration)**. In theory, one of these beauties can do the work of five or six single-range micrometers. The trouble is, they're awkward to use when measuring little parts, and changing the anvils is a hassle.

How to read a micrometer

The outside micrometer is without a doubt the most widely used precision measuring tool. It can be used to make a variety of highly accurate measurements without much possibility of error through misreading, a problem associated with other measuring instruments, such as vernier calipers.

Like any slide caliper, the outside micrometer uses the "double contact" of its spindle and anvil **(see illustration)** touching the object to be measured to determine that object's dimensions. Unlike a caliper, however, the micrometer also features a unique precision screw adjustment which can be read with a great deal more accuracy than calipers.

Why is this screw adjustment so accurate? Because years ago toolmakers discovered that a screw with 40 precision machined threads to the inch will advance one-fortieth (0.025) of an inch with each complete turn. The screw threads on the spindle revolve inside a fixed nut concealed by a sleeve.

On a one-inch micrometer, this sleeve is engraved longitudinally with exactly 40 lines to the inch, to correspond with the number of threads on the spindle. Every fourth line is made longer and is numbered one-tenth inch, two-tenths, etc. The other lines are often staggered to make them easier to read.

The thimble (the barrel which moves up and down the sleeve as it rotates) is divided into 25 divisions around the circumference of its beveled edge and is numbered from zero to 25. Close the micrometer spindle until it touches the anvil: You should see nothing but the zero line on the sleeve next to the beveled edge of the thimble. And the zero line of the thimble should be aligned with the horizontal (or axial) line on the sleeve. Remember: Each full revolution of the spindle from zero to zero advances or retracts the spindle one-fortieth or 0.025-inch. Therefore, if you rotate the thimble from zero on the beveled edge to the first graduation, you will move the spindle 1/25th of 1/40th, or 1/25th of 25/1000ths, which equals 1/1000th, or 0.001-inch.

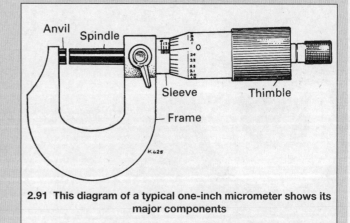

2.91 This diagram of a typical one-inch micrometer shows its major components

Remember: Each numbered graduation on the sleeve represents 0.1-inch, each of the other sleeve graduations represents 0.025-inch and each graduation on the thimble represents 0.001-inch. Remember those three and you're halfway there.

For example: Suppose the 4 line is visible on the sleeve. This represents 0.400-inch. Then suppose there are an additional three lines (the short ones without numbers) showing. These marks are worth 0.025-inch each, or 0.075-inch. Finally, there are also two marks on the beveled edge of the thimble beyond the zero mark, each good for 0.001-inch, or a total of 0.002-inch. Add it all up and you get 0.400 plus 0.075 plus 0.002, which equals 0.477-inch.

Some beginners use a "dollars, quarters and cents" analogy to simplify reading a micrometer. Add up the bucks and change, then put a decimal point instead of a dollar sign in front of the sum!

2.92 The dial indicator is indispensable for measuring endplay in a transmission, as well as other critical measurements

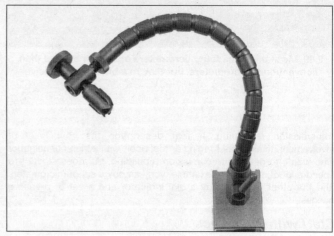

2.93 Get an adjustable, flexible fixture like this one, and a magnetic base, to ensure maximum versatility from your dial indicator

Dial indicators

The dial indicator **(see illustration)** is another measuring mainstay. It's indispensable for measuring endplay in a transmission and can also be used for engine work. Make sure the dial indicator you buy has a probe with at least one inch of travel, graduated in 0.001-inch increments.

Buy a dial indicator set that includes a flexible fixture and a magnetic stand **(see illustration)**. If the model you buy doesn't have a magnetic base, buy one separately. Make sure the magnet is plenty strong. If a weak magnet comes loose and the dial indicator takes a tumble on a concrete floor, you can kiss it good-bye. Make sure the arm that attaches the dial indicator to the flexible fixture is sturdy and the locking clamps are easy to operate.

Some dial indicators are designed to measure depth or flatness **(see illustration)**. They have a removable base that straddles a hole. To measure the flatness of your valve body halves or the transmission case, you'll also need a U-shaped bridge for your dial indicator.

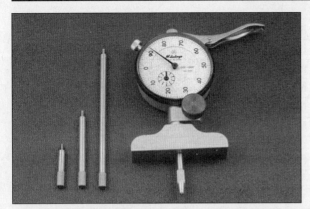

2.94 This dial indicator is designed to measure depth or flatness. It has a removable base that straddles a hole. To measure the flatness of your valve body, pump halves or the transmission case you'll need a U-shaped bridge

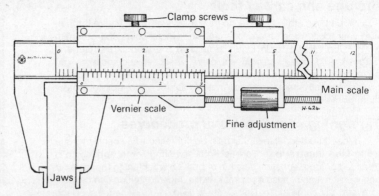

2.95 Vernier calipers aren't quite as accurate as micrometers, but they're handy for quick measurements, are relatively inexpensive, and because they've got jaws that can measure internal and external dimensions, they're versatile

Calipers

Vernier calipers **(see illustration)** aren't quite as accurate as a micrometer, but they're handy for quick measurements and they're relatively inexpensive. Most calipers have inside and outside jaws, so you can measure the inside diameter of a hole, or the outside diameter of a part.

Better-quality calipers have a dust shield over the geared rack that turns the dial to prevent small metal particles from jamming the mechanism. Make sure there's no play in the moveable jaw. To check, put a thin piece of metal between the jaws and measure its thickness with the metal close to the rack, then out near the tips of the jaws. Compare your two measurements. If they vary by more than 0.001-inch, look at another caliper - the jaw mechanism is deflecting.

If your eyes are going bad, or already are bad, vernier calipers can be difficult to read. Dial calipers **(see illustration)** are a better choice. Dial calipers combine the measuring capabilities of micrometers with the convenience of dial indicators. Because they're much easier to read quickly than vernier calipers, they're ideal for taking quick measurements when absolute accuracy isn't necessary. Like conventional vernier calipers, they have both inside and outside jaws which allow you to quickly determine the diameter of a hole or a part. Get a six-inch dial caliper, graduated in 0.001-inch increments.

2.96 Dial calipers are a lot easier to read than conventional vernier calipers, particularly if your eyesight isn't as good as it used to be!

How to read a vernier caliper

On the lower half of the main beam, each inch is divided into ten numbered increments, or tenths (0.100-inch, 0.200-inch, etc.). Each tenth is divided into four increments of 0.025-inch each. The vernier scale has 25 increments, each representing a thousandth (0.001) of an inch.

First read the number of inches, then read the number of tenths. Add to this 0.025-inch; for each additional graduation. Using the English vernier scale, determine which graduation of the vernier lines up exactly with a graduation on the main beam. This vernier graduation is the number of thousandths which are to be added to the previous readings.

For example, let's say:
1) *The number of inches is zero, or 0.000-inch;*
2) *The number of tenths is 4, or 0.400-inch;*
3) *The number of 0.025's is 2, or 0.050-inch; and*
4) *The vernier graduation which lines up with a graduation on the main beam is 15, or 0.015-inch.*
5) *Add them up:*
   0.000
   0.400
   0.050
   0.015

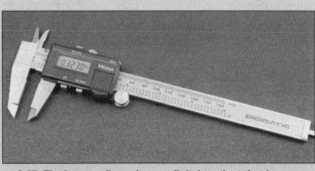

2.97 The latest calipers have a digital readout that is even easier to read than a dial caliper - another advantage of digital calipers is that they have a small microchip that allows them to convert instantaneously from inch to metric dimensions

6) *And you get:*
   0.46-inch
That's all there is to it!

The latest calipers **(see illustration)** have a digital LCD display that indicates both inch and metric dimensions. If you can afford one of these, it's the hot setup.

Storage and care of tools

Good tools are expensive, so treat them well. After you're through with your tools, wipe off any dirt, grease or metal chips and put them away. Don't leave tools Lying around in the work area. General purpose hand tools - screwdrivers, pliers, wrenches and sockets - can be hung on a wall panel or stored in a tool box. Store precision measuring instruments, gauges, meters, etc. in a tool box to protect them from dust, dirt, metal chips and humidity.

Tightening sequences and procedures

Most threaded fasteners should be tightened to a specific torque value (see illustration). Torque is the twisting force applied to a threaded component such as a nut or bolt. Overtightening the fastener can weaken it and cause it to break, while undertightening can cause it to eventually come loose. Bolts, screws and studs, depending on the material they are made of and their thread diameters, have specific torque values. Be sure to follow the torque recommendations closely. For fasteners not assigned a specific torque, a general torque value chart is presented here as a guide. These torque values are for dry (unlubricated) fasteners threaded into steel or cast iron (not aluminum). As was previously mentioned, the size and grade of a fastener determine the amount of torque that can safely be applied to it. The figures listed here are approximate for Grade 2 and Grade 3 fasteners. Higher grades can tolerate higher torque values.

If fasteners are laid out in a pattern - such as oil pump bolts, oil pan bolts, valve body bolts, etc. - loosen and tighten them in sequence to avoid warping the component. Where it matters, we'll show you this sequence. If a specific pattern isn't that important, the following rule-of-thumb guide will prevent warping.

First, install the bolts or nuts finger-tight. Then tighten them one full turn each, in a criss-cross or diagonal pattern. Then return to the first one and, following the same pattern, tighten them all one-half turn. Finally, tighten each of them one-quarter turn at a time until each fastener has been tightened to the proper torque. To loosen and remove the fasteners, reverse this procedure.

Metric thread sizes	Ft-lbs	Nm
M-6	6 to 9	9 to 12
M-8	14 to 21	19 to 28
M-10	28 to 40	38 to 54
M-12	50 to 71	68 to 96
M-14	80 to 140	109 to 154

Pipe thread sizes		
1/8	5 to 8	7 to 10
1/4	12 to 18	17 to 24
3/8	22 to 33	30 to 44
1/2	25 to 35	34 to 47

U.S. thread sizes		
1/4 – 20	6 to 9	9 to 12
5/16 – 18	12 to 18	17 to 24
5/16 – 24	14 to 20	19 to 27
3/8 – 16	22 to 32	30 to 43
3/8 – 24	27 to 38	37 to 51
7/16 – 14	40 to 55	55 to 74
7/16 – 20	40 to 60	55 to 81
1/2 – 13	55 to 80	75 to 108

2.98 Standard torque values for various bolt sizes

How to remove broken fasteners

Sooner or later, you're going to break off a bolt inside its threaded hole. There are several ways to remove it. Before you buy an expensive extractor set, try some of the following cheaper methods first.

First, regardless of which of the following methods you use, be sure to use penetrating oil. Penetrating oil is a special light oil with excellent penetrating power for freeing dirty and rusty fasteners. But it also works well on tightly torqued broken fasteners.

If enough of the fastener protrudes from its hole and if it isn't torqued down too tightly, you can often remove it with Vise-grips or a small pipe wrench. If that doesn't work, or if the fastener doesn't provide sufficient purchase for pliers or a wrench, try filing it down to take a wrench, or cut a slot in it to accept a screwdriver (see illustration). If you still can't get it off - and you know how to weld - try welding a flat piece of steel, or a nut, to the top of the broken fastener. If the fastener is broken off flush with - or below - the top of its hole, try tapping it out with a small, sharp punch. If that doesn't work, try drilling out the broken fastener with a bit only slightly smaller than the inside diameter of the hole. For example, if the hole is 1/2-inch in diameter, use a 15/32-inch drill bit. This leaves a shell which you can pick out with a sharp chisel.

If THAT doesn't work, you'll have to resort to some form of screw extractor, such as an E-Z-Out (see illustration). Screw extractors are sold in sets which can remove anything from 1/4-inch to 1-inch bolts or studs. Most extractors are fluted and tapered high-grade steel. To use a screw extractor, drill a hole

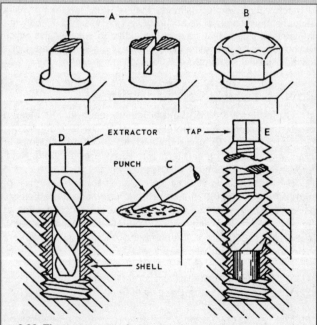

2.99 There are several ways to remove a broken fastener

A	File it flat or slot it	D	Use a screw extractor (like an E-Z-Out)
B	Weld on a nut		
C	Use a punch to unscrew it	E	Use a tap to remove the shell

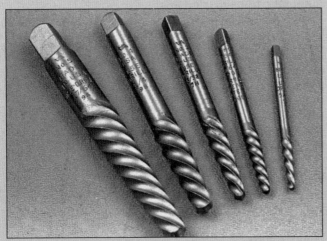

2.100 A typical assortment of E-Z-Out extractors

**2.101 When screwing in the E-Z-Out, make sure
it's centered properly**

slightly smaller than the O.D. of the extractor you're going to use (Extractor sets include the manufacturer's recommendations for what size drill bit to use with each extractor size). Then screw in the extractor **(see illustration)** and back it - and the broken fastener - out. Extractors are reverse-threaded, so they won't unscrew when you back them out.

A word to the wise: Even though an E-Z-Out will usually save your bacon, it can cause even more grief if you're careless or sloppy. Drilling the hole for the extractor off-center, or using too small, or too big, a bit for the size of the fastener you're removing will only make things worse. So be careful!

How to repair broken threads

Sometimes, the internal threads of a nut or bolt hole can become stripped, usually from overtightening. Stripping threads is an all-too-common occurrence, especially when working with aluminum parts, because aluminum is so soft that it easily strips out. Overtightened pan bolts are the most common cause of stripped threads.

Usually, external or internal threads are only partially stripped. After they've been cleaned up with a tap or die, they'll still work. Sometimes, however, threads are badly damaged.

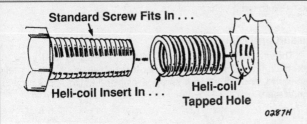

2.102 To install a Heli-Coil, drill out the hole, tap it with the special included tap and screw in the Heli-Coil

When this happens, you've got three choices:

1) *Drill and tap the hole to the next suitable oversize and install a larger diameter bolt, screw or stud.*

2) *Drill and tap the hole to accept a threaded plug, then drill and tap the plug to the original screw size. You can also buy a plug already threaded to the original size. Then you simply drill a hole to the specified size, then run the threaded plug into the hole with a bolt and jam nut. Once the plug is fully seated, remove the jam nut and bolt.*

3) *The third method uses a patented thread repair kit like Heli-Coil or Slimsert. These easy-to-use kits are designed to repair damaged threads in straight-through holes and blind holes. Both are available as kits which can handle a variety of sizes and thread patterns. Drill the hole, then tap it with the special included tap. Install the Heli-Coil* **(see illustration)** *and the hole is back to its original diameter and thread pitch.*

Regardless of which method you use, be sure to proceed calmly and carefully. A little impatience or carelessness during one of these relatively simple procedures can ruin your whole day's work and cost you a bundle if you wreck an expensive case.

Component disassembly

Disassemble components carefully to help ensure that the parts go back together properly. Note the sequence in which parts are removed. Make note of special characteristics or marks on parts that can be installed more than one way, such as a grooved thrust washer on a shaft. It's a good idea to lay the disassembled parts out on a clean surface in the order in which you removed them. It may also be helpful to make sketches or take instant photos of components before removal.

When you remove fasteners from a component, keep track of their locations. Thread a bolt back into a part, or put the washers and nut back on a stud, to prevent mix-ups later. If that isn't practical, put fasteners in small boxes. A cupcake or muffin tin, or an egg crate, is ideal for this purpose - each cavity can hold the bolts and nuts from a particular area (i.e. oil pan bolts, valve body bolts, transmission mount bolts, etc.). A pan of this type is helpful when working on assemblies with very small parts, such as the valve body or governor. Mark each cavity with paint or tape to identify the contents.

When you unplug the connector(s) between two wire harnesses, or even two wires, it's a good idea to identify the two halves with numbered pieces of masking tape - or a pair of matching pieces of colored electrical tape - so they can be easily reconnected.

Gasket sealing surfaces

Gaskets seal the mating surfaces between two parts to prevent lubricants, fluids, vacuum or pressure from leaking out between them. Age, heat and pressure can cause the two parts to stick together so tightly that they're difficult to separate. Often, you can loosen the assembly by striking it with a soft-face hammer near the mating surfaces. You can use a regular hammer if you place a block of wood between the hammer and the part, but don't hammer on cast or delicate parts that can be easily damaged. When a part refuses to come off, look for a fastener that you forgot to remove.

Don't use a screwdriver or prybar to pry apart an assembly. It can easily damage the gasket sealing surfaces of the parts, which must be smooth to seal properly. If prying is absolutely necessary, use an old broom handle or a section of hard-wood dowel.

Once the parts are separated, carefully scrape off the old gasket and clean the gasket surface. If some gasket material refused to come off, soak it with rust penetrant or treat it with a special chemical to soften it, then scrape it off carefully with a razor blade. The mating surfaces must be clean and smooth when you're done. Never use a gasket sealer when reassembling any internal transmission component.

Automotive chemicals and lubricants

A wide variety of automotive chemicals and lubricants - ranging from cleaning solvents and degreasers to lubricants and protective sprays for rubber, plastic and vinyl - are available.

Cleaners

Brake system cleaner

Brake system cleaner removes brake dust, grease and brake fluid from brake parts like disc brake rotors, where a spotless surface is essential. It leaves no residue and often eliminates brake squeal caused by contaminants. Because it leaves no residue, brake cleaner is often used for cleaning transmission parts as well.

Carburetor and choke cleaner

Carburetor and choke cleaner is a strong solvent for gum, varnish and carbon. Most carburetor cleaners leave a dry-type lubricant film which will not harden or gum up. So don't use carb cleaner on electrical components.

Degreasers

Degreasers are heavy-duty solvents used to remove grease from the outside of the transmission and from chassis components. They're usually sprayed or brushed on. Depending on the type, they're rinsed off either with water or solvent.

Demoisturants

Demoisturants remove water and moisture from electrical components such as alternators, voltage regulators, electrical connectors and fuse blocks. They are non-conductive, non-corrosive and non-flammable.

Electrical cleaner

Electrical cleaner removes oxidation, corrosion and carbon deposits from electrical contacts, restoring full current flow. It can also be used to clean spark plugs, carburetor jets, voltage regulators and other parts where an oil-free surface is necessary.

Lubricants

Moly penetrants

Moly penetrants loosen and lubricate frozen, rusted and corroded fasteners and prevent future rusting or freezing.

Automatic transmission fluid

Automatic transmission fluid is a chemically formulated lubricant that contains additives to make the fluid more slippery under certain operating conditions. It also normally contains a wide variety of additives to prevent corrosion and reduce foaming and wear in automatic transmissions.

Petroleum Jelly

Petroleum jelly is pure, clear petroleum base grease or jelly it is safe and idea for lubricating seals, holding small parts during assembly.

Silicone lubricants

Silicone lubricants are used to protect rubber, plastic, vinyl and nylon parts.

White grease

White grease is a heavy grease for metal-to-metal applications where water is present. It stays soft under both low and high temperatures (usually from -100 to +190-degrees F), and won't wash off or dilute when exposed to water. Another good "glue" for holding parts in place during assembly.

Sealants

Anaerobic sealant

Anaerobic sealant is much like RTV in that it can be used either to seal gaskets or to form gaskets by itself. It remains flexible, is solvent resistant and fills surface imperfections. The difference between an anaerobic sealant and an RTV-type sealant is in the curing. RTV cures when exposed to air, while an anaerobic sealant cures only in the absence of air. This means that an anaerobic sealant cures only after the assembly of parts, sealing them together.

RTV sealant

RTV sealant is one of the most widely used gasket compounds. Made from silicone, RTV is air curing, it seals, bonds, waterproofs, fills surface irregularities, remains flexible, doesn't shrink, is relatively easy to remove, and is used as a supplementary sealer with almost all low and medium temperature gaskets.

Thread and pipe sealant

Thread and pipe sealant is used for sealing hydraulic and pneumatic fittings and vacuum lines. It is usually made from a teflon compound, and comes in a spray, a paint-on liquid and as a wrap-around tape.

Chemicals

Anaerobic locking compounds

Anaerobic locking compounds are used to keep fasteners from vibrating or working loose and cure only after installation, in the absence of air. Medium strength locking compound is used for small nuts, bolts and screws that may be removed later. High-strength locking compound is for large nuts, bolts and studs which aren't removed on a regular basis.

Anti-seize compound

Anti-seize compound prevents seizing, galling, cold welding, rust and corrosion in fasteners. High-temperature anti-seize, usually made with copper and graphite lubricants, is used for exhaust system and exhaust manifold bolts.

Safety first!

Essential DOs and DON'Ts

Regardless of how enthusiastic you may be about getting on with the job at hand, take the time to ensure that your safety is not jeopardized. A moment's lack of attention can result in an accident, as can failure to observe certain simple safety precautions. The possibility of an accident will always exist, and the following points should not be considered a comprehensive list of all dangers. Rather, they are intended to make you aware of the risks and to encourage a safety-conscious approach to all work you carry out on your vehicle.

DON'T rely on a jack when working under the vehicle. Always use approved jackstands to support the weight of the vehicle and place them under the recommended lift or support points.

DON'T attempt to loosen extremely tight fasteners (i.e. wheel lug nuts) while the vehicle is on a jack - it may fall.

DON'T start the engine without first making sure that the transmission is in Neutral (or Park where applicable) and the parking brake is set.

DON'T remove the radiator cap from a hot cooling system - let it cool or cover it with a cloth and release the pressure gradually.

DON'T attempt to drain the transmission oil until you are sure it has cooled to the point that it will not burn you.

DON'T touch any part of the engine or exhaust system until it has cooled sufficiently to avoid burns.

DON'T siphon toxic liquids such as gasoline, antifreeze and brake fluid by mouth, or allow them to remain on your skin.

DON'T inhale brake lining or clutch disc dust - it is potentially hazardous (see Asbestos below)

DON'T allow spilled oil or grease to remain on the floor - wipe it up before someone slips on it.

DON'T use loose-fitting wrenches or other tools which may slip and cause injury.

DON'T push on wrenches when loosening or tightening nuts or bolts. Always try to pull the wrench toward you. If the situation calls for pushing the wrench away, push with an open hand to avoid scraped knuckles if the wrench should slip.

DON'T attempt to lift a heavy component alone - get someone to help you.

DON'T rush or take unsafe shortcuts to finish a job.

DON'T allow children or animals in or around the vehicle while you are working on it.

DO wear eye protection when using power tools such as a drill, sander, bench grinder, etc. and when working under a vehicle.

DO keep loose clothing and long hair well out of the way of moving parts.

DO make sure that any hoist used has a safe working load rating adequate for the job.

DO get someone to check on you periodically when working alone on a vehicle.

DO carry out work in a logical sequence and make sure that everything is correctly assembled and tightened.

DO keep chemicals and fluids tightly capped and out of the reach of children and pets.

DO remember that your vehicle's safety affects that of yourself and others. If in doubt on any point, get professional advice.

Asbestos

Certain friction, insulating, sealing, and other products - such as brake linings, brake bands, clutch linings, torque converters, gaskets, etc. - contain asbestos. Extreme care must be taken to avoid inhalation of dust from such products since it is hazardous to health. If in doubt, assume that they do contain asbestos.

Batteries

Never create a spark or allow a bare light bulb near a battery. They normally give off a certain amount of hydrogen gas, which is highly explosive.

Always disconnect the battery ground (-) cable at the battery before working on the fuel or electrical systems.

If possible, loosen the filler caps or cover when charging the battery from an external source (this does not apply to sealed or maintenance-free batteries). Do not charge at an excessive rate or the battery may burst.

Take care when adding water to a non maintenance-free battery and when carrying a battery. The electrolyte, even when diluted, is very corrosive and should not be allowed to contact clothing or skin.

Always wear eye protection when cleaning the battery to prevent the caustic deposits from entering your eyes.

Fire

We strongly recommend that a fire extinguisher suitable for use on fuel and electrical fires be kept handy in the garage or workshop at all times. Never try to extinguish a fuel or electrical fire with water. Post the phone number for the nearest fire department in a conspicuous location near the phone.

Fumes

Certain fumes are highly toxic and can quickly cause unconsciousness and even death if inhaled to any extent. Gasoline vapor falls into this category, as do the vapors from some cleaning solvents. Any draining or pouring of such volatile fluids should be done in a well ventilated area.

When using cleaning fluids and solvents, read the instructions on the container carefully. Never use materials from unmarked containers.

Never run the engine in an enclosed space, such as a garage. Exhaust fumes contain carbon monoxide, which is extremely poisonous. If you need to run the engine, always do so in the open air, or at least have the rear of the vehicle outside the work area.

Gasoline

Remember at all times that gasoline is highly flammable. Never smoke or have any kind of open flame around when working on a vehicle. But the risk does not end there. A spark caused by an electrical short circuit, by two metal surfaces contacting each other, or even by static electricity built up in your body under certain conditions, can ignite gasoline vapors, which, in a confined space, are highly explosive. Do not, under any circumstances, use gasoline for cleaning parts. Use an approved safety solvent. Also, DO NOT STORE GASOLINE IN A GLASS CONTAINER - use an approved metal or plastic container only!

Always disconnect the battery ground (-) cable at the battery before working on any part of the fuel system or electrical system. Never risk spilling a fuel on a hot engine or exhaust component.

Household current

When using an electric power tool, inspection light, etc., which operates on household current, always make sure that the tool is correctly connected to its plug and that, where necessary, it is properly grounded. Do not use such items in damp conditions and, again, do not create a spark or apply excessive heat in the vicinity of fuel or fuel vapor.

Secondary ignition system voltage

A severe electric shock can result from touching certain parts of the ignition system (such as the spark plug wires) when the engine is running or being cranked, particularly if components are damp or the insulation is defective. In the case of an electronic ignition system, the secondary system voltage is much higher and could prove fatal.

Keep it clean

Get in the habit of taking a regular look around the shop to check for potential dangers. Keep the work area clean and neat. Sweep up all debris and dispose of it as soon as possible. Don't leave tools lying around on the floor.

Be very careful with oily rags. Spontaneous combustion can occur if they're left in a pile, so dispose of them properly in a covered metal container.

Check all equipment and tools for security and safety hazards (like frayed cords). Make necessary repairs as soon as a problem is noticed - don't wait for a shelf unit to collapse before fixing it.

Accidents and emergencies

Shop accidents range from minor cuts and skinned knuckles to serious injuries requiring immediate medical attention. The former are inevitable, while the latter are, hopefully, avoidable or at least uncommon. Think about what you would do in the event of an accident. Get some first aid training and have an adequate first aid kit somewhere within easy reach.

Think about what you would do if you were badly hurt and incapacitated. Is there someone nearby who could be summoned quickly? If possible, never work alone just in case something goes wrong.

If you had to cope with someone else's accident, would you know what to do? Dealing with accidents is a large and complex subject, and it's easy to make matters worse if you have no idea how to respond. Rather than attempt to deal with this subject in a superficial manner, buy a good First Aid book and read it carefully. Better yet, take a course in First Aid at a local junior college.

Environmental safety

At the time this manual was being written, several state and federal regulations governing the storage and disposal of oil and other lubricants, gasoline, solvents and antifreeze were pending (contact the appropriate government agency or your local auto parts store for the latest information). Be absolutely certain that all materials are properly stored, handled and disposed of. Never pour used or leftover oil, solvents or antifreeze down the drain or dump them on the ground. Also, don't allow volatile liquids to evaporate - keep them in sealed containers. Air conditioning refrigerant should never be expelled into the atmosphere. Have a properly equipped shop discharge and recharge the system for you.

Chapter 3
Automatic transmission fundamentals

Simply put, any transmission's function, be it manual or automatic, is to transfer the rotational energy of the engine to the rear wheels of the vehicle so you can move down the road. The most basic example of a transmission is a bicycle chain. Think of your legs as the "engine" and the chain and sprockets as the "transmission."

wheels, a set of controls (the hydraulic system) to sense when it's the correct time for a gearchange and a planetary geartrain that can shift gears without disengaging the engine from the transmission (**see illustration**).

Gear ratios

Most power sources have an optimum range of rpm (revolutions per minute) when they are most efficient. Using our bicycle example, think about riding up a very steep hill in high gear: your legs will be straining against the pedals, which will be hardly moving - you'll groan and sweat, but make little progress. Likewise, if you're riding downhill in low gear, you'll be moving your legs so fast that it will be difficult to apply any force with your legs during the short time that each pedal is moving down.

In this example, your legs during bicycle riding are like an automobile engine. Like your legs, engines have a certain range of rpm during which they'll operate efficiently without strain, generally between about 2,000 and 4,000 rpm. In order to move a vehicle both quickly down the freeway and slowly down a residential street while maintaining rpm within this range, varying gear ratios are necessary.

If you can remember your first drive in a vehicle with a manual transmission, you'll probably remember alternately bogging the engine by selecting too high a gear and winding out the engine by selecting too low a gear. Automatic transmissions use a torque converter to maintain a continuous fluid coupling between the engine and rear

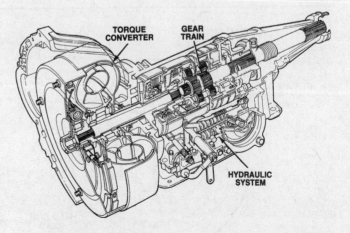

3.1 The automatic transmission uses a torque converter instead of a clutch, a planetary geartrain that can shift gears while power is still applied to the rear wheels and a sophisticated hydraulic system that controls shifting

PLANETARY GEARSET

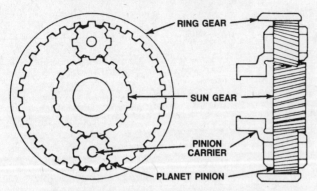

3.2 A front and side view of a planetary gearset

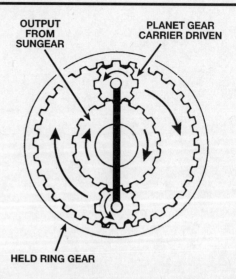

3.3 A planetary gearset providing major gear reduction

Planetary gearsets

Planetary gearsets allow gearchanges without disconnecting the engine from the drive wheels with a clutch, as with a manual transmission. These gearsets are so named because of the way they operate - planet gears within a ring gear rotate around a sun gear **(see illustration)**. Gear changes with planetary gearsets are made by holding one member of the set (the planet carrier, ring gear or sun gear) and driving another. Any member of a planetary gearset can play any part in transmitting power by being held or driven. The planet gears are held in a *planet carrier*, which keeps the planet gears evenly spaced between the ring and sun gears.

Operation of a simple planetary gearset

Let's look at the way a simple planetary gearset operates. If the ring gear is held and the sun gear is rotated, the planet gears will "walk" around the sun gear and rotate the planet carrier in the same direction as the sun gear, but at a much slower speed than the sun gear (major gear reduction) **(see illustration)**. If the sun gear is held and the ring gear is rotated, the planet gears will walk around the sun gear at a somewhat slower speed than the ring gear (minor gear reduction) **(see illustration)**. By holding the planet carrier and driving the sun gear, the ring gear is turned in the opposite direction (reverse and gear reduction) **(see illustration)**. Direct drive can be achieved by locking any two elements of the planetary gearset together.

The compound planetary gearset

Some planetary gearsets are *compound*, meaning more than one set of planetary gears share a single sun gear. The most common compound gearset is the Simpson planetary gearset. This gearset uses two planetary assemblies on a single sun gear, which is attached to the transmission output shaft. This arrangement of gears allows for more possible gear ranges than the simple planetary gearset described above.

Apply devices

To make an automatic transmission work, methods must be provided to hold members of the planetary gearsets and provide the shifts into different gear ranges. We call these components *apply devices* because they apply the various gear ranges. There are three apply devices: Clutches, bands and one-way clutches.

Clutches

Well, you caught us. There really *are* clutches in automatic transmissions. However, the clutches are of much smaller diameter than the big clutch plate in a manual-transmission vehicle, and the

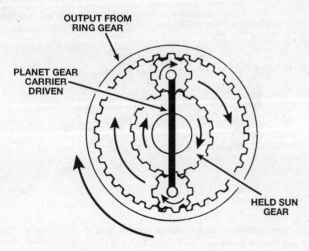

3.4 A planetary gearset providing minor gear reduction

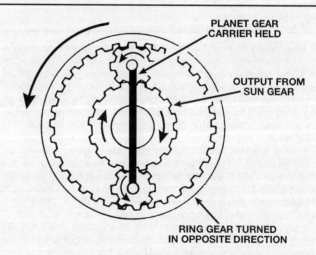

3.5 A planetary gearset providing reverse gear and gear reduction

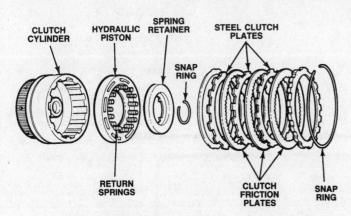

3.6 A typical clutch pack and actuating piston assembly - exploded view

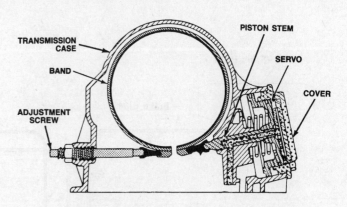

3.7 A typical band and servo assembly - cutaway view

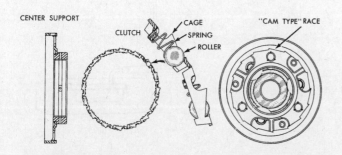

3.8 A typical roller clutch assembly - when the outer race is rotating clockwise in relation to the inner race, the rollers are in the notched area of the cam-type race and the two races rotate independently; however, when the outer race is rotating counter-clockwise in relation to the inner race, the rollers move up their ramps, locking the inner and outer races together

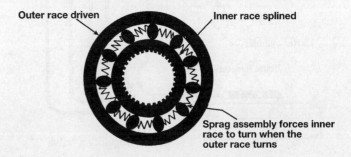

3.9 Sprag-type clutches are stronger than roller clutches - the dog-bone shaped sprags allow the inner race to turn independently when it is rotating clockwise in relation to the outer race but lock the races together when the inner race is rotating counter-clockwise in relation to the outer race

clutches in automatic transmissions consist of multiple friction plates. They are often referred to as "clutch packs." These clutches are very similar to motorcycle multiple-plate clutches, having a set of friction plates sandwiched together with a set of plain steel plates. The friction plates are made of an asbestos-type friction material. The friction plates are attached to one driving member while the steel plates are attached to another. When the clutch piston applies force to squeeze the sandwich of plates together, the clutch applies and the two members are locked together. When the piston releases force, the clutch return springs force the piston up, allowing the plates to freely rotate, releasing the two members from each other **(see illustration).**

Like other components in automatic transmissions, the clutch packs operate in an environment of transmission fluid, which prevents excessive wear to the friction plates, rinses away worn clutch material and cools the clutch assembly so it does not overheat and become less effective.

Bands

Bands, like clutches, use a friction surface of an asbestos-type material that's attached to the inside surface of a thin, flexible steel shell. As its name implies, the band encircles the drum of a planetary drive assembly. When a servo piston applies force to one of the ends of the band (the other end is held stationary), the drum is clamped securely by the band and held stationary **(see illustration).** When the piston force is released, the band expands and the drum is allowed to rotate freely.

One-way clutches

As alternatives to bands or disc-type clutches, one-way clutches are used in automatic transmissions to provide a simpler method of applying and releasing a particular gear range. These devices do not use hydraulic pressure, but instead use a simple mechanism that allows rotation in one direction only. Not only are these apply/release devices simpler, they are actually preferred in some situations, since they are faster in their apply/release cycles than are hydraulic-type devices, since hydraulic devices must build up and release fluid pressure, causing a brief delay.

Two types of clutches are used in the vehicles covered by this manual. The roller-type clutch **(see illustration)** is the most common. This type of clutch uses roller-type bearings that are held into pockets when the inner or outer drum is rotating in one direction, but, when the drum is turned the other direction, the rollers move up ramps, locking the rollers against the other drum. Sprag-type clutches **(see illustration)** use the same principle as roller-type clutches, but use sprags (dog-bone shaped locking devices) instead of rollers. Since the sprags are taller when rotated in one direction than when they are rotated in the other direction, they allow freewheeling in one direction and lock-up in the other direction.

Roller-type clutches are generally used in normal-duty applications, but sprags are preferred in high-performance applications, since they provide a stronger lock-up. In the transmissions covered by this manual, only some early-model THM400 transmissions came originally equipped with sprag-type clutches. A common race-type modification to the THM350 transmission is to install a sprag-type clutch in place of the roller-type clutch.

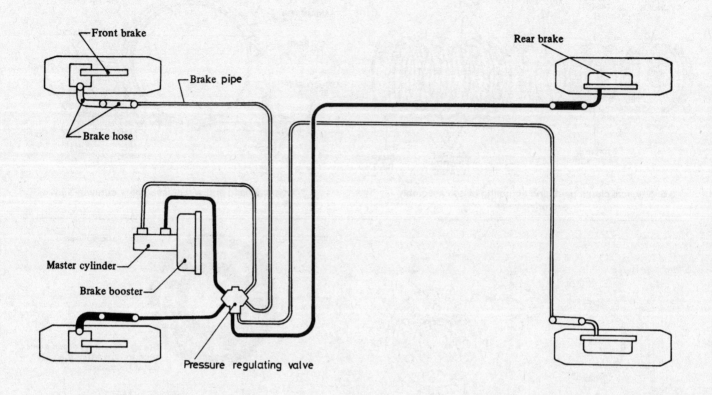

3.10 Hydraulics are also used for automotive brake systems - imagine how complex this simple brake system would be if it were actuated mechanically

The hydraulic system

Hydraulic basics

Shifting in an automatic transmission is controlled through hydraulics. Hydraulics rely on the *non-compressibility* of liquids to transmit power. Unlike air or other gasses, which can be compacted in devices like an air compressor or automotive engine to store energy in the form of pressure, liquids can only *transmit* forces that try to compress them. An example of this property of liquids has been observed by many mechanics when a blown head gasket or other malfunction causes a cylinder of an automotive engine to fill with a liquid (like oil or coolant) when it's towards the bottom of its compression stroke. When the driver attempts to start the engine, the engine immediately stops when the piston tries to compress the liquid against the top of the combustion chamber. Depending on the force generated by the starter, the steel connecting rod will often bend, but under no circumstances will the liquid compress! While this phenomenon, generally referred to as *hydrostatic lock* can cause serious damage in this situation, it can be very beneficial when harnessed in an automatic transmission.

Shift parameters

If you've driven cars with manual transmissions you know that you don't always shift at the same road speed and engine rpm. If you're climbing a hill, you'll "hold out" a shift, bringing the vehicle to a higher rpm and road speed before shifting, then, if the hill gets steeper and the engine starts "bogging," you downshift to a lower gear to allow the engine to operate at a more efficient rpm range. If you're trying to accelerate quickly, you'll allow the engine to rev higher and develop

more horsepower before you shift. Automatic transmissions consider these operating conditions automatically and make shifting decisions for you, so many individual actions must happen to make sure each shift takes place at the correct rpm, at the correct road speed and with force sufficient to match the amount of load on the engine.

Needless to say, the shifting decisions made by an automatic transmission are complex. Carrying out an automatic transmission's duties requires a versatile method of transmitting force.

Simplifying with hydraulics

Because liquids are non-compressible, they can be employed to transmit force in situations where levers and cables would be awkward or wouldn't work at all. Automotive brake systems **(see illustration)** use hydraulics to transmit the force of your foot on the brake pedal to all four wheels, proportion the force so there's the correct front-to-rear balance and multiply the brake-pedal-force many times to permit moderate foot pressure to stop a two-ton vehicle. Without hydraulics, a complex system of cables and levers would be required, employing cams and/or bellcranks to proportion force from front to rear, and gearing would be necessary to multiply force. Such a system would be very heavy and so complex as to be unsafe. Since the operations of an automatic transmission are much more complex than this brake-system example, you can see why hydraulics are so necessary.

A basic transmission hydraulic system

To develop an understanding of basic transmission functions, we'll look at the most basic type of transmission possible - one planetary gearset and one band. The hydraulic circuit to actuate the band consists of transmission fluid, a pump to generate pressure from the fluid, a pressure regulator valve to keep pressure constant in the circuit, a shift valve and a shift servo **(see illustration)**.

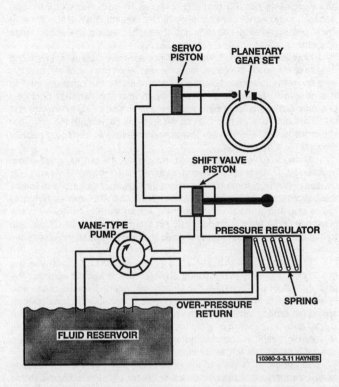

3.11 This simple hydraulic system provides two gear ranges - neutral and drive. By manually moving the shift valve piston to the right, fluid pressure generated by the pump will move the servo piston to the right, tightening the band on the planetary gearset. When the pump generates excessive pressure, the pressure regulator spring is compressed and excess pressure is returned to the fluid reservoir

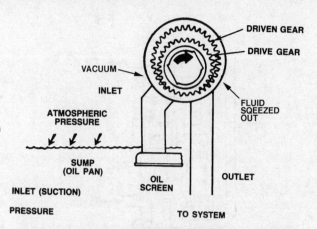

3.12a The most common type of pump in an automatic transmission is the gear-type pump. When the gears rotate, vacuum is created at the inlet and fluid is squeezed out at the outlet

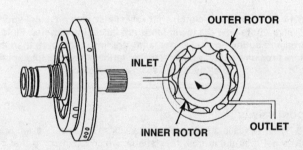

3.12b Rotor-type pumps work by the same principle as gear-type pumps - the only difference is the shapes of the components

The pump

Pumps in automatic transmission hydraulic systems are generally *positive displacement* pumps driven by the engine. A positive displacement pump is one which has the same output per revolution regardless of pump speed or pressure already developed in the system. Positive-displacement pumps include piston, gear and rotor-type pumps **(see illustrations)**. Because of their size, piston-type pumps are not used in automatic transmissions, but gear- and rotor-type pumps are common. Gear- and rotor-type pumps are also used as oil pumps in engine lubrication systems (another type of hydraulic system), so if you understand the workings of a lubricating oil pump, you're well on your way to understanding automatic transmission pumps.

Vane-type pumps are also used in automatic transmissions. Vane-type pumps use sliding vanes in place of gears or rotors, but operate by a similar principle. The vane holder rotates while the housing remains stationary, and the fluid between the vanes is forced through the pump to the outlet. The vanes are free to slide in and out of the vane housing in their slots and are held against the housing in operation by centrifugal force. A primary advantage of the vane-type pump is that, when the not-quite-circular housing is rotated, output per revolution can be varied.

The pressure regulator

Since most pumps generate the same output-per-revolution regardless of speed or pressure already in the hydraulic circuit, it is necessary to regulate the pressure so it does not get too high and damage components **(see illustration 3.11)**. A basic pressure regulator employs a piston and a spring that compresses at a specific

pressure to allow some oil to flow back to the reservoir, bypassing the hydraulic circuit and thus reducing pressure. By using a pressure regulator with a spring calibrated to a pressure much lower than the pump's output, constant pressure can be maintained in the system. When the engine is at low speed, the pressure regulator will be nearly closed, while at high engine speed the pressure regulator will be nearly open. But high speed or low speed, a constant pressure is maintained in the hydraulic system.

The shift valve

Although more complex in a real automatic transmission (actual operation will be discussed in detail later), the shift valve in our example is simply a piston that can be moved to uncover a passage leading to the shift servo **(see illustration 3.11)**.

The servo

The pressure applied to the servo piston when the shift valve is opened moves the servo piston against the band, which in turn immobilizes the drum of the planetary gearset and provides output **(see illustration 3.11)**.

Components for automatic operation

The basic hydraulic circuit just described helped us understand the operation of a simple transmission, but this transmission is so basic that it requires the shift valve to be moved manually, and the shift firmness could not be controlled. The information that follows discusses the hydraulic components necessary to provide fully automatic operation in a modern automatic transmission.

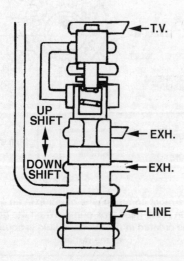

3.14 This converter clutch shift valve illustrates a typical spool valve - note how the lower lands are larger in diameter. Fluid pressure acting against larger lands applies more force than the same pressure acting against smaller lands. This principle applies to all hydraulic valves and pistons

Spool valves

Most valves in an automatic transmission are spool valves. Spool valves get their name from their shape, which is similar to that of a sewing-thread-type spool. However, unlike a sewing-thread spool, most automatic transmission spool valves have several *lands* (the larger-diameter part of the spool) to allow fluid pressure to act on several different parts of the valve. Many spool valves have different-sized lands to allow fluid pressure to act differently upon different parts of the valve **(see illustration)**. Since a large-diameter land has more surface area on its face than a smaller-diameter land, fluid pressure applied to the face of the larger-diameter land will have more force on the spool valve than an equal fluid pressure applied to the face of the smaller-diameter land.

Spool-type valves are used for the governor, throttle valve, vacuum modulator valve, manual valve and automatic shift valves.

The governor

The governor monitors transmission output shaft speed (road speed), controlling the pressure of fluid acting on the shift valves to permit shifts to take place at the correct road speed. The governor does this by using centrifugal force to restrict the amount of transmission fluid that escapes from the governor as engine speed increases. Since more fluid escaping results in less pressure against the shift valves, the shift valves remain closed until the governor can restrict the escaping fluid enough to raise the pressure sufficiently to counteract the force of the shift-valve spring and allow the shift valve to open.

An additional benefit of the governor is that it also raises pressure at the band servos and clutch-pack pistons as speed increases. Lower band apply pressures at lower speeds permit smooth shifts in normal driving (since lower pressure allows for a bit more slippage as the band or clutch applies). As road speed increases, the amount of pressure needed to apply a band or clutch pack is greater. Using the lower pressure that allowed a smooth shift at lower speeds would cause a great deal more slippage as the band or clutch applied and would likely allow more slippage when more load was placed on the transmission (such as in hill climbing or acceleration). Simply put,

higher speeds require higher pressures to hold the clutches and bands. The governor permits these higher pressures while still allowing lower pressures at low speeds and therefore keeping low-speed shifts smooth.

Now let's examine how a governor normally operates. When the vehicle is stopped, the governor is "at rest" with the spool valve all the way up in the governor housing. In this position, the pressure inlet to the governor is closed or slightly open and the exhaust port and pressure outlet are fully open. With the exhaust port fully open, you can see that any pressure that gets to the shift valves through the governor pressure outlet will be very low since pressure is escaping rapidly through the exhaust port.

As the vehicle begins moving, rotation of the output shaft (either in forward or reverse) causes the governor to rotate. This rotation causes centrifugal force to act against the governor weights and forces the weights away from the governor body. As the weights begin to move out, the arms on the weights, acting through hinges on the governor body, lever the spool valve in the governor down. This starts to close off the exhaust port and open the pressure inlet, which causes outlet pressure to rise.

Two sets of weights are used on the governor to increase the governor's accuracy in regulating pressure at low vehicle speeds. The primary weights, which have lighter springs holding them back are also heavier and move first, at very low vehicle speeds. Once the governor speed becomes high enough, the primary weights bottom against their stops, and the secondary weights act alone to move the spool valve. At very high vehicle speeds, the exhaust port is fully closed, allowing very high pressures to the pressure outlet.

An additional feature of the governor is that governor pressure is routed through a passage in the lower center of the spool valve to the bottom of the valve, near the drive gear. This pressure opposes the force of the centrifugal weights and helps to stabilize the governor operation at steady speeds.

The throttle valve

When climbing a hill, a driver finds he has press down the accelerator farther to maintain the same road speed. Also, when the driver needs to accelerate quickly, she will press the accelerator down farther. Both of these actions require a downshift, but the operation of the transmission, as discussed up to now, will not provide it. The throttle valve provides this function by monitoring engine throttle position and allowing lower-speed shifts when the vehicle speed is relatively low compared with the engine throttle opening.

The throttle valve in the transmission provides a fluid pressure that also acts against the shift valves, but in opposition to it. To understand operation of the throttle valve, we'll first examine the most simple type of throttle valve: the mechanical valve that's used in THM200, 200-4R, 350 and 700 transmissions. Basically, the mechanical valve in the transmission is operated through a cable that attaches to the throttle linkage on the engine's carburetor or throttle body. The valve itself is a spool-type valve that uses a spring and plunger to oppose mainline pressure acting through its inlet port. When the engine throttle valve is opened, the cable pulls the lever arm and compresses the spring, applying pressure to the throttle valve in the transmission. This causes the valve to move to the left and open the outlet port **(see illustration)**. The throttle pressure outlet port is connected to many parts of the transmission. Some of the fluid pressure is sent to the other side of the throttle valve to act against the opening pressure, preventing the valve from opening all at once and also permitting the valve to stabilize at various positions between fully open and fully closed, depending on position of the engine throttle valve.

Fluid pressure from the throttle-valve outlet is also routed to the opposite side of the shift valves to balance governor pressure against throttle position and allow shifts to occur at the correct time (this will be discussed further under the heading "The automatic shift valve"). Throttle pressure is also routed to the apply devices that are in operation (bands, accumulators and/or pistons) to supplement apply pressure, thus preventing slippage, since the transmission is under

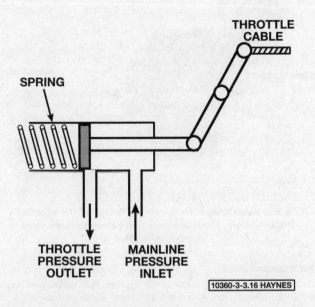

3.16 The throttle valve varies fluid pressure in the transmission based on the position of the throttle in the carburetor or throttle body

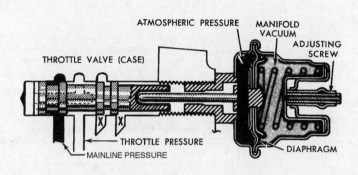

3.17 Vacuum modulators provide the same function as throttle valves, except engine manifold vacuum is used instead of throttle position to determine the load on the engine

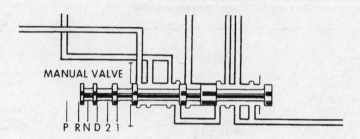

3.18 The manual valve is a spool valve that directs fluid pressure based on the position of the shift lever in the passenger compartment

much higher load during hill climbing and acceleration than it is during normal cruising.

The vacuum modulator

The vacuum modulator that is used on some transmissions has the same function and operates very similarly to the throttle valve. The difference is that the modulator operates using engine vacuum rather than a mechanical linkage **(see illustration).**

When the engine is operating normally (such as when idling or cruising), the vacuum in the engine's intake manifold is very high. When the engine is under load (such as during acceleration or hill climbing), the vacuum is lower. A tube connects the intake manifold to one side of a rubber diaphragm in the vacuum modulator on the transmission. Atmospheric pressure operates on the other side of the diaphragm. The diaphragm is connected to the throttle spool valve in the transmission. When engine vacuum is high (engine load low), the diaphragm moves to the right and closes the inlet and outlet ports of the throttle valve. When engine vacuum is low (engine load high), the diaphragm moves to the left and opens the inlet and outlet ports, increasing transmission throttle pressure.

The manual valve

Simply put, the manual valve in an automatic transmission is a spool valve connected by linkage or a cable to the shift lever inside the passenger compartment. The manual valve, which is connected to the manual lever on the side of the transmission **(see illustration)**, directs fluid flow within the transmission to provide the correct type of operation for the selected range. For example, when Neutral or Park are selected, fluid is directed to an exhaust port that sends pressure back to the transmission pan so no apply devices are engaged. When Drive is selected, fluid is directed to the Low gear clutch piston and to the 1-2 shift valve.

The automatic shift valve

Earlier, when discussing operation of a basic transmission hydraulic system, the shift valve had to be moved manually to select a gear. Automatic transmissions perform this operation by sensing vehicle speed and throttle position to determine the correct shift point. Basically, an automatic shift valve is a simple spool valve that balances pressure from the governor output against spring pressure and fluid pressure from the throttle valve (or vacuum modulator) output **(see illustration).** When governor pressure overcomes spring and throttle pressure, the shift takes place.

The valve body

The valve body is the hydraulic "brain" of the automatic transmission **(see illustration).** The valve body houses most of the hydraulic valves - the shift valves, manual valve, throttle valve, converter lock-up valve, etc. - used in the transmission. Additionally, the valve body has many passages that connect together the drilled galleries within the transmission.

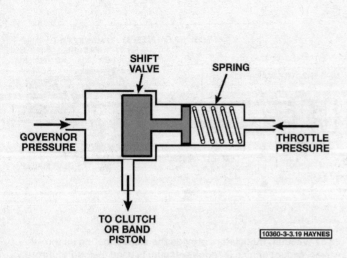

SHIFT
VALVE   SPRING

GOVERNOR
PRESSURE   THROTTLE
PRESSURE

TO CLUTCH
OR BAND
PISTON

10360-3-3.19 HAYNES

**3.19 Automatic shift valves balance governor fluid pressure
against throttle fluid pressure and spring pressure. When
governor pressure overcomes the opposing force,
the shift takes place**

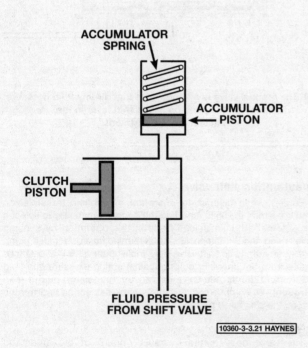

ACCUMULATOR
SPRING

ACCUMULATOR
PISTON

CLUTCH
PISTON

FLUID PRESSURE
FROM SHIFT VALVE

10360-3-3.21 HAYNES

**3.21 Separate-piston type accumulators use a spring-loaded
piston to absorb fluid shock as a band or clutch applies**

**3.20 The valve body is the hydraulic "brain" of the automatic
transmission - it contains the shift valves, manual valve
and throttle valve**

The accumulator

In a transmission hydraulic system, when fluid under pressure is sent to a servo piston, it arrives with great force. If allowed to act directly against the servo piston, a phenomenon known as *fluid shock* would occur. Fluid shock is the same phenomenon sometimes found in household plumbing systems that causes pipes to rattle when a valve is opened. Since liquid is not compressible, the entire force of the pressurized liquid hits the pipes (or, in a transmission, the servo piston) all at once. In a household plumbing system, this force causes the pipes to rattle. In an automatic transmission, it causes vibration and harsh shifting. To prevent this from happening, accumulators are used. In automatic transmissions, accumulators are either separate or integral piston types.

The operation of a separate piston-type accumulator is relatively self-evident **(see illustration).** When fluid pressure is applied to the circuit, much of the force is absorbed by the accumulator piston. The accumulator piston spring will absorb force until the spring behind it is fully compressed, when full pressure will act against the servo piston. By the time the spring is compressed, there will be no engagement shock. In some applications, fluid shock can be further reduced by applying a lower auxiliary pressure to the spring side of the servo to help supplement spring pressure.

The integral piston-type accumulator operates similarly to the separate piston-type, except that both the accumulator piston and the servo piston occupy the same cylinder bore in the transmission. These types of accumulator systems are usually arranged so that the accumulator piston is part of the apply-pressure circuit for a different servo. In the illustration, you can see that the accumulator piston for the 1-2 clutch is installed in the same bore as the low-reverse servo piston. When the low-reverse band and the 1-2 clutch are both released, accumulator pressure is applied to the spring side of the accumulator piston, which forces the accumulator piston against the servo piston and holds the servo in the released position. When the 1-2 clutch is applied, part of the fluid from that circuit is routed into the accumulator through internal passages in the accumulator piston. The fluid enters the area between the accumulator and servo pistons and forces the accumulator piston up, to the top of its travel, against accumulator and spring pressure. This cushions the pressure increase when the 1-2 clutch is applied, much the same as with an independent accumulator. During accumulator operation, 1-2 clutch pressure works against the spring side of the low-reverse servo piston. This pressure holds the servo in the released position.

Working examples of hydraulic systems

In operation, there is a great deal of interaction among the components in a hydraulic system. The shift valves, by balancing

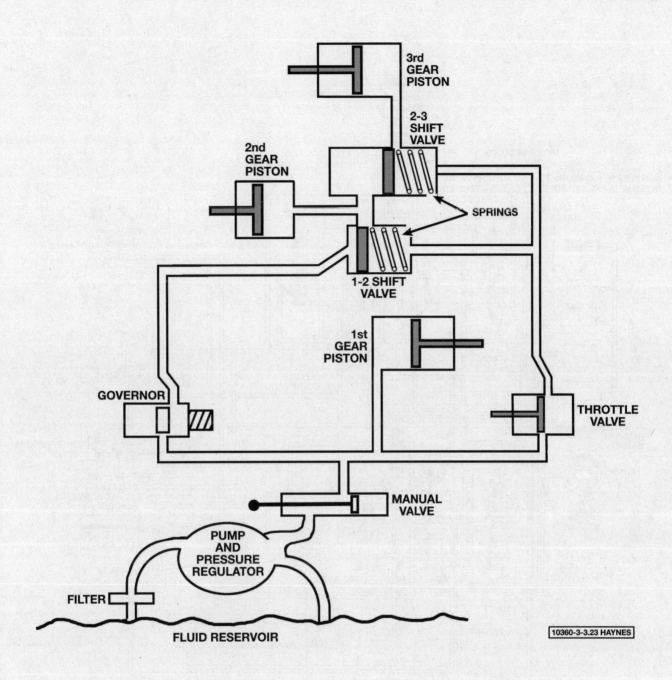

3.23 This schematic of an automatic transmission hydraulic system is overly simplified to show basic functions

governor and throttle pressures not only assure a shift occurs at the right speed, but also that the shift will have the correct amount of firmness. For example, in looking at the first, simplified example **(see illustration),** you'll see that pressing the accelerator to the floor will not only cause a shift to occur at a higher speed, but also assure it is firmer. This is because pressing the throttle to the floor will make the throttle valve apply greater fluid pressure to the right side of the shift valve. This will mean it will take greater governor pressure against the left side of the shift valve to make the shift take place. This means a higher road speed for the shift, but it also means higher pressure will

act against the piston when the shift does take place, limiting slippage during high power output by the engine. Conversely, light throttle pressure will allow shifts at lower speeds, but will also apply less pressure to the piston, allowing a less harsh shift for smooth transition in normal driving.

The next example **(see illustration)** is an actual transmission hydraulic system. It is included here as a learning aid to help you understand the intricacies of a modern hydraulic system. While fairly complex, a little time studying the interaction of components will give you a broader understanding of hydraulic systems.

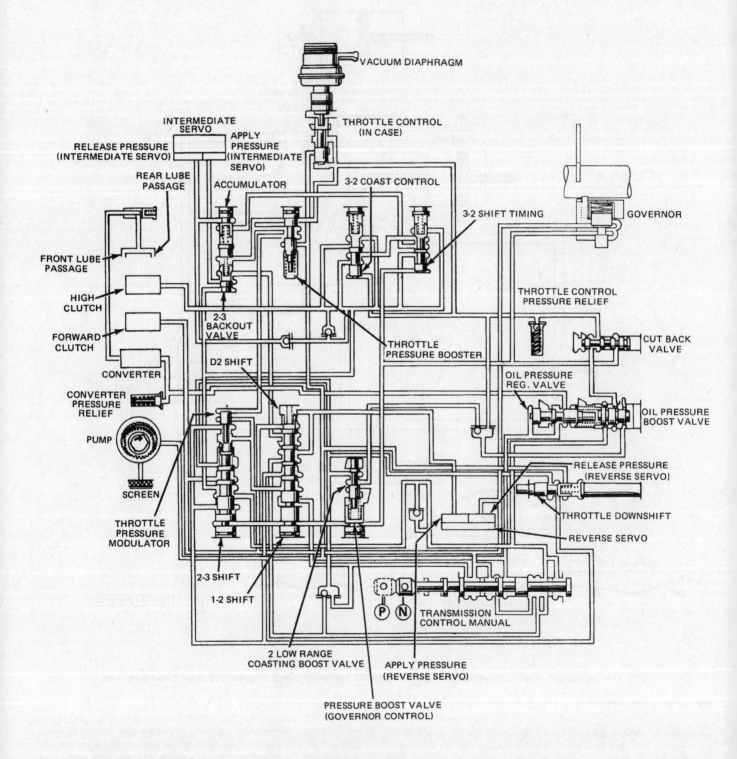

3.24 Spend some time studying this typical hydraulic system schematic. It will help you better understand the functioning of an automatic transmission

3.25 The torque converter is a fluid coupler that replaces the clutch in a manual transmission

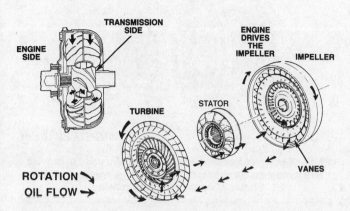

3.26 Here is both a cutaway and exploded view of a typical torque converter

The torque converter

The torque converter **(see illustration)** replaces the clutch used in manual transmissions. Since planetary gearsets are meshed at all times and can be "shifted" without interrupting power delivery to the rear wheels, a disengaging-type clutch is not necessary. However, a means of allowing the engine to idle in gear with the vehicle motionless must be provided. Also, to help provide for smooth gear shifts at low-speed, part-throttle driving and to reduce wear on clutches and bands during these driving conditions, some *slippage* (when the engine is momentarily allowed to operate at a slightly higher speed without affecting road speed) must also be provided. The torque converter is a very flexible power transmitter that provides all these functions and more.

The basic principle of torque converter operation can be observed by placing the blades of two electric fans opposite each other and turning on one of the fans. If one of the fans is turned on, the force of the air column produced will act upon the motionless blades of the other fan. The blades of the fan that is turned off will begin turning and will accelerate and finally reach a speed approaching the speed of the fan that's powered.

To put this principle into automotive terms, imagine the blades of one fan are attached to the rear of the engine's crankshaft and the blades of the other fan are attached to the driveshaft, which is connected to the rear wheels. Start the engine and we're ready to drive down the road, right? Not quite. Remember that, since air is compressible, it is not efficient at transmitting power. This is why the blades of an automotive torque converter are sealed in a case that's filled with transmission fluid, which is non-compressible. The fluid is capable of transmitting driving force efficiently enough to provide power to the rear wheels and move the vehicle.

However, there's a big difference between just *moving* a vehicle and moving it *efficiently*, achieving good fuel economy and low-speed torque. To achieve this efficiency, torque converters use some unique design features. First, the inside of a torque converter does not look like two sets of fan blades facing each other **(see illustration)**. The *impeller* (the part attached to the engine crankshaft, which GM sometimes calls a *pump*) and the *turbine* (the part attached to the transmission) look more like two bundt-cake pans facing each other. Inside both are dividers that create individual cavities shaped like slices of bundt cake that are cut at angles. The purpose of these shapes is to allow the transmission fluid to circulate, in a circular motion, between the turbine and impeller. The angled cavities in the impeller force fluid out of the impeller when the engine rotates it, like a fan, but, unlike our fan example, the angled cavities in the turbine redirect the remaining fluid force back to the impeller. Greater

efficiency is achieved by this circular motion of fluid since it takes full advantage of the force generated by the impeller. Force is not lost like in the fan example, where the airflow not used to rotate the idle fan is lost.

The stator

When the vehicle is cruising down the road and the impeller and turbine are rotating at approximately the same speed, this fluid coupling works well. But, think hard about the motion of the fluid in this arrangement of parts when the vehicle is accelerating, particularly when it's accelerating from a stop. Since the fluid returning from the turbine, after acting upon it, will be redirected against the impeller, which is turning at a higher speed than the turbine, the redirected fluid flow will actually be counterproductive, interfering with turbine fluid flow and reducing the efficiency of the fluid coupling.

To solve this problem, a third member, called the *stator*, is necessary. The stator has blades angled to reverse the direction of fluid flow as it leaves the turbine so that it will again act against the impeller, in the direction of rotation, and therefore assist the engine in turning the impeller. To further aid in redirecting fluid flow, the stator rotates on a one-way roller clutch so that it's free to rotate in the direction of engine rotation but not in the opposite direction. This allows the stator to remain efficient when the turbine is turning, and not just when it's standing still. The re-direction of fluid flow results in an actual multiplication of the torque developed by the engine during acceleration, particularly from a stop. Torque converters are so efficient that, during acceleration from a stop, the torque delivered to the transmission is frequently *twice* the torque developed by the engine.

Variable-pitch stators

During 1965 through 1967, some THM400 transmissions in Buicks, Oldsmobiles and some Cadillacs came equipped with *variable-pitch* stators. This system allows the angle of the stator blades to be changed during transmission operation. Since normal stators represent a compromise between good torque multiplication at low speeds and high efficiency during cruising, the ability to vary stator blade angle in operation is desirable.

This system uses stator blades that can pivot upon shafts and that are actuated hydraulically. A switch on the carburetor senses when the throttle is fully open. When in this position, an electric solenoid opens a valve that allows transmission fluid pressure to move the stator blades to maximum angle. When at part-throttle, the blades move to a minimum angle.

Variable stators did result in slightly improved efficiency, but were discontinued because of little public interest.

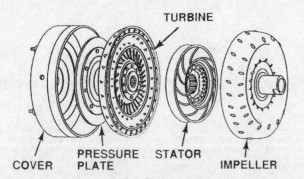

TURBINE

COVER   PRESSURE   STATOR   IMPELLER
         PLATE

3.27 Lock-up torque converters use a pressure plate to provide a direct mechanical connection between the engine and rear wheels when the vehicle is cruising

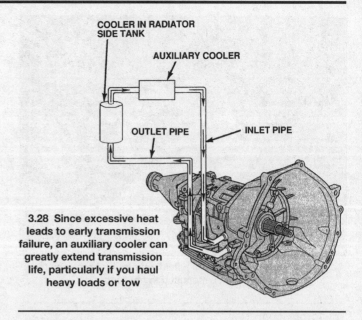

COOLER IN RADIATOR
SIDE TANK

AUXILIARY COOLER

OUTLET PIPE   INLET PIPE

3.28 Since excessive heat leads to early transmission failure, an auxiliary cooler can greatly extend transmission life, particularly if you haul heavy loads or tow

The lock-up converter

Beginning in the 1980's, the transmissions covered by this manual began being equipped with lock-up torque converters. The purpose of the lock-up converter is to provide for direct drive when the vehicle is in high gear and cruising at part-throttle. Since there is always some slippage in the viscous coupling of a torque converter, some power is lost and fuel economy suffers. By providing a direct mechanical coupling through the transmission during cruising, the lock-up converter helps improve fuel economy during cruising.

A lock-up converter has a pressure plate within the converter housing, just in front of the impeller/turbine assembly **(see illustration).** The pressure plate has friction material on its front. When the vehicle is cruising and lock-up is desired, an electric solenoid is energized which opens the converter clutch valve in the valve body. This allows fluid pressure to act upon the rear of the pressure plate. The pressure plate is then forced against a machined surface on the converter cover and, like on a manual-transmission-type clutch, the pressure plate and converter cover become as one assembly. Since the pressure plate is splined to the transmission input shaft, a direct mechanical link through the torque converter is established. When lock-up is no longer required, a port opens that allows the pressurized fluid to exhaust. Fluid then flows out from in front of the pressure plate through centrifugal force and the pressure plate moves away from the converter housing, re-establishing the fluid coupling.

Lock-up on all but late 1979 and early 1980 models is controlled by the vehicle's Electronic Control Module (ECM). When this computer senses the engine is warm, the vehicle is traveling over 35 miles per hour in high gear and at a steady speed, lock-up is initiated. When speed falls below 35 miles per hour, the brakes are applied, a lower gear is selected or the vehicle is accelerated quickly, fluid is exhausted to end lock-up. The inputs to the computer that control lock-up are: the coolant temperature sensor, the vehicle speed sensor, the throttle position sensor and a brake-off switch (that tells the computer when the brakes are applied).

The first lock-up control system that was used in late 1979 and early 1980 did not use the ECM. This system is operated through electric and vacuum controls. This system uses a governor pressure switch, a low vacuum switch to sense when the vehicle is cruising (lock-up is only permitted when vacuum is high), an engine thermal vacuum switch to sense engine temperature (lock-up is only permitted when the engine is warm) and a brake-off switch that turns off lock-up when the brakes are applied. This very early system was discontinued because of its complexity and reliance on vacuum hoses and the mechanical condition of the engine (low engine vacuum can cause malfunctions).

The fluid cooler

Slippage within an automatic transmission generates heat, and heat is the greatest enemy of any automatic transmission. Heat causes

fluid to break down, losing its lubricating and heat-transfer properties, and heat also causes clutch friction material to varnish, causing still more slippage. Since transmission fluid is in contact with virtually all components within an automatic transmission, cooling the fluid will ultimately cool the transmission. Fluid coolers circulate pressurized fluid through lines (usually steel tubes) to the radiator. A separate transmission fluid chamber within the radiator bottom or side tank is in constant contact with engine coolant. Since normal engine coolant temperature is lower than normal transmission fluid temperature, the transmission fluid chamber transfers heat to the engine coolant, cooling the transmission fluid.

This "heat exchanger" works well under normal conditions, but if the engine overheats, the transmission will likewise overheat. Also, if the transmission is slipping excessively and building up excessive heat, the engine will also overheat. To overcome these problems and extend transmission life by reducing operating temperature, it is wise to install an auxiliary transmission cooler in your vehicle, especially if the vehicle is used for towing or moving heavy loads **(see illustration).** Installation of an auxiliary transmission cooler is covered in Chapter 9.

The parking pawl

When PARK is selected, an actuating rod within the transmission actuates a pawl that moves into contact with teeth on the outside of the direct-clutch drum. This mechanically locks the output shaft so the vehicle cannot move.

The final drive

On RWD vehicles, the final drive is more commonly known as the differential and is mounted in the rear axle housing. Final drive/differential set-ups on RWD vehicles typically consist of a ring and pinion gear which are known as hypoid type gears. Hypoid type gears are used when the power from the motor must be transmitted to the driveaxles at a 90 degree angle, such is the case on most RWD vehicles and some FWD vehicles that have the engine mounted longitudinally in the vehicle. Regardless of the type of vehicle, the final drive/differential is always the last set of gears that power from the engine is transferred through on its way to the driveaxles. The majority of FWD vehicles today have transversely mounted engines, therefore power from the engine is transmitted parallel with the driveaxles, which allows the manufacturers to employ simple helical type gears mounted in the transaxle as the final drive to apply power to the driveaxles.

Chapter 4   Transmission identification

Transmissions covered by this manual

This manual covers the THM200-4R, THM350, THM375B, THM400 and THM700-R4 automatic transmissions used in rear-wheel drive cars and light trucks and the THM 125/125C/3T40 and 440-T4/4T60 transaxles used in front wheel drive cars produced by General Motors.

THM200-4R

The THM200-4R transmission was used in GM rear-wheel drive cars equipped with the 3.8L V6, as well as 307 and 350 cubic inch (Oldsmobile-built) and 301 cubic inch (Pontiac-built) V8 engines from 1981 through 1989. If the car meets the preceding criteria and is equipped with a four-speed overdrive automatic transmission (identified by two drive ranges on the shift indicator, the first one circled by a large O), it is most likely a THM200-4R. If you have a 350 V8 engine and are not sure whether it is built by Oldsmobile or Chevrolet, see the information under THM700-R4 below.

THM350

The THM350 was used in medium-duty applications from 1969 through 1989. This transmission can be found in Buick, Oldsmobile, Pontiac and Chevrolet cars as well as Chevrolet and GMC light trucks through 1987 and in some Cadillacs from 1980 through 1989. Generally speaking, this transmission is used with engines of moderate to moderately large displacement, generally in-line six-cylinder, V6 and small-block V8 engines.

THM375B

The THM375B transmission is basically a heavier duty version of the THM350. Both transmissions are outwardly identical, and the internal parts layout of the THM375B is identical to that of a heavier duty version of the THM350.

THM400

The THM400 transmission is the heavy-duty GM transmission used from 1964 through 1990. This transmission is used by the same manufacturers as the THM350, with the additions of AMC, Jaguar, Rolls Royce and Bentley. This transmission is used on large-displacement engines with high torque output and/or in large vehicles, especially those with towing packages. Virtually all rear-wheel drive Cadillacs produced from 1965 through 1979 are equipped with this transmission. Additionally, most Buick, Oldsmobile, Pontiac and Chevrolet full-size rear-wheel drive cars with large-displacement V8 engines use this transmission. Many Chevrolet and GMC trucks also use this transmission.

THM700-R4

The THM700-R4 four-speed transmission is used in GM cars and light trucks with 2.8L, 3.1L and 4.3L V6 engines and Chevrolet-built V8 engines (displacements of 305, 350 and 454 cubic inches) built from 1982 through 1992. (The 350 engine referred to here is not to be confused with the 350 cubic inch Oldsmobile-built engine, which was in many Buick, Oldsmobile, Pontiac and Cadillac cars built during these years. The Oldsmobile-built engine is easily distinguished from the Chevrolet-built engine by the aluminum coolant bypass tube that comes out of the thermostat housing and hooks down, where a short hose connects it to the water pump. The Chevrolet-built engine has only the upper radiator hose connected to the thermostat housing.)

THM 125/125C and 3T40

The THM 125/125C was used in front wheel drive applications from 1980 through 1989 when it was renamed by General Motors the 3T40 transaxle. The 3T40 transaxle was used in front wheel drive vehicles from 1990 through 1994. This three-speed transaxle can be found in Buick, Oldsmobile, Pontiac and Chevrolet models and in Cadillac Cimarron models from 1982 through 1989. Generally speaking, the THM 125/125C/3T40 transaxles were used with a variety of four and six cylinder engine combinations in compact and intermediate sized vehicles.

THM 440-T4/4T60

The THM 440-T4 was General Motors first version of a four-speed front wheel drive transaxle. It was first introduced in 1984 and was used through 1990 when it was renamed by General Motors the 4T60 transaxle. The THM 440-T4/4T60 transaxle can also be found in Buick, Oldsmobile, Pontiac and Chevrolet models and in Cadillac models through 1993. Generally speaking, this four-speed transaxle is used with a variety of engine combinations in intermediate and full size vehicles.

Visual identification

The quickest and easiest way to identify the type of transmission you have is to climb under the vehicle (make sure it's safely supported!) and look at the shape of the transmission pan bolted to the bottom of the transmission. The accompanying drawings show the shapes of GM transmission pans (see illustrations). Note that THM200 and THM250 transmissions, both of which are not covered by this manual, have basically the same pan shape as the THM350, and that the 3T40 FWD transaxle which is covered by this manual has the same pan shape as the THM 125/125C. The 4T60 also uses the same pan shape as the THM 440-T4 since it is the same transaxle with a new name.

The THM200 is easily distinguished from the THM350 by the words METRIC and HYDRAMATIC DIV. of GMC that are stamped into the bottom of the pan in large letters. The THM350 does not have any words stamped into the pan.

The THM250 is used in Vegas, Astres, Sunbirds, Starfires, Skyhawks and Monzas equipped with four-cylinder engines from mid-1973 through 1981. In these vehicles, the transmission has four large holes in the housing, in the torque converter area, for cooling. These small-car transmissions are air cooled - they have no transmission cooler in the radiator. The THM250 is also used in some Nova, Camaro and Malibu models with six-cylinder engines in 1974 and 1975, and on

A

B

C

D

E

4.1a This chart identifies GM automatic transmissions based on the shape of the transmission pan. Note that the Powerglide transmission is not covered by this manual - its pan shape is included here for reference purposes only

A   THM700-R4   B   THM400   C   THM350   D   THM200-4R   E   Powerglide

some intermediate cars in the early to mid 1980's. In these larger cars, there are no holes in the housing and a conventional transmission cooler is used. An easy way to tell whether you have a THM250 is by looking for an adjusting screw for the intermediate band - it's just behind the transmission cooler fittings on the right side of the transmission case, pointing downward. THM350 transmissions do not have an adjusting screw in this location. Also, on 1980 and later THM250 transmissions with lock-up torque converters, the transmission pan is deeper than the standard pan used on THM350 transmissions. Also, the pan is ribbed, instead of flat steel, as on the THM350.

Another derivative-type transmission is the THM375 (which is totally different from the THM375B discussed earlier). This transmission is based on the THM400 design, and thus has the same unusually shaped transmission pan. This transmission has 375-THM cast in large letters on the bottom of the tailshaft housing, just behind the transmission mount. Basically, the transmission is a lighter-duty version of the THM400. It was used from 1972 through 1976 in some full-size models. This transmission is also not covered by this manual.

Aside from the different types of torque converters implemented on different model years the 125/125C and the 3T40 transaxles are essentially the same in design and identical in pan shape. These transaxles can only be properly identified by the VIN code on the transmission.

The THM 440-T4 and the 4T60 transaxles are also essentially the same in design to each other and identical in pan shape. Transaxles with the identical pan shapes can only be identified by the VIN code and the model year located on the transaxle.

Please note that this manual does not cover the electronic version of the THM 700-R4 (4L60-E) or the electronic version of the THM 440-T4 (4T60-E).

Identifying by VIN

While not normally necessary during overhaul, it is sometimes important to verify if your vehicle has its originally installed transmission. It is common for transmission shops to exchange an already rebuilt transmission of the same type in place of your ailing old transmission. This allows them to get you back on the road quicker. So long as they've done their job correctly, this is not a problem.

If you need to identify the transmission to the chassis, you can take advantage of a number that the manufacturer used to identify certain components with a specific vehicle. Every transmission covered by this manual has a derivative of the primary Vehicle Identification Number (VIN) stamped into the transmission case. The primary VIN is stamped onto a steel plate at the front of the dashboard, visible from outside the vehicle by looking through the windshield on the driver's side. Some early model transmissions use the last six digits of the primary VIN number on the transmission. Later models use the last eight digits plus the third digit of the primary VIN stamped on the transmission case **(see illustration)**. Check the VIN derivative on the transmission case with the primary VIN number on the dashboard, If

they match, the transmission is the one originally installed in your vehicle. If not, the transmission has been swapped.

On THM350 transmissions, the VIN derivative is in one of three locations:

1) *Stamped into the driver's side of the housing, near the manual (shifter) shaft.*
2) *Stamped into the right side of the housing, just above the transmission pan.*
3) *Stamped onto a boss just behind the bellhousing on the passenger's side of the transmission.*

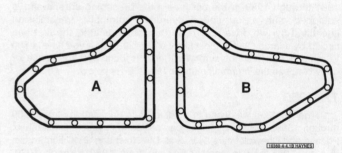

4.1b This chart identifies GM front wheel drive automatic transmissions based on the shape of the transmission pan

A   THM 125/125C and 3T40
B   THM 440-T4/4T60

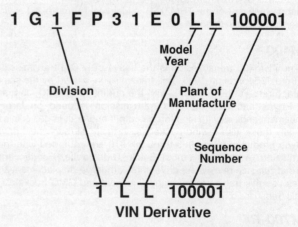

4.2 Later models have a 9 digit derivative of the VIN stamped into the transmission case

On THM400 transmissions, the VIN derivative is stamped onto the machined surface just above the transmission pan on the driver's side.

On THM200-4R transmissions, the VIN derivative is stamped into the housing on the driver's side of the transmission, just above the transmission pan, toward the rear of the pan.

On THM700-R4 transmissions, the VIN derivative is stamped onto a boss just behind the bellhousing on the passenger's side of the transmission. It may also be located just above the transmission pan on the driver's side or just behind the governor cover, stamped on the vertical surface where the main housing meets the tailshaft housing.

On most THM 125/125C and 3T40 transaxles, the VIN derivative is stamped onto the top of the case side cover near the transaxle ID tag. On early THM 125 models, the VIN derivative is stamped onto the transaxle oil pan rail near the dipstick tube.

On THM 440-T4/4T60 transaxles the VIN derivative is stamped onto the top of the case side cover near the transaxle ID tag. On early THM 125 models, the VIN derivative is stamped onto the transaxle oil pan rail near the dipstick tub

Identifying by transmission code

All GM-built transmissions come from the factory with an identification code stamped onto the transmission directly or on a metal tag attached to the transmission (see illustrations). This code can be used to accurately identify the transmission. The code chart in this chapter can be used to identify the type of transmission you have based on this code. Note that some transmission types listed in this chart have a "C" suffix, such as THM350C. The "C" identifies the transmission as having a lock-up torque converter.

AA, THM200-4R, THM400
AAH, THM440-T4
AB, THM400
ABH, THM440-T4
AC, AD, AE, THM400
AF, THM350
AFH, THM440-T4
AG, THM350
AH, THM200-4R, THM350, THM400
AJ, THM350,
AL, THM400
AM, THM400
AN, THM350, THM400
ANH, THM440-T4
AO, THM200-4R
AP, THM200-4R
ARC, THM3T40
AS, THM200, THM200C
AT, THM400
ATH, THM440-T4
AWH, THM440-T4
AX, THM200
AY, AZ, THM400
AYC, THM3T40
B, THM250
BA, THM200, THM400, THM440-T4
BAH, THM440-T4
BB, BC, THM400, THM440-T4
BD, THM200C, THM440-T4
BDH, THM440-T4
BF, THM125C
BFH, THM125C, THM440-T4
BH, THM200, THM200C, THM440-T4
BHC, THM125C
BHH, THM440-T4
BJC, THM125C
BJH, THM440-T4
BK, THM200C, THM200-4R, THM375 ('74-'76)
BKH, THM440-T4
BL, THM200, THM125C
BLC, THM125, THM125C
BM, THM200-4R
BMH, THM440-T4
BP, THM125C
BQ, THM200-4R
BR, THM200, THM200-4R
BRH, THM440-T4
BS, THM440-T4
BT, THM200-4R, THM400
BTH, THM440-T4
BU, THM200, THM400

BUC, THM3T40
BW, THM200, THM400
BWH, THM440-T4
BXH, THM440-T4
BY, THM200-4R
BYC, THM3T40
BYH, THM440-T4
BZ, THM200, THM200C
BZC, THM125C
C3, THM125C
CA, THM125C, THM200, THM200C
CAH, THM440-T4
CB, THM125, THM125C, THM200C
CBC, THM125C, THM350
CC, THM125 THM200, THM200C
CD, THM125, THM125C, THM200
CE, THM125, THM125C, THM200C
CF, THM125C
CFH, THM440-T-4
CG, THM125
CH, THM200-4R, THM400
CHC, THM3T40
CI, THM125C
CJ, THM125, THM 125C
CJC, THM125C
CK, THM125C THM200C
CL, THM125C THM475
CLC, THM125, THM125C
CLH, THM440-T4
CM, THM125C, THM440-T4
CMC, THM125C
CMH, THM440-T4
CN, THM200, THM200C
CO, THM200C
CP, THM125
CPC, THM125C
CQ, THM200-4R
CR, THM200, THM200-4R
CRC, THM125C
CRH, THM440-T4
CS, THM200, THM200C
CT, THM125, THM125C
CTC, THM125C
CTH, THM440-T4
CU, THM125C THM200, THM200-4R
CUC, THM125C
CV, THM125, THM200, THM200C
CW, CX, THM125C, THM200C, THM440-T4
CWC THM3T40
CWH, THM440-T4
CXC, THM125C
CXH, THM440-T4

CY, THM200, THM200C
CZ, THM200C
CZH, THM440-T4
DO, THM400
EA, THM125
EB, EF, THM125C
EG, THM200-4R
EI, EK, EL, EM, EN, EP, EQ, EW, EZ, THM125C
FA, FB, FC, THM400
FBH, THM440-T4
FCH, THM440-T4
FD, FE, FF, THM400
FG, FH, FI, THM400
FJ, FK, FL, THM400
FJH, THM440-T4
FM, FN, FO, THM400
FP, FO, FR, THM400
FS, FT, FV, THM400
FSH, THM440-T4
FW, FX, FY, THM400
FZ, THM400
HA, HB, THM200C
HAC, THM3T40
HC, HD, THM125C, THM200C
HCC, THM3T40
HE, THM200C, THM200-4R
HF, THM200C
HFC, THM125C
HG, THM200-4R
HH, THM200C
HHC, THM125C, THM3T40
HI, THM125C
HK, HL, THM200C
HKC, THM3T40
HLC, THM125C
HM, HR, HS, THM125C
HRC, THM125C
HT, THM200, THM440-T4
HTC, THM3T40
HU, HV, HW, HX, THM125C
HWC, THM125C, THM3T40
HXC, THM3T40
HY, THM125C
HYC, THM125C, THM3T40
HZ, THM200C
HZC, THM125C, THM3T40
JA, JB, THM350
JAC, THM125C
JC, THM350
JD, THM350
JDC, THM125C

JE, THM350
JFC, THM125C
JH THM350
JJ, JK, JL THM350
JKC, THM125C, THM3T40
JMC, THM125C
JN, THM350
JNC, THM125C
JPC, THM125C
JR, JS, THM350
JRC, THM3T40
JSC, THM125C
JUC, THM125C
JWC, THM125C
JXC, THM125C
JY, THM200C
JYC, THM3T40
KA, THM350, THM350C
KB, THM350
KC, THM350, THM350C
KCC, THM3T40
KD, THM350, THM350C
KDC, THM125C, THM3T40
KE, THM250 ('73-'77), THM350, THM350C
KF, THM350
KH, THM350, THM400
KHC, THM125C
KJ, THM350,
KK, THM350, THM350C, THM375 ('74-'76)
KKC, THM3T40
KL, THM350, THM350C
KMC, THM3T40
KN, THM350C, THM350
KP, THM350
KS, THM350, THM350C
KT, THM350C, THM350
KV, THM350
KW, THM350
KX, THM350,
KXC, THM3T40
KY, THM350C
LA, THM350, THM350C
LB, THM350C
LC, THM350, THM350C
LD, THM250 ('73-'77), THM350, THM350C
LE, THM350
LH, THM350C
LJ, THM350
LJC, THM3T40
LK, THM350
LKC, THM3T40
LM, LS, LT, THM350
LSC, THM125C
LUC, THM3T40
LYC, THM3T40
M2, M4, M5, THM700-R4
M6, M7, THM700-R4
MA, THM350C, THM350
MC, THM250 ('73-'77), THM350C, THM700-4R
MD, THM350, THM700-R4
ME, THM250
MG, THM300
MH, MJ, MK, THM700-R4
MP, THM350
MT, THM350
NC, THM350
OB, OC, OD, THM400
OF, THM200-4R, THM400
OG, THM200-4R

OH, THM200-4R,
OI, THM200C
OJ, THM200-4R,
OM, THM200-4R,
ON, THM400
OO, THM200-4R
OP, THM125C
OR, OS, THM200, THM200C
OT, THM200C
OU, THM125C, THM200C
OW, THM200, THM200C
OX, OY, THM200C
OZ, THM200, THM200C, THM200-4R
P2, THM125
P3, THM125C
PA, PB, PC, THM200
PBC, THM3T40
PD, THM125C, THM200C
PDC, THM125C, THM3T40
PE, PF, THM125C, THM200C
PG, THM125C, THM200, THM200C
PH, THM200, THM200-4R
PI, PJ, PK, PL, PN, PO, THM125C
PJC, THM3T40
PKC, THM125C
PMC, THM125C
PNC, THM125C, THM3T40
POC, THM125C
PPC, THM125C, THM3T40
PQ, THM700-R4
PRC, THM3T40
PS, THM200C
PSC, THM125C
PTC, THM125C, THM3T40
PUC, THM125C
PV, THM200
PVC, THM125C
PW, THM125C, THM200C
PWC, THM125C
PX, PY, THM200
PZ, THM125 THM200
PZC, THM125C
RAC, THM125C, THM3T40
RCC, THM3T40
RLC, THM125C
RTC, THM125C
RUC, THM3T40
RVC, THM125C
SA, THM125C
T2, T3, T4, THM350C
T5, THM700-R4
T6, THM350C, THM700-R4
T7, T9, THM350C
TA, THM250C, THM350, THM350C
TAC, THM125C, THM3T40
TB, THM250C, THM350C
TBC, THM125C, THM3T40
TC, THM250C, THM350, THM350C, THM700-R4
TD, THM350, THM350C
TE, THM350, THM350C, THM400, THM700-R4
TF, THM350
TG, THM250C
TH, THM350C, THM700-R4
THC, THM3T40
TJ, THM700-R4
TK, THM350, THM350C, THM700-R4
TKC, THM3T40
TL, THM350C, THM700-R4

TN, THM350, THM350C THM700-R4
TNC, THM125C
TO, THM350C
TP, THM350, THM350C, THM700-R4
TR, THM350, THM350C
TRC, THM125C, THM3T40
TS, THM350, THM350C, THM700-R4
TT, THM250C
TV, THM350C
TW, THM350C, THM700-R4
TX, THM350, THM350C
TY, THM350C
TZ, THM350, THM350C
V4, THM350
V6, THM350C
VA, VC, VD, THM350C
VE, THM350C
VH, THM350C, THM700-R4
VJ, THM350C, THM700-R4
VK, VL, VN, THM350C
VP, THM350C
VS, VW, VZ, THM350C
WA, WB, THM350, THM350C
WBH, THM440-T4
WC, WD, THM350, THM350C
WE, THM350C
WF, THM350
WG, THM350
WH, WJ, THM350C
WK, THM250C, THM350, THM350C
WKH, THM125C
WL, THM250C, THM350, THM350C
WLH, THM440-T4
WM, WN, WO, THM350C
WP, THM350C
WRH, THM440-T4
WS, WT, THM350C
WUH, THM440-T4
WW, WX, THM350C
WZ, THM350C
XA, THM250C, THM350, THM350C
XB, THM250C, THM350
XC, XD, THM250, THM250C, THM350C
XE, THM350C
XF, THM700-R4
XH, XK, XK, THM250C
XL, THM250C
XM, XN, THM350C
XP, THM250C, THM350C
XR, THM350C
XS, THM250C, THM350C
XW, XX, THM350C
XXC, THM125C, THM3T40
XXH, THM3T40
Y3, Y4, Y6, THM700-R4
Y7, Y8, Y9, THM700-R4
Y, THM250
YA, THM700-R4
YBH, THM440-T4
YD, THM700-R4
YF, THM700-R4
YG, THM700-R4
YH, THM700-R4
YJH, THM440-T4
YK, THM700-R4
YL, THM700-R4
YN, THM700-R4
YP, THM700-R4
YT, THM700-R4
ZR, THM200-4R

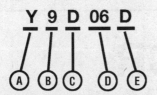

4.3 On THM350 transmissions built by Chevrolet, the identification code is stamped into the side (usually the right side) of the transmission pan. It works like this:

A   Assembly plant (Y = Toledo, B = Parma, X = Cleveland)
B   Last number of model year (assumes you know the decade of production [in this case, 1979])
C   Month produced (A = January, B = February, C = March, D = April, E = May, H = June, K = July, M = August, P = September, R = October, S = November, T = December)
D   Day of month (the sixth in this case)
E   Shift (D = Day, N = Night)

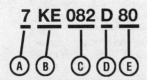

4.5 On later THM350 transmissions built by Buick, the identification code is stamped into the governor cover (it's a steel dome on the left rear of the transmission, secured by a wire bail). The code works like this:

A   ID number (1978 through 1981 models only) (5 = 1978, 6 = 1979, 7 = 1980, 8 = 1981) (not on all models)
B   Model type (see chart for identification)
C   Day of year built (1-365)
D   Shift built (D = Day, N = Night)
E   Model year

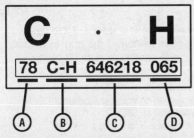

4.7 On THM400 transmissions, the transmission code is stamped onto a plate that's attached to the transmission case. The code works like this:

A   Model year
B   Model type (see chart for identification)
C   Transmission serial number (not the VIN)
D   Day of year built (1-365) (not on all transmissions)

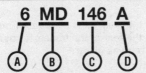

4.9 On 1985 and 1986 THM700-R4 transmissions, the code works like this:

A   Model year
B   Model type (see chart for identification)
C   Day of year built (1-365)
D   Shift (D = Day, N = Night, A&B = First shift, C&H = Second shift)

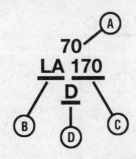

4.4 On early THM350 transmissions built by Buick, the number is stamped into the accumulator cover, which is just above the center of the pan on the right side of the transmission. The code works like this:

A   Last two digits of model year
B   Model type (see chart for identification)
C   Day of year built (1-365)
D   Shift built (D = Day, N = Night)

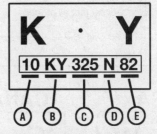

4.6 On 1982 and later THM350 transmissions built by Buick, the transmission code is stamped into a plate that's attached to the right side of the transmission case. The code works like this:

A   Model year (9 = 1982, 10 = 1983, 11 = 1984, 12 = 1985, 13 = 1986, 14 = 1987)
B   Model type (see chart for identification)
C   Day of year built (1-365)
D   Shift (D = Day, N = Night)
E   Year built

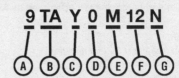

4.8 On THM700-R4 transmissions, the ID code is stamped into the transmission case on the right side, just above the transmission pan. Through 1984, the code works like this:

A   Model year (9 = 1982, 10 = 1983, 11 = 1984)
B   Model type (see chart for identification)
C   Assembly plant (Y = Toledo, B = Parma, X = Cleveland)
D   Last digit of calendar year
E   Month produced (A = January, B = February, C = March, D = April, E = May, H = June, K = July, M = August, P = September, R = October, S = November, T = December)
F   Day of month built
G   Shift (D = Day, N = Night)

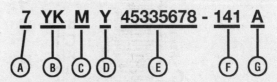

4.10 On 1987 and 1988 THM700-R4 transmissions, the code works like this:

A   Last digit of model year (7 or 8)
B   Model type (see chart for identification)
C   Transmission type (M = 700-R4)
D   Assembly plant (Y = Toledo, B = Parma, X = Cleveland)
E   Transmission serial number (not the VIN)
F   Day of year built (1-365)
G   Shift (A&B = First shift, C&H = Second shift)

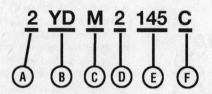

4.11 On 1989 and later THM700-R4 transmissions, the code works like this:

A   Last digit of model year
B   Model type (see chart for identification)
C   Transmission type (M = 700-R4)
D   Last digit of calendar year (not all models)
E   Day of year built (1-365)
F   Shift built (A&B = First shift, C&H = Second shift)

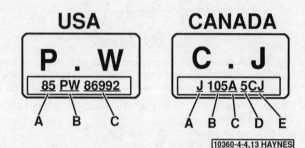

4.13 On all 125/125C and 3T40 transaxles the code is stamped onto a plate that's attached to the top of the transaxle case side cover. On early models the codes read as follows:

US models
A   Model year
B   Model type (see chart for identification)
C   Transaxle serial number (not the VIN)

Canadian models
A   Assembly plant (J = Windsor Canada)
B   Day of year built (1-365)
C   Shift (A = first shift, B = Second shift, C = Third shift)
D   Model year (assumes you know the decade of production)
E   Model type (see chart for identification)

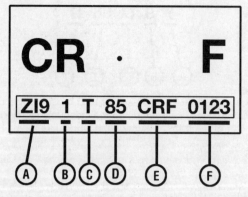

4.12 On 200-4R transmissions, the number is stamped onto a plate that's attached to the right side of the transmission, at the rear

A   Day of year built (1-365)
B   Shift (1 = First shift, 2 = Second shift, 3 = Third shift)
C   Assembly plant (T = Three Rivers)
D   Last two digits of model year
E   Model type (see chart for identification)
F   Transmission serial number (not the VIN)

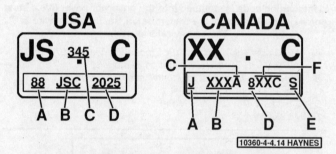

4.14 Later model 125/125C and 3T40 transaxles use a 3 digit code to identify the transaxle. Later model codes read as follows:

US models
A   Model year
B   Model type (see chart for identification)
C   Day of year built (1-365)
D   Transaxle serial number (not the VIN)

Canadian models
A   Assembly plant (J = Windsor Canada)
B   Day of year built (1-365)
C   Shift (A = first shift, B = Second shift, C = Third shift)
D   Model year (assumes you know the decade of production)
E   Model type (see chart for identification)
F   No meaning

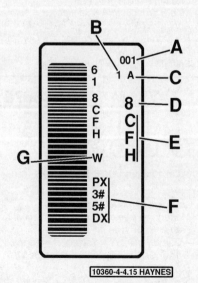

4.15 On THM 440-T4/4T60 transaxles the codes are printed on a sticker that is affixed to the rear of the transaxle case. The codes read as follows:

A   Day of year built (1-365)
B   Assembly Line (1, 2, 3, 4 etc...)
C   Shift (A = first shift, B = Second shift, C = Third shift)
D   Model year (assumes you know the decade of production)
E   Model type (see chart for identification)
F   Transaxle serial number (not the VIN)
G   Assembly plant (W = Warren Michigan)

Chapter 5 Troubleshooting

Introduction

The purpose of this chapter is to help you determine, first of all, if your transmission actually needs an overhaul, or if it can be repaired in the vehicle. If an overhaul is unavoidable, it's best to identify the possible problem area, or areas, before you begin teardown so you can inspect the problem area thoroughly. You should have a basic understanding of your transmission's operating fundamentals, and how the components interact to achieve shifting, to totally benefit from the symptom-based troubleshooting sections we give you in this Chapter **(see Chapter 3 for more information, if necessary)**.

Always start by checking the following items before you begin any in-depth troubleshooting (all items do not apply to all transmissions):
a) *Check the transmission fluid for proper level and color.*
b) *Check to see if the manual linkage is properly installed and adjusted (see Chapter 6).*
c) *Check the throttle valve or detent cable for proper installation and adjustment (see Chapter 6).*
d) *Check the vacuum modulator vacuum hose for proper installation. Make sure the hose is not cracked or broken and vacuum is reaching the modulator.*
e) *Check the engine timing and idle speed is set correctly.*
f) *Check to make sure there are no engine vacuum leaks.*

After you have completed all the above checks, perform a thorough road test.

Fluid examination

General information

General Motors automatic transmissions are designed to operate with the fluid level between the ADD ONE PINT and the HOT FULL marks on the dipstick indicator, with the fluid at normal operating temperature **(see illustration)**. The normal operating temperature is attained by driving the car for 8 to 15 miles or running the engine approximately 10 minutes, while shifting through the gears several times during this period. The fluid temperature should reach 150 to 200-degrees F when normal operating temperature is reached.
Note: *If the car has been driven for a long period of time or the fluid temperature is over 200-degrees F, you must wait for the fluid to cool down before you can accurately check the fluid level.*

Examining the fluid color and odor

The normal color of automatic transmission fluid (ATF) is deep red or orange red and should not be black, brown or pink. The best way to check the color of the ATF is to use white paper. Remove the dipstick and wipe the fluid off of the dipstick onto the white paper, this will allow you to see the true color of the fluid as it is absorbed into the paper. Inspect the paper for the proper color and for black, brown or metal specks.

If the color of the ATF is a green/brown shade and does not have a burned odor, this indicates that regular maintenance is need to prevent possible transmission damage.

If the color of the ATF is a black or brown shade and has a burned

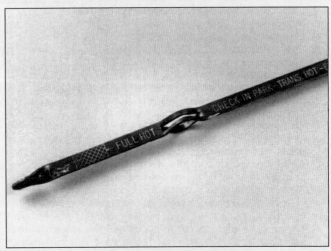

5.1 Follow the directions stamped on the dipstick to get an accurate reading - use only Dexron II™ or equivalent high quality transmission fluid

odor, this indicates that the transmission has been overheated or possibly burned. With this type of fluid condition the transmission has probably been damaged and servicing of the fluid and filter at this point may not help.

If the color of the ATF has a pink shade or milky feel to it, the transmission oil cooler in the radiator is leaking water or coolant into the transmission through the oil cooler lines. Repair or replacement of the transmission cooler is necessary before servicing the transmission. After the leak has been repaired, the transmission will require servicing and flushing. Unfortunately this does not mean the problem has been solved. Damaged may have occurred and flushing might only be successful if only water has contaminated the transmission. If coolant has contaminated the system, flushing and servicing will not cure the problem. The ethylene glycol in the antifreeze breaks down the bonding material in the bands and clutch discs, causing the friction material to tear apart. This will cause severe transmission damage and failure.

If the ATF is red but has bubbles or is foamy the fluid level is to high and the internal parts of the transmission are not being properly lubricated. To remedy this problem drain the excess transmission fluid from the pan or use a suction gun and hose to remove fluid through the fill tube.

If the transmission is operating properly, but there are tiny particles in the fluid, this is considered normal. If large amounts of particles are found, they're most likely from worn bushings, bands, clutches and/or friction material. If excessive material is found remove the pan and filter, inspect for aluminum, brass or bronze flakes or friction material, this indicates extreme wear and internal damage **(see illustration)**.

If the ATF has a burned or bad odor, regardless of color, this indicates the fluid has overheated and possible clutch or band failure may have occurred. To test for burned fluid, put a small amount of fluid from the dipstick on your fingers and rub it together. If it smells like burned oil, the fluid has been overheated. Typically, burned fluid will be dark brown or black.

Road test

General information

After you have performed the preliminary inspection outlined in the Introduction, the road test is next. A properly conducted road test is a valuable tool in diagnosing the transmission. Again, you must have a basic understanding of how the transmission operates to totally benefit from the road test **(see Chapter 3)**.

When you perform the road test, it's helpful to record the actual shift points for each gear. During the road test check for:

  a) *Vibrations*
  b) *Unusual noises*
  c) *Poor shift quality*
  d) *Slippage*
  e) *Erratic shift pattern*

A lightly traveled road is ideal for conducting the road test. Take advantage of your areas natural features, such as curves and hills that could enhance the problem and make it easier to diagnose.

During the road test you should check the following major points:

  a) *Operate the transmission in all gear ranges to check for differences in shifting and for slippage.*
  b) *Check that you have all upshift, downshift, coasting downshift, manual downshift and engine braking capabilities.*
  c) *Note the quality of each shift. Is it firm, soft, harsh or mushy?*
  d) *Check and record the speeds at which all upshifts and downshifts take place.*
  e) *Watch the engine speed for sudden engine speed increase indicating slippage. If this occurs in a gear it usually indicates a clutch, band or one-way clutch has a problem.*

Note: *If there is a delay on initial engagement when the transmission is placed into gear, the check valve in the oil pump is probably stuck or*

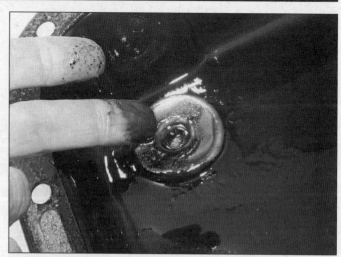

5.2 If material is found on the dipstick remove the oil pan and filter and look for large particles in the pan

sticking and has allowed the fluid to drain from the converter into the transmission oil pan.

How to conduct a road test

Begin the road test from a stop with the gear selector in the Drive or Overdrive position, if equipped. Be sure that the engine and transmission are both at normal operating temperature. Accelerate the car moderately. Record all the upshift points. The 1-2, 2-3 and 3-4 (on overdrive transmissions) shifts should occur while you are accelerating, but shift points should vary depending on how quickly you accelerate.

To test for part throttle downshift, accelerate the vehicle to approximately 45-mph in high gear, then quickly depress the accelerator half way (you only want to open the throttle half way). The transmission should downshift one gear. Repeat the procedure, opening throttle fully, to test the full throttle downshift. Depending on the speed and transmission model, the transmission may downshift one or two gears. Test for a coasting downshift by decelerating from cruising speed to a complete stop. You should feel the transmission downshift from 4-3 (if equipped), 3-2 and finally 2-1. Make a note of the downshift speeds.

To check the operation of manual second or manual low, accelerate from a standing start with the gear selector in the range you wish to check. For manual second, there should be a 1-2 upshift. The transmission should stay in second gear after the 1-2 upshift regardless of the vehicle speed, and provide engine braking on deceleration. No 2-3 upshift should occur. When manual low is selected the transmission will remain in the low gear and provide engine braking on deceleration. No 1-2 upshift should occur.

Check the manual 3-2 downshift quality by moving the selector lever from Drive to manual second at a moderate speed. Observe the shift quality and check for engine braking. Some transmissions, such as the THM400, will shift into manual second then into manual low when manual low is selected.

The last two operations to check are Neutral and Reverse. Stop the car and place the selector lever into the Neutral position and listen for noise. Feel for vehicle movement; there should be no engagement of the transmission in Neutral or the Park position. Finally, place the gear selector lever in Reverse. Check the transmission operation in Reverse, both at idle and part throttle.

Take the information you have gathered on the road test and compare it to the applicable chart listed as follows. Use the chart to narrow the problem down to a specific component or apply device in the transmission by noting the components that are applied in the particular problem range. For example, if your transmission has no second gear, but low and high gear are OK; a problem with the intermediate band is indicated.

Road Test Application Chart

THM200-4R

Range	Band Applied	Clutch Applied
Park/Neutral	No band applied	No clutch applied
Overdrive range 1st gear	No band applied	Forward clutch applied, overdrive roller clutch holding and low roller clutch holding
Overdrive range 2nd gear	Intermediate band applied	Forward clutch applied, overdrive roller clutch holding
Overdrive range 3rd gear	No band applied	Direct clutch applied, forward clutch applied and overdrive roller clutch holding
Overdrive range 4th gear	No band applied	Direct clutch applied, forward clutch applied and fourth clutch applied
Manual Low	No band applied	Forward clutch applied, overrun clutch applied and low-reverse clutch applied
Manual Second	Intermediate band applied	Forward clutch applied and overrun clutch applied
Manual Third	No band applied	Forward clutch applied, overrun clutch applied and direct clutch applied
Reverse	No band applied	Direct clutch applied, low-reverse clutch applied and overdrive roller clutch holding

THM350

Range	Band Applied	Clutch Applied
Neutral	No band applied	No Clutch Applied
Drive range 1st gear	No band applied	Forward clutch applied, low roller clutch holding
Drive range 2nd gear	No band applied	Forward clutch applied, intermediate clutch applied and intermediate roller clutch holding
Drive range 3rd gear	No band applied	Forward clutch applied, direct clutch applied and intermediate clutch applied
Manual Low	No band applied	Forward clutch applied and low-reverse clutch applied
Manual Second	Intermediate band	Forward clutch applied, intermediate clutch applied and intermediate roller clutch holding
Reverse	No band applied	Direct clutch applied and low-reverse clutch applied

THM400

Range	Band Applied	Clutch Applied
Neutral	No band applied	No clutch applied
Drive range 1st gear	No band applied	Forward clutch applied, intermediate clutch applied and low roller clutch holding
Drive range 2nd gear	No band applied	Forward clutch applied, intermediate clutch applied and intermediate sprag holding
Drive range 3rd gear	No band applied	Forward clutch applied, direct clutch applied and intermediate clutch applied
Manual Low	Rear band applied	Forward clutch applied and low roller clutch holding
Manual Second	Front band applied	Forward clutch applied, intermediate clutch applied and intermediate sprag holding
Reverse	Rear band applied	Direct clutch applied

THM700-R4

Range	Band Applied	Clutch Applied
Park/Neutral	No band applied	No clutch applied
Overdrive range 1st gear	No band applied	Forward clutch applied, low roller clutch holding and forward sprag holding
Overdrive range 2nd gear	2-4 band applied	Forward clutch applied and forward sprag holding
Drive range 3rd gear	No band applied	Forward clutch applied, 3-4 clutch applied and forward sprag holding
Overdrive range 4th gear	2-4 band applied	Forward clutch applied and 3-4 clutch applied
Manual Low	No band applied	Forward clutch applied, overrun clutch applied and low roller clutch holding
Manual Second	2-4 band applied	Forward clutch applied and overrun clutch applied
Manual Third	No band applied	Forward clutch applied, overrun clutch applied and 3-4 clutch applied
Reverse	No band applied	Reverse input clutch applied and low-reverse clutch applied

THM125/125C and 3T40

Range	Band Applied	Clutch Applied
Neutral	No band applied	No Clutch Applied
Drive range 1st gear	No band applied	Forward clutch applied, roller clutch holding
Drive range 2nd gear	Intermediate band applied	Forward clutch applied
Drive range 3rd gear	No band applied	Forward clutch applied, direct clutch applied
Manual Low	No band applied	Forward clutch applied, roller clutch holding and low-reverse clutch applied
Manual Second	Intermediate band applied	Forward clutch applied
Reverse	No band applied	Direct clutch applied and low-reverse clutch applied

Road Test Application Chart (continued)

THM440-T4/4T60

Range	Band Applied	Clutch Applied
Park/Neutral	No band applied	No clutch applied
Overdrive range 1st gear	1-2 band applied	Input clutch applied, input sprag holding
Overdrive range 2nd gear	1-2 band applied	2nd clutch applied, input sprag over-running
Overdrive range 3rd gear	No band applied	2-3 clutch applied, third roller clutch holding
Overdrive range 4th gear	No band applied	2-3-4 clutches applied, third roller clutch over-running
Manual Low	1-2 band applied	Input clutch applied, third clutch applied, input sprag holding and third roller clutch holding
Manual Second	1-2 band applied	2nd clutch applied, input sprag over-running
Manual Third	No band applied	Input clutch applied, 2-3 clutches applied, input sprag holding and third roller clutch holding
Reverse	Reverse band applied	Input clutch applied, input sprag holding

5.3 The oil pressure test gauge hose fitting threads into the transmission test port, the dial on the gauge should read up to 300 psi

5.4 Oil pressure test port location for the THM350

Oil pressure test

General information

An automatic transmission is a hydraulically operated device, therefore adequate oil pressure must be maintained for correct operation of all the internal components. The oil pump creates oil pressure and supplies transmission fluid to the components through the oil circuits of the transmission. The pressure is regulated by a pressure regulator device in the oil pump body.

A hydraulic pressure test is an accurate way to pinpoint the specific causes of transmission pressure related problems. As with the road test, having some idea of the possible causes of a problem before you remove the transmission might save you from unnecessary work.

There are many oil circuits in the transmission, and several sub-systems such as the throttle pressure system and the governor system. They all have one thing in common; they are supplied by main line oil pressure (or simply line pressure) by the oil pump. When an oil pressure test is performed, typically it's the line pressure that's checked. Line pressure is also known as control pressure and is used to activate and hold the clutches and bands and provide the pressure to move the control valves. Throttle pressure is line pressure directed and controlled at and by the throttle valve. The throttle valve is connected to the engine by mechanical linkage, a cable or a vacuum modulator. Throttle pressure increases with the engine load and

throttle opening. It interacts with the governor pressure to control shift points. Governor pressure is line pressure that is increased in relation to vehicle road speed and regulated by the governor valve. The governor valve is a centrifugal operated valve driven off of the output shaft and works in conduction with throttle pressure to control shift points. If the line pressure is high or low, it can affect the entire transmission because it supplies the pressure to regulate shifting.

5.5 Oil pressure test port location for the THM400

5.6 Oil pressure test port location for the THM200-4R and the THM700-R4

5.7 Oil pressure test port location for the THM 125/125C and the 3T40

5.8 Oil pressure test port location for the THM 440-T4/4T60

How to perform an oil pressure test

To perform an oil pressure test you'll need an oil pressure gauge and a tachometer (see illustration). The gauge must be capable of reading up to 300 psi and equipped with a heavy duty hose with a 1/8-inch NPT fitting. The hose must be at least 10 feet long if you're planning to read the gauge from inside the vehicle.

Locate the test port plug on the side of the transmission and remove the plug (see illustrations). If necessary raise the vehicle and support it securely on jackstands to access the transmission test port from under the vehicle. Install the oil pressure gauge into the line pressure test port and tighten the fitting securely. Start the engine and allow the engine and transmission to reach normal operating temperature. Firmly apply the brake, shift the transmission into gear, slowly raise the engine speed to 1000 rpm and record the test pressure. Return the engine to idle, shift to the next range and perform the test in each of the indicated ranges. Do not take more than 20 seconds to record the pressure in any one range and do not exceed two minutes total test time. Compare your readings with the normal oil pressure from the applicable chart below.

Oil Pressure Test Chart

THM350 and 400 (@ 1000 rpm with the brakes applied)*

Range	Normal oil pressure
Neutral	55 to 75 psi
Low or D2	
THM400	130 to 160 psi
THM350	85 to 110 psi
Drive	60 to 90 psi
Reverse	85 to 150 psi

THM200-4R and 700-R4 (@ 1000 rpm with the brakes applied)*

Range	Normal oil pressure
Neutral	55 to 75 psi
Low or D2	
THM200-4R	110 to 160 psi
THM700-R4	85 to 190 psi
Drive	55 to 75 psi
Reverse	85 to 140 psi

THM125/125C and 3T40 (@ 1000 rpm with the brakes applied)*

Range	Normal oil pressure
Neutral, Drive	55 to 85 psi
Low, D2 or Intermediate	95 to 185 psi
Reverse	95 to 150 psi

THM440-T4/4T60 (@ 1250 rpm with the brakes applied)*

Range	Normal oil pressure
Neutral, Reverse	61 to 180 psi
D1	137 to 192 psi
D2, D3, D4	61 to 150 psi

Caution: Do not exceed 2 minutes running time.

*Note: The line pressure readings listed above are a compilation of approximate readings listed by the manufacturer at the time this manual was written. General Motors Corporation releases new updated material from time-to-time on specific models and makes of transmissions. Therefore, it is best to consult your dealer service department for any updated technical material that might apply to your specific model transmission.

Typical diagnosis of high or low oil pressure

Note: *Not all conditions apply to all transmissions.*
1   Check the transmission fluid level and condition.
2   Check the oil filter for:

a) *Blockage or a restriction.*
b) *Cracks in the filter body or intake tube.*
c) *Intake tube plugged.*
d) *O-ring cut or missing from intake tube to case.*

3   Check the modulator for:

a) *Vacuum line disconnected or leaking.*
b) *Modulator valve stuck.*
c) *Damaged modulator.*

4   Check the oil pump assembly for:

a) *Stuck pressure regulator valve or weak spring.*
b) *Pressure regulator spacer missing.*
c) *Rotor guide omitted or incorrectly installed.*
d) *Rotor or gear cracked, broken or worn excessively.*
e) *TV boost valve, reverse boost valve or sleeve stuck, damaged or installed incorrectly.*
f) *Plugged orifice hole in the pressure regulator valve.*
g) *Sticking slide or excessive rotor clearance.*
h) *Pressure relief valve or ball not seated or damaged.*
i) *Wrong pump cover or porosity in the pump cover or body.*
j) *Pump faces are not flat.*
k) *Pump-to-case gasket installed incorrectly.*

5   Check the TV exhaust ball for sticking or damage.
6   Check the throttle lever, bracket, cable and linkage for binding, incorrect installation or damage.
7   Check the valve body for:

a) *Manual valve scoring or damaged.*
b) *Spacer plate or gaskets damaged, missing or improperly installed.*
c) *Valve body face or case not flat.*
d) *TV valve or TV limit valve sticking.*
e) *Modulated downshift valve, Line bias valve or 2-3 shift valve stuck.*
f) *Check balls missing or installed incorrectly.*
g) *Line bias valve binding in the open or closed position.*

8   Check the detent cable or system for:

a) *Stuck detent valve or cable.*
b) *Shorted or damaged detent switch, solenoid or wiring.*

9   Check the case, forward clutch, direct clutch, accumulator and servo for internal leakage.

Symptom-based troubleshooting

You can make an accurate diagnosis of a transmission problem from the symptom-based troubleshooting information listed as follows. This section lists the common symptoms along with their possible causes and items to check. Remember that many common transmission problems can be caused a variety of different components or systems. The troubleshooting information listed in this section can be helpful in inspecting the transmission components during an overhaul to determine the exact cause of the failure.

The information listed is general for all transmission types covered by this manual. Not all items apply to all transmission types, you must be familiar with your particular transmission components to make the correct diagnosis. For example; a defective modulator will not apply to a THM700-R4 because it's not equipped with a vacuum modulator system. Use the information from this section along with your road test results and oil pressure readings together to make a competent diagnosis.

Oil leaks

1   Check the oil pan for loose or missing bolts, a damaged or incorrectly installed gasket or a bent or warped sealing flange.
2   Check the oil filler pipe for a damaged or missing seal.

3   Check the throttle valve cable for an improperly installed or damaged seal.
4   Check the driveshaft (RWD) or driveaxle (FWD) seal(s) for an improperly installed or damaged seal.
5   Check the driveshaft yoke (RWD) or the inboard housing on the driveaxle (FWD) for scoring or grooves.
6   Check the speedometer driven gear for a damaged shaft seal or O-ring seal.
7   Check the manual shaft for a damaged or incorrectly installed seal.
8   Check the case for a loose or missing line pressure tap plug.
9   Check the case for cracks or porosity.
10   Check the oil pump for loose or missing attaching bolts or a damaged front pump seal or housing O-ring.
11   Check the servo cover or accumulator cover for a damaged O-ring seal.
12   Check the governor cover for a damaged O-ring seal.
13   Check the vacuum modulator for a damaged O-ring seal.

No movement in Drive range

1   Check the fluid for proper level, color and condition.
2   Check the manual linkage for proper adjustment.
3   Check the oil filter for a plugged or restricted screen or a damaged or missing O-ring seal.
4   Check the oil pump for a stuck pressure regulator or damaged pump drive tangs.
5   Check the overdrive unit for a damaged roller clutch.
6   Check the forward clutch for worn or burned clutch plates, damaged piston or seals, a forward clutch housing retainer and check ball not sealing or damaged or a forward clutch feed passage plugged or restricted.
7   Check the roller clutch for damaged rollers, missing springs or incorrect installation (backwards).

High or low shift points

1   Check the fluid for proper level, color and condition.
2   Check the TV cable for binding, pinched cable, bent or damaged linkage or incorrect adjustment.
3   Check the TV exhaust ball for sticking or damage.
4   Check the throttle lever, bracket and linkage for binding, incorrect adjustment or damage.
5   Check the governor assembly for a damaged or missing shaft-to-cover seal ring or a damaged or missing cover gasket.
6   Check the oil pump assembly for:

a) *Pressure regulator valve or TV boost valve stuck or damaged.*
b) *Pump slide sticking.*

7   Check the valve body assembly for:

a) *Sticking line bias valve, TV limit valve, modulated TV upshift or downshift valves, or a sticking throttle valve plunger.*
b) *Sticking or stuck 1-2, 2-3, 3-4 throttle valves, or pressure regulator valve.*
c) *Spacer plate or gaskets incorrectly installed or damaged.*

8   Check the case for:

a) *Damaged valve body surface.*
b) *Governor filter plugged or damaged.*
c) *2-4 servo assembly accumulator damaged.*
d) *2-4-servo piston seals cut or damaged.*
e) *2-4 servo assembly apply pin damaged or incorrect length.*
f) *2-4 band burned or anchor pin not engaged.*

Will not shift out of 1st gear

1   Check the fluid for proper level, color and condition.
2   Check the governor assembly for:

a) *Governor valve sticking.*
b) *Governor drive gear worn, damaged or retaining pin missing.*
c) *Governor weights or springs binding, missing or damaged.*
d) *Exhaust check balls missing or damaged.*

3   Check the valve body for:

a) *1-2 shift valve sticking.*
b) *Spacer plate or gaskets are incorrectly installed or damaged.*

4   Check the case for:

a) *Valve body face warped or damaged.*
b) *Governor filter plugged or damaged.*

5   Check the 2-4 servo assembly for:

a) *Apply passages in case plugged or restricted.*
b) *Servo pin or pin bore nicked or burred.*
c) *The 4th servo piston in backwards.*

6   Check the 2-4 band assembly for a damaged or worn band or a band not engaged in the anchor pin.

7   Check the intermediate or 2nd clutch for:

a) *Piston seals leaking.*
b) *Intermediate roller clutch damaged.*
c) *Housing check ball assembly damaged.*

8   Check the reverse reaction drum for:

a) *Damaged splines.*
b) *Missing drum plates*

Slips in 1st gear or during 1-2 shift

1   Check the fluid for proper level, color and condition.
2   Check the intermediate clutch for damaged piston seals or burned clutch plates.
3   Check the forward clutch assembly for:

a) *Worn clutch plates.*
b) *Damage to the forward clutch piston.*
c) *Missing, cut or damaged forward clutch piston seals.*
d) *Input housing to forward clutch housing O-ring cut, missing or damaged.*
e) *Damage to the forward clutch housing.*
f) *Forward clutch housing retainer and ball not sealing or damaged.*

4   Check the forward accumulator for:

a) *Damaged, cut or missing piston seal.*
b) *Abuse valve stuck.*
c) *Accumulator piston out of it's bore.*
d) *Defects in the accumulator piston or auxiliary valve body.*

5   Check the oil pump for:

a) *Auxiliary accumulator valve tube leaking, missing or not seated in pump cover.*
b) *Turbine shaft seals cut, damaged or missing.*

6   Check the valve body for:

a) *Stuck 1-2 accumulator valve.*
b) *Damaged face, lands or passages that interconnect.*
c) *Damaged, missing or incorrectly installed spacer plate or gaskets.*
d) *Loose valve body bolts.*

7   Check the TV cable for proper movement, adjustment or a broken cable.

8   Check the low roller clutch for:

a) *Damage to lugs, inner ramps or inner splines.*
b) *Free moving rollers.*
c) *Plugged lube passages*
d) *Inadequate spring tension.*

9   Check the 1-2 accumulator assembly for:

a) *Defective piston, accumulator cover or pin assembly.*
b) *Damaged ring grooves or seals on piston.*
c) *Broken 1-2 accumulator spring or piston stuck in bore.*
d) *Valve body to the spacer plate gasket at the 1-2 accumulator cover missing or damaged.*

10   Check the 2-4 servo assembly for incorrect servo piston installation.
11   Check the oil pressure (see oil pressure test).

Slipping, rough, early or late 1-2 shift

1   Check the fluid for proper level, color and condition.

2   Check the engine for:

a) *Properly tuned and running smoothly.*
b) *Vacuum lines connected to modulator valve and proper engine source.*

3   Check the throttle cable, lever and bracket assembly for:

a) *Binding or incorrect installation.*
b) *TV cable broken, binding or incorrectly adjusted.*

4   Check the governor assembly for:

a) *Governor valve sticking.*
b) *Governor drive gear worn, damaged or retaining pin missing.*
c) *Governor weights or springs binding, missing or damaged.*

5   Check the valve body for:

a) *Sticking or stuck throttle valve or 1-2 shift valve train.*
b) *Sticking or stuck line bias valve, TV plunger or TV limit valve or 1-2 accumulator valve.*
c) *Damaged face, lands or passages that interconnect.*
d) *Damaged, missing or incorrectly installed spacer plate, gaskets or bolts loose.*
e) *1-2 shift check ball missing or sticking.*

6   Check the intermediate servo assembly for:

a) *Damaged or missing servo piston or piston to case oil seal ring.*
b) *Bleed cup missing in case.*
c) *Incorrect apply pin or leak between pin and case.*

7   Check the 2-3 accumulator for a stuck piston, missing or broken piston spring or damaged bore.

8   Check the 2-4 servo assembly for:

a) *Apply pin too long or too short.*
b) *Seal missing, cut or damaged on 2nd servo apply piston.*
c) *Oil passages restricted or missing.*
d) *Damage to servo bore in the case.*

9   Check the 1-2 accumulator for:

a) *Defects, nicks or burrs in the 1-2 accumulator piston or housing.*
b) *1-2 accumulator piston stuck or spring missing.*
c) *1-2 accumulator housing bolts loose.*
d) *Piston seal or groove damaged.*
e) *Oil passages restricted or missing.*

10   Check the intermediate band for:

a) *Improper alignment, burned or extremely worn.*
b) *Wrong selection of apply pin or leak between pin and case.*

11   Check the 2-4 band for improper alignment or extreme wear.
12   Check the oil pump assembly and case for warped machined surfaces.
13   Check the case cover for internal leakage.

No 2-3 shift or slipping, rough or late 2-3 shift

1   Check the fluid for proper level, color and condition.
2   Check the engine for:

a) *Properly tuned and running smoothly.*
b) *Vacuum lines connected to modulator valve and proper engine source.*

3   Check the converter for internal damage.
4   Check the governor assembly for:

a) *Valve stuck.*
b) *Drive gear retaining pin missing or loose.*
c) *Governor weights binding.*
d) *Governor driven gear damaged.*
e) *Governor support pin in case too long or too short.*
f) *Thrust bearing/washer damage.*
g) *Leaking governor pipes.*
h) *Governor driven gear stirpped*

5   Check the oil pump for a scored stator shaft support sleeve.
6   Check the center support for:

a) *Plugged direct feed passages.*
b) *Damaged or missing oil seal rings.*

7 Check the direct clutch or the third clutch for:
a) Damaged or missing inner oil seal ring on piston.
b) Damaged or missing center oil seal ring on the direct clutch hub.
c) Damaged or missing check ball or retainer on the direct clutch piston.
d) Damaged or missing direct clutch housing, piston or clutch plates.
e) Direct clutch backing plate snap ring out of groove.
f) Release spring guide incorrectly installed, preventing the piston check ball from seating in retainer.
g) Burned direct clutch plates.
h) Case to support bolts not tight causing a leak.

8 Check the intermediate servo assembly for:
a) Broken servo to case oil seal ring or missing on intermediate servo piston.
b) Damaged or missing intermediate servo.
c) Plugged exhaust hole in case between servo piston and seal rings.
d) Bleed orifice cup plug missing from intermediate servo pocket in case.

9 Check the 1-2 servo assembly for:
a) Servo bore cup plug missing.
b) Servo release ball capsule leaking or stuck.
c) Leaking pipes

10 Check the valve body for:
a) Proper adjustment of the throttle valve cable.
b) Stuck or sticking accumulator valve, throttle valve and plunger, TV limit valve or 2-3 shift valve sticking.
c) Damaged, missing or incorrectly installed spacer plate or gaskets.
d) Check ball(s) not seating, damaged or missing.

11 Check the input housing for:
a) Worn clutch plates.
b) Too much clutch plate travel.
c) Cut or damaged piston seals
d) Defects in the clutch housing or piston.
e) Apply passages plugged or restricted.
f) Forward clutch piston retainer and ball assembly not seating.
g) Sealing balls in housing loose or missing.

12 Check the case for:
a) Accumulator retainer and ball assembly not seating.
b) Accumulator cup plug leaking or missing.
c) Accumulator exhaust check valve for proper seating in case.
d) Case to governor shaft sleeve missing or damaged.
e) Defects in the case channels or castings.

13 Check the check balls for:
a) The 3-2 exhaust check ball installed incorrectly or missing.
b) The accumulator check ball installed incorrectly or missing, cut or damaged.

15 Check the transmission internal speed sensor for damage.
16 Check the third roller clutch for:
a) Damaged cage or rollers.
b) Damaged springs.
c) Misassembled input sungear shaft.

No 3-4 shift or slipping, rough or late 3-4 shift
1 Check the fluid for proper level, color and condition.
2 Check the governor for:
a) Governor valve sticking.
b) Governor drive gear worn or damaged.
c) Governor support pin in the case is incorrect.
d) Governor weights or springs binding, missing or damaged.
3 Check the oil pump assembly for:
a) Warped pump body or cover surface.
b) Pump cover retainer and ball assembly missing or damaged.
4 Check the valve body for:
a) Incorrectly adjusted or missing throttle valve cable.
b) Sticking or binding accumulator valve, 3-2 control valve, TV limit valve, 1-2 or 2-3 shift valve train.

c) Sticking or binding throttle valve and plunger.
d) Bent or damaged manual valve link.
e) Damaged, missing or incorrectly installed spacer plate or gaskets.

5 Check the 2-4 servo assembly for:
a) Band apply pin installed incorrectly.
b) Servo seals damaged or missing.
c) Defects in the pistons, cover or case.
d) Orifice cup plug missing or plugged.
e) 3rd accumulator retainer and ball assembly leaking.
f) Defects in the 3-4 accumulator piston or bore.

6 Check the center support for:
a) Cracks or pin holes in the center support.
b) Loose center support bolts.
c) Damaged fourth clutch piston seals or surface.
d) Burned forth clutch plates.

7 Check the case for:
a) 3rd accumulator retainer and ball assembly leaking.
b) Defects in the 3-4 accumulator piston or bore.
c) 3-4 accumulator piston or seal damaged.
d) Orifice cup plug missing or plugged.
e) Oil passages restricted or plugged.

8 Check the input housing assembly for:
a) Worn clutch plates.
b) Too much clutch plate travel.
c) Cut or damaged piston seals
d) Defects in the clutch housing or piston.
e) Apply passages plugged or restricted.
f) Forward clutch piston retainer and ball assembly not seating.
g) Sealing balls in housing loose or missing.

9 Check the 2-4 band assembly for wear or incorrectly installed.

No movement in reverse or slips in reverse
1 Check the fluid for proper level, color and condition.
2 Check the input housing for:
a) 3-4 apply ring stuck in the applied position.
b) Forward clutch not releasing.
c) Missing, cut or damaged turbine shaft seals.
3 Check the throttle valve cable for incorrect adjustment or binding.
4 Check the manual valve link for proper installation or possibly broken or missing.
5 Check the center support for:
a) Loose or missing attaching bolts.
b) Passages plugged or blocked.
c) Damaged or worn oil seal rings or grooves.
6 Check the oil pump assembly for:
a) Missing cup plug.
b) Missing or damaged retainer and ball assembly.
c) Damaged stator seal rings or ring grooves.
d) Scored or damaged stator shaft sleeve.
e) Stuck converter clutch valve or incorrectly installed or damaged reverse boost valve.
f) Oil passages restricted.
g) Pump faces warped.
7 Check the valve body assembly for:
a) Stuck or sticking 2-3 shift valve, throttle valve, TV limit valve, line bias valve or reverse boost valve.
b) Improperly adjusted manual link.
c) Damaged, missing or incorrectly installed spacer plate or gaskets.
8 Check the forward, direct or input clutch and housing for:
a) Burned clutch plates or clutches not releasing.
b) Cracked piston or housing.
c) Damaged or missing inner or outer piston seal.
d) Missing or damaged check balls.
9 Check the reverse input clutch assembly for:
a) Worn clutch plates or too much clutch plate travel.

b) Cracked weld on the reverse input housing and drum assembly.
c) Clutch plate retaining ring out of groove.
d) Return spring assembly retaining ring out of groove.
e) Damaged or cut seals or defects in the apply piston.
f) Apply passage plugged or restricted.
g) Incorrectly installed Beleville plate.

10 Check the rear servo and accumulator for:

a) Servo piston seal ring damaged or missing.
b) Servo piston stuck or damaged in bore.
c) Short band apply pin damaged or incorrectly installed.

11 Check the auxiliary valve body for:

a) Stuck low overrun valve.
b) Missing, restricted or damaged orifice cup plug.

12 Check the rear band for:

a) Burned or broken band.
b) Apply pin or anchor pins incorrectly installed.

13 Check the low-reverse clutch for:

a) Worn clutch plates.
b) Damaged seals or defects in the pistons.
c) Incorrectly in stalled return spring assembly retaining ring.
a) Apply passage restricted.

14 Check the input and reaction carrier for:

a) Damaged pinions.
b) Internal gear or sun gear damage.

15 Check the input sprag for proper assembly.
16 Check the reverse reaction drum for damaged splines.
17 Check for damaged or broken drive link chain.
18 Check the reverse band for damage.

No (or delayed) part throttle downshifts

1   Check the TV cable and bracket assembly for correct installation, bent or loose.
2   Check the 2-4 servo assembly for:

a) Incorrectly installed or missing servo cover retaining ring.
b) Missing or broken 4th apply piston.
c) Missing or damaged servo inner housing.

3   Check the governor assembly for:

a) Stuck governor valve.
b) Binding or sticking governor weights.

4   Check the valve body assembly for:

a) Stuck throttle valve, 3-2 control valve or TV modulated downshift valve.
b) Blocked 4-3 valve body sequence channel.
c) Damaged, missing or incorrectly installed spacer plate or gaskets.

5   Check the vacuum modulator system for proper operation.

No engine braking in manual 3-2-1

1   Check the external linkage for proper adjustment.
2   Check the valve body for:

a) Stuck 4-3 sequence valve or throttle valve.
b) Damaged, missing or incorrectly installed spacer plate or gaskets.
c) Incorrectly installed check ball.
d) Damaged blow-off valve assembly.

3   Check the servo assembly for a damaged or missing servo cover to case oil seal.
4   Check the intermediate band for:

a) Anchor pin broken or off.
b) Band burned or broken.

5   Check the low-reverse clutch assembly for:

a) Piston seals damaged or missing.
b) Clutch housing snap ring out of case.
c) Housing or piston cracked or defective.
d) Cup plug or rubber seal missing or damaged between case and low/Reverse clutch housing.
e) Leaking pipes.

6   Check the case for defects in casting or cracks.
7   Check the input clutch assembly for:

a) Damaged turbine shaft seal rings.
b) Plugged or improperly drilled turbine shaft oil passages.
c) Loose or missing turbine shaft sealing balls.
d) Defects in the forward or overrun clutch pistons.
e) Burned overrun clutches.
f) Damaged or cut overrun piston seals.
g) Overrun piston checkball not sealing.

Converter clutch does not apply

1   Check the electrical system for:

a) 12 volts supplied to transmission.
b) Damaged outside electrical connector.
c) Damaged inside wiring harness or solenoid.
d) Electrical short in wiring.
e) Bad ground or no ground to solenoid.
f) Damaged or wrong pressure switches.

2   Check the valve body for a stuck converter clutch shift valve or throttle valve.
3   Check the converter for internal damage.
4   Check the oil pump assembly for:

a) Converter clutch valve stuck or installed backwards.
b) Incorrect installation of the converter clutch valve retaining ring.
c) Incorrect installation of the pump to case gasket.
d) Restricted or plugged orifice cup plug.
e) Cut or damaged solenoid "O" ring seal.
f) Uneven or too much bolt torque.

5   Check the input housing and shaft for:

a) Cut or damaged turbine shaft "O" ring seal
b) Restricted or damaged turbine shaft retainer and ball assembly.

6   Check the torque converter clutch solenoid for a blocked screen.
7   Check for damaged seals on the turbine speed shaft.
8   Check the torque converter assembly for internal damage.

Converter clutch shudder or does not release

1   Check the torque converter assembly for internal damage.
2   Check the oil pump assembly for:

a) Oil pressure too low.
b) Converter clutch valve stuck.
c) Restriction in oil passages.
d) Cup plug in release passage missing.

3   Check the oil filter for:

a) Leaks or cracks in the filter body.
b) Restriction in the filter neck.
c) "O" ring seal cut or damaged.

4   Check the input housing and shaft for:

a) Turbine shaft "O" ring cut or damaged.
b) Turbine shaft retainer and ball assembly restricted or damaged.

5   Check the converter clutch solenoid for a grounded solenoid or wiring (this will cause the converter clutch not to release) or blocked screen.
6   Check the engine for proper tune.

Drive range in neutral

1   Check the forward clutch for:

a) Clutch assembly not releasing.
b) Burned or fused solid clutch plates.
c) Sticking exhaust check ball.

2   Check the manual linkage and valve link for proper installation or link disconnected.
3   Check the case for cracks or machined surfaces warped.

Takes off in 2nd or 3rd gear

1   Check the governor assembly for a stuck valve or governor support pin too long or missing.
2   Check the forward clutch sprag assembly for improper assembly or installed backwards.
3   Check the valve body for:
 a) *1-2 shift valve or throttle valve sticking in the upshift position.*

Does not lock in Park

1   Check the parking linkage for:
 a) *Linkage incorrectly adjusted.*
 b) *Bent or damaged actuator rod assembly.*
 c) *Actuator rod spring binding or improperly crimped.*
 d) *Actuator rod not attached to inside detent lever.*
 e) *Parking lock bracket lock bracket damaged or not torqued properly.*
 f) *Inside detent lever not torque properly.*
 g) *Detent roller and spring assembly incorrectly installed or not torqued properly.*
 h) *Parking pawl binding or damaged.*

Transmission has ratcheting noise when shifted to Park

1   Check the parking pawl for a broken, damaged or weak return spring.

Oil comes out of the breather vent

1   Check the oil pump for the chamfer in the oil pump body being too large.
2   Check the valve body for a stuck TV limit valve.
2   Check the fluid level for excessive fluid level.
3   Check the Thermo element for:
 a) *Improper pin heights.*
 b) *Incorrect installation.*
 c) *Does not close when hot.*
5   Check for plugged drain back holes on the drive sprocket support.

Vibration in reverse and whining noise in park

Check the oil pump for broken gears or vane rings.

Chapter 6 Maintenance, adjustments and in-vehicle repairs

Fluid and filter change

1   Changing the transmission fluid and filter is the single most important thing you can do to prolong the life of your transmission. Check you owner's manual for the manufacturer's recommended service intervals. Although some factory recommendations are often less frequent, we recommend you change fluid and filter at least every 30,000 miles. Service the transmission sooner (every 15,000 miles) if the fluid shows signs of overheating (dark color, burnt smell), if the vehicle is operated in extreme heat conditions, used for towing or operated in continuous stop-and-go driving situations.

2   Before beginning, make sure you have all the necessary tools and supplies to complete the job. You'll need a large drain pan, the proper pan gasket and filter and at least four quarts of Dexron II Automatic Transmission Fluid (ATF). If your transmission is equipped with a deep pan, you'll need more ATF, possibly six quarts or more.

3   The transmission fluid should be warm when drained, but not so hot as to burn yourself, so, when the vehicle is cold, drive the vehicle a few miles to warm-up the fluid. Park the vehicle on a level cement or asphalt surface, raise the vehicle and support it securely on jackstands.

4   Place the drain pan under the transmission and loosen all the bolts 2 to 3 turns. Fluid should begin draining from around the pan; if not, tap the sides of the pan gently with a rubber mallet to break the gasket seal. Begin removing the bolts from the front of the pan, then work down the sides to the rear. The idea here is to allow the pan to hinge down from the rear, draining the fluid from the front edge **(see illustration)**. After most of the fluid has drained, remove the rear bolts,

6.1 With the rear bolts in place but loose, pull the front of the pan down to let the fluid drain

carefully remove the pan and drain the remaining fluid from the pan.

5   On THM350 transmissions, remove the two screws retaining the filter to the valve body. On THM400 transmissions, remove the single mounting bolt. On all other transmission types, pull the filter straight down to disengage the pick-up pipe from the transmission. Separate the filter from the retaining clip, if equipped.

6.2 Inspect the inside of the pan for contamination and metal filings - the clutch material shown in this pan indicates normal wear

6.3 The gasket surfaces of the transmission and the oil pan must be carefully cleaned before reassembly

6.4 Some models have an O-ring on the filter spout; it may not come out when the filter is removed and you will have to reach up into the opening to retrieve it

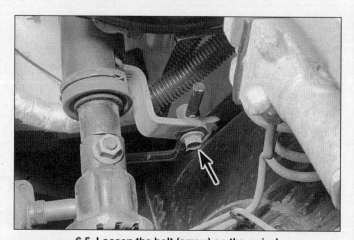

6.5 Loosen the bolt (arrow) on the swivel

6   Inspect the inside of the pan for pieces of metal or friction material that may indicate a problem **(see illustration)**. A small amount of clutch material is normal, but pieces of metal or piles of clutch material generally mean the transmission is close to failing. Remove all traces of gasket material from the transmission and oil pan sealing surfaces and clean the inside of the pan thoroughly with solvent. Wipe the transmission and pan sealing surfaces with lacquer thinner or acetone and allow them to air-dry **(see illustration)**.

7   Inspect the oil pan for damage. Hammer out any dents and straighten the sealing flange, if necessary. Tap the bolt holes with the rounded end of a ball-peen hammer to eliminate any indentations caused by previous overtightening of the bolts.

8   On THM350 transmissions, install a new gasket on the filter and install the filter, tightening the screws securely - note that the filter can only be installed one way and some filters are marked "front." On all others, install the new O-ring on the filter filler pipe, lubricate the O-ring with clean ATF and install the filter into the transmission. Make sure the old O-ring was removed with the old filter and not stuck in the transmission **(see illustration)**. On THM350 or THM400 transmissions with deep pans, make sure the spacer is between the filter and the valve body and tighten the bolt to 96 in-lbs.

9   Install a new gasket on the oil pan. Gasket sealant is not recommended, although RTV sealant may be used between the gasket and oil pan, if desired. Install the oil pan and tighten the bolts to 10-15 ft-lbs. **Caution:** *Do not overtighten the oil pan bolts or leaks may develop.*

10   Lower the vehicle and, on most models, add three quarts of Dexron II ATF through the filler tube - use of a two-to-three foot long funnel is

highly recommended. Add four quarts if equipped with a deep pan.

11   Start the engine and allow the engine and transmission to begin to warm-up. Check the fluid level and add fluid, bringing the level to the "Cold" mark on the dipstick. With the parking brake firmly applied and the drive wheels blocked, shift the transmission through all the gear ranges several times. Allow the engine and transmission to reach normal operating temperature and add fluid, if necessary, bringing the fluid level half way between the "Cold" and "Hot" marks on the dipstick. **Caution:** *Do not overfill the transmission or leaks may develop.*

12   Test drive the vehicle, noting transmission operation and check the fluid level once more. Monitor the fluid level closely the next few trips.

Shift linkage adjustment

Rear wheel drive
Column-shift models

1   Loosen the swivel lock-screw on the linkage rod **(see illustration)**.

2   Place the shift lever on the steering column in the Neutral position. **Note:** *Do not use the shift indicator to locate neutral, but instead rotate the lever until it drops into the Neutral gate.*

3   Raise the vehicle and place it securely on jackstands. Be sure to block the wheels and set the parking brake securely, since you'll be disengaging the Park system.

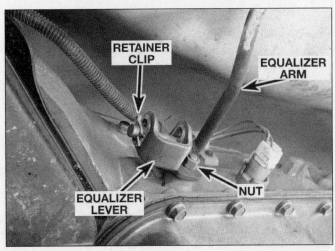

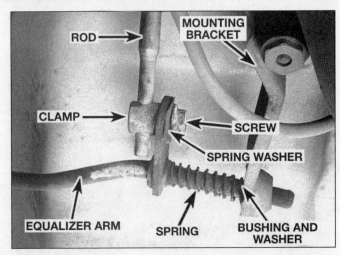

6.6 Typical column-type shift linkage components

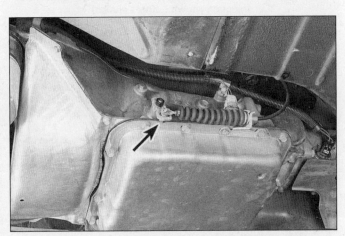

6.7 Loosen the cable locknut at the transmission lever

6.8 Shift cable retaining nut on early model transaxles

4   Working under the vehicle, place the lever on the transmission in Neutral by rotating the lever fully clockwise to the Park position, then counterclockwise two detents to the Neutral position (see illustration).
5   Hold the rod and tighten the swivel lock-screw securely.
6   Lower the vehicle, and, with the parking brake still set, shift the transmission through all ranges, making sure it fully engages in the Park position.
7   Shift the transmission back to the Neutral position. Again, don't rely on the indicator - shift into Park, then back two detents. Check the shift indicator. If the indicator needle is not aligned with the center of the N, adjust the shift indicator as follows:

   a) Working inside the vehicle, remove the necessary steering column trim pieces to gain access to the shift bowl (the part of the column that rotates when the shift lever is moved).
   b) Slide the cable clip in the desired direction to center the indicator.
   c) Replace the trim pieces.

8   Pressing firmly on the brake pedal, try to start the vehicle in each gear. Verify that the engine starts in Park and Neutral only. If the vehicle starts in positions other than Park and Neutral, the neutral start switch is damaged or out of adjustment. See the Haynes Automotive Repair Manual for your specific vehicle for the adjustment and replacement procedure.

Floor-shift models

9   Raise the vehicle and place it securely on jackstands. Be sure to block the wheels and set the parking brake securely, since you'll be disengaging the Park system.
10   Loosen the cable locknut at the shift lever on the transmission

(see illustration).
11   Loosen the swivel locknut on the backdrive rod.
12   Rotate the transmission lever to the Park position.
13   Place the floor shift lever in the Park position.
14   Push up on the backdrive rod, hold it lightly against its stop and tighten the swivel nut securely. Push the floor shift lever forward against its stop and tighten the cable locknut securely.
15   Pressing firmly on the brake pedal, try to start the vehicle in each gear. Verify that the engine starts in Park and Neutral only. Shift to Park and verify that the ignition key can easily be removed from the lock cylinder. If the key cannot be easily removed, readjust the backdrive rod.

Front wheel drive

Note: Some models are equipped with a nut on the cable end at the transaxle lever that must be loosened while the correct shifting position is located, while other models are equipped with a cable adjuster on the shift cable grommet at the transaxle bracket.

Cable retaining nut type

16   Place the shift control lever in the passenger compartment in the Neutral position.
17   Working in the engine compartment, loosen the shift cable retaining nut at the transaxle lever (see illustration).
18   Place the manual lever on the transaxle in Neutral by rotating the lever fully clockwise to the Park position, then counterclockwise two detents to the Neutral position.
19   Tighten the shift cable retaining nut at the transaxle lever.

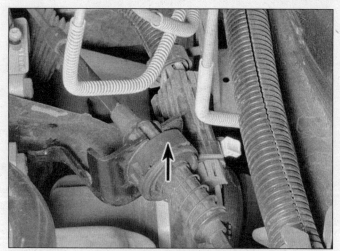

6.9 The shift cable adjuster on later model transaxles is held in place by the transaxle bracket – depress the lock tab (arrow) to allow spring tension to automatically adjust the cable

6.10 Throttle Valve (TV) cable adjuster assembly (Tuned Port Injection shown - others similar)

1   Re-adjust tab   2   Slider

Cable adjuster type

20   Place the shift control lever in the passenger compartment in the Neutral position.

21   Working in the engine compartment, place the manual lever on the transaxle in Neutral by rotating the lever fully clockwise to the Park position, then counterclockwise two detents to the Neutral position while depressing the locking tab on the side of the cable adjuster **(see illustration)**.

22   Release the locking tab on the side of the cable adjuster to adjust the shift cable in the cable mounting bracket.

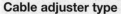

Throttle Valve (TV) cable adjustment and replacement

Note: *On a THM350 transmission the TV cable is also referred to as the detent or downshift cable, because its main function is controlling part/full throttle downshifts. On the THM200-4R, THM700-R4, THM 125/125C and THM 3T40 transmissions, the TV cable controls line pressure and shift points besides part/full throttle downshifts. Its* function is similar to the 350 modulator and detent cable combined. NEVER operate a THM200-4R, THM700-R4, THM 125/125C or the THM 3T40 transmissions with a broken or disconnected TV cable or damage to the transmission may occur. The THM400 has no TV cable.

Adjustment

1   Several different types of TV cable adjusting mechanisms have been used over the years, but all are adjusted in basically the same manner. The cable adjuster is located near the carburetor or throttle body on most models **(see illustration)**, but the adjuster on early models may be located under the dash near the throttle pedal.

2   With the engine Off, release the cable lock and push the cable housing into the slider **(see illustration)**. If it has a self adjusting tab, hold the tab down, push the cable in and release the tab. Manually open the throttle to the wide-open-throttle position, the cable will ratchet out of the slider to the proper adjustment position. Snap the cable lock down (if equipped) and release the throttle. After the adjustment is made check to see if the cable operation is free **(see illustration)**.

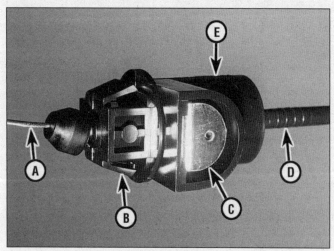

6.11 On most models, depress the throttle valve (TV) cable release tab and pull the slider back until it rests on its stop - release the tab and open the throttle completely

| A | TV cable | C | Release tab | E | Slider |
| B | Locking lugs | D | Cable casing | | |

6.12 To check for free operation, pull forward on the throttle valve (TV) inner cable, feeling for smooth operation through the full range of travel - the cable should retract evenly and rapidly when released

6.13 Detach the throttle (TV) cable from the throttle lever by pulling it forward, off the mounting lug

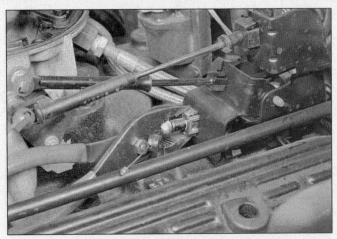

6.14 Pinch the locking tangs of the TV cable housing with a pair of pliers and push the housing through the bracket

Replacement

3   Disconnect the cable end from the carburetor or throttle body **(see illustration)**.
4   Depress the lock tabs at the slider bracket and push the cable through the bracket **(see illustration)**.
5   Raise the vehicle and support it securely on jackstands.

6.15 Remove the screw and washer holding the cable to the transmission. Pull the cable up and disconnect the cable from the link

6   Remove the cable end retaining screw and pull the cable up out of the transmission. Disconnect the cable eye from the TV link **(see illustration)**.
7   Replace the TV cable seal at the transmission. Install the cable and adjust as described above.

Seal replacement

Note: *The TV cable, modulator and governor cover seals are covered in the related section of this Chapter. See the appropriate transmission overhaul chapter for replacement of the accumulator or servo cover seals.*

Rear wheel drive
Extension housing seal

1   Raise the vehicle and support it securely on jackstands.
2   Remove the driveshaft.
3   Pry out the seal with a seal removal tool; or use a large screwdriver and hammer to tap around the circumference of the seal, bending it in until it can be pried out with the screwdriver **(see illustration)**.
4   Lubricate the seal lip with ATF. Using a seal driver, a large socket or a section of pipe the exact diameter of the outer metal portion of the seal, drive the seal squarely into the bore with a hammer until it's flush with the end of the extension housing **(see illustration)**.
5   Install the driveshaft and lower the vehicle.

6.16 Using a seal removal tool or a long screwdriver to carefully pry the seal out of the rear of the transmission

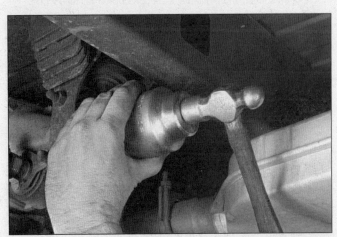

6.17 A large socket or piece of pipe works well for installing the seal - the socket should contact the outer edge of the seal

6.18 Slowly twist the speedometer gear housing to remove the assembly

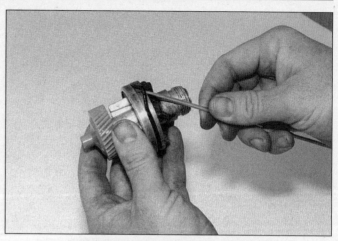

6.19 Use a small pick to remove the seal

Speedometer gear seal

6   Raise the vehicle and support it securely on jackstands.

7   Disconnect the speedometer cable from the housing.

8   Remove the housing retaining bolt and retainer.

9   Twist the housing back-and-forth to free the seal and pull it straight out of the case **(see illustration)**.

10   Remove the speedometer gear from the housing. Inspect the speedometer gear for nicks, damaged teeth or a worn shaft and replace it if necessary. Be sure you replace it with the exact replacement gear (indicated by color or the number of teeth) or your speedometer calibration will be effected.

11   Using a small screwdriver, pry out the retaining ring and shaft seal from the housing.

12   Install a new shaft seal and install the retaining ring. Lubricate the gear shaft with ATF and install the gear into the housing.

13   Replace the housing O-ring **(see illustration)** and install the housing into the transmission case.

14   Connect the speedometer cable and lower the vehicle.

Front wheel drive

Driveaxle seals

15   Refer to your Haynes auto repair manual and remove the driveaxle.

16   Pry the seal from the transaxle case with a large screwdriver or pry bar **(see illustration)**. Be careful not to damage the case.

15   Coat the outer edge of the new seal with oil or grease, then position it in the bore and carefully drive it in with a hammer and large socket (if a socket isn't available, a section of pipe will also work).

6.20 Dislodge the metal-type driveaxle oil seal by working around the outer circumference with a chisel and hammer, then pry the seal out

16   Lubricate the seal lip with multi-purpose grease or clean transmission lubricant, then install the driveaxle.

Speedometer driven gear seal (mechanical driven)

19   The speedometer driven gear is located on top of the transmission by the governor.

20   Disconnect the speedometer cable from the driven-gear assembly.

21   Remove the bolt and the retaining tab, then pull the driven-gear from the governor housing cover.

22   Remove the O-ring from the driven-gear assembly.

23   Coat the new O-ring with clean engine oil and install it on the driven gear assembly.

24   The remainder of reassembly is otherwise the reverse of disassembly.

All models

Filler tube seal

25   Remove the dipstick from the tube. Raise the vehicle and support it securely on jackstands.

26   Remove the bellhousing bolt retaining the tube.

27   Pull the tube straight-out of the transmission case.

28   Remove the seal from the case and install a new seal **(see illustration)**.

29   Lubricate the seal with ATF and press the tube into the seal until it's fully seated.

30   Replace the bellhousing bolt, lower the vehicle and check the transmission fluid level.

6.21 Remove the seal and lubricate the new one with a light coat of ATF

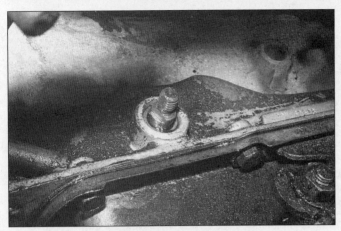

6.22 With the linkage and/or the neutral safety switch removed you can see the seal

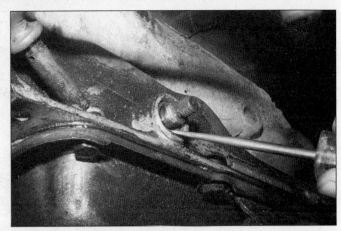

6.23 Take a sharp pick and push it into the shaft seal, carefully prying the seal out

Selector shaft seal

31 On rear wheel drive vehicles, raise the vehicle and support it securely on jackstands. On front wheel drive vehicles, locate the end of the shift cable in the engine compartment.

32 Disconnect the shift linkage from the transmission selector lever. Remove the nut retaining the selector lever and remove the lever from the selector shaft. On front wheel drive models, it will also be necessary to remove the neutral safety switch **(see illustration)**.

33 Using the special seal removal tool, thread the tool into the seal and withdraw the seal from the case. If a seal removal tool is not available, tap a sharp pick into the seal body and pry the seal out. Be very careful not to damage the manual shaft **(see illustration)**.

34 Lubricate the seal lip with ATF and install the seal using the special seal driver or an appropriate size deep socket **(see illustration)**.

35 Install the shift linkage lever to the selector shaft, connect the linkage and lower the vehicle.

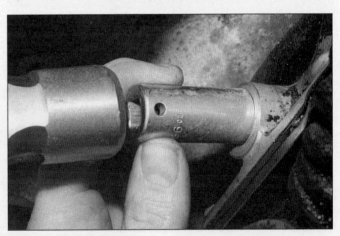

6.24 Tap the seal in until it's properly seated

Vacuum modulator replacement

1 On rear wheel drive vehicles, raise the vehicle and support it securely on jackstands.

2 Locate the vacuum modulator. On THM 350 and 400 transmissions the vacuum modulator is located at the right rear of the transmission case which must be accessed from below the vehicle. On

THM 440-T4/4T60 transaxles the vacuum modulator is located on the left side of the transmission case facing the front of the vehicle which can be accessed from above in the engine compartment.

3 Disconnect the vacuum line at the modulator. Inspect the rubber section of hose for cracks or deterioration, replace if necessary **(see illustration)**.

4 Remove the modulator bolt and clamp and remove the modulator **(see illustrations)**.

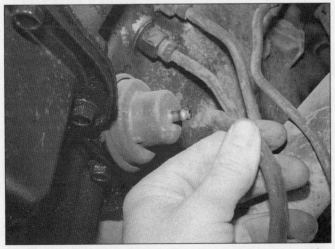

6.25 Remove the vacuum line from the modulator and check for cracks, breaks or fluid in the line

6.26 Vacuum modulator clamp bolt – THM440-T4/4T60

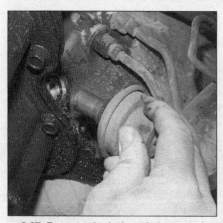

6.27 Remove the bolt and clamp that holds the modulator and rotate the valve out

6.28 Make sure the O-ring is lubricated and the surface is clean before you install the modulator

6.29 Removing the governor cover on a THM 400

5   Remove the modulator O-ring and replace it with a new one. Lubricate the O-ring and reinstall the modulator **(see illustration)**.
6   Attach the vacuum line, lower the vehicle (if necessary) and check the vacuum line at the intake manifold. Replace the rubber section if it's cracked or deteriorated.

Governor replacement

1   Raise the vehicle and support it securely on jackstands.
2   On a THM350 or THM700-R4 transmission, unsnap the retaining bail (if equipped) and remove the governor cover by tapping around the outer edge with a large screwdriver and hammer. Be careful not to damage the cover or transmission case.
3   On a THM400, THM 125/125C/3T40 and THM 440-T4/4T60 transmissions, remove the governor cover retaining screws and remove the cover **(see illustrations)**.
4   On a THM200-4R, remove the oil pan (see Section 1) and remove the governor cover retaining bolts.
5   Withdraw the governor from the case using a slight twisting motion **(see illustrations)**.
6   Inspect the governor gear for damage. Inspect the governor weights, springs, valve and check balls (if equipped) for damage and freedom of movement. Check the governor sleeve for nicks, scoring or damage **(see illustration)**.
7   If the governor valve shows any signs of damage or sticking, replace it. If the governor gear is damaged, refer to the appropriate transmission overhaul chapter for replacement.

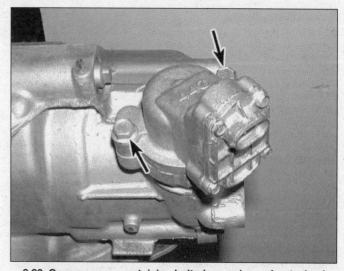

6.30 Governor cover retaining bolts (arrows) on a front wheel drive transaxle

8   Installation is the reverse of removal. Install a new O-ring or gasket on the governor cover (if equipped) and on THM350 and THM700-R4 transmissions, apply a small amount of non-hardening Permatex or Loctite cup plug sealer around the outer edge of the cover.

6.31 Remove the governor with a slight twisting motion

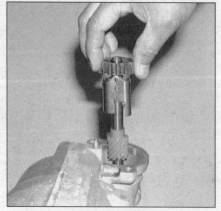

6.32 Removing the governor on front wheel drive transaxle

6.33 Inspect the lands for scoring and the governor weights for sticking

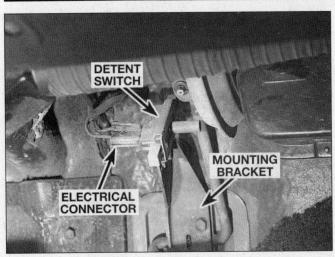

6.34 THM400 downshift switch details

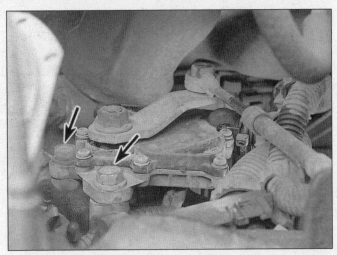

6.35 Neutral start switch retaining bolts (arrows) -
front wheel drive models

Downshift switch replacement and adjustment (THM400 models only)

Replacement

1   The downshift switch (or detent switch) has been located at several different locations over the many years of THM400 production. It's usually located at the carburetor or under the dash attached to the accelerator linkage. On some early models it may be mounted on the firewall.
2   Located the downshift switch, disconnect the electrical connector, remove the mounting bolt and replace the switch **(see illustration)**.

Adjustment

3   Most later model under-dash switches (1968 and later) are self-adjusting. After installation push the plunger all the way forward and depress the accelerator to the floor (with the engine not running). The switch will self-adjust.
4   The easiest way to adjust all other switches is with a test light. Connect a test light to the switch terminal and ground. Depress the accelerator; the switch contacts should close and the test light should come on at approximately 60-degrees of throttle opening. If it doesn't loosen the switch mounting screws and adjust the switch until it does.

Neutral Start switch – adjustment and replacement (front wheel drive models only)

Adjustment

1   Shift the transaxle into Neutral.
2   Working in the engine compartment, loosen the switch retaining bolts **(see illustration)**.
3   Insert a 3/32-inch drill bit into the outer service hole of the switch body, then rotate the switch in either direction until the drill bit aligns with the inner service hole on the switch shaft. The Neutral position on the switch is indicated when the inner and outer holes are aligned with the drill bit **(see illustration)**.
4   Tighten the mounting bolts and verify that the engine will start only in Neutral or Park.

Replacement

5   Working in the engine compartment, detach and set aside any components which interfere with access to the neutral safety switch.
6   Trace the wire harness from the Neutral start switch to the connector and unplug it. Also detach any wiring harness retaining clips that would interfere with the removal of the switch.
7   Remove the nut and detach the shift lever from the transaxle.
8   Remove the bolts and detach the switch.
9   To install the switch, line up the flats on the shift shaft with the flats in the switch and lower the switch onto the shaft.
10   Install the switch mounting bolts loosely and adjust the switch as described above.

Torque Converter Clutch (TCC) solenoid - replacement

1   Drain the transmission fluid as described in the fluid and filter change Section of this Chapter.
2   On THM 200-4R, THM 350C and THM 700-R4 rear wheel drive transmissions remove the transmission filter.
3   On front wheel drive transmissions, remove the necessary components to allow removal of the side (valve body) cover. On THM440-T4/4T60 transaxles it will be necessary to remove the left driveaxle to allow removal of the side cover. Remove the bolts and detach side (valve body) cover. **Note:** *On some models it may be necessary to lower the left side of the engine cradle and the transaxle to allow the removal of the side cover.*

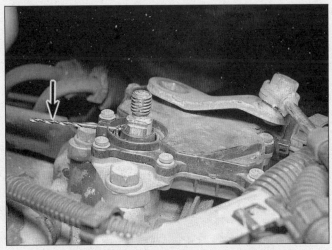

6.36 Align the outer notch on the neutral safety switch
with the inner notch on the shaft using a drill bit
(shift lever removed for clarity)

6.37 Location of the TCC solenoid on THM 200-4R and
THM700-R4 transmissions

6.38 TCC solenoid mounting bolt (arrow) –
THM 125/125C and 3T40

6.39 TCC solenoid mounting bolts (arrows) – THM 440-T4/4T60

4   Remove the Torque Converter Clutch (TCC) solenoid bolts and
pull the solenoid out of the case **(see illustrations)**. Remove the wiring
harness from the retainers and disconnect the harness connectors
from the pressure switches and the case plug. Remove the solenoid
and harness as an assembly.
5   Install the new solenoid in position and reconnect the new
harness assembly.
6   Install the solenoid mounting bolts and torque them to 96 in-lbs.
7   The remainder of installation is the reverse of removal. Clean the
transmission pan thoroughly and follow the installation procedures and
fluid recommendations outlined in the fluid and filter change Section of
this Chapter.

Chapter 7
Transmission removal and installation

This is the dirtiest part of the overhaul (don't wear clothes you care about!) and the part that will require the most planning - read through this entire Chapter before beginning work, since you'll need some special tools and equipment. The most important piece of equipment is a transmission jack, which can usually be rented from an equipment rental yard. During removal and installation, the higher you can safely raise the vehicle, the easier and cleaner the job will be.

Removal

Rear wheel drive

1   Disconnect the negative cable from the battery, then remove the transmission fluid dipstick. Place the gear selector lever in Neutral. On four-wheel drive models, get inside the vehicle and remove the range-

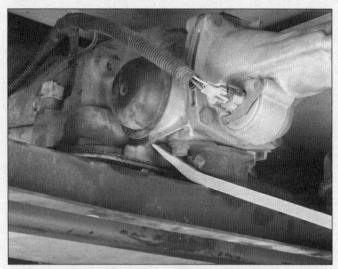

7.1 To check the transmission mount for wear, place a large
screwdriver or pry bar between the crossmember and one of
the mounting bolts and try to pry up on the transmission -
it shouldn't move much. Excessive movement means
the transmission mount needs replacement

7.2 To disconnect the detent cable, remove this bolt, . . .

7.3 . . . pull the cable housing out of the transmission case and
slip the link out of the cable eye

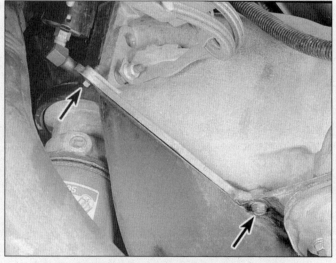

7.4a To detach the torque converter cover, remove the
four bolts - the two shown on this side (arrow)
and two on the other side. Then . . .

selector shift boot and knob. If accessible through the opening,
disconnect the range-selector rod from the lever.

2   Raise the vehicle and support it securely on jackstands. Since the
transmission will need to be slid out from under the vehicle, support
both the front and rear of the vehicle with four sturdy jackstands. Raise
the vehicle as high as safely possible.

3   Before removing the transmission, check the transmission mount
to see if it will need replacement. To check the mount, insert a large
screwdriver or pry bar into the space between the transmission and
the crossmember and try to pry the transmission up slightly (see illustration). The transmission should not move away from the insulator
much. If the mount moves appreciably or there is any separation of the
rubber, the mount is worn out; remove the mount from the transmission in Step 27 and replace it on installation. **Note:** *Transmission
mounts are subjected to considerable stress and transmission fluid
leaks cause them to deteriorate rapidly. It's wise to replace the mount
routinely at overhaul time.*

4   Drain the transmission fluid (see Chapter 6) and reinstall the pan.
On models with cable-type shifting, do not reinstall the bolts that hold

the cable bracket to the pan. On four-wheel drive models, also drain
the transfer case lubricant. Note that some full-time transfer cases do
not have a drain plug, so you'll have to remove the cover plate on the
front side of the transfer case to drain it.

5   On all except THM400 models, disconnect the detent or TV cable
from the carburetor (see Chapter 6). Remove the cable housing bolt
from the transmission (see illustration). Pull the cable housing up and
slip the link out of the cable eye (see illustration). Position the cable
safely out of the way.

6   Remove the torque converter cover (see illustrations).

7   Mark the torque converter and the driveplate with a scribe or
chalk so they can be installed in the same position (see illustration).

8   Remove the driveplate-to-torque converter bolts (see illustration). Turn the crankshaft (in a clockwise direction only, viewed
from the front) for access to each bolt.

9   Disconnect the wires from the electrical terminals on the starter
motor, then remove it (see illustrations).

10   Remove the driveshaft (see illustrations); if the vehicle is
equipped with four-wheel drive, remove the front driveshaft also.

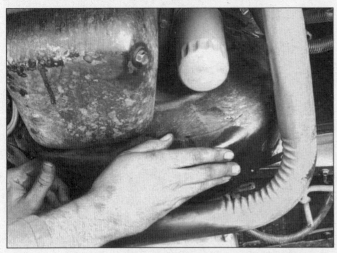

7.4b . . . carefully work the cover toward one side to remove it. Sometimes it's a tight fit, but it will come out!

7.5 To ensure proper reassembly, mark the relationship between the driveplate and the torque converter

7.6 Remove the torque converter-to-driveplate retaining bolts (here a special tool is being used to prevent the flywheel from turning, but a socket and breaker bar on the crankshaft vibration damper center bolt will also work)

7.7a Remove the nuts and disconnect the wires from these two terminals on the starter motor, labeled A and B. Some starters also have a third wire terminal, like B in this photo, but on the other side of A. If there's a wire connected to the third terminal, remove it also

7.7b Two bolts retain the starter to the engine - remove them with a socket, extension and ratchet

7.8a Before removing the driveshaft, mark the relationship between the driveshaft and differential yoke

7.8b Use a large screwdriver or prybar to immobilize the U-joint, as shown, then remove the bolts. A screwdriver or prybar in this position can also be used to separate the joint after the bolts are removed

7.8c After loosening all four bolts, remove the retaining straps . . .

7.8d . . . then lower the rear of the driveshaft and, on two-wheel drive models, slide the driveshaft to the rear - the slip-yoke on the driveshaft will simply slide out of the rear of the transmission. Four-wheel drive models generally have bolt-on joints at both ends of a driveshaft. Once the driveshaft is removed, wrap electrical tape around the U-joint so the bearing cups do not fall off while the driveshaft is out of the vehicle

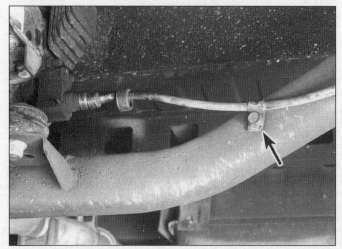

7.9 On earlier models, unscrew the speedometer cable sleeve (shown already unscrewed near the left end of the cable), then remove the cable housing retaining bolt. Pull the cable out of the transmission

11   If the vehicle has a speedometer cable, disconnect it **(see illustration)**. If it has a vehicle speed sensor, unplug the electrical connector **(see illustration)**.

12   Unplug any remaining wire harness connectors from the transmission **(see illustration)**.

13   On THM350 and THM400 transmissions, disconnect the vacuum hose from the modulator (right side of the transmission) **(see illustration)**. Disconnect the steel vacuum tube from the clip(s) on the transmission and position the tube to the side, out of the way.

14   Look at the exhaust system to see if it will interfere with transmission removal. Often you can remove the transmission without disturbing the exhaust system, but sometimes you'll have to disconnect the pipe(s) from the exhaust manifold(s) **(see illustration)**. If clearance still looks tight, disconnect the exhaust system hangers and remove the exhaust system from the vehicle.

15   Disconnect the shift linkage **(see illustration)** or cable **(see illustration)**.

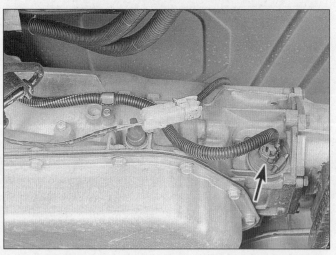

7.10 Later models have a speed sensor in place of a speedometer cable - disconnect the electrical connector (arrow)

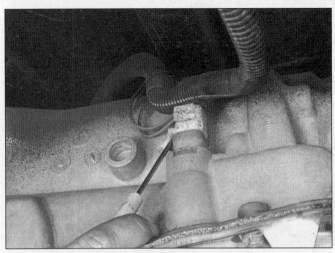

7.11 On models since about 1980, you'll also have a torque converter clutch electrical connector to disconnect - it's usually on the left side of the transmission, and you'll also have to remove the wiring harness retaining bolt just above it

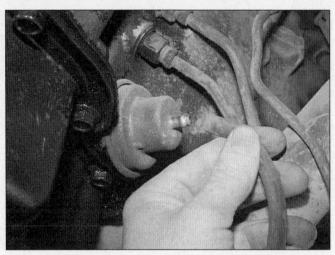

7.12 Remove the hose from the vacuum modulator

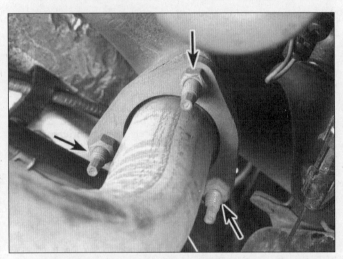

7.13 It is often necessary to disconnect the exhaust pipes from the exhaust manifolds. The arrows point to three bolts used to secure this pipe to its manifold, but some models may have only two bolts

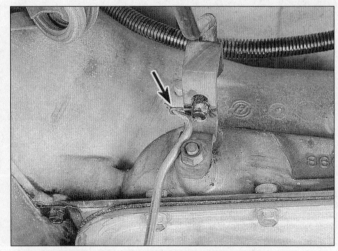

7.14 On most models a spring clip secures the shift linkage to the manual lever on the transmission - here a prying tool is being used to remove the clip

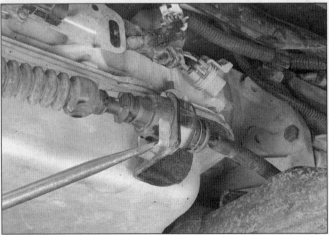

7.15 Models with floor shifters generally use a shift cable - the bracket is secured by two of the transmission pan bolts. The cable can be disconnected by removing the retainer clip

Four-wheel drive models only

Note: *We recommend removing the transfer case before removing the transmission, as described here, since the transmission/transfer case assembly can be very cumbersome to remove together as a unit.*

16   Remove the skid plate under the transfer case, if equipped. Also unbolt and remove the transfer case-to-engine support strut(s). Some models have only one, but many later models have two.

17   If not already done, disconnect the shift linkage from the transfer case. On some models, the shift rod snaps into place on the transfer case lever and can be disconnected by prying it loose with a screwdriver. On other models you'll have to remove a clip or a nut.

18   Support the transfer case with a jack, preferably a jack designed for this purpose. Use safety chains to secure the transfer case to the jack.

19   Remove the bolts and/or nuts securing the transfer case to the transmission.

20   Make a final check that all cables, wires and shift linkage are disconnected from the transfer case, then move the jack to the rear until the transfer case input shaft is clear of the transmission. Lower the transfer case and remove it from under the vehicle.

7.16 A special transmission jack, like the one shown here, is the only safe way to remove an automatic transmission

7.17 Some transmissions have a damper, like the one shown here. It is retained by two bolts and nuts

7.18 Remove the nut from the transmission mount-to-crossmember stud

7.19a Four bolts and nuts are used to retain the crossmember to the frame rails - two on each side. Sometimes the bolt heads are right out in the open, as shown here, but . . .

All rear wheel drive models

21   Support the engine with a jack. Use a block of wood under the oil pan to spread the load. Keep the engine supported during the entire time the transmission is out of the vehicle so you don't strain the engine mounts.

22   Support the transmission with a jack - preferably a jack made for this purpose (see illustration). Safety chains will help steady the transmission on the jack.

23   A transmission-to-rear axle torque strut is used on some Camaro/Firebird, Corvette and Vega models. Unbolt this strut from the transmission and axle and remove it.

24   If equipped; unbolt and remove the transmission damper (see illustration). On some models it will also be necessary to remove the transmission-to-engine support strut.

25   Remove the rear transmission mount-to-crossmember nut (see illustration).

26   Remove the four (two per side) crossmember-to-frame nuts and bolts (see illustrations).

27   Raise the transmission with the jack enough to allow removal of the crossmember. If you'll be replacing the transmission mount, unbolt and remove it at this time (see illustration).

7.19b . . . usually the bolt heads will be hiding inside holes, as shown here. You'll have to use a socket, extension and ratchet to get at them

7.20 Two bolts (arrows) secure the transmission mount to the transmission

7.21 With the transmission safely supported, remove the transmission-to-engine bolts (arrows) - note that the upper right bolt also secures the transmission dipstick tube bracket

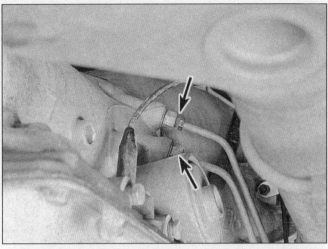

7.22 After lowering the transmission, use a flare-nut wrench to disconnect the cooler lines (arrows) and plug them to prevent fluid loss. It may be necessary to use a back-up wrench on the transmission-side fittings to prevent twisting the lines

28   Remove the transmission-to-engine bolts **(see illustration)**.
29   Lower the transmission slightly and, using a flare-nut wrench, unscrew the flare-nuts on the transmission fluid cooler lines from the fittings on the transmission case **(see illustration)**. It may also be necessary to use a back-up wrench to hold the fittings threaded into the transmission case steady while you unscrew the flare-nuts on the lines. After disconnecting the lines, plug the cooler lines to prevent fluid leakage. An easy way to plug the lines is to connect a short piece of 3/8-inch diameter fuel hose between the two disconnected lines.
30   Remove the transmission dipstick tube by pulling it straight up, out of the transmission housing.
31   Move the transmission to the rear to disengage it from the engine block dowel pins and make sure the torque converter is detached from the driveplate. Secure the torque converter to the transmission so it won't fall out during removal. One way to secure the torque converter is to clamp a pair of Vise Grips onto the transmission housing, just in front of the torque converter. Another way is to bolt a long 15 mm or 9/16-inch combination wrench onto the front of the transmission, using one of the lower transmission-to-engine bolt holes **(see illustration)**. Use a large washer on the bolt and put it through the box end of the wrench, with the angle on the wrench pointing toward the rear of the vehicle. Place the open end of the wrench near the center of the torque

converter. When you put the bolt into the transmission bolt hole, put a nut on the other end and tighten it, the wrench will press against the converter, holding it securely in the transmission.

Front wheel drive

Note: *The engine on front wheel drive vehicles must be supported from above when the transaxle is removed. This is done with a bar-type fixture that rests on the fender flanges, or an engine hoist. The engine is suspended from the fixture or hoist with brackets or chains so the transaxle can be removed. In addition, automatic transaxles are heavy and awkward to handle and a transmission jack should be used to remove and install the unit because the transaxle will not balance on a regular floor jack. The engine support fixture, engine hoist and a transmission jack can be rented from some auto parts stores and most equipment rental companies.*
32   Disconnect the negative cable from the battery.
33   Raise the vehicle and support it securely on jackstands.
34   Drain the transmission fluid.
35   Remove the torque converter cover **(see illustrations)**.
36   Mark the torque converter-to-driveplate relationship with white paint so they can be installed in the same position.

7.23 A combination wrench bolted to one of the mounting bolt holes will secure the torque converter during removal

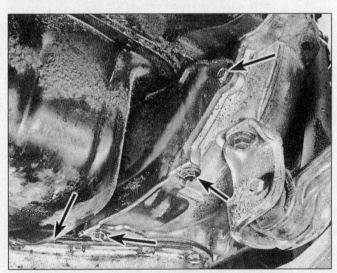

7.24a Torque converter shield mounting bolts (arrows) on early model transaxles

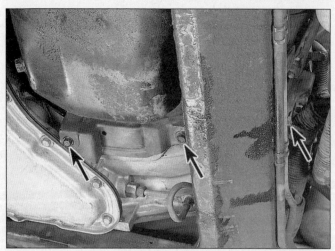

7.24b Torque converter shield mounting bolts (arrows) on later model transaxles

7.25 Lock the driveplate starter ring gear teeth with a screwdriver and remove the torque converter bolts

37   Remove the torque converter-to-driveplate bolts **(see illustration)**. Turn the crankshaft pulley bolt for access to each bolt.
38   Remove the starter motor.

7.26a The engine must be supported from above - the best way is with a three bar support fixture like this one

7.26b If an engine support tool is not available, connect a chain to the lifting eyes and raise the weight off the engine mounts with an engine hoist

39   Disconnect the driveaxles from the transaxle.
40   Disconnect the speedometer/speed sensor.
41   Disconnect the wire harness from the transaxle.
42   On models so equipped, disconnect the vacuum hose(s).
43   Remove any exhaust components which will interfere with transaxle removal.
44   Disconnect the TV cable from the transaxle.
45   Disconnect the shift linkage from the transaxle.
46   Remove the dipstick tube.
47   Support the engine from above using a three bar support fixture or an engine hoist **(see illustrations)**.
48   Remove the transaxle mount nuts and bolts.
49   Remove any chassis or suspension components which will interfere with transaxle removal. **Note:** *Some models will require removing the engine cradle or the front crossmember to allow sufficient clearance for transaxle removal* **(see illustration)**.
50   Support the transaxle with a jack - preferably a special jack made for this purpose. Safety chains will help steady the transaxle on the jack.
51   Remove the bolts securing the transaxle to the engine. If equipped, remove the transaxle cradle **(see illustration)**.
52   Pry the transaxle back to disengage it from the engine block dowel pins and make sure the torque converter is detached from the driveplate **(see illustration)**. Secure the torque converter to the transaxle so it will not fall out during removal.

7.27 Removing the engine cradle - on some models you can separate (arrows) the left side of the engine cradle from the right side of the cradle

7.28 Some models are equipped with a transaxle cradle which must be removed – upper mounting bolts shown, lower nuts not visible in this photo

7.29 Pry the transaxle bellhousing away from the engine with a large screwdriver

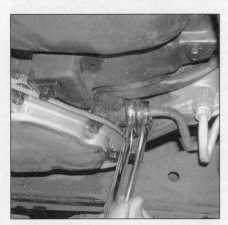

7.30a Use a flare nut wrench on the tube nut and an open end wrench on the fitting adapter to avoid damaging the cooler lines – THM 440-T4/4T60 shown

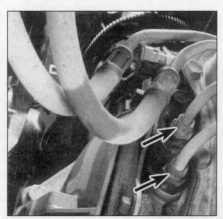

7.30b The transaxle cooler lines on THM 125/125c and 3T40 transmissions are located next to the side (valve body) cover

7.31 On some models, it may be necessary to move the suspension components aside for clearance when removing the transaxle

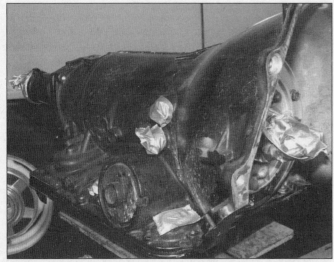

7.32 Cover all openings in the transmission before cleaning to prevent entry of water and dirt

53   Lower the transmission slightly, disconnect and plug the transmission cooler lines and lower the transmission from the vehicle (see illustrations).

Cleaning

The transmission you've just removed has undoubtedly accumulated a lot of grease and grime. To make the overhaul a cleaner experience for you and to prevent any of this crud from winding up inside the transmission, it's essential to clean the transmission now.

Steam cleaning is the best method, but this expensive equipment is not normally available to the do-it-yourselfer. Aerosol cleaning solvents are readily available from auto parts stores. These solvents that spray on and hose off do an adequate job and represent the most cost-effective alternative to steam cleaning.

Before cleaning, seal up all openings in the transmission - at the input shaft, output shaft, TV cable hole, etc. - so no solvent or water winds up inside the transmission (see illustration). Then follow the solvent manufacturer's label instructions. Generally, you'll spray on the solvent, allow it to soak in for about ten minutes, then scrub the surfaces with a stiff brush (be sure to wear gloves!). When all grime has been loosened, spray off the solvent with a garden hose and allow the transmission to air-dry.

7.33 Drill-operated pumps work well for flushing coolers - set up like this, the pump will circulate solvent from the container, through the cooler and back again to another container

7.34 Support the converter with both hands and slide it straight out of the transmission. Some fluid may drain out during removal, so be prepared to tilt the converter rear-side-up as soon as it clears the input shaft

7.35 Overturn the converter in a bucket or similar container to drain it

Flushing the transmission cooler

The transmission cooler in your radiator, as well as the lines leading to and from it, now contain burned transmission fluid and debris such as clutch material and metal particles that were deposited by your failing transmission. If you don't flush out this gunk, it will wind up inside your newly rebuilt transmission and possibly damage it - flushing the cooler is essential at overhaul time.

The best way to flush the cooler is with a special tank-type flushing machine. Transmission shops have these machines, but it's generally not practical to tow your vehicle into a shop just to have the cooler and lines flushed.

The best at-home method we found is to use an electric drill-powered fluid pump. These pumps are commonly available from hardware stores at a reasonable price. Fill up a bucket or similar container with solvent and connect the suction side of the pump to a short hose, placing the other end of the hose in the bucket. Connect another short hose between the pump outlet and one of the cooler lines, then connect a hose from the other cooler line, placing the other end of the hose in the bucket **(see illustration)**. Run the pump until the solvent coming out of the return line comes out clean. Then disconnect the pump and blow compressed air through the cooler line until no more solvent comes out the other line. If solvent does not flow through to the return line, the cooler is plugged, and you'll need to either replace the radiator or take the cooler to a transmission shop to have it unplugged.

After flushing the cooler with solvent and blowing it out with compressed air, use the pump to circulate some new ATF through the cooler. This will ensure that all solvent has been purged from the cooler. If you don't have a drill-powered pump, an alternative method is to use a hand-type pump, such as the kind that come with large containers of gear oil.

Before assuming your cooler is now good to go, check to see if there is a leak. Generally speaking, a leak will cause transmission fluid in the engine coolant and/or coolant in the transmission fluid (which will generally show up as fluid that looks like a strawberry milkshake). To test the cooler, securely plug the end of one of the cooler lines, then apply compressed air at about 30 psi to the other line. Remove the radiator cap and look for bubbles in the engine coolant. Any bubbles at all are an indication there is a leak and the cooler will need to be repaired or the radiator replaced. Continue to apply pressure for ten minutes or so while you watch the radiator opening.

Flushing and inspecting the torque converter

Note: *We recommend routinely replacing the torque converter at overhaul time. Torque converters generally are well worn by overhaul time, and it would be a shame to destroy a newly overhauled transmission by re-installing a failing converter that's sending pieces of metal throughout the transmission. Remanufactured torque converters are generally available at a reasonable price.*

After removing the transmission and placing it on your workbench, remove the torque converter. The torque converter is easily removed from the transmission by supporting it securely and pulling it straight out of the front pump **(see illustration)**. Immediately after removing the converter, turn it front side down so no fluid leaks out. Next, overturn the converter in a bucket or pan that can hold at least four quarts and allow the converter to drain **(see illustration)**.

If you're planning to re-use the same torque converter, it's important to flush it thoroughly so no burned fluid, metal particles or clutch material wind up in your newly rebuilt transmission. Transmission shops have a machine that flushes the converter with solvent while it spins the turbine to assure good agitation that will break loose particles of gunk. You can simulate this operation at home (though not nearly as well) by filling the converter with solvent and using snap-ring pliers to spin the turbine (the last splined hub you see when looking down the opening) as best you can. After letting the converter sit for

7.36 Inspect the hub area (arrow) carefully. This is where the front seal rides, so it must be smooth, with no ridge. The converter must be replaced if this surface has a groove or nicks that won't polish out with 600-grit sandpaper

7.37 Operation of the stator one-way clutch can be checked with large snap-ring pliers

about an hour, spin the turbine with the pliers and drain the solvent, then repeat the whole operation until the solvent comes out clean. If any metal particles come out of the converter, the converter must be replaced. Finally, repeat the procedure with new ATF.

First check the drive lugs on the converter. There should be three welded-on nuts that allow the driveplate to be bolted to the converter. If these lugs are cracked, bent, loose or have damaged threads, it's best to replace the converter rather than try to repair the lugs. Since the lugs assure correct alignment with the driveplate, vibration can result from a damaged or deformed lug.

Next, check the converter hub for scoring or nicks **(see illustration)**. Light scoring can be removed by polishing with 600-grit sandpaper (cover the opening to make sure nothing enters the converter during polishing), but any significant scoring means the converter will have to be replaced. Since the transmission front seal rides on the converter hub, a worn or damaged hub means your freshly overhauled transmission will almost surely leak.

Check also for leaks and damage to the converter case. Any dents or cracks will necessitate converter replacement. Check very carefully and look for signs of leakage, particularly at the weld that runs the circumference of the converter and the weld that attaches the hub to the rear shell of the converter.

The first operational check is for correct functioning of the stator one-way clutch. This check can be done with a large pair of snap-ring pliers **(see illustration)** or with the transmission front pump cover (refer to the appropriate Part of Chapter 8 to remove the front pump cover). Place the converter front-side down on your workbench. Using the pump cover or snap-ring pliers, quickly rotate the stator hub (the second splined hub you can see through the opening). It should turn freely when its rotated clockwise, but you should feel a slight resistance when turned in the counter-clockwise direction. Also, there should be no binding or noise when the stator is rotated clockwise. It the converter fails to operate as described, replace it.

Next check converter endplay. With the converter still front-side down, hook a special tool under the turbine hub at the bottom of the converter opening **(see illustration)**. Zero the dial indicator, then pull up on the tool until the maximum reading is obtained. The reading should not exceed 0.050 inch. A less-exact way to take this measurement is to bend a small hook at the bottom of a piece of very stiff wire. Hook the wire under the turbine hub and place a steel ruler across the converter opening. Scratch a mark on the wire where ruler crosses it, then pull up on the wire and mark it again. The distance between the two marks is converter endplay. Again, the measurement should not exceed 0.050 inch.

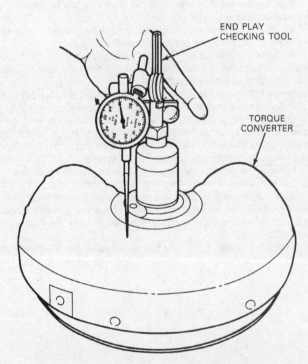

7.38 Measuring converter endplay with a special tool

Now check for stator-to-impeller interference. Referring to the appropriate Part of Chapter 8, remove the front pump assembly from the transmission and place it on the workbench, shaft-side up. Carefully place the converter over the shaft, twisting it to make sure the splines engage correctly. Now hold the pump assembly and rotate the converter counter-clockwise. If the converter binds or makes a scraping noise during this test, replace it.

Finally, check for stator-to-turbine interference. Referring to the appropriate Part of Chapter 8, remove the front pump and input shaft/front clutch assembly. With the converter front-side down, install the front pump assembly, making sure the splines fully engage, then install the input shaft, again making sure the splines engage correctly. Hold the converter and pump while rotating the input (turbine) shaft. The turbine should rotate freely in both directions. If there is any binding or scraping noises, the converter must be replaced.

Installation

1   Prior to installation, make sure the torque converter hub is securely engaged in the pump. It is often easiest to do this with the transmission tilted so the front is facing up (if the transmission is chained to a transmission jack, this can be done safely on the jack). Wipe some transmission fluid on the converter hub to lubricate the front seal, then carefully place the converter over the input shaft. Rotate the converter while supporting it in the center, and the converter should slide into place, one "click" at a time. When the converter is fully installed, the drive lugs on the converter will be engaged in the front pump and you should not be able to put your fingers between the converter and the pump. To verify the converter is fully engaged, place a straightedge across the front of the transmission bellhousing and measure the distance from the front of the converter to the straightedge - it should be one inch or more **(see illustration)**. Once the converter is fully engaged, secure it in place using one of the methods described in the last step of the removal procedure in this Chapter.

2   With the transmission secured to the jack, raise it into position. Be sure to keep it level so the torque converter doesn't slide out. Connect the transmission fluid cooler lines.

3   Turn the torque converter until the marks on the converter and driveplate are aligned.

4   Move the transmission towards the engine carefully until the dowel pins engage with the holes in the bellhousing.

5   Install the transmission housing-to-engine bolts. Tighten them securely. Also install the dipstick tube at this time. Be sure to use a new O-ring or tube seal on installation.

6   Install the driveplate-to-torque converter bolts and tighten them to 35 ft-lbs. **Note:** *Install all of the bolts before tightening any of them.*

7   On rear wheel drive vehicles, Install the crossmember and lower the mount studs into their holes on the crossmember. On front wheel drive vehicles, install any steering, suspension and chassis components removed. Tighten the bolts and nuts securely.

8   Remove the jacks supporting the transmission and the engine.

9   On four-wheel drive models, secure the transfer case to the jack and raise it into position. Align the transfer case input shaft with the splines on the transmission output shaft, install a new gasket, then join the transmission and transfer case. Install the transfer case mounting bolts and braces.

10   Install the starter motor. On four-wheel drive models, install the

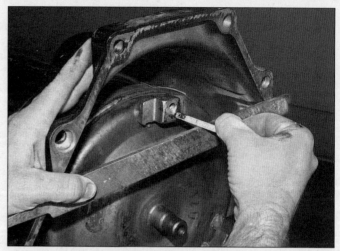

7.39 Hold a straightedge across the front of the transmission and measure the distance between the straightedge and the mounting face of the torque converter - if the converter is fully seated, the distance will be one inch or more

skid plate (if equipped).

11   Connect the vacuum hose(s) (if equipped).

12   Connect the shift linkage and detent/TV cable. Be sure to use a new O-ring or seal at the base of the detent cable housing. Be careful when installing the new O-ring, since the plastic at the bottom of the cable housing breaks very easily.

13   Plug in the transmission wire harness connectors.

14   Install the torque converter cover.

15   On rear wheel drive vehicles, install the driveshaft(s). On front wheel drive vehicles install the driveaxles.

16   Connect the speedometer cable or speed sensor electrical connector.

17   Adjust the shift linkage or cable (see Chapter 6).

18   Install any exhaust system components that were removed or disconnected.

19   Lower the vehicle.

20   Fill the transmission (and transfer case on four-wheel drive models) with the recommended fluid as described in Chapter 6.

Chapter 8   Part A
Disassembly, inspection and assembly THM200-4R transmission

Introduction

The THM200-4R is a four-speed automatic transmission manufactured for rear-wheel drive vehicles. The major components of this transmission are:

a) Lock-up torque converter
b) Vane-type oil pump
c) Control valve assembly
d) Compound planetary gear set
e) Overdrive planetary gear set
f) Five separate multiple disc clutch packs
g) Two roller clutches
h) Intermediate band

Follow the photographic sequence for disassembly, inspection and assembly. The model shown is a typical transmission of this type. Differences do exist between models and many changes have been made over the years, so perform each step in order and lay the components out on a clean work bench in the EXACT ORDER of removal to prevent confusion during reassembly. Many snap-rings and clutch plates are similar in size, but must not be interchanged. Keep the individual parts together with the component from which they were removed to avoid mix-ups. Save all old parts and compare them with the new part to ensure they are an exact match before reassembly. Pay particular attention to the stack-up of the various clutch packs. Differences do exist between models, as your transmission may not match the stack-up shown. Note the exact location of the check balls in the case as well as the valve body. Save all the old parts until the overhaul is complete and the transmission has been thoroughly road tested; old components can be useful in diagnosing any problems that may arise.

The THM200-4R is a metric dimensioned transmission; use metric tools on the fasteners. Special tools are required for some procedures. Alternate procedures are shown where possible, but some procedures can only be accomplished with special tools. Read through the entire overhaul procedure before beginning work to familiarize yourself with the procedures and identify any special tools that may be needed. Thoroughly clean the exterior of the transmission before beginning disassembly.

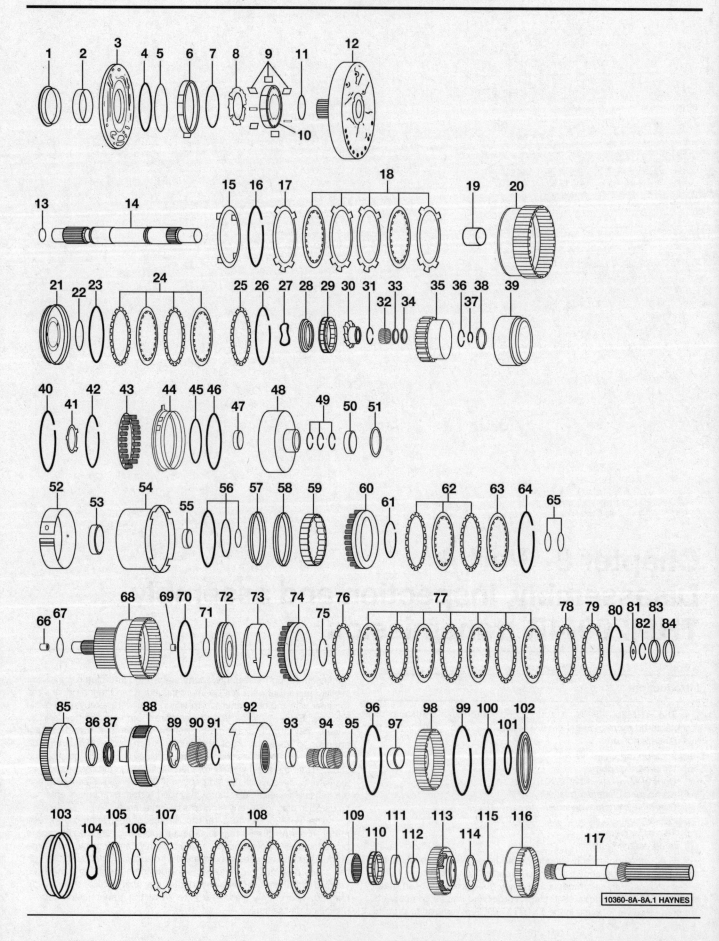

10360-8A-8A.1 HAYNES

8A.1 Exploded view of the typical THM200-4R internal components

1 Front seal	60 Direct clutch release spring assembly
2 Pump body bushing	61 Snap-ring
3 Pump body	62 Direct clutch plates
4 Oil seal ring	63 Direct clutch backing plate
5 O-ring seal	64 Retaining ring
6 Pump slide	65 Oil seal rings
7 Pump vane ring	66 Forward clutch housing bushing
8 Rotor guide	67 Thrust washer
9 Pump vanes	68 Forward clutch housing
10 Pump rotor	69 Cup plug
11 Pump vane ring	70 Forward clutch piston outer seal
12 Pump cover	71 Forward clutch piston inner seal
13 O-ring	72 Forward clutch piston
14 Input shaft	73 Forward clutch apply ring
15 Oil deflector	74 Forward clutch spring assembly
16 Retaining ring	75 Snap-ring
17 Fourth gear clutch backing plate	76 Waved clutch plate
18 Fourth gear clutch plates	77 Forward clutch plates
19 Overrun clutch bushing	78 Waved clutch plate
20 Overrun clutch housing	79 Forward clutch backing plate
21 Overrun clutch piston	80 Retaining ring
22 Overrun clutch inner seal	81 Thrust washer (selective)
22 Overrun clutch outer seal	82 Snap-ring
24 Overrun clutch plates	83 Thrust washer (selective)
25 Overrun clutch backing plate	84 Thrust washer
26 Retaining ring	85 Front internal gear
27 Overrun clutch release spring (waved)	86 Front internal gear bushing
28 Spring retainer	87 Thrust bearing assembly
29 Overdrive roller clutch assembly	88 Front planetary carrier assembly
30 Overdrive roller clutch cam	89 Thrust bearing assembly
31 Snap-ring	90 Front sun gear
32 Overdrive sun gear	91 Snap-ring
33 Overdrive carrier bushing	92 Input drum
34 Thrust bearing assembly	93 Rear sun gear bushing
35 Overdrive planetary carrier assembly	94 Rear sun gear
36 Snap-ring	95 Thrust washer
37 Snap-ring	96 Retaining ring
38 Thrust bearing assembly	97 Low-reverse housing bushing
39 Overdrive internal gear	98 Low-reverse clutch housing
40 Retaining ring	99 Spacer
41 Thrust washer	100 Low-reverse piston outer seal
42 Retaining ring	101 Low-reverse piston inner seal
43 Fourth gear clutch spring assembly	102 Low-reverse piston
44 Fourth gear clutch piston	102 Clutch apply ring
45 Fourth gear clutch inner seal	104 Release spring (waved)
46 Fourth gear clutch outer seal	105 Spring retainer
47 Center support bushing	106 Snap-ring
48 Center support	107 Wave plate
49 Oil seal rings	108 Low-reverse clutch plates
50 Center support bushing	109 Low roller clutch race
51 Thrust washer	110 Low roller clutch assembly
52 Intermediate band	111 Thrust bearing
53 Direct clutch housing bushing	112 Rear carrier bushing
54 Direct clutch housing	113 Rear planetary carrier assembly
55 Direct clutch housing bushing	114 Thrust washer
56 Direct clutch piston seals	115 Thrust bearing assembly
57 Direct clutch piston	116 Rear internal gear
58 Direct clutch apply ring	117 Output shaft
59 Release spring guide	

Transmission disassembly

8A.3 Place the transmission on a sturdy workbench and begin disassembly by removing the external components. Tap the output shaft oil seal in with a large screwdriver and hammer and pry the seal from the case

8A.4 Remove the speedometer gear adapter and gear assembly

8A.5 Remove the intermediate servo cover retaining ring by prying it out of the groove through one of the slots

8A.6 Using a pair of adjustable pliers, twist the cover to break it loose and remove the intermediate servo cover

8A.7 Remove the servo cover O-ring

8A.8 Remove the outer servo piston . . .

8A.9 . . . and withdraw the inner servo piston and band apply pin assembly

8A.10 Turn the transmission over with the oil pan facing up. Remove the transmission oil pan . . .

8A.11 . . . and withdraw the oil filter and O-rings from the case (the O-rings may stick in the case bore)

8A.12 Disconnect the electrical connector from the transmission case plug by prying the retaining clip open with a small screwdriver

8A.13 Remove the TCC solenoid bolts, pull the solenoid out of the pump, disconnect the pressure switch(es) and remove the wiring harness assembly

8A.14 Remove the bolt retaining the TV linkage and carefully set the bracket, link and lever assembly aside. Note the assembly of the linkage, bracket and link for later reassembly

8A.15 Remove the detent spring and roller assembly from the valve body

8A.16 Remove the remaining valve body bolts and carefully lift the valve body free of the case while disconnecting the manual valve link from the detent lever and manual valve

8A.17 Remove the manual valve from the valve body so it doesn't fall out and set the valve body aside. Retrieve the check balls, which will be left sitting on the spacer plate

8A.18 Remove the 1-2 accumulator housing from the case . . .

8A.19 . . . and remove the piston and spring from the housing

8A.20 Remove the accumulator plate and separate the valve body spacer plate and gaskets from the case. Retrieve the check balls from the case, making note of their exact locations

8A.21 Remove the 3-4 accumulator piston, pin and spring from the case (note the installed order of the piston and spring, on some models the piston is installed first)

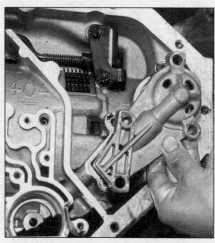

8A.22 Remove the bolts retaining the governor cover, remove the cover and gasket . . .

8A.23 . . . and withdraw the governor assembly from the case

8A.24 Remove the oil pump-to-case bolts and, using the special puller, pull the pump free from the case

8A.25 Remove the pump and stator shaft assembly from the case and set the assembly aside

8A.26 Remove the pump-to-housing thrust washer from either the backside of the pump or from inside the case

8A.27 Remove the oil deflector plate

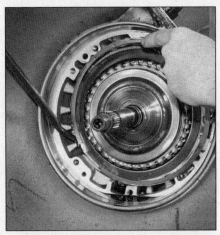

8A.28 Remove the fourth gear clutch retaining ring by prying it from the case lugs

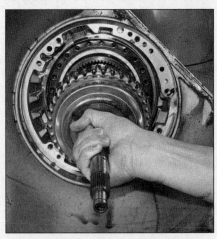

8A.29 Grasp the input shaft and remove the overdrive unit from the case

8A.30 Separate the fourth gear clutch plates from the overdrive unit and remove the one remaining steel plate from the case

8A.31 Remove the overdrive internal gear from the case and remove the thrust bearing from inside the gear

8A.32 Turn the internal gear over and remove the thrust washer from the backside of the gear or from the top of the center support

8A.33 Remove the fourth clutch spring retaining ring from the groove in the center support. A special tool is available to compress the spring retainer, making removal of the retaining ring easier, but it can be accomplished by pressing the retainer down by-hand

8A.34 Remove the fourth clutch spring assembly . . .

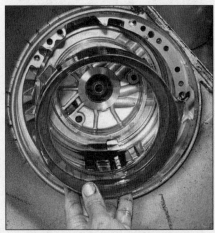

8A.35 . . . and fourth clutch piston from the case

8A.36 Using a 10-mm socket, remove the two center support bolts

8A.37 Remove the center support-to-case beveled retaining ring

8A.38 Remove the center support. A special tool is available to bump the center support free. If the tool is not available, bump the output shaft forward to free the center support from the case

8A.39 Remove the fourth clutch inner . . .

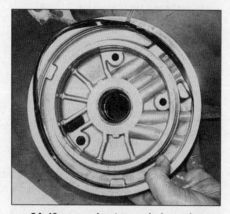

8A.40 . . . and outer seals from the center support

8A.41 Remove the center support-to-direct clutch thrust washer

8A.42 A special tool is available to remove the direct and forward clutch assemblies together. If the tool is not available, remove the direct clutch housing

8A.43 Remove the intermediate band . . .

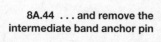

8A.44 . . . and remove the intermediate band anchor pin

8A.45 Remove the forward clutch housing

8A.46 Remove the output shaft-to-forward clutch shaft selective washer from the end of the output shaft

8A.47 Remove the output shaft snap-ring . . .

8A.48 . . . and remove the front internal gear

8A.49 Remove the selective washer . . .

8A.50 . . . and the thrust washer from the internal gear

8A.51 Remove the needle thrust bearing from the front carrier assembly . . .

8A.52 . . . and remove the front carrier assembly

8A.53 Remove the thrust washer from the front sun gear . . .

8A.54 . . . and remove the front sun gear

8A.55 Remove the input drum and rear sun gear assembly . . .

8A.56 . . . and remove the thrust washer from the backside

8A.57 Remove the low-reverse clutch housing-to-case beveled retaining ring

8A.58 The low-reverse clutch housing is very difficult to remove and a special low-reverse clutch housing removal tool is necessary

8A.59 Insert the tool into the housing and lock the tool into place. Rock the housing back-and-forth with the tool and pull the low-reverse clutch housing from the case

8A.60 Remove the low-reverse clutch housing spacer ring from the case lugs

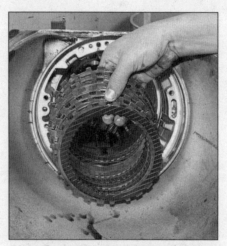

8A.61 Grasp the output shaft and remove the remainder of the rear unit parts from the case. Separate the low-reverse clutch plates from the assembly

8A.62 Remove the low roller clutch and rear carrier assembly from the output shaft and remove the low roller clutch inner race

8A.63 Remove the low roller clutch from the rear carrier assembly

8A.64 Remove the thrust bearing from inside the carrier assembly

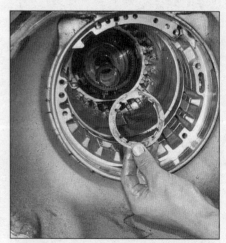

8A.65 Remove the four-tabbed thrust washer from the backside of the carrier assembly

8A.66 Remove the needle thrust bearing from inside the rear internal gear . . .

8A.67 . . . and remove the rear internal gear from the output shaft. The rear internal gear is pressed on the output shaft on some models and cannot be removed

8A.68 Remove the overrun clutch retaining ring from the overrun clutch housing

8A.69 Remove the overdrive carrier snap-ring from the input shaft

8A.70 Remove the overdrive carrier from the input shaft. Invert the carrier and remove the overdrive sun gear from the overdrive carrier

8A.71 Remove the overrun clutch housing from the input shaft and remove the overrun clutch pack from the housing

8A.72 Remove the snap-ring from the overrun clutch hub . . .

8A.73 . . . and remove the overdrive roller clutch cam and roller assembly from the overrun clutch housing. Be careful not to loose any rollers from the roller clutch

8A.74 Remove the overrun clutch release spring retainer . . .

8A.75 . . . and the wave spring from the overrun housing

8A.76 Remove the overrun clutch piston . . .

8A.77 . . . and remove the inner and outer seals from the piston

8A.78 Remove the direct clutch retaining ring from the direct clutch housing . . .

8A.79 . . . and remove the direct clutch pack from the housing - note the number of plates for reassembly reference

8A.80 Mount the housing in a spring compressor or press, compress the spring retainer and remove the snap-ring

8A.81 Remove the direct clutch release spring assembly . . .

8A.82 . . . and the spring guide from the housing

8A.83 Remove the direct clutch piston . . .

8A.84 . . . and remove the direct clutch apply ring from the piston. Remove the inner and outer seals from the piston

8A.85 Remove the direct clutch piston center seal from the hub inside the housing

8A.86 Remove the thrust washer from the forward clutch housing

8A.87 Invert the housing, remove the forward clutch retaining ring . . .

8A.88 . . . and remove the forward clutch pack from the housing

8A.89 Mount the forward clutch housing in a spring compressor or press, compress the spring retainer and remove the snap-ring

8A.90 Remove the forward clutch release spring assembly . . .

8A.91 . . . and the forward clutch piston from the housing

8A.92 Remove the apply ring from the forward clutch piston . . .

8A.93 . . . and remove the forward clutch inner and outer seals

8A.94 Remove the low-reverse clutch apply ring from the low-reverse piston

8A.95 Remove the snap-ring from the low-reverse housing hub . . .

8A.96 . . . and remove the spring retainer . . .

8A.97 . . . and low-reverse clutch wave spring

8A.98 Remove the low-reverse piston from the housing . . .

8A.99 . . . and remove the inner and outer seals from the piston

Component inspection and subassembly

Using an approved cleaning solvent, clean and dry all the components thoroughly, including the case. Do not use rags to wipe the components dry, as lint from the rag may lodge in the oil passages, causing a valve to stick.

Inspect the following components and repair or replace as necessary:

a) *Case* - Inspect the exterior of the case for damage, cracks and porosity (a porous casting will cause fluid leaks). Check the valve body mating surfaces on the case and valve body for damage and flatness (use a precision straightedge to check for flatness - any warpage means the valve body or case will have to be machined or replaced). Check all the oil passages, the accumulator bore, the servo bore, the speedometer bore and the governor bore for damage. Check all threaded holes for damage or stripped threads (repair thread damage as described in Chapter 2). Check the oil cooler line fittings for damage. Check the interior of the case for damaged retaining ring grooves or case lugs - if any are damaged the case will have to be replaced. Check the output shaft bushing for wear (if necessary, replace the bushing, as described in Chapter 2). Inspect the manual linkage and the park-lock linkage for damage.

b) *Overdrive unit and center support* - Inspect all the bushings and thrust washers for wear or damage. Check the center support for cracks and check the oil ring grooves for damage. Check the piston and spring retainer for cracks or damage. Inspect the input shaft for damaged splines. Check the oil seal rings and snap-ring grooves for damage. Inspect the check-ball assembly for freedom of movement. Inspect the overrun clutch plates for wear or heat damage. Check the overrun clutch housing, piston, spring and retainer for cracks, damage or distortion. Inspect the overdrive roller clutch assembly for damaged rollers, springs or cam. Inspect the overdrive sun gear and carrier for damaged gear teeth or splines. Inspect the roller clutch race for wear or damage. Inspect the pinion gears for damaged thrust washers, rough bearings and for cracked or chipped teeth. Check the endplay of each pinion - it should be between 0.009 and 0.025-inch.

c) *Direct clutch, forward clutch and intermediate band assemblies* - Inspect all the clutch plates or wear or heat damage. Inspect all the bushings and thrust washers for wear or damage. Inspect the direct clutch housing for cracks, damaged lugs or damaged snap-ring grooves. Check the piston, spring guide and spring assembly for cracks, damage or collapsed springs. Check the piston check-balls for freedom of movement. Inspect the forward clutch housing for damaged lugs or snap-ring grooves. Check the shaft journals for wear or damage. Inspect the oil seal rings for damage - DO NOT remove the Teflon oil seal rings unless they are damaged. Inspect the piston, retainer and spring assembly for cracks or damage or distortion. Inspect the intermediate band for burning, flaking or cracks. If the band is severely damaged or burned check the servo pin length with the special Intermediate Band Apply Pin Gauge J-25014, or equivalent. Servo pins are available in different sizes at a dealership parts department.

d) *Front planetary gear unit* - Inspect all the bushings and thrust washers for wear or damage. Inspect the front internal gear for worn or damaged splines and for chipped or broken teeth. Inspect the front carrier pinions for damaged teeth or bearings. Check each pinion gear for endplay - it should be between 0.009 and 0.027-inch. Inspect the front sun gear for worn or damaged splines and teeth. Check the thrust bearing surface for wear or scoring. Check the thrust bearing for roughness. Inspect the rear sun gear and input drum cracks, worn or damaged splines and cracked or chipped teeth.

e) *Low-reverse clutch assembly* - Inspect the low-reverse clutch plates for wear or signs of overheating. Check the low roller clutch assembly for worn or damaged rollers or springs. Check the races for scoring or damage. Check the low-reverse clutch housing for a plugged oil feed hole. Check for worn or damaged bushings or splines. Inspect the clutch apply ring and piston for cracks and check the spring retainer for damage.

f) *Rear planetary gear unit* - Inspect the output shaft for damaged splines, snap-ring grooves and worn or damaged journals. Check the governor drive gear teeth for damage. Inspect the rear internal gear for damaged splines or teeth. Check the bearing wear surfaces for scoring and check the parking pawl lugs for damage. Inspect the rear carrier for a worn or damaged bushing. Inspect the pinion gears for damaged teeth or bearings. Check the pinion gear endplay - it should be between 0.009 and 0.027-inch. Check the thrust bearings and washers for wear of damage.

Oil pump assembly

The THM200-4R oil pump is essentially the same as the THM700-R4 oil pump. See the "Oil pump assembly" section in Chapter 8 Part D for the photographic assembly sequence.

Disassemble the oil pump, removing the slider, rotor and vanes from the pump body. Use a small screwdriver to pry the slider spring out of the body. Be very careful; the slider spring is under high pressure, place a clean shop towel over the spring to prevent it from flying out. Remove the pressure regulator valve train, the converter clutch valve train, the pressure relief ball and spring (if necessary) and the oil pump cover screen. Lay the valves and springs out on a clean, lint-free towel in the exact order of removal to prevent confusion on assembly. Clean and dry the cover, body and all internal components. Inspect the valves and remove any burrs with a fine lapping compound; inspect the springs for damage or distortion; inspect the valve bores for damage; inspect the capsulated check balls for freedom of movement. Replace any damaged components. Inspect the pump pocket, cover, pump rotor, vanes and slider very carefully. If the pump body pocket and cover are damaged or scored, it may be

necessary to replace the complete pump assembly. If a new rotor and slider are to be installed in the original pump body, use a micrometer to measure the thickness of the original rotor and slider. Install a rotor and slider of the same thickness; selective-fit parts are available at a dealership parts department.

Control valve assembly

Complete disassembly of the valve body is not necessary unless the valve body has been contaminated. Clean the valve body using an approved solvent and air dry (DO NOT use rags to dry the valve body, as lint from the rag may cause a valve to stick). Check each valve for freedom of movement in its bore by prying the valve against its spring with a small screwdriver or pick. The valve should snap back when pressure is released. If a stuck valve is encountered, remove the individual valve and components for further cleaning and inspection. Nicks and burrs may be removed by lapping the valve with a fine lapping compound.

If complete disassembly of the valve body is required, lay the valve body on a clean workbench and use clean tools to disassemble and wash the valve body with clean solvent. Remove the valves from the valve body, one at a time. Lay out the valves, springs and bushings in their proper order on a clean lint-free towel. Cleanliness and meticulous care in keeping the valves in order cannot be over-stressed. A tapered number 49 drill bit is useful in removing any stubborn roll-pins you may encounter.

Governor

Clean the governor with an approved cleaning solvent and air dry. Inspect the governor for damage. Inspect the governor cover for scoring. Check the governor gear for damaged teeth. The gear may be replaced by removing the retaining ring with a small screwdriver, then sliding the washer and gear off the shaft.

Transmission assembly

An automatic transmission is a precision piece of equipment. Install each component as shown, and do not force any component into place. If it doesn't fit properly, find out why and rectify the situation. Maintain a clean workplace and lubricate all moving parts as they are installed. Lubricate the thrust washers, bearings and bushings with clean automatic transmission fluid (ATF) or petroleum jelly. use petroleum jelly to retain thrust washers and check balls in their proper location as the component is installed. Dip all friction plates in ATF before installation.

8A.102 Inspect the governor seal ring for damage. If damaged, carefully cut it off without damaging the groove and install a new seal ring

8A.103 Inspect the governor weights and springs for freedom of movement. Check for the presence of two check balls and inspect the shaft for damage

8A.104 Drive out the old rear case bushing and install a new bushing with the appropriate size driver

8A.105 Install a new rear oil seal

8A.106 Install a new case electrical connector and O-ring. Press it in until the retaining tabs lock in place

8A.107 Drive the low-reverse cup plug/seal from the case with a 3/8-inch diameter rod or punch. DO NOT install the new seal at this time

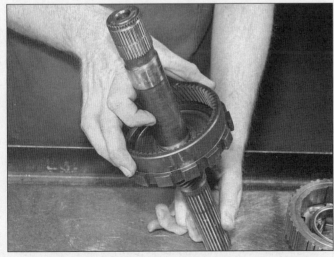

8A.108 Install the rear internal gear onto the output shaft, if removed

8A.109 Install the rear internal gear thrust bearing with the inside diameter race against the internal gear. Lubricate the bearing with ATF

8A.110 Install the four-tabbed thrust washer on the rear carrier. Retain the thrust washer with petroleum jelly

8A.111 Lubricate the thrust bearings and pinions with ATF and install the rear carrier into the rear internal gear

8A.112 Install the low-roller clutch race thrust washer into the rear carrier

8A.113 Install the low roller clutch into the rear carrier, pressing the rollers in as you install the assembly

Note

Transmission assembly is best accomplished with the transmission case secured in the vertical position. Also, the output shaft must be supported during preliminary assembly. Special tools are available to support the case and output shaft. If the tools are not available, develop some means of supporting the output shaft in position. After installing the rear gear unit and output shaft assembly, look through the parking pawl slot in the case and adjust the output shaft so the parking pawl lugs on the rear internal gear are aligned with the parking pawl tooth

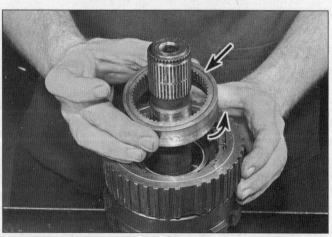

8A.114 Install the inner race with the splined end up - identified by the groove in the top surface (arrow). Rotate the race in a counterclockwise direction as you press it into position. Lubricate the assembly with ATF

8A.115 Install the rear unit assembly into the transmission case

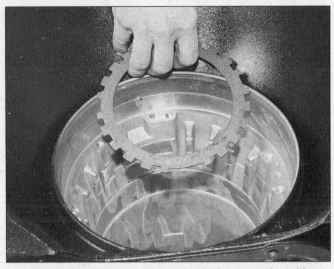

8A.116 Install the low-reverse clutch plates, starting with a steel plate . . .

8A.117 . . . and alternating friction plates and steel plates. Dip the friction plates in ATF before installing

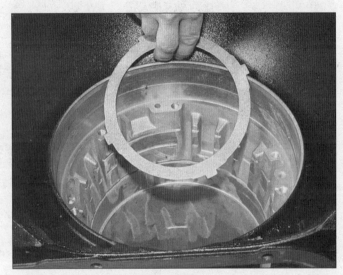

8A.118 Install the low-reverse clutch waved plate on top of the last steel plate

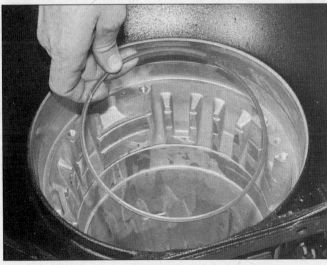

8A.119 Install the low-reverse clutch spacer ring . . .

8A.120 . . . engaging the ring fully in the case lugs (arrow)

8A.121 Install the inner and outer lip seals onto the low-reverse clutch piston with the seal lips facing into the housing bore

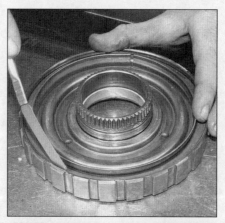

8A.122 Lubricate the seals with ATF and install the piston into the housing. Work the seal lips in with a seal installation tool and press the piston in until fully seated. Make sure the clutch apply ring is in place

8A.123 Install the waved release spring . . .

8A.124 . . . and the spring retainer with the cupped side over the spring

8A.125 Depress the spring retainer and install the snap-ring into the groove in the housing. Make sure the snap-ring is fully seated in the groove

8A.126 Lock the low-reverse clutch housing onto the special installation tool and install the housing into the case. Align the oil feed hole (arrow) with the lubrication passage in the case

8A.127 Press the low-reverse housing into the case lugs until it clears the retaining ring groove (arrow). It may be necessary to adjust the output shaft to allow the housing to seat past the retaining ring groove. Also it may be necessary to rotate the low roller clutch race to align the splines - use the rear sun gear and input drum as a tool to rotate the roller clutch race

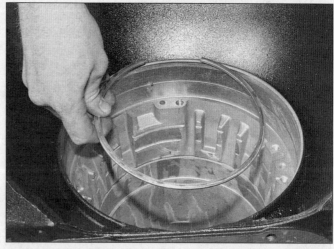

8A.128 Install the low-reverse clutch housing retaining ring with the beveled side up

8A.129 Install the four-tabbed thrust washer onto the input drum, engaging the tabs into the slots in the drum. Retain the thrust washer with petroleum jelly

8A.130 Install the rear sun gear/input drum, seating it on the low-reverse clutch housing

8A.131 Install the front sun gear with the flat side facing up (arrow). The side with the groove faces the rear sun gear snap ring

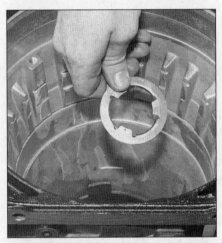

8A.132 Install the front sun gear needle thrust bearing with the needle bearings against the front sun gear and the three-tabbed flange fitting inside the sun gear

8A.133 Install the front carrier, meshing the splines with the output shaft and seating it on the sun gear

8A.134 Install the thrust bearing onto the front carrier with the inside diameter race against the carrier. Retain the thrust bearing with petroleum jelly

8A.135 Make sure the snap-ring groove in the output shaft is above the front carrier hub (arrow). If it isn't adjust the output shaft higher

8A.136 Install the front internal gear meshing the teeth with the front carrier pinions and seating it on the thrust bearing

8A.137 Install the front internal gear thrust washer . . .

8A.138 . . . placing it inside the internal gear hub (arrow)

8A.139 Install the selective thrust washer . . .

8A.140 . . . and install the output shaft snap-ring. Be very careful not to over extend the snap-ring

8A.141 Make sure the snap-ring is fully seated in the output shaft groove (arrow). It may be necessary to adjust the output shaft to expose the snap-ring groove. Once this snap-ring is installed, the output shaft support may be removed

Note

Mount a dial indicator to the transmission case and check the rear unit endplay. Position the needle of the indicator on the end of the output shaft. Push the output shaft down and zero the indicator. Push the output shaft up and measure the endplay. Rear unit endplay should be between 0.004 to 0.025-inch. If it isn't change the selective washer located between the front internal gear thrust washer and the output shaft snap-ring. Selective washers are available at a dealership parts department

8A.142 Install the front unit selective washer into the end of the output shaft

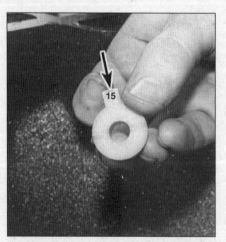

8A.143 Front selective washers are identified by color and by a number imprinted on the tab (arrow) - install the same size as original if no major components have been replaced

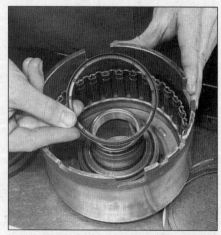

8A.144 Install the center lip seal on the direct clutch housing hub with the lip facing up

8A.145 Install the inner and outer lip seals on the direct clutch piston with the lips facing into the housing bore

8A.146 Install the apply ring onto the piston, if removed. Lubricate the seals and bore with ATF and install the piston into the housing. Be careful not to cut the outer seal on the snap-ring groove; use a seal protector if available

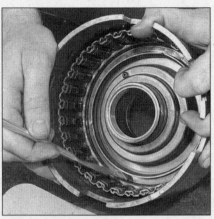

8A.147 Press the piston into the bore while working the seal lips in with a seal installation tool. With the piston properly installed, you should be able to rotate the piston in the bore

8A.148 Install the spring guide into the housing. Make sure the slot in the bottom of the guide is placed over the piston check ball assembly

8A.149 Install the release spring assembly, fitting the springs into the pockets in the guide

8A.150 Compress the spring retainer with a spring compressor or press and install the snap-ring. Make sure it's seated in the groove and inside the four tabs on top of the retainer (arrows)

8A.151 Install a direct clutch steel plate into the housing . . .

8A.152 . . . followed by a friction plate; dip the friction plates in ATF before installing. Alternate steel plates and friction plates until all the direct clutch plates are installed. The number of plates installed is dependent on the model of transmission; install the exact number removed originally

8A.153 Install the direct clutch pressure plate with the smooth finished side down against the last friction plate

8A.154 Install the direct clutch retaining ring, seating it in the groove in the housing. Make sure you have the correct ring, the various retaining rings are similar in size. Make sure there is sufficient clearance in the clutch pack for the friction plates to turn freely in the housing, then align the friction plate splines with a small screwdriver

8A.155 Install the inner and outer lip seals onto the forward clutch piston with the seal lips facing into the housing bore

8A.156 Install the apply ring, if removed, lubricate the seals and bore with ATF and install the piston into the forward clutch housing

8A.157 Work the seal lips in with a seal installation tool and press the piston into the housing until it's fully seated. With the piston properly installed you should be able to rotate the piston in the bore

8A.158 Install the spring assembly onto the piston

8A.159 Compress the spring retainer with a spring compressor or press and install the snap-ring. Make sure it's seated in the groove and inside the four tabs on top of the retainer (arrows)

8A.160 Install the forward clutch waved plated (if equipped) into the housing

8A.161 Dip the friction plates in ATF and install the remaining clutch plates, alternating friction and steel plates until all the forward clutch plates are installed. Clutch stack-up may vary with different models, so make certain the parts are installed as they were originally

8A.162 Install the pressure plate with the chamfered side up and the smooth side against the last plate

8A.163 Install the forward clutch retaining ring, seating it in the groove. Make sure there is sufficient clearance in the clutch pack for the friction plates to turn freely in the housing

8A.164 Install new sealing rings onto the forward clutch shaft. Make sure the scarf-cut ends are overlapped properly and the rings turn freely in the grooves. Retain the rings in the grooves with petroleum jelly

8A.165 Install the direct clutch-to-forward clutch thrust washer, retaining the washer to the hub with petroleum jelly

8A.166 Lower the assembled direct clutch over the forward clutch hub, engaging the splines on the forward clutch housing with the friction plates in the direct clutch housing. Spin the direct clutch housing as you slowly lower it to engage all the clutch plates. When the two assemblies are properly seated the bottom of the direct clutch housing will be 5/8-inch from the bottom of the forward clutch housing

8A.167 Install the intermediate band anchor into the hole in the case

8A.168 Install the intermediate band in the case, engaging the band with the anchor pin and positioning the apply lug inline with the servo bore (arrow)

8A.169 Grasp the forward clutch shaft and lower the assembly into the case (a special tool is available to hold the assembly, making this step easier). Engage the slots in the direct clutch housing with the tabs on the input drum

8A.170 The properly assembled direct clutch and forward clutch assembly sits squarely in the case, inside the intermediate band and seated on the front carrier assembly thrust bearing

8A.171 Install the cast-iron oil seal rings on the center support hub. Make sure to interlock the ends of the rings. Seat the rings in the grooves and retain them with petroleum jelly

8A.172 Install the center support-to-direct clutch thrust washer over the center support hub and retain the washer with petroleum jelly

8A.173 Install the center support inner and outer lip seals with the seal lips facing down. Lubricate the seals with ATF

8A.174 Install the center support into the case with the center support bolt holes (arrows) aligned with the holes in the case. Seat the center support on the direct clutch hub, install the bolts and tighten them finger tight

8A.175 Install the center support retaining ring with the beveled side up

8A.176 Make sure the center support retaining ring is seated fully in the groove (arrow)

Note

Check the front unit end play as follows: Install a dial indicator into the case with the needle positioned on the end of the forward clutch shaft. Lever the output shaft forward, eliminating the rear unit end play. Zero the indicator, pull the forward clutch shaft up and read the front unit end play (a special tool is available to grip the forward clutch shaft). Front unit end play should be between 0.022 to 0.051-inch; if is isn't change the output shaft-to-forward clutch shaft thrust washer (see illustration 8A.143) to bring the end play within specifications

8A.177 Tighten the center support bolts (arrows) to 18 ft-lbs

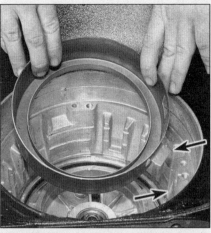

8A.178 Lubricate the fourth clutch piston with ATF and install the piston into the center support, aligning the tab on the piston with the wide space in the case lugs (arrows)

8A.179 Install the fourth clutch spring and retainer assembly onto the piston

8A.180 Compress the spring retainer with your fingers and install the retaining ring (a special tool is available to compress the springs, if necessary)

8A.181 Make sure the retaining ring is seated fully in the groove (arrow)

8A.182 Install the internal gear-to-support thrust washer with the tangs fitted down over the center support hub. Retain the thrust washer with petroleum jelly

8A.183 Install the overdrive internal gear, engaging the splines with the forward clutch shaft

8A.184 Install the internal gear-to-carrier thrust bearing with the large diameter race against the carrier

8A.185 Install inner and outer seals onto the overrun clutch piston with the seal lips facing into the overrun clutch housing bore

8A.186 Lubricate the seals and bore with ATF and install the piston into the housing. Work the seal lips in with a seal installation tool

8A.187 Install the waved release spring over the hub . . .

8A.188 . . . and install the spring retainer with the cupped side down over the waved spring

8A.189 Install the overdrive roller clutch cam into the roller clutch assembly as shown (the side of the roller clutch with the roller spring locating tangs faces down)

8A.190 Install the roller clutch assembly onto the overrun clutch housing hub

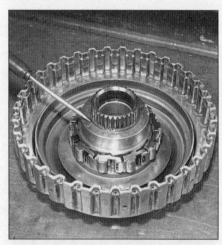

8A.191 Press the roller clutch cam down and install the thin snap-ring. Make sure the snap-ring is fully seated in the groove

8A.192 Install an overrun clutch steel plate into the housing . . .

8A.193 . . . followed by a friction plate (dip the friction plates in ATF before installing). Alternate steel and friction plates

8A.194 Install the overrun clutch backing plate with the chamfered side up

8A.195 Install the retaining ring, sealing it into the groove in the housing. Make sure there is sufficient clearance in the clutch pack for the friction plates to turn freely in the housing.

8A.196 Install the overdrive sun gear onto the overrun clutch hub with the chamfered spline end facing up (arrow)

8A.197 Align the overrun clutch friction plate splines and install the overdrive carrier into the housing. Engage the splines in the carrier with all the friction plates. Rotate the overdrive carrier counterclockwise as you seat it over the roller clutch

8A.198 When properly installed the overdrive carrier will be fully seated into the overrun clutch housing

8A.199 Grasp the overdrive carrier and overrun clutch assembly, holding them together with one hand and insert the input shaft into the assembly with the other hand. (DO NOT replace the input shaft oil seal rings (arrows) unless they are damaged. The top ring is solid and requires special tools for replacement. Lubricate the rings with petroleum jelly

8A.200 Turn the assembly upside down and install a NEW overdrive carrier-to-input shaft snap-ring (usually provided with the overhaul kit). Make sure it's fully seated in the groove

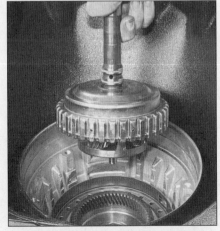

8A.201 Grasp the input shaft and lower the assembly into the case, engaging the overdrive carrier pinions into the internal gear

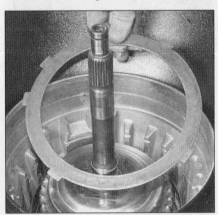

8A.202 Install a fourth clutch steel plate, engaging the tabs into the case lugs

8A.203 Dip the friction plates in ATF and install one friction plate

8A.204 Install two steel plates next to each other. . .

8A.205 . . . followed by the remaining friction plate

8A.206 Install the thicker fourth clutch backing plate

8A.207 Install the fourth clutch retaining ring, seating it in the groove in the case. Make sure there is sufficient clearance for the friction plates to turn freely

8A.208 Install the oil deflector plate with the tangs facing up

8A.209 Install two oil pump alignment bolts and place the oil pump gasket into the case. Make sure all the holes line-up; the gasket will only go on one way

8A.210 Install the stator shaft flange selective thrust washer. Retain the washer with petroleum jelly

8A.211 Install the pump cover O-ring seal with the stripe facing out. Lubricate the seal with ATF

8A.212 Carefully lower the pump onto the alignment bolts. Make sure the pump is aligned properly with the oil filter bore (arrow) facing the valve body surface. Press the pump down until fully seated, remove the alignment bolts and install the oil pump bolts finger-tight

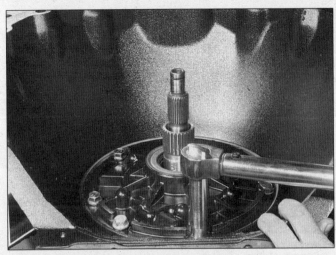

8A.213 Tighten the oil pump bolts to 18-ft-lbs. Rotate the input shaft as you tighten the bolts. If you are unable to rotate the shaft before the pump is fully tightened, a thrust washer could be out-of-place or a hub may not be splined in a clutch plate - remove the pump and rectify the situation before proceeding

8A.214 Mount a dial indicator to the case and place the needle on the end of the input shaft. Lift up on the input shaft with approximately 3-lbs of force and zero the indicator. Lift up with approximately 20-lbs of force and read the end play. Overdrive unit endplay should be between 0.004 and 0.027-inch - if it isn't change the stator shaft flange selective thrust washer to bring the end play within specifications

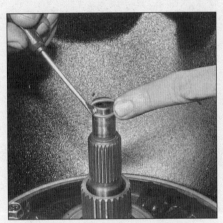

8A.215 Replace the input shaft-to-converter O-ring

8A.216 Place the transmission on a sturdy workbench with the valve body surface up. Install a new O-ring on the servo cover and install the outer servo piston into the cover (do not replace the piston seals unless they are damaged)

8A.217 Place the inner servo piston into the outer piston with the cupped side facing out (lubricate the seals with petroleum jelly)

8A.218 Install the servo cushion spring, pin assembly and inner spring into the piston assembly

8A.219 Align the intermediate band apply lug with the servo bore by prying the band over with one screwdriver while aligning the apply lug with another thin screwdriver inserted through the bore hole. Leave the screwdriver shown on the right holding the band in position until the servo has been installed

8A.220 Lubricate the seals and bore with petroleum jelly and install the servo assembly

8A.221 Press the servo cover in past the snap-ring groove and install the retaining ring with the ring ends installed near the slots in the case

8A.222 Install the governor into the governor bore, engaging the driven gear with the output shaft

8A.223 Install the governor cover gasket . . .

8A.224 . . . and install the governor cover. Tighten the bolts to 18 ft-lbs

8A.225 Install the 3-4 accumulator spring and piston with the cupped side down over the spring. Lubricate the piston seal with petroleum jelly (on some models, the piston is installed first, cupped side up, then the spring)

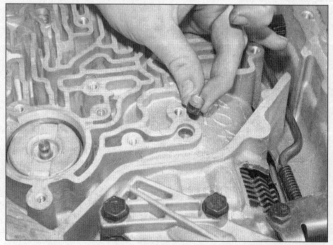

8A.226 Install a new low-reverse clutch housing cup seal into the oil passage with the seal end down into the case

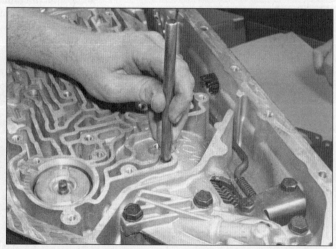

8A.227 Drive the seal into the bore with a 3/8-inch diameter rod until the seal is firmly seated against the low-reverse clutch housing

8A.228 Install the check balls into the case oil passages in the locations shown. Install TV exhaust check ball (A), if one was originally installed in that location. Make sure the intermediate servo check ball (B) is located in the capsule and is clean and moves freely

8A.229 Install two valve body alignment bolts and place the spacer plate-to-case gasket over the bolts

8A.230 Coat the spacer plate with a thin film of ATF and install the spacer plate over the alignment bolts . . .

8A.231 . . . and the spacer plate-to-valve body gasket

8A.232 Install the 1-2 accumulator plate and tighten the bolts finger-tight

8A.233 Install the 1-2 accumulator piston into the accumulator housing with the cupped side facing up. Lubricate the seal with petroleum jelly

8A.234 Install the 1-2 accumulator spring into the housing. Retain the spring in the housing with petroleum jelly

8A.235 Place the accumulator housing-to-plate gasket in position . . .

8A.236 . . . install the accumulator assembly and tighten the bolts finger-tight

8A.237 Install the three check balls into the valve body oil passages in the locations shown (arrows). Retain the check balls with petroleum jelly

8A.238 Lower the valve body over the alignment bolts and engage the manual valve with the detent link. Seat the valve body assembly onto the spacer plate and gaskets

8A.239 Remove the alignment bolts and install the valve body bolts finger tight. Install the TCC solenoid and wiring harness assembly, connecting the terminals to the pressure switch and case connector. Secure the wiring harness and oil pipe in their proper clips. Install the TV linkage and detent roller assembly and tighten the bolts finger tight

8A.240 Beginning in the center and working out in a spiral pattern, tighten the valve body, accumulator and TCC solenoid bolts to 108 in-lbs

8A.241 Install a new oil filter and seal, pressing it firmly down until seated. Install the oil pan gasket and oil pan. Tighten the oil pan bolts to 12 ft-lbs

8A.242 Turn the transmission over onto the oil pan. Install a speedometer gear shaft seal into the adapter, retaining the seal with the retaining ring

8A.243 Install an O-ring onto the adapter, lubricate the seal, O-ring and speedometer gear shaft with ATF, insert the gear into the adapter and install the assembly into the transmission case. Install the retainer and bolt. Install the torque converter and the transmission is ready for installation into the vehicle

Chapter 8 Part B
Disassembly, inspection and assembly
THM350 transmission

Introduction

The THM350 is a three-speed automatic transmission manufactured for rear-wheel drive vehicles. The major components of this transmission are:

a) Torque convertor
b) Gear-type oil pump
c) Control valve assembly
d) Four multiple-disc clutch packs
e) Two planetary gear sets
f) Two roller clutches
g) Intermediate band

Follow the photographic sequence for disassembly, inspection and assembly. The model shown is a typical transmission of this type. Differences do exist among models and many changes have been made over the years, so perform each step in order and lay the components out on a clean work bench in the EXACT ORDER of removal to prevent confusion during reassembly. Many snap-rings and clutch plates are similar in size, but must not be interchanged. Keep the individual parts together with the component from which they were removed to avoid mix-ups. Save all old parts and compare them with the new part to ensure they are an exact match before reassembly. Pay particular attention to the stack-up of the various clutch packs. Differences do exist between models and your transmission may not match the stack-up shown. Note the exact location of the check balls in the case. Save all the old parts until the overhaul is complete and the transmission has been thoroughly road tested; old components can be useful in diagnosing any problems that may arise.

Basic hand tools can be used for most procedures. although some special tools are required. Alternate procedures are shown where possible, but some procedures can only be accomplished with special tools. Read through the entire overhaul procedure before beginning work to familiarize yourself with the procedures and identify any special tools that may be needed. Thoroughly clean the exterior of the transmission before beginning disassembly.

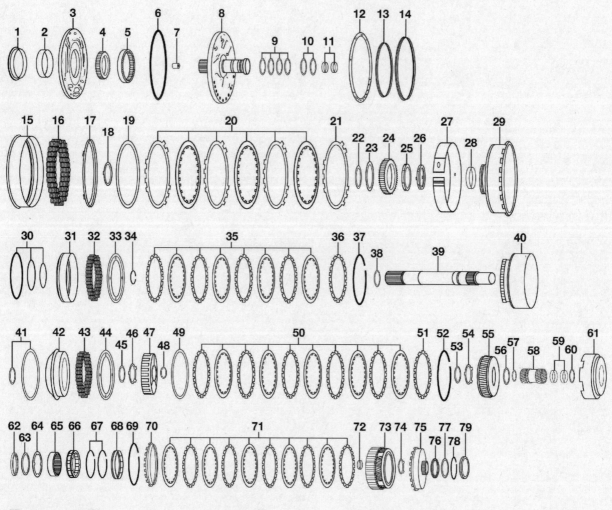

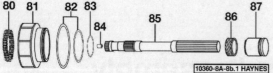

8B.0 Exploded view of the typical THM350 internal components

1 Front seal	22 Snap-ring	44 Spring retainer	66 Roller clutch
2 Pump body bushing	23 Retainer	45 Snap-ring	67 Snap-rings
3 Pump body	24 Outer race	46 Thrust washer	68 Outer race
4 Drive gear	25 Intermediate roller clutch	47 Front ring gear	69 Retaining ring
5 Driven gear	26 Inner race	48 Bushing	70 Clutch support
6 O-ring	27 Intermediate band	49 Cushion spring	71 Low-reverse clutch plates
7 Bushing	28 Bushing	50 Forward clutch plates	72 Bushing
8 Pump cover	29 Direct clutch drum	51 Pressure plate	73 Rear reaction carrier
9 Sealing rings (hook-type)	30 Piston seals	52 Retaining ring	74 Thrust washer
10 Sealing rings (Teflon)	31 Direct clutch piston	53 Snap-ring	75 Output ring gear
11 Bushings	32 Return springs	54 Thrust washer	76 Ring
12 Gasket	33 Spring retainer	55 Output carrier	77 Thrust bearing
13 Intermediate clutch piston	34 Snap-ring	56 Thrust bearing	78 Snap-ring
inner seal	35 Direct clutch plates	57 Race	79 Spring retainer
14 Intermediate clutch piston	36 Pressure plate	58 Sun gear	80 Return springs
outer seal	37 Retaining ring	59 Bushings	81 Low-reverse clutch piston
15 Intermediate clutch piston	38 Thrust bearing	60 Snap-ring	82 Piston seals
16 Return springs	39 Input shaft	61 Input drive shell	83 Spring seat retainer
17 Spring retainer	40 Forward clutch drum	62 Thrust washer	84 Bushing
18 Thrust washer	41 Piston seals	63 Snap-ring	85 Output shaft
19 Cushion spring	42 Forward clutch piston	64 Thrust washer	86 Speedometer gear
20 Intermediate clutch plates	43 Return springs	65 Inner race	87 Sleeve
21 Pressure plate			

Transmission disassembly

8B.1 Using a large screwdriver pry the rear seal from the extension housing

8B.2 Remove the speedometer adapter and driven gear

8B.3 Remove the extension housing from the case

8B.4 Push the speedometer gear retaining clip down and carefully tap the gear off the output shaft. Be careful not to damage the gear

8B.5 A special speedometer drive gear puller is available to remove the gear without damage

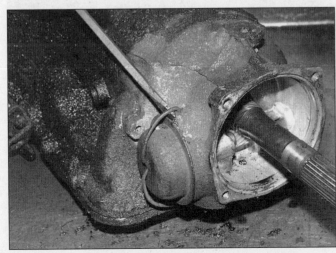

8B.6 If equipped, pry the bail from the governor cover . . .

8B.7 . . . and tap the cover off with a large screwdriver

8B.8 Withdraw the governor from the case

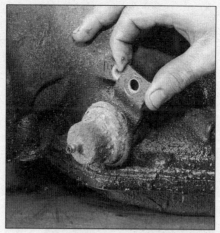

8B.9 Remove the vacuum modulator retainer . . .

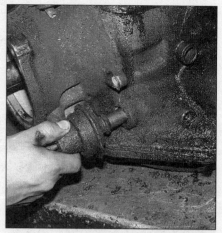

8B.10 . . . and pull the vacuum modulator from the case

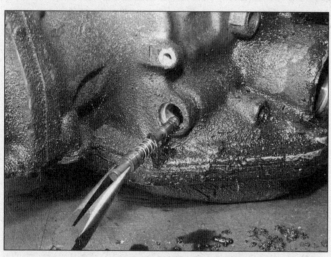

8B.11 Using a pair of needle-nose pliers, remove the modulator valve

8B.12 Insert a small punch or nail into the hole behind the accumulator cover snap-ring and pry the snap-ring from the case

8B.13 Remove the 1-2 accumulator cover and O-ring . . .

8B.14 . . . and the 1-2 accumulator spring

8B.15 Use a pair of snap-ring pliers to grasp the inside of the 1-2 accumulator piston and withdraw it from the case - DO NOT remove the Teflon oil seal rings; if they are damaged, replace the piston assembly

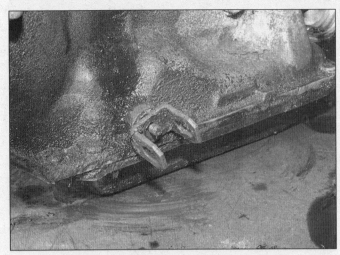

8B.16 Remove the manual shaft linkage lever

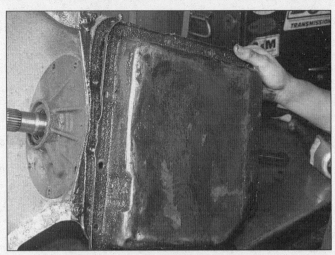

8B.17 Remove the transmission oil pan

8B.18 Remove the oil filter

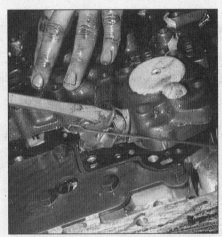

8B.19 Pry the actuator pin from the detent valve lever and remove the detent control link. Note how the detent control link is installed so there's no confusion on reassembly

8B.20 First remove the manual lever detent roller and spring assembly, then remove all the valve body bolts

8B.21 Lift the valve body off and disconnect the manual valve S-link. Carefully remove the manual valve from the valve body and set it aside

8B.22 Compress the 2-3 accumulator piston and remove the E-clip

8B.23 Remove the 2-3 accumulator piston . . .

8B.24 . . . and spring - DO NOT remove the Teflon oil seal ring from the piston; if it's damaged, replace the piston assembly

8B.25 Remove the spacer support plate . . .

8B.26 . . . and the valve body gaskets and spacer plate

8B.27 Remove the intermediate servo piston, apply pin and spring - DO NOT remove the Teflon oil seal ring from the piston; if it's damaged, replace the piston assembly

8B.28 Using a small magnet, remove the check balls from the case - Note carefully the location of each check ball

8B.29 Remove the park lock bracket

8B.30 Pry the manual shaft retainer from the manual shaft

8B.31 Remove the range selector jam-nut from the manual shaft

8B.32 Remove the parking pawl actuator rod and range lever assembly

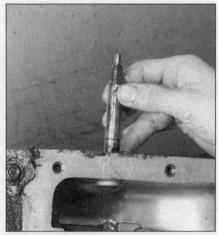

8B.33 Remove the manual shaft from the case. If the manual shaft will not pull through the case easily, deburr the shaft with a flat file

8B.34 Remove the oil pump bolts, install slide-hammers into the threaded holes and bump the pump loose from the case

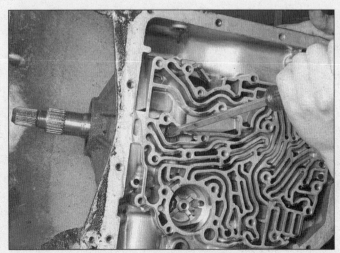

8B.35 If slide-hammers are not available, pry the pump loose with a large screwdriver or prybar. Be careful not to damage the case

8B.36 Place the pump assembly on the bench and remove the five oil pump bolts (arrows)

8B.37 Separate the pump body from the pump cover. Remove the intermediate clutch piston spring retainer, springs and piston. Remove the lip seal from the piston. Remove the selective thrust washer from the hub

8B.38 Remove the oil pump rotors from the pump body. Some models may have a priming valve and spring - don't lose it

8B.39 Pry the oil seal from the pump cover

8B.40 Use a long screwdriver to unhook the intermediate band anchor from the case

8B.41 Grasp the input shaft and withdraw the complete clutch pack assembly and band from the case

8B.42 Remove the intermediate clutches . . .

8B.43 . . . the intermediate band . . .

8D.44 . . . and the direct clutch drum from the forward clutch/input shaft assembly

8B.45 Remove the direct clutch drum-to-forward clutch housing thrust bearing

8B.46 Pry the direct clutch pressure plate retaining ring out of the groove with a small screwdriver

8B.47 Remove the direct clutch plates from the drum

8B.48 Using a spring compressor, compress the spring retainer and remove the snap-ring. Release the spring pressure slowly. If a spring compressor isn't available, use two C-clamps to compress the spring retainer

8B.49 Remove the spring assembly . . .

8B.50 . . . and the direct clutch piston

8B.51 Remove the inner and outer seals from the piston

8B.52 Turn the drum over and remove the intermediate overrun clutch snap-ring

8B.53 Remove the retainer . . .

8B.54 . . . the outer race . . .

8B.55 . . . and the roller clutch assembly

8B.56 Remove the forward clutch pressure plate retaining ring . . .

8B.57 . . . and remove the forward clutch plates from the housing

8B.58 Compress the forward clutch spring retainer and remove the snap-ring

8B.59 Remove the spring retainer and springs. Note the color code of the springs and do not mix them with the direct clutch springs

8B.60 Remove the forward clutch piston . . .

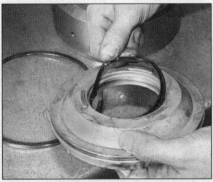

8B.61 . . . and remove the inner and outer seals from the piston

8B.62 Remove the forward clutch housing-to-input ring gear thrust washer

8B.63 Remove the input ring gear from the case

8B.64 Remove the input ring gear-to-output carrier thrust bearing

8B.65 Remove the output carrier-to-output shaft snap-ring . . .

8B.66 . . . and remove the output carrier assembly from the case

8B.67 Remove the sun gear shell. . .

8B.68 . . . and the sun gear shell thrust washer

8B.69 Pry the low-reverse roller clutch retaining ring from the case lugs

8B.70 It may take some effort, but grasp the output shaft and pull the low-reverse clutch support assembly from the case

8B.71 If you encounter difficulty in clearing the case lugs with the support, use a pair of snap-ring pliers to turn the support as you pull on the output shaft

8B.72 Retrieve the clutch support retaining spring from inside the case

8B.73 Invert the assembly on the bench and remove the output shaft and ring gear assembly from the reaction carrier

8B.74 Remove the output ring gear-to-case thrust bearing (it may be in the case)

8B.75 Remove the output ring gear-to-reaction carrier thrust bearing from inside the ring gear

8B.76 Remove the reaction carrier assembly . . .

8B.77 . . . and the low-reverse clutch plates from the low-reverse roller clutch support

8B.78 Using a small screwdriver, pry the roller clutch retaining ring from the support

8B.79 Turn the support assembly over . . .

8B.80 . . . and push the inner race and roller clutch assembly out of the support

8B.81 You'll need a special spring compressor to remove the low-reverse piston

8B.82 Lock the compressor in the case lugs, compress the low-reverse clutch piston spring retainer and remove the snap-ring

8B.83 Release the spring pressure, remove the tool and remove the spring retainer and springs

8B.84 Set the case upright and carefully apply air pressure to the reverse oil passage . . .

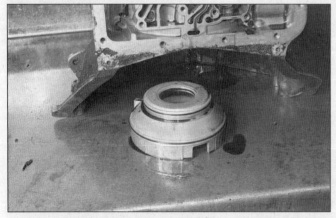

8B.85 . . . to blow the piston out of the case. Be very careful not to injure yourself; the piston will come out with some force (place some rags on the bench to prevent damaging the piston)

8B.86 Remove the inner, outer and center seals from the piston

Component inspection and subassembly

Using an approved cleaning solvent, clean and dry all the components thoroughly, including the case. Do not use rags to wipe the components dry, lint from the rag may lodge in the oil passages causing a valve to stick.

Inspect the following transmission components and repair or replace as necessary:

a) *Case: Inspect the exterior of the case for damage, cracks and porosity. Check the valve body surface for damage and flatness. Check all the oil passages, the accumulator bore, the speedometer bore and the governor bore for damage. Check all threaded holes for damage. Damaged threads may be repaired by drilling, tapping and installing thread inserts. Check the oil cooler line fittings for damage. Check the interior of the case for damaged retaining ring grooves. Check the case lugs for excessive wear. Check the output shaft bushing for wear. Inspect the manual linkage and the park lock linkage for damage.*

b) **Intermediate clutch pack, overrun brake band and roller clutch assembly** - Inspect the condition of the clutch plates. Check for signs of overheating. Check the friction plates for wear, pitting, cracking or flaking. Check the intermediate band for wear or damage. Inspect the intermediate overrun roller clutch for damaged rollers or springs. Check the race finish for scoring, wear or damage.

c) **Direct and forward clutch assemblies** - Inspect the condition of the clutch plates. Check for signs of overheating. Check the friction plates for wear, pitting, cracking or flaking. Check the pistons for damage. Check the return springs for damage or signs of overheating. Check the bushings for wear or damage. Check the check balls for damage and freedom of movement. Check the input shaft for scoring or damages splines.

d) **Output carrier, input ring gear and sun gear** - Inspect the output carrier, input ring gear and sun gear drive shell for damaged teeth or splines. Check for worn bushings. Check the needle thrust bearings for wear or damage. Inspect the pinion gear bearings for wear or damage. Check the endplay of each pinion gear - it should be between 0.009 and 0.024-inch.

e) **Low-reverse clutch pack and roller clutch assembly** - Inspect the condition of the clutch plates. Check for signs of overheating. Check the friction plates for wear, pitting, cracking or flaking. Inspect the roller clutch for worn or damage rollers. Check the springs for damage. Check the race finish for scoring, wear or damage.

f) **Output shaft and reaction carrier** - Inspect the output shaft for damages splines, scoring or worn bushings. Check the reaction carrier for damaged gear teeth or worn needle bearings. Check the needle thrust bearings for wear or damage. Inspect the pinion gear bearings for wear or damage. Check the endplay of each pinion gear - it should be between 0.009 and 0.024-inch.

Oil pump assembly

Clean the oil pump components with solvent and air dry. Inspect the gears and gear pocket for scoring or damage. Check the hub for damaged sealing ring grooves. Inspect the stator shaft bushings for wear or damage. Inspect the pump cover and body faces for nicks or burrs and make sure the oil passages and lubrication holes are not restricted. Place the pump body over the cover and check for warpage. Try to insert a feeler gage between the two mating surfaces around the circumference of the pump - there should be no gap greater than 0.003-inch.

Control valve assembly

Lay the control valve assembly on a clean work surface and begin removing the valves from the valve body. Working on one valve at a time, remove the roll pin and bore plug. Withdraw the bushings, valves and springs and lay them out on a clean lint-free towel in the EXACT order of removal. Keep them in the proper orientation to the valve body. Remove the E-clip from the accumulator piston and remove the piston and spring (use a small C-clamp to depress the piston if necessary). Clean all the bushings, valves and springs. Check the valves and bushings closely for scoring, cracks or damage. Check the

8B.88 Drive out the pump body bushing and install a new bushing in the pump body

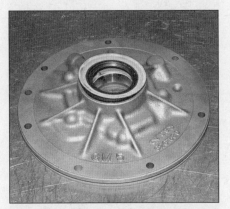

8B.89 Install a new front pump oil seal in the pump body

8B.90 Replace the stator shaft bushings, if worn or damaged

8B.91 Install the front stator shaft bushing 1/4-inch below the top of the stator shaft. Install the rear stator shaft bushings with the inside bushing 1-1/32 inch below the top surface of the pump hub and the outside bushing 0.010-inch below the chamfer - Make sure the bushings do not block the oil delivery hole (arrow)

8B.92 Install the pump gears into the pump body with the offset drive tangs on the drive gear (arrow) facing to the rear, away from the seal. Lubricate the gears and pump body pocket liberally with ATF. Install the priming valve and spring, if equipped.

8B.93 Install the inner and outer lip seals on the intermediate clutch piston with the seal lips facing into the pump cover bore

8B.94 Lubricate the seals and bore with ATF and install the piston. Use a seal installation tool to work the seal lips into the bore. Press the piston in until it's fully seated - you should be able to turn the piston in the bore, if installed properly

8B.95 Place the intermediate clutch return springs onto the posts, evenly spaced around the piston

8B.96 Install the spring retainer and place the bolts through the holes

8B.97 Place the pump cover over the pump body and align the bolt holes. Draw the two halves together and install the bolts finger-tight

8B.98 Install the alignment band around the pump assembly, align the bolt holes and tighten the band

8B.99 Tighten the pump bolts to 18 to 20 ft-lbs

Note
If an alignment band is not available, the pump can be aligned by placing the assembled pump upside-down into the transmission case (without the O-ring installed). Align the bolt holes with a screwdriver or pick and tighten the bolts

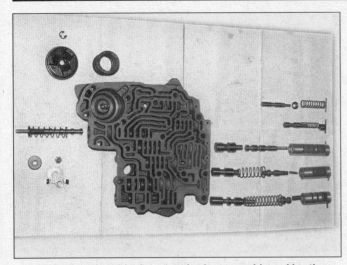

8B.101 Disassemble the control valve assembly and lay the components out on a clean lint-free towel. Clean and inspect the valve body and components. Check each valve for nicks or burrs. Finally, reassemble the valve body and check each valve for freedom of movement in its bore

springs for collapsed or distorted coils. Check the accumulator piston and teflon ring for damage. It is not necessary to replace the accumulator teflon ring unless it is damaged (the replacement ring will be cast iron). Finally check the valve body bores for scoring or damage and begin reassembly.

Governor

Inspect the governor weights for freedom of movement. Check the weight springs for distortion or damage. Check the governor valve for freedom of movement. Check the governor sleeve for nicks, scoring or damage. Check the governor gear for nicks or damaged teeth. See THM400 governor section for gear replacement procedures, if necessary.

Transmission assembly

An automatic transmission is a precision fit piece of equipment. Install each component as shown, do not force any component into place. If it doesn't fit properly, find out why and rectify the situation. Maintain a clean work place and lubricate all moving parts as they are installed. Lubricate thrust washers and bearings with automatic transmission fluid (ATF) or petroleum jelly. Use petroleum jelly to retain thrust washers and check balls in their proper location as the component is installed. Dip all friction plates in ATF before installation.

Forward clutch assembly

8B.104 Install the inner and outer seals on the forward clutch piston with the seal lips facing into the housing bore

8B.105 Lubricate the seals and the housing bore with ATF and install the piston into the housing

8B.106 Work the seal lips into the housing with a seal installation tool. If the piston is properly installed you will be able to rotate the piston in the bore

8B.107 Install the springs in the pockets and spring retainer over the springs

8B.108 Compress the spring retainer with a spring compressor or two C-clamps and install the snap-ring

8B.109 Release the spring compressor and make sure the snap-ring is seated in the groove and is inside the four tabs in the retainer (arrow)

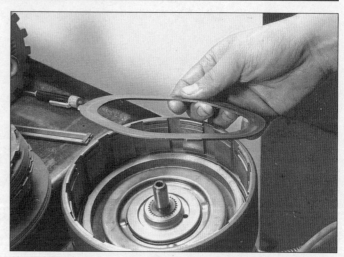

8B.110 Install the cushion spring and a steel plate in the housing . . .

8B.111 . . . followed by a friction plate. Dip all friction plates in ATF before installation. Alternate steel plates and friction plates until all forward clutch plates are installed

8B.112 Install the forward clutch pressure plate . . .

8B.113 . . . and retaining ring. Make sure the retaining ring is seated in the groove

8B.114 Check the clearance between the top plate and the pressure plate with a feeler gauge. For optimum performance the clearance should be held between 0.015 to 0.030-inch. If the clearance is not as specified, different thickness pressure plates are available at a dealership parts department

Direct clutch and intermediate overrun roller clutch assembly

8B.117 Install the inner and outer seals onto the direct clutch piston with the seal lips facing into the housing bore. Install the center seal in the direct clutch drum with the seal lip facing up

8B.118 Lubricate the seals and housing bore with ATF and install the piston into the housing

8B.119 Work the seal lips into the housing bore with a seal installation tool. If the piston is properly installed you will be able to rotate the piston in the bore

8B.120 Install the springs in the pockets and spring retainer over the springs

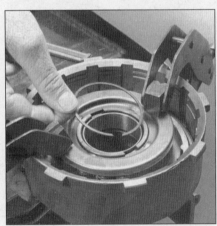

8B.121 Compress the spring retainer with a spring compressor or two C-clamps and install the snap-ring

8B.122 Release the spring compressor and make sure the snap-ring is seated in the groove and is inside the four tabs in the retainer (arrow)

8B.123 Install a steel plate in the housing followed by a friction plate. Dip all friction plates in ATF before installation. Alternate steel plates and friction plates until all direct clutch plates are installed

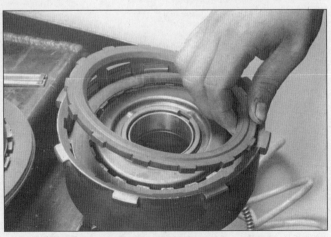

8B.124 Install the direct clutch pressure plate . . .

8B.125 . . . and retaining ring. Make sure the retaining ring is seated in the groove

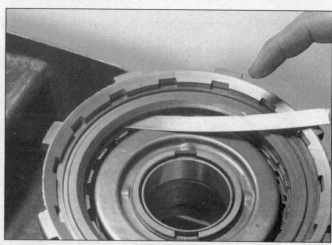

8B.126 Check the clearance between the top plate and the pressure plate with a feeler gauge. For optimum performance the clearance should be held between 0.060 to 0.080-inch. If the clearance is not as specified, different thickness pressure plates are available at a dealership parts department

8B.127 Turn the direct clutch housing over and install the intermediate overrun roller clutch onto the inner race - if a roller happens to fall out, install it from inside the cage to avoid damaging the spring

8B.128 When installed properly the four lube holes are facing up (arrows)

8B.129 Install the outer race, rotating it in a counterclockwise direction as you set it in place

8B.130 Install the retainer and the retaining ring, seating the retaining ring in the groove

8B.131 When properly assembled, the outer race will rotate in a counterclockwise direction only and will lock-up if you attempt to turn it clockwise

Low-reverse roller clutch assembly

8B.133 Install the roller clutch into the low-reverse support -
If a roller falls out during assembly, install it from the
outside-in to avoid damaging the springs

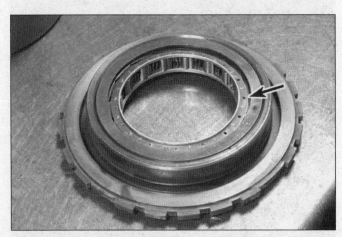

8B.134 When installed properly the lube holes (arrow) will face to
the rear of the transmission

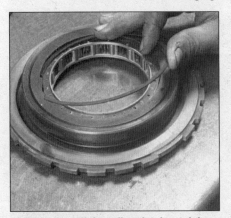

8B.135 Install the roller clutch retaining
ring in the support groove

8B.136 Install the inner race, turning it
counterclockwise to engage the rollers

8B.137 With the low-reverse roller clutch
assembled properly, the inner race will
only rotate counterclockwise
(as viewed from the backside)

Final assembly

Final assembly of the transmission is easier with the transmission
positioned vertically. If a holding fixture is not available, secure the
transmission case to a sturdy workbench in an upright position.

8B.138 Install the three square-cut seals
on the low-reverse piston

8B.139 Lubricate the seals with ATF and
install the piston in the case. Align the tab
on the piston (arrow) with the notch in the
case. This will place the cut-out in the
piston adjacent to the parking pawl

8B.140 Seat the piston firmly in the case
and install the piston return springs
onto the posts

8B.141 Install the spring retainer with the cupped side over the springs

8B.142 A special low-reverse piston spring compressor is necessary to compress the springs

8B.143 Install the spring compressor, locking it into the case lugs

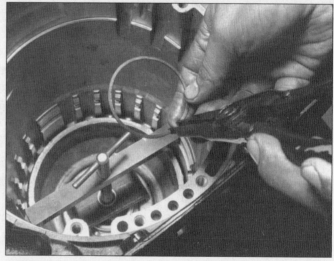

8B.144 Compress the spring retainer and install the snap-ring

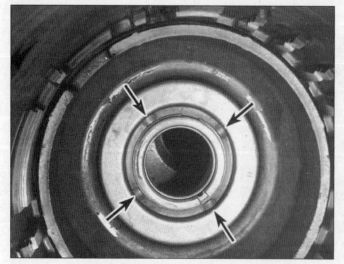

8B.145 Remove the spring compressor and make sure the snap-ring is fully seated in the groove and inside the four retainer tabs (arrows)

8B.146 Install the output ring gear onto the output shaft, meshing the splines

8B.147 Install a new output shaft snap-ring (usually provided in the overhaul kit) onto the output shaft to retain the ring gear. Do not over-stress the snap-ring and make sure it's fully seated in the groove

8B.148 Install a new plastic output shaft bushing (usually provided in the overhaul kit) into the end of the shaft. Press it in until it's fully seated

8B.149 Install the reaction carrier-to-output ring gear needle thrust bearing with the outer lip facing up. Retain the bearing with petroleum jelly

Note

Early models may use a three-tabbed thrust washer instead of a needle thrust bearing between the reaction carrier and the output ring gear. Install the three-tabbed washer, retaining it with petroleum jelly, if equipped

8B.150 Install the output ring gear-to-case needle thrust bearing with the inner lip facing toward the rear of the transmission. Retain the bearing with petroleum jelly

8B.151 Lubricate the pinion gears and thrust bearings with ATF and install the reaction carrier assembly into the output ring gear, meshing the pinions into the ring gear teeth

8B.152 Set the reaction carrier/output shaft assembly into the case. Rotate the output shaft in the case - it must turn freely, with no binding or rough spots

8B.153 Install the low-reverse clutch plates, starting with a steel plate and alternating friction plates until all the low-reverse plates are installed. Dip the friction plates in ATF before installation and mesh the splines with the reaction carrier. The number of plates used depends on the model - install the exact number of plates originally removed

8B.154 Liberally apply petroleum jelly to the clutch support retaining spring . . .

8B.155 . . . and install it into the wide space between case lugs with the open end up (arrow)

8B.156 Install the low-reverse roller clutch/support assembly, aligning the splines with the case lugs. Press the support assembly down firmly seating it past the support retaining spring and engaging the roller clutch inner race with the reaction carrier

8B.157 Install the low-reverse clutch support retaining ring, seating it fully in the case groove. Install the retaining ring with the end against the retaining spring (arrow)

Note

Check the low roller clutch again - the inner race should only rotate clockwise - if it turns counterclockwise, the roller clutch is installed upside down and the transmission will not operate in Drive

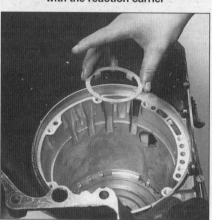

8B.158 Install the four-tab sun shell thrust washer, engaging the tabs with the roller clutch inner race. Retain the washer with petroleum jelly

8B.159 Lubricate the bushings with ATF and install the sun gear drive shell, seating it on the thrust washer and engaging the teeth with the reaction carrier. Rotate the sun shell - it should turn freely in both directions

8B.160 Install the four-tab thrust washer onto the output carrier (some models may use a needle thrust bearing instead; install the needle thrust bearing with the lip facing down, if equipped). Retain the thrust washer or bearing with petroleum jelly

8B.161 Lubricate the pinion gears and thrust washer with ATF and install the output carrier into the sun shell, meshing the pinion gears with the sun gear teeth until fully seated

8B.162 Install a new output shaft snap-ring (usually provided in the overhaul kit) to retain the output carrier to the output shaft. Do not overstress the snap-ring and make sure it's fully seated in the groove

8B.163 Install the three-tab thrust washer onto the input ring gear. Retain the washer with petroleum jelly

8B.164 Lubricate the bushing and thrust washer with ATF and install the input ring gear onto the output carrier assembly, meshing the ring gear teeth with the output carrier pinion gears

8B.165 Rotate the ring gear - it should turn freely in both directions but more resistance will be felt in the counterclockwise direction

8B.166 Install the forward clutch needle thrust bearing with black-oxide inner race against the forward clutch housing

8B.167 Place the direct clutch drum over the input shaft and lower it onto the forward clutch hub. Engage the direct clutch plates into the splines as you rotate the housing. When properly installed the direct clutch drum will sit level and spin freely on the forward clutch housing

8B.168 Holding the assembly by the input shaft, lower the clutch assembly into the case. Rotate the housing, engaging the forward clutch plates onto the input ring gear splines

8B.169 When properly installed, the tabs on the direct clutch drum will engage the slots in the sun gear drive shell (arrow)

8B.170 Install the intermediate band over the clutch housing

8B.171 Use a screwdriver to engage the band anchor into the case boss properly (arrow). Insert a long, thin screwdriver through the servo hole in the case to center the other end of the band

8B.172 Install the intermediate clutch pressure plate with the flat face up. Engage the tabs with the case splines - it will only go in one way

8B.173 Dip the friction plates in ATF and install the friction plates . . .

8B.174 . . . and steel plates, alternating each plate and ending with a steel plate

8B.175 Install the intermediate clutch cushion spring

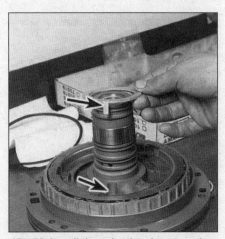

8B.176 Install the selective thrust washer over the oil pump hub. Engage the tab with the slot in the pump (arrows). Later models may use a selective shim and a needle thrust bearing instead of the washer

8B.177 Install new direct clutch and forward clutch sealing rings onto the pump hub (arrows). Hook the ends together properly and check the rings for freedom of movement in the grooves. If the rings do not spin freely use a small file to deburr the grooves

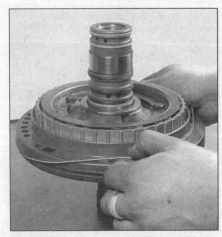

8B.178 Install a new pump O-ring with the stripe facing out. Lubricate the O-ring, sealing rings and thrust washer liberally with ATF

8B.179 Install two pump alignment bolts in opposite sides of the case (arrows) . . .

8B.180 . . . and install the oil pump-to-case gasket, aligning the holes in the gasket with the case holes

8B.181 Lubricate the case bore and clutch housings with ATF. Align the pump with the bolt holes and set the pump over the alignment bolts. Press the pump into the case by hand until fully seated. Rotate the input shaft as you seat the pump; if the shaft binds before the pump is fully seated, a thrust washer is out of place or a clutch plate is not engaged - remove the clutch assembly and correct this condition before proceeding

8B.182 Mount a dial indicator to the case with the needle positioned on the end of the input shaft. Zero the indicator, lever the shaft up and down and check the endplay. Correct endplay should be between 0.015 to 0.030-inch. If it's not, remove the pump and change the selective thrust washer with one of a different size. Selective thrust washers are available at a dealership parts department

8B.183 When the endplay is correct, remove the alignment bolts, install new sealing washers on the pump bolts, install the bolts and tighten them to 20 ft-lbs

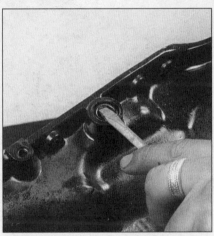

8B.184 Place the transmission on the workbench in a horizontal position. Pry the manual shaft seal from the case

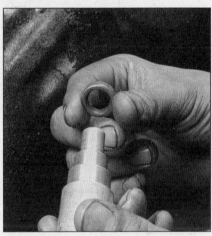

8B.185 Install a new manual shaft seal with the appropriate size driver (a deep socket may be used)

8B.186 Drive the seal into the bore until seated

8B.187 Install the park-lock bracket and tighten the bolts to 29 ft-lbs

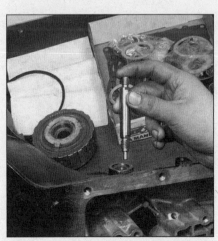

8B.188 Lubricate the manual shaft with ATF and install the shaft

8B.189 Connect the detent lever with the park-lock rod and install the linkage assembly, engaging the actuating rod with the parking pawl

8B.190 Slip the manual shaft through the detent lever, engaging the slot. Install the jam-nut and tighten it to 30 ft-lbs

8B.191 Install the manual shaft retaining clip securely over the shaft

8B.192 Install new metal rings on the 1-2 accumulator piston if it originally had metal rings. If it has Teflon rings, DO NOT remove the Teflon rings. Lubricate the rings with ATF and install the piston in the case bore as shown

8B.193 Install the 1-2 accumulator spring

8B.194 Install the 1-2 accumulator cover O-ring into the case

8B.195 Lubricate the O-ring with ATF and install the cover

8B.196 Depress the cover and install the retaining ring in the groove (a special tool is available to depress the spring; it makes the job much easier, but is not entirely necessary)

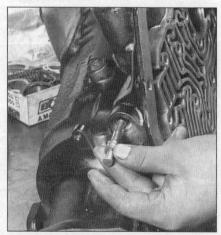

8B.197 Lubricate the modulator valve with ATF and install it into the case. Make sure it moves freely in the bore

8B.198 Install the O-ring on the modulator, lubricate with ATF and install it into the case (a new modulator is recommended anytime the transmission is rebuilt)

8B.199 Install the modulator retainer and tighten the bolt to 12 ft-lbs

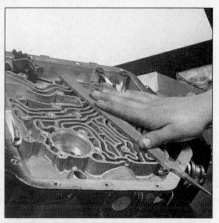

8B.200 Run a flat file over the valve body surface to remove any burrs. Blow the surface and passages out with compressed air to remove any metal filings

8B.201 Install the check balls in the locations shown (retain the balls with petroleum jelly) - Install a check ball in location "A" ONLY if equipped with a lock-up torque converter

8B.202 Install the intermediate servo piston spring into the case

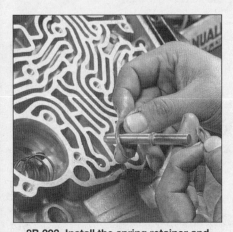

8B.203 Install the spring retainer and washer over the pin as shown and install the assembly into the case, retaining the spring

8B.204 Install a new metal ring on the intermediate servo piston if originally equipped with a metal ring. If equipped with a Teflon ring DO NOT remove the Teflon ring. Lubricate the ring with ATF and install the piston, dished side up, over the pin

8B.205 Install two alignment bolts into the threaded holes . . .

8B.206 . . . and place the valve body-to-case gasket . . .

8B.207 . . . the spacer plate . . .

8B.208 . . . and the spacer plate-to-valve body gaskets
over the alignment bolts

8B.209 Install the spacer support plate and tighten
the bolts finger-tight

8B.210 Install the manual valve and link in the valve body, lower
the valve body over the alignment bolts and engage
the manual valve link with the detent lever

8B.211 Install the valve body bolts finger-tight, then
install the detent roller and spring

8B.212 Tighten the valve body bolts, spacer support bolts and detent spring bolt to 12 ft-lbs, working from the center out and tightening the detent spring last

8B.213 Install a new oil filter and gasket. Tighten the screws securely

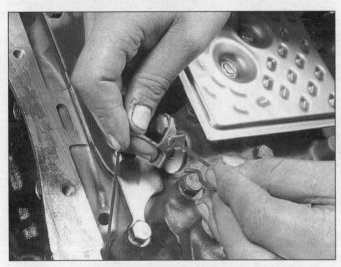

8B.214 Connect the detent control valve wire to the detent control linkage and connect the linkage to the detent valve with the spring clip

8B.215 Install a new oil pan gasket. Install the oil pan and tighten the oil pan bolts to 12 ft-lbs

8B.216 Place the speedometer drive gear retaining clip into the hole in the output shaft

8B.217 Slip the gear over the output shaft and slide it over the retainer . . .

8B.218 . . . until the retainer springs catch the backside of the gear (arrow)

8B.219 Drive a new bushing squarely into the extension housing . . .

8B.220 . . . followed by a seal

8B.221 Place a new O-ring over the extension housing, lubricate with ATF and install the extension housing. Tighten the bolts to 35 ft-lbs

8B.222 Lubricate the governor bore with ATF and install the governor

8B.223 Install a new O-ring on the cover and install the cover

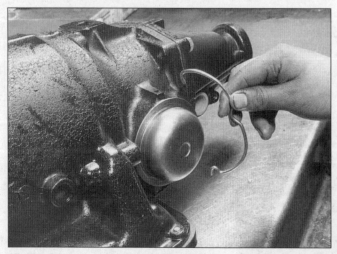

8B.224 Tap the outer edge of the cover with a soft-faced hammer until it's seated and install the bail, if equipped

8B.225 Install the speedometer gear with new seals and install new seals into the dipstick and detent cable holes. Install the torque converter and the transmission is ready for installation into the vehicle

Chapter 8 Part C
Disassembly, inspection and assembly
THM400 transmission

Introduction

The THM400 is a three-speed automatic transmission manufactured for rear-wheel drive vehicles. The major components of this transmission are:

a) *Torque converter*
b) *Gear-type oil pump*
c) *Control valve assembly*
d) *Two bands*
e) *Three separate multiple disc clutch packs*
f) *Two roller clutches (or one roller clutch and one sprag, depending on model)*
g) *Compound planetary gear set*

Follow the photographic sequence for disassembly, inspection and assembly. The model shown is a typical transmission of this type. Differences do exist between models and many changes have been made over the years, so perform each step in order and lay the components out on a clean work bench in the EXACT ORDER of removal to prevent confusion during reassembly. Many snap-rings and clutch plates are similar in size, but must not be interchanged. Keep the individual parts together with the component from which they were removed to avoid mix-ups. Save all old parts and compare them with the new part to ensure they are an exact match before reassembly. Pay particular attention to the stack-up of the various clutch packs. Differences do exist between models and your transmission may not match the stack-up shown. Note the exact location of the check balls in the case. Save all the old parts until the overhaul is complete and the transmission has been thoroughly road tested; old components can be useful in diagnosing any problems that may arise.

Basic hand tools can be used for most procedures, although some special tools are required. Alternate procedures are shown where possible, but some procedures can only be accomplished with special tools. Read through the entire overhaul procedure before beginning work to familiarize yourself with the procedures and identify any special tools that may be needed. Thoroughly clean the exterior of the transmission before beginning disassembly.

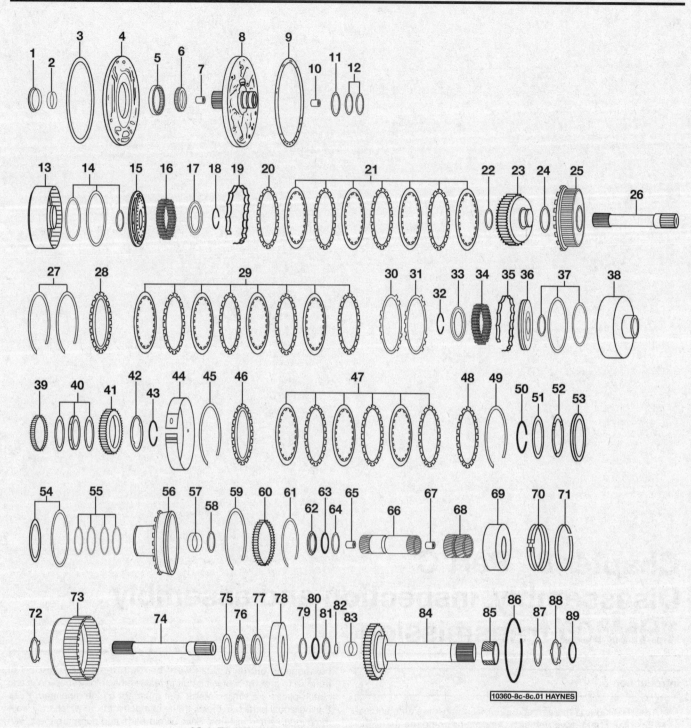

8C.1 Exploded view of the typical THM400 internal components

1	Front seal	12	Sealing rings	23	Forward clutch hub
2	Pump body bushing	13	Forward clutch housing	24	Thrust washer
3	O-ring	14	Forward clutch piston seals	25	Direct clutch hub
4	Pump body	15	Forward clutch piston	26	Input shaft
5	Pump driven gear	16	Piston release springs	27	Retaining rings
6	Pump drive gear	17	Release spring retainer	28	Direct clutch backing plate
7	Bushing	18	Snap-ring	29	Direct clutch plates
8	Pump cover	19	Apply ring	30	Waved clutch plate
9	Gasket	20	Forward clutch waved plate	31	Dished clutch plate
10	Bushing	21	Forward clutch plates	32	Snap-ring
11	Thrust washer	22	Thrust washer	33	Release spring retainer

Transmission disassembly

8C.2 Begin disassembly by removing the vacuum modulator

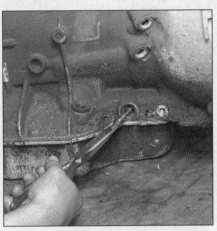

8C.3 Withdraw the modulator valve from the case

8C.4 Remove the four bolts, then the governor cover . . .

8C.5 . . . and withdraw the governor from the case

8C.6 Remove the speedometer gear adapter and gear and remove the extension housing

8C.7 Remove the transmission oil pan, remove the bolt retaining the transmission oil filter (arrow) and withdraw the filter from the case

34 Piston release springs	53 Intermediate clutch piston	72 Thrust washer
35 Apply ring	54 Intermediate clutch piston seals	73 Output carrier assembly
36 Direct clutch piston	55 Oil seal rings	74 Main shaft
37 Direct clutch piston seals	56 Center support	75 Thrust bearing race
38 Direct clutch housing	57 Bushing	76 Thrust bearing
39 Intermediate clutch roller assembly	58 Thrust washer	77 Thrust bearing race
40 Sprag assembly	59 Retaining ring	78 Rear internal gear
41 Intermediate clutch race	60 Low roller clutch assembly	79 Thrust bearing race
42 Intermediate clutch retainer	61 Reaction drum spacer	80 Thrust bearing
43 Snap-ring	62 Thrust bearing race	81 Thrust bearing race
44 Intermediate (front) band assembly	63 Thrust bearing	82 Snap-ring
45 Retaining ring	64 Thrust bearing race	83 Bushing
46 Intermediate clutch backing plate	65 Bushing	84 Output shaft
47 Intermediate clutch plates	66 Sun gear shaft	85 Speedometer drive gear
48 Waved clutch plate	67 Bushing	86 Retaining ring
49 Center support retaining ring	68 Sun gear	87 Thrust washer
50 Snap-ring	69 Reaction carrier assembly	88 Selective thrust washer
51 Intermediate clutch spring assembly	70 Rear band	89 O-ring
52 Intermediate clutch guide	71 Front internal gear ring	

8C.8 Remove the valve body retaining bolts

8C.9 Lift the valve body up and disconnect the manual valve linkage from the manual valve

8C.10 Pry the valve body-to-governor pipes free from the case

8C.11 Separate the valve body from the transmission and remove the manual valve from the valve body

8C.12 Remove the governor pipes from the valve body

8C.13 Remove the valve body gasket and set the valve body aside for later cleaning, disassembly and inspection

8C.14 Remove the rear servo cover and gasket . . .

8C.15 . . . and withdraw the rear servo, accumulator piston and spring from the case

8C.16 Separate the accumulator piston and spring from the rear servo piston

8C.17 Remove the front servo piston, retainer and spring

8C.18 Remove the detent solenoid from the case and disconnect the lead from the electrical connector

8C.19 Remove the valve body spacer plate and gaskets

8C.20 Remove the check balls from the case. Note the location of each ball for reassembly (arrows)

8C.21 Using a thin walled, 12-point, 3/8-inch deep socket, remove the center support bolt

8C.22 Remove the oil pump bolts

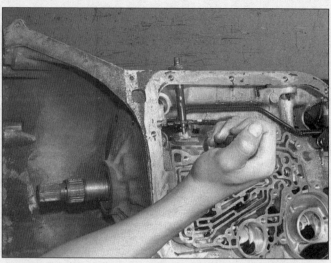

8C.23 Use two slide-hammers threaded into the front pump bolt holes to bump the pump loose from the case. If the slide-hammers are not available, insert a large screwdriver or prybar behind the front pump as shown . . .

8C.24 . . . and pry the pump loose from the case

8C.25 Remove the pump cover-to-body bolts and separate the pump halves

8C.26 Remove the gears from the pump body

8C.27 Using a large screwdriver, pry the old seal from the pump cover

8C.28 Grasp the input shaft and remove the forward clutch assembly from the case

8C.29 Invert the forward clutch assembly and remove the retaining ring from the direct clutch driving hub

8C.30 Separate the direct clutch driving hub from the forward clutch assembly

8C.31 Remove the forward clutch hub from the housing and . . .

8C.32 . . . remove the thrust washers from on top . . .

8C.33 . . . and inside the forward clutch hub

8C.34 Remove the forward clutch plates

8C.35 Mount the forward clutch housing in a press

8C.36 Depress the spring retainer, remove the snap-ring and release the press

8C.37 Remove the spring retainer and all the springs from the housing

8C.38 Remove the forward clutch piston from the housing

8C.39 Remove the apply ring, if it comes loose from the piston

8C.40 Remove the inner and outer seals from the forward clutch piston

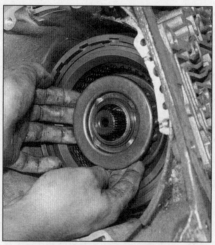

8C.41 Grasp the spring retainer and withdraw the direct clutch assembly from the case

8C.42 Remove the retaining ring . . .

8C.43 . . . and remove the direct clutch pack from the housing

8C.44 Mount the direct clutch housing in a spring compressor or press and remove the snap-ring, spring retainer, springs, direct clutch piston and seals in the same manner as the forward clutch

8C.45 Invert the direct clutch housing and remove the snap-ring retaining the intermediate roller clutch

8C.46 Remove the retainer . . .

8C.47 . . . and, while rotating the race clockwise, remove the roller clutch outer race

8C.48 Lift the intermediate roller clutch or sprag (depending on model) off the inner race. Be careful not to dislodge the rollers

8C.49 Reach into the case and withdraw the front band

8C.50 Pry the intermediate clutch retaining ring from the case lugs and remove the retaining ring

8C.51 Reach into the case and remove the intermediate clutch pack

8C.52 Pry the center support retaining ring from the case lugs . . .

8C.53 . . . and remove the retaining ring; note that this retaining ring is chamfered

8C.54 Reach in and grasp the center support and remove it from the case

8C.55 Remove the intermediate clutch snap ring . . .

8C.56 . . . and remove the intermediate clutch spring retainer, springs and spring guide

8C.57 Remove the intermediate clutch piston . . .

8C.58 . . . and remove the inner and outer seals

8C.59 Turn the center support over and remove the thrust bearing upper race, if its stuck to the center support

8C.60 Also remove the center support-to-reaction drum thrust washer

8C.61 Remove the sun gear shaft from the case and remove the thrust bearing and race from the shaft

8C.62 Remove the reaction carrier assembly from the case

8C.63 Remove the low roller clutch from the reaction carrier

8C.64 Remove the sun gear

8C.65 Grasp the mainshaft and lift the rear gear unit from the case

8C.66 Remove the silencing ring from the output carrier

8C.67 Remove the thrust washer from inside the output carrier

8C.68 Invert the assembly and remove the thrust washer from the output shaft

8C.69 Using a small screwdriver, pry off the output shaft-to-rear internal gear retaining ring . . .

8C.70 . . . and separate the output shaft from the rear internal gear assembly

8C.71 Remove the output shaft needle thrust bearing and races

8C.72 Separate the output carrier assembly from the rear internal gear and main shaft assembly . . .

8C.73 . . . and remove the sun gear-to-rear internal gear thrust bearing and races

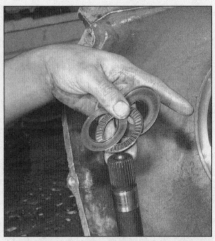

8C.74 Make sure you retrieve all three pieces of the bearing assembly

8C.75 Remove the selective case washer from the rear of the case

8C.76 Remove the low-reverse band from the case

8C.77 Some models are equipped with a center support spacer ring. Pry the spacer ring from the case lugs and remove the ring

8C.78 Using a pair of needle-nose pliers or side-cutters, remove the selector shaft retaining pin

8C.79 Loosen the jam-nut with an open-end wrench . . .

8C.80 . . . and remove the selector shaft from the case

8C.81 If the selector shaft is difficult to remove the end may be mushroomed - file the end of the shaft where it has contacted the detent lever

8C.82 Remove the park-lock linkage

8C.83 Remove the case electrical connector, knocking it out from the inside

Component inspection and subassembly

Using an approved cleaning solvent, clean and dry all the components thoroughly, including the case. Do not use rags to wipe the components dry, lint from the rag may lodge in the oil passages causing a valve to stick.

Inspect the following transmission components and repair or replace as necessary:

a) **Case:** Inspect the exterior of the case for damage, cracks and porosity. Check the valve body surface for damage and flatness. Check all the oil passages, the servo bore, the speedometer bore and the governor bore for damage.

Check all threaded holes for damage. Damaged threads may be repaired by drilling, tapping and installing thread inserts. Check the oil cooler line fittings for damage.

Check the interior of the case for damaged retaining ring grooves. Check the case lugs and band anchor pins for excessive wear. Check the output shaft bushing for wear. Inspect the manual linkage and the park lock linkage for damage.

b) **Forward, direct and intermediate clutch assemblies:** Inspect the input shaft for damaged splines. Inspect the check balls for looseness and the seal rings for damage.

Check the clutch housings, pistons, springs, spring retainers, clutch plates, backing plates and retainer rings for wear or damage. Check for nicks or burrs in the lip seal areas. Check the intermediate roller clutch assembly for wear, broken springs, spline damage and race finish wear. Check the housing and drum for worn bushings.

Check the direct clutch housing band apply surface for damage. Lay a steel ruler or straightedge across the surface and inspect for dishing. Inspect the intermediate band assembly and servo for damage or wear.

c) **Center support and gear unit assembly:** Inspect the center support for a worn or damaged bushing. Check the roller clutch inner race for wear or galling, and make sure the lubrication passage is clear. Check the oil seal ring grooves for nicks or damage.

Check for stripped splines, cracked or broken gear teeth, damaged or worn thrust bearings and bushings on the sun shaft, sun gear, main shaft, rear internal gear, reaction carrier, output carrier and output shaft. Check the low roller clutch for damaged rollers, springs or cage. Inspect the rear band for wear or damage. Check the band surface on the reaction carrier for signs of overheating or damage. If the band is extremely damaged or burned, check the band apply pin length with the special Band Apply Pin Tool (Kent-Moore J-21370, or equivalent).

Check the reaction carrier and output carrier pinion gears for broken teeth, damaged bearings or worn washers. Check the pinion endplay with a feeler gauge; it should be between 0.009 and 0.024-inch on all pinions.

Oil pump

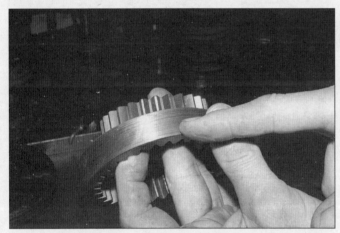

8C.85 Check the drive gear and driven gear for scoring, broken teeth or other damage. Note how the outer race of this driven gear is scored - it will cause a pump whine if reused

8C.86 Install a new gear set in place of the damaged gears. Always replace the gears as a set

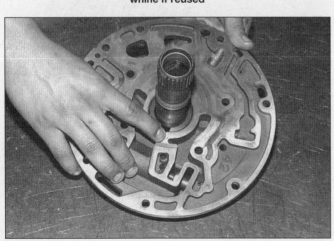

8C.87 Inspect the face of the pump cover for scores or nicks. Also inspect the stator shaft for damaged splines

8C.88 Inspect the pump cavity for scoring at the gear face . . .

8C.89 . . . and at the outer edge of the cavity. Check the threaded holes for damaged threads. If any part of the pump body or cover is damaged, replace the pump assembly

8C.90 Remove the sealing rings from the pump cover

8C.91 Remove the hook-type ring by depressing the ring and unhooking the locking tabs

8C.92 Check the sealing ring grooves for damage by working a new sealing ring around the groove. the ring should spin freely with about 0.002-inch clearance

8C.93 Small nicks or tight spots in the ring groove can be restored with a small file

8C.94 Remove the pressure regulator valve snap-ring . . .

8C.95 . . . and withdraw the pressure regulator boost valve, spring retainer, spacer and pressure regulator valve. Remove the retaining pin and the bore plug

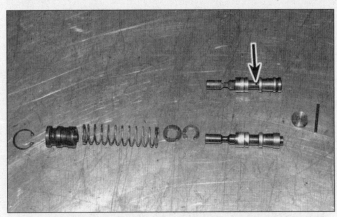

8C.96 Clean the parts thoroughly and check the valves for scoring or damage. Inspect the bore in the pump cover for nicks or damage. Check the pressure regulator valve and boost valve for freedom of movement - they should easily slide in and out of their bores. Two types of pressure regulator valve have been used, early model valves have a hole (arrow) while later model valves are solid

8C.97 If a solid pressure regulator valve is used, the pump cover must have a hole in this location. Do not use a solid valve with a cover which has no hole or vice-versa - the hole must be either in the valve or the cover, but not both

8C.98 Using a cape chisel or bushing removal tool, remove the pump body bushing

8C.99 Inspect the stator shaft front and rear bushings and replace if necessary. Drive the front stator shaft bushing out from the rear (a threaded bushing remover and slide hammer can also be used to remove the stator bushings)

8C.100 Drive the rear bushing out from the front

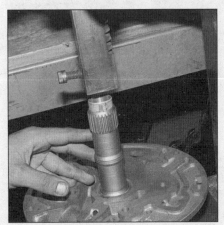

8C.101 Press the new bushings into the pump cover (a bushing driver and hammer can also be used to install the bushings, but a press installs them squarely into the bore)

8C.102 The appropriate size driver is needed to seat the front bushing

8C.103 The bushing is properly seated about 1/4-inch below the splined end of the stator shaft

8C.104 Install the rear stator
shaft bushing . . .

Note
*After new stator shaft
bushings are installed,
place the pump cover over
the transmission input
shaft and check for proper
fit. The cover should spin
freely on the shaft with no
binding or rough spots*

8C.105 . . . pressing it in with the appropriate drivers until it is
properly seated in the pump cover

8C.106 Install the pressure regulator valve, bore plug and
retaining pin into the pump cover

8C.107 Install the pressure regulator spring spacer or spacers over
the valve (either one or two spacer are used depending on the
model - installing two spacers will increase the transmission
line pressure)

8C.108 Install the spring retainer with the tabs toward
the spring . . .

8C.109 . . . and install the pressure regulator spring

8C.110 Install the pressure regulator boost valve in the bushing. Use petroleum jelly to retain the valve in the bushing

8C.111 Install the boost valve assembly and snap-ring into the bore. Make sure the snap-ring is fully seated in the groove

8C.112 Install the pump body bushing. Press or drive it into the bore with the appropriate tools

8C.113 Install the oil seal

8C.114 Run a flat file over the pump body to remove any nicks or burrs on the surface (be sure to clean any metal filings from the pump body)

8C.115 Install the driven gear in the pump body, then install the drive gear with the offset drive lugs (arrow) to the rear of the transmission (away from the seal). If there are any alignment marks on the gears, align them together and position them up

8C.116 Using feeler gauges and a straightedge, check the pump gear-to-body clearance. It should be between 0.0008 and 0.0035-inch

8C.117 Lubricate the pump gears liberally with ATF and align the pump cover with the pump body

8C.118 Bring the two halves together and install the bolts finger tight. Note the locations of the long bolts

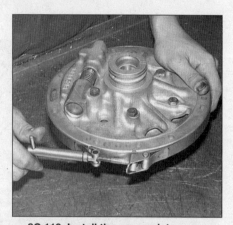

8C.119 Install the appropriate pump alignment band around the pump assembly

8C.120 Check the alignment of the pump-to-transmission case bolt holes and tighten the alignment band

8C.121 Tighten the five pump assembly bolts to 18 ft-lbs

Control valve assembly

Lay the control valve assembly on a clean work surface and begin removing the valves from the valve body. Working on one valve at a time, remove the roll pin and bore plug. Withdraw the bushings, valves and springs and lay them out on a clean lint-free towel in the EXACT order of removal. Keep them in the proper orientation to the valve body. Remove the E-clip from the accumulator piston and remove the piston and spring (use a small C-clamp to depress the piston if necessary). Clean all the bushings, valves and springs. Check the valves and bushings closely for scoring, cracks or damage. Check the springs for collapsed or distorted coils. Check the accumulator piston and teflon ring for damage. It is not necessary to replace the accumulator teflon ring unless it is damaged (the replacement ring will be cast iron). Finally, check the valve body bores for scoring or damage and begin reassembly.

8C.123 Coat the valves with ATF and assemble the valves and springs into their respective bushings or bores. Use an appropriate sized aluminum rod to seat the valves

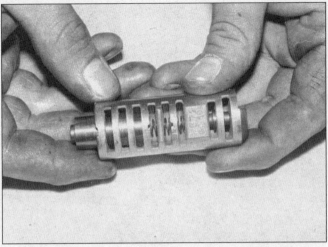

8C.124 Verify that the valve moves freely in the bushing bore

8C.125 Install the bore plug (note that the bore pug must be positioned properly to receive the roll pin) and install the roll pin flush with the valve body face

8C.126 After all the valves are installed, check each valve for freedom of movement by gently prying the valve against its spring with a small screwdriver - the valve should snap back when pressure is released

8C.127 Lubricate the sealing ring with ATF and install the accumulator spring and piston

8C.128 Press the piston into the bore and install the E-clip (a C-clamp can be used to depress the piston)

8C.129 If the governor gear needs replacement, mount the governor in a holding fixture and drive out the roll pin with an appropriate size punch

Governor

Inspect the governor weights for freedom of movement. Check the weight springs for distortion or damage. Check the governor valve for freedom of movement. Check the governor sleeve for nicks, scoring or damage. Check the governor gear for nicks or damaged teeth.

Transmission assembly

An automatic transmission is a precision fit piece of equipment. Install each component as shown, do not force any component into place. If it doesn't fit properly, find out why and rectify the situation. Maintain a clean work place and lubricate all moving parts as they are installed. Lubricate thrust washers and bearings with automatic transmission fluid (ATF) or petroleum jelly. Use petroleum jelly to retain thrust washers and check balls in their proper location as the component is installed. Dip all friction plates in ATF before installation.

8C.130 Remove the gear

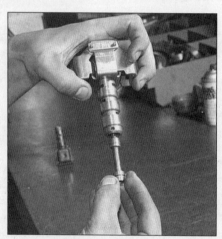

8C.131 With the gear removed you can remove the governor valve and inspect it more closely

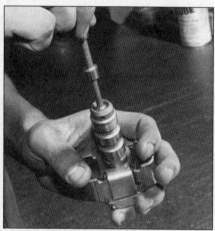

8C.132 Insert the governor valve into the sleeve assembly and check it for freedom of movement

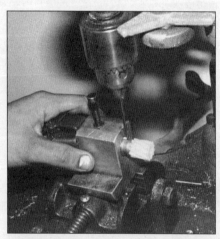

8C.133 Press on a new gear, mount the governor in the holding fixture and using the hole in the sleeve as a guide, drill a hole through the gear. If the hole in the sleeve is enlarged, drill a new hole 90-degrees from the original

8C.134 Install a new roll pin

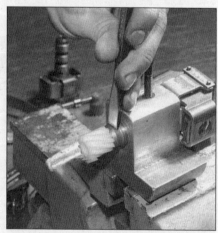

8C.135 Stake the roll pin on each side of the sleeve

Center support and gear unit

8C.136 Apply petroleum jelly to the outside race of the rear internal gear-to-sun gear thrust bearing and install the race with the flange facing forward or up

8C.137 Install the needle thrust bearing . . .

8C.138 . . . and the inside race with the inner flange facing down; use petroleum jelly to lubricate and retain the parts

8C.139 Invert the rear internal gear and install the output shaft-to-sun gear thrust bearing inside race with the inner flange facing up

8C.140 Install the needle thrust bearing . . .

8C.141 . . . and the outer race with the flange facing down, cupped over the bearing; use petroleum jelly to lubricate and retain the parts

8C.142 Place the output carrier assembly over the mainshaft, meshing the pinion gears into the rear internal gear

8C.143 Invert the assembly and install the output shaft , meshing the splines into the output carrier

8C.144 Install the output shaft-to-output carrier retaining ring. Make sure it's fully seated in the groove

8C.145 Install the yoke seal (arrow), if equipped

8C.146 Install the output shaft-to-case thrust washer; seat the tabs of the washer into the holes and use petroleum jelly to lubricate and retain the washer

8C.147 Invert the assembly and install the output carrier-to-reaction carrier thrust washer; use petroleum jelly to lubricate and retain the washer

8C.148 Install the silencing ring onto the output carrier

8C.149 Install the reaction drum spacer (if equipped) and low roller clutch into the reaction carrier. Lubricate the roller clutch with ATF

8C.150 Install the reaction carrier onto the output carrier

8C.151 Install the sun gear with the flat side (arrow) facing forward or up

8C.152 Install the sun gear shaft with the long splines down, engaging them with the splines in the sun gear (removed for clarity)

8C.153 Install the four sealing rings onto the center support, locking the ring ends together; check the rings for freedom of movement in their grooves (the grooves can be enlarged slightly with a small file if necessary)

8C.154 Install the inner and outer seals onto the intermediate clutch piston; make sure the seal lips face the proper direction (seal lips always face the pressure)

8C.155 Lubricate the seals with ATF and install the piston into the center support, line-up the dimples in the piston with the contact area of the center support; use a seal protector for the inner seal if possible

8C.156 Use a feeler gauge or seal installation tool to work the outer seal into the bore; depress the piston until it's fully seated

8C.157 Install the intermediate clutch spring guide . . .

8C.158 . . . and the intermediate clutch release springs into the guide pockets

8C.159 Install the spring retainer over the springs

8C.160 Depress the spring retainer with your thumbs and install the snap-ring

8C.161 Check all the springs to make sure they're seated properly under the retainer

8C.162 Install the center support-to-reaction drum thrust washer, retaining it in place with petroleum jelly

8C.163 Install the center support thrust bearing race with the inner flange fitted into the center support bore. Retain the race with petroleum jelly

8C.164 Install the center support needle thrust bearing and race into the reaction drum. Make sure the flange on the race is fitted around the outside edge of the needle bearing. Lubricate the needle bearing with ATF

8C.165 Lubricate the low roller clutch with ATF and install the center support into the reaction carrier using a twisting motion. When holding the reaction carrier, the low roller clutch should allow the center support to be rotated only counterclockwise

Direct clutch assembly

8C.166 Install the inner and outer seals onto the direct clutch piston with the seal lips facing into the drum

8C.167 Install the direct clutch center seal into the housing with the seal lip facing the piston

8C.168 Lubricate the seals with ATF and install the direct clutch piston into the housing, working the seal lips in with a feeler gage or seal installation tool. Press the piston in until fully seated and rotate it within the housing; check for binding which would indicate a doubled-over seal lip

8C.169 Install the direct clutch release springs into the pockets

8C.170 Install the spring retainer with the dished side up. Using a spring compressor or press depress the retainer and install the snap-ring

8C.171 Install the intermediate roller clutch onto the cam on the backside of the direct clutch housing

8C.172 Lubricate the roller clutch and outer race with ATF and install the outer race, turning it clockwise as you press it into place

8C.173 Install the intermediate clutch retainer with the dished side up . . .

8C.174 . . . and install the snap-ring. Make sure the snap-ring is seated in the groove. When properly installed the intermediate roller clutch outer race will not rotate counterclockwise; if it does, it's installed upside-down

8C.175 Make sure the apply ring is installed on the piston (if equipped) and install the wave plate (if equipped) or a steel plate . . .

Note

Some models may be equipped with a dished plate instead of a waved plate. If equipped with a dished plate, install the dished plate followed by a steel plate

8C.176 . . . followed by a friction plate. Lubricate all plates with ATF before assembly

8C.177 Install the direct clutch backing plate . . .

Note

You can air-check the direct clutch by placing the assembly over the center support hub and applying air pressure to the oil feed hole (left of bolt hole). Applying air pressure to the oil feed hole will activate the direct clutch piston, forcing it against the clutch plates

8C.178 . . . and the retaining ring. Make sure the retaining ring is seated in the groove

8C.179 Using a feeler gauge, check the direct clutch pack clearance. It should be approximately 0.060 to 0.080-inch

Forward clutch assembly

8C.180 Assembly of the forward clutch piston is essentially the same as the direct clutch. Install the center lip seal in the housing with the seal lip facing up, into the piston

8C.181 Install the inner and outer seals onto the piston with the seal lips facing into the housing. Lubricate the seals with ATF and install the piston into the housing, working the seal lips in with a feeler gauge or seal installation tool. Press the piston in until fully seated and rotate it within the housing; check for binding which would indicate a doubled-over seal lip. Install he springs into the pockets. Install the retainer (dished side up), compress the retainer and install the snap-ring

8C.182 Install the thrust washer on the outside of the forward clutch hub. Retain the washer with petroleum jelly

8C.183 Install the bronze thrust washer on the inside of the forward clutch hub. Retain the washer with petroleum jelly

8C.184 Install the forward clutch hub into the forward clutch housing

8C.185 Make sure the apply ring is installed onto the piston (if equipped) and install the waved plate or dished plate (if equipped with a dished plate, install a steel plate next)

8C.186 Lubricate the plates with ATF and alternate friction and steel plates

8C.187 Install the direct clutch hub and retaining ring

Note

You can air-check the forward clutch by placing the assembly over the oil pump hub and applying air pressure to the oil feed hole (the one next to the bolt hole in the large cluster of holes). Applying air pressure to the oil feed hole will activate the forward clutch piston, forcing it against the clutch plates

Final assembly

8C.188 Using a single-edged razor blade, clean the valve body gasket surface of any remaining gasket material

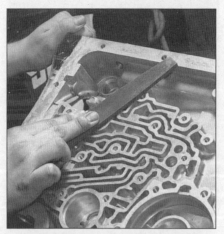

8C.189 Lightly run a flat file across the valve body surface to remove any burrs. Clean the surface of any metal filings

8C.190 Using a cape chisel or bushing removal tool, drive out the rear case bushing . . .

8C.191 . . . and install a new bushing with the appropriate size bushing driver

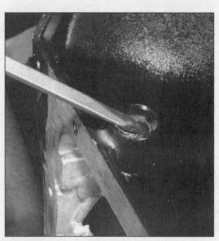

8C.192 Carefully pry the manual shaft seal from the case . . .

8C.193 . . . and drive in a new seal with the appropriate size driver (use a deep socket if the driver is not available)

8C.194 Lubricate the seal with ATF and install the manual shaft. Install the detent lever/park rod assembly, inserting the park rod in the bracket and engaging the slot in the detent lever with the manual shaft

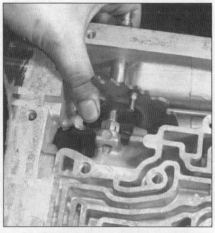

8C.195 Install the retaining nut and tighten it securely

8C.196 Insert the retaining pin through the hole in the case so it retains the manual shaft in place

8C.197 Bend the end of the pin up slightly and cut off the excess. Rotate the manual shaft back-and-forth several times to make sure it operates smoothly and is actuating the parking pawl. Finally position it so the parking pawl is retracted

8C.198 Install the modulator valve in the case. Make sure the valve operates freely and does not bind in the case

8C.199 Install the vacuum modulator with a new O-ring. A new modulator is recommended any time the transmission is rebuilt. Install the retaining bracket and tighten the bolt securely

8C.200 Check the case vent tube. If it's broken, install a new tube and . . .

8C.201 . . . drive it in until its flush with the case

8C.202 Install a new case connector and O-ring (arrow)

8C.203 The internal transmission components are best assembled with the transmission positioned vertically. If a holding fixture is not available, position the case off the ground, allowing clearance for the output shaft and secure it to a sturdy workbench. Install the rear selective thrust washer . . .

8C.204 . . . engaging the three tabs in the case slots (arrows). Retain the washer with petroleum jelly and lubricate the thrust face with ATF

8C.205 Install the rear band into the case, engaging the two holes in the band (arrows) . . .

8C.206 . . . with the two rear band anchor lugs in the case (arrows). Insert a small rod or thin screwdriver through the rear servo hole in the case and center the band

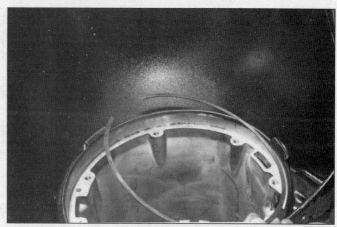

8C.207 Some models are equipped with a center support spacer ring. Do not confuse the spacer (which is 0.040-in thick and flat on both sides) with the center support-to-case retaining ring (beveled on one side) or the intermediate clutch backing plate retaining ring (which is 0.093-inch thick)

8C.208 Install the spacer in the bottom groove of the case lugs with the gap directly under the intermediate band anchor pin (arrow)

8C.209 The entire center support and gear unit must be held by the main shaft as it is lowered into the case. The assembly is quite heavy and a special holding tool (Kent-Moore J-21795, or equivalent) is available to support the unit. If the holding tool is not available, wrap the end of the mainshaft with duct-tape to protect the splines and clamp a large pair of locking pliers to use as a handle

8C.210 Align the center support bolt hole with the hole in the case and carefully lower the gear unit into the case in one smooth motion

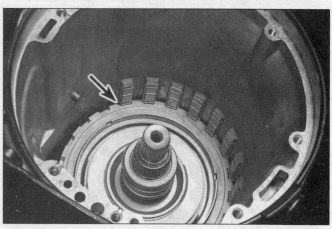

8C.211 Tap the center support down with the blunt end of a hammer handle until the top of the support is below the retaining ring groove (arrow). Make sure the center support bolt hole is properly aligned with the hole in the case

8C.212 Install the center support retaining ring with the beveled edge up and the gap under the intermediate band anchor pin

8C.213 Stake the retaining ring with a hammer and large screwdriver in several places around the case, seating it fully in the groove

Note

Check the rear unit endplay as follows: Turn the transmission over (with the output shaft pointing up) and mount a dial indicator to one of the extension housing bolt holes. Place the indicator needle on the end of the output shaft and zero the indicator. Pull the output shaft up and read the endplay. It should be between 0.007 and 0.019-inch. If it isn't remove the gear unit from the case and change the rear selective thrust washer. Selective thrust washers are available at a dealership parts department

8C.214 When the endplay is properly adjusted, install the center support bolt (arrow). Load the center support by inserting a medium-size screwdriver into the lube passage adjacent to the bolt and prying the center support counterclockwise; tighten the center support bolt to 20 to 25 ft-lbs. Be very careful not to nick the case with the screwdriver, but if you do, remove any burrs before proceeding

8C.215 Install the intermediate clutch plates, starting with the waved plate (if equipped) or a steel plate. Dip the friction plates in ATF and alternate friction and steel plates until all the intermediate clutch plates are installed

8C.216 Install the intermediate clutch backing plate with the ridged side up

8C.217 Install the retaining ring, seating it fully in the groove with the gap opposite the intermediate band anchor pin (arrow)

8C.218 Install the front band indexing the hole in the band over the anchor pin in the case (arrow). Make sure the apply lug is aligned with the servo hole

8C.219 Align the splines in the intermediate clutch plates and install the direct clutch assembly. Hold the drum straight and rotate it slightly to engage the clutch plates. It may be necessary to hold the front band in place with a screwdriver

8C.220 When the direct clutch assembly is installed properly and fully seated, the splines on the inside of the drum will be flush with the end of the sun shaft (arrow)

8C.221 Make sure the thrust washer is still in place on the back of the drum and install the forward clutch assembly indexing the hub in the direct clutch plates. Rotate the input shaft as you engage the clutch plates until the assembly is seated on the mainshaft

8C.222 Install two oil pump alignment bolts and the oil pump gasket onto the case

8C.223 Install the selective thrust washer over the pump hub retaining it with petroleum jelly

8C.224 Install the oil seal rings into the grooves, hooking the ends of the seals together. Rotate the rings in the grooves, making sure the rings fit freely in the grooves, then retain them with petroleum jelly

8C.225 Install the oil pump cover O-ring seal with the stripe facing out and lubricate it with ATF

8C.226 Align the bolt holes and install the pump over the alignment bolts, pressing it into place. Rotate the input shaft as you seat the pump. If the input shaft cannot be rotated, there is a problem with either the direct or forward clutch assemblies. Correct this condition before fully seating the pump

8C.227 Mount a dial indicator with the needle resting on the end of the input shaft. Zero the indicator and lever the input shaft up-and-down to check the front unit endplay. Load the output shaft forward to remove the rear unit endplay as you measure the front unit endplay. It should be between 0.003 and 0.024-inch. If it isn't remove the pump and change the selective thrust washer on the pump hub - selective washers are available at a dealership parts department

8C.228 Once the endplay is correct, install new sealing washers on the pump bolts, install the pump bolts and tighten them to 18 to 20 ft-lbs

8C.229 Place the transmission on the workbench with the valve body surface facing up. Install a new seal on the rear servo piston

8C.230 Install new metal rings on the 1-2 accumulator piston. If the piston originally had teflon rings, DO NOT remove the teflon rings unless they are damaged

8C.231 Lubricate the seals with ATF and install the 1-2 accumulator piston into the servo piston

8C.232 Install the accumulator spring onto the servo assembly. . .

8C.233 . . .and install the servo assembly into the transmission case

8C.234 Install the servo cover gasket . . .

8C.235 . . . and servo cover. Install the bolts and tighten them gradually to 18 to 20 ft-lbs

8C.236 Install a new metal ring on the intermediate servo piston. If the piston originally had a teflon ring DO NOT remove the teflon ring unless it's damaged

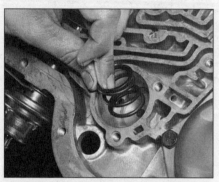

8C.237 Install the intermediate servo spring into the servo bore

8C.238 Install the spring retainer . . .

8C.239 . . . and the servo pin. Make sure the E-clip is installed on the pin

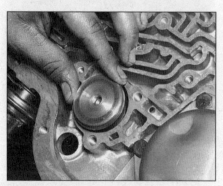

8C.240 Lubricate the piston seal with ATF and install the intermediate servo piston with the dished side down

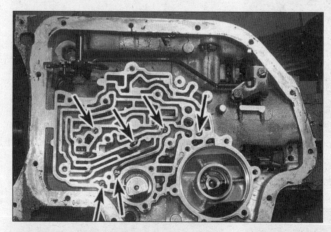

8C.241 Install the six check balls in the locations shown. Retain the check balls with petroleum jelly

8C.242 Install two valve body alignment bolts and install the valve body-to-case gasket over the bolts

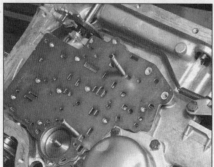

8C.243 Install the spacer plate . . .

8C.244 . . . and the spacer plate-to-valve body gasket

8C.245 Install the detent solenoid and gasket; tighten the bolts finger tight (a new detent solenoid is recommended any time the transmission is rebuilt)

8C.246 Install the governor screen, open end into the case, in the location shown (arrow)

8C.247 Install the manual valve in the valve body

8C.248 Lower the valve body assembly over the alignment bolts guiding the governor tubes into position . . .

8C.249 . . . and engaging the manual valve with the linkage

8C.250 Remove the alignment bolts and install all the valve body bolts finger tight. Tap the governor pipes down, seating them into the case

8C.251 Install the detent spring and roller, engaging it with the detent lever

8C.252 Tighten the valve body bolts, detent spring and detent solenoid bolts to 8 to 10 ft-lbs. Connect the detent solenoid wire to the case connector

8C.253 Install the O-ring on the filter intake pipe, lubricate the O-ring with ATF and install the filter. Be sure and install the spacer, if equipped with a deep pan. Install the oil pan gasket and oil pan. Tighten the oil pan bolts to 12 ft-lbs

8C.254 Lubricate the governor bore with ATF and install the governor

8C.255 Install the governor cover and gasket. Tighten the bolts to 18 ft-lbs

8C.256 Install a new speedometer driven gear shaft seal into the speedometer adapter

8C.257 Retain the seal with the small retaining ring

8C.258 Lubricate the gear shaft and bore with ATF, and install the gear in the adapter

8C.259 Install a new O-ring on the adapter, lubricate with ATF and install the speedometer driven gear and adapter assembly into the case

8C.260 Install the retainer and tighten the bolt securely

8C.261 Press a new bushing into the extension housing . . .

8C.262 . . . and install a new seal

8C.263 Install the extension housing and gasket onto the case and tighten the bolts to 22 ft-lbs. Install the torque converter (see Chapter 7) and the transmission is ready for installation into the vehicle

Chapter 8   Part D
Disassembly, inspection and assembly THM700-R4 transmission

Introduction

The THM700-R4 is a four-speed automatic transmission manufactured for rear-wheel drive vehicles. The major components of this transmission are:

a) Lock-up torque converter
b) Vane-type oil pump
c) Control valve assembly
d) 2-4 band
e) Five separate multiple disc clutch packs
f) One sprag clutch
g) One roller clutch
h) Two planetary gear sets

Follow the photographic sequence for disassembly, inspection and assembly. The model shown is a typical transmission of this type. Differences do exist between models and many changes have been made over the years, so perform each step in order and lay the components out on a clean work bench in the EXACT ORDER of removal to prevent confusion during reassembly. Many snap-rings and clutch plates are similar in size, but must not be interchanged. Keep the individual parts together with the component from which they were removed to avoid mix-ups. Save all old parts and compare them with the new part to ensure they are an exact match before reassembly. Pay particular attention to the stack-up of the various clutch packs. Differences do exist between models and your transmission may not match the stack-up shown. Note the exact location of the check balls in the case as well as the valve body. Save all the old parts until the overhaul is complete and the transmission has been thoroughly road tested; old components can be useful in diagnosing any problems that may arise.

The THM700-R4 is a metric dimensioned transmission; use metric tools on the fasteners. Special tools are required for some procedures. Alternate procedures are shown where possible, but some procedures can only be accomplished with special tools. Read through the entire overhaul procedure before beginning work to familiarize yourself with the procedures and identify any special tools that may be needed. Thoroughly clean the exterior of the transmission before beginning disassembly.

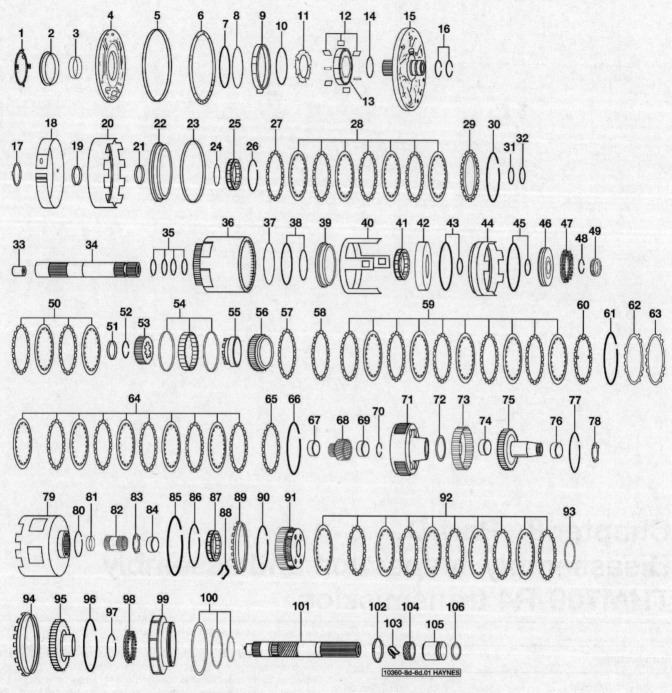

8D.1 Exploded view of the typical THM700-R4 internal components

1 Oil seal retainer	13 Pump rotor
2 Oil seal	14 Pump vane ring
3 Pump body bushing	15 Pump cover
4 Pump body	16 Seal rings
5 O-ring	17 Pump-to-drum thrust washer
6 Gasket	18 2-4 band
7 Slide seal wear plate	19 Reverse input drum front bushing
8 Slide O-ring	20 Reverse input housing assembly
9 Pump slide	21 Reverse input drum rear bushing
10 Pump vane ring	22 Reverse input clutch piston
11 Rotor guide	23 Reverse input clutch outer seal
12 Pump vanes	24 Reverse input clutch inner seal

25	Reverse input clutch spring assembly
26	Reverse input clutch spring retainer ring
27	Reverse input clutch waved plate
28	Reverse input clutch plates
29	Reverse input clutch backing plate
30	Reverse input clutch retaining ring
31	Input shaft bearing assembly
32	Input shaft selective thrust washer
33	Check ball assembly
34	Turbine shaft
35	Turbine shaft oil seal rings
36	Input housing
37	Input O-ring
38	3-4 clutch piston seals
39	3-4 clutch piston
40	3-4 clutch apply ring
41	3-4 clutch spring assembly
42	Forward clutch housing
43	Forward clutch piston seals
44	Forward clutch piston
45	Overrun clutch piston seals
46	Overrun clutch piston
47	Overrun clutch spring assembly
48	Overrun clutch spring retainer snap-ring
49	Input housing seal
50	Overrun clutch plates
51	Input sun gear bearing
52	Overrun clutch snap-ring
53	Overrun clutch hub
54	Forward sprag assembly
55	Sprag retainer and race
56	Forward sprag clutch outer race
57	Forward clutch apply plate
58	Forward clutch waved plate
59	Forward clutch plates
60	Forward clutch backing plate
61	Forward clutch backing plate retainer
62	3-4 clutch retainer ring
63	3-4 clutch apply plate
64	3-4 clutch plates
65	3-4 clutch backing plate
66	3-4 clutch backing plate retainer
67	Input sun gear front bushing
68	Input sun gear
69	Input sun gear rear bushing
70	Input carrier snap-ring
71	Input planetary carrier assembly
72	Input carrier thrust bearing
73	Input internal gear
74	Reaction carrier shaft front bushing
75	Reaction carrier shaft
76	Reaction carrier shaft rear bushing
77	Reaction shaft retainer ring
78	Reaction shaft thrust washer
79	Reaction sun shell
80	Reaction sun gear retainer ring
81	Reaction sun bushing
82	Reaction sun gear
83	Reaction shell thrust washer
84	Low-reverse roller clutch race
85	Low-reverse support retainer ring
86	Low-reverse roller assembly retainer ring
87	Low-reverse roller clutch
88	Low-reverse clutch support retainer spring
89	Low-reverse support assembly
90	Low-reverse roller assembly retainer ring
91	Reaction planetary carrier assembly
92	Low-reverse clutch plates
93	Reaction carrier thrust bearing
94	Internal reaction gear
95	Internal reaction gear support
96	Reaction gear support retainer ring
97	Low-reverse clutch retainer ring
98	Low-reverse clutch spring assembly
99	Low-reverse clutch piston
100	Low-reverse clutch seals
101	Output shaft
102	Reaction gear support bearing
103	Speedometer drive gear clip
104	Speedometer drive gear
105	Output shaft sleeve
106	Output shaft seal

Transmission disassembly

8D.2 Remove the bolt and pull out the speedometer gear housing and gear (already removed in this photo). Remove the four rear extension housing bolts and housing. Using a hammer and drift, tap the rear seal from the housing from the inside.

8D.3 Remove the servo cover retaining ring by prying through one of the slots with a screwdriver

8D.4 Grasp the servo cover with a pair of pliers, twist back-and-forth and pull the cover straight out. If the cover is difficult to remove, pull it out far enough to hook the O-ring with a small screwdriver through the slot; cut the O-ring and pull it from the cover

8D.5 Remove the servo assembly and the servo return spring from the case. Remove the fourth apply piston from inside the cover, then remove the inner housing from the 2nd apply piston (inner housing is being held in this photo, with the 2nd apply piston below it. The fourth apply piston and cover are at left)

8D.6 Remove the governor cover by tapping it off with a large screwdriver and hammer

8D.7 Withdraw the governor from the case

8D.8 Remove the oil pan bolts and oil pan. Note the clutch material and metal in this pan, indicating why this transmission needs an overhaul

8D.9 Grasp the oil filter and pull it straight out

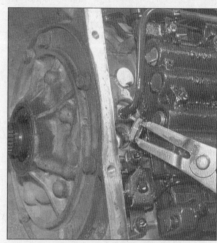

8D.10 Retrieve the oil filter seal, if it remains in the pump body

8D.11 Carefully pry the oil pipe from the valve body and case and remove the oil pipe

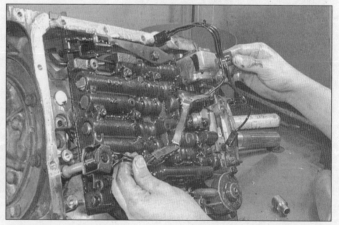

8D.12 Remove the Torque Converter Clutch (TCC) solenoid bolts and pull the solenoid out of the case. Remove the wiring harness from the retainers, disconnect the harness connectors from the pressure switches and case plug and remove the solenoid and harness assembly

8D.13 Remove the accumulator bolts and the 1-2 accumulator assembly. Remove the 1-2 accumulator spring and note that the large end was installed into the piston

8D.14 Remove the 1-2 accumulator piston from the accumulator housing

8D.15 Remove all of the valve body bolts. Note the position of the wiring harness clips, retaining washer and the filter retaining clip. Remove the oil passage cover, if equipped

8D.16 Remove the bolt and the manual detent spring

8D.17 Remove the Throttle Valve (TV) lever and bracket assembly. Disconnect the TV cable link from the lever, noting how it was installed

8D.18 Lift the control valve (valve body) assembly from the case while disconnecting the manual valve link from the manual valve

8D.19 Remove the manual valve from the valve body

8D.20 Remove the bolts and the auxiliary valve body (if equipped)

8D.21 Remove the auxiliary valve body end cover . . .

8D.22 . . . and remove the accumulator spring and piston

8D.23 Remove the spacer plate and spacer plate gaskets

8D.24 Remove the 3-4 accumulator spring . . .

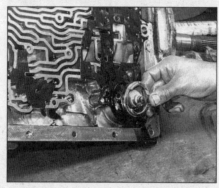

8D.25 . . . and piston from the case

8D.26 Retrieve all the check balls from the valve body and case, noting their location. A magnetic tool is helpful for removing steel balls

8D.27 Using an open-end wrench, remove the manual shaft-to-detent lever retaining nut . . .

8D.28 . . . pry the retaining clip from the shaft . . .

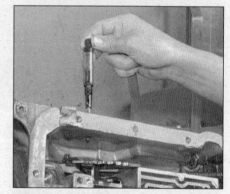

8D.29 . . . and withdraw the manual shaft from the case

8D.30 Lift the detent lever and park-lock rod assembly from the case

8D.31 Remove the bolts and the park-lock bracket from the case

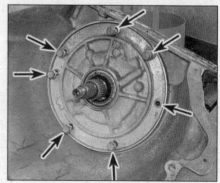

8D.32 Remove the bolts from the oil pump (arrows)

8D.33 Using the appropriate puller, pull the oil pump from the case. If a puller is not available, gently pry between the pump cover and the input drum until the pump is free Remove the pump assembly and set it aside for later disassembly

8D.34 Grasp the input shaft and remove the reverse clutch and input clutch assembly and set them aside

8D.35 Remove the 2-4 band anchor pin from the case . . .

8D.36 . . . and remove the 2-4 band

8D.37 Remove the input sun gear

8D.38 Remove the input carrier-to-output shaft snap-ring (if the case is being disassembled in the vertical position, the input shaft may fall out when the snap-ring is removed if the input shaft is not supported)

8D.39 Remove the input carrier assembly . . .

8D.40 . . . and remove the thrust washer from the backside

8D.41 Remove the input internal gear/reaction carrier shaft assembly . . .

8D.42 . . . and remove the thrust washer from the reaction sun shell

8D.43 Remove the reaction sun shell . . .

8D.44 . . . and the thrust washer

8D.45 Remove the low-reverse support-to-case retaining ring by gently prying it from the lugs

8D.46 Grasp the output shaft and lift the low-reverse support/reaction carrier assembly from the case

8D.47 Retrieve the low-reverse clutch retainer spring from the case

8D.48 Invert the assembly on the bench and remove the output shaft

8D.49 Remove the internal reaction gear . . .

8D.50 . . . and the thrust bearing assembly

8D.51 Remove the reaction planetary carrier assembly . . .

8D.52 . . . and the reaction sun gear

8D.53 Separate the low-reverse clutch plates and steel discs for cleaning and inspection. Count the number of plates and discs used on your transmission and write these numbers down for assembly reference

8D.54 Remove the roller clutch assembly retaining ring . . .

8D.55 . . . and separate the support assembly from the roller clutch

8D.56 Separate the low-reverse roller clutch from the inner race

8D.57 A special low-reverse clutch spring compressor is required to compress the spring retainer

8D.58 Install the special tool (it locks into the case lugs), compress the low-reverse spring assembly and remove the snap-ring with snap-ring pliers

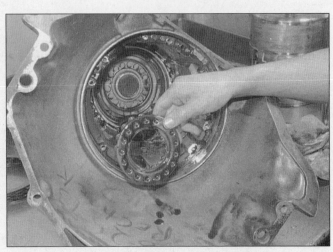

8D.59 Remove the spring assembly

8D.60 Place the case on end and gently apply air pressure to the low-reverse clutch apply passage, blowing the low-reverse piston from the case. Pad the area beneath the piston with a bed of rags so it will not be damaged when it falls out). Warning: *Do not place your hand below the piston - air pressure can cause the piston to be ejected violently! Also, always wear eye protection when using compressed air!*

8D.61 Remove the inner and outer lip seals from the low-reverse piston

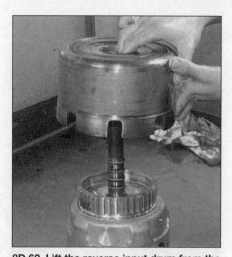

8D.62 Lift the reverse input drum from the input shaft assembly

8D.63 Invert the drum on the bench and remove the reverse input clutch retaining ring

8D.64 Remove the reverse input clutch backing plate, friction plates, steel discs and the waved plate. Separate the plates for cleaning and inspection

8D.65 Place the drum in a spring compressor or press, depress the spring retainer and remove the snap-ring

8D.66 Remove the reverse input clutch spring assembly

8D.67 Remove the reverse input clutch piston . . .

8D.68 . . . and remove the inner and outer seals from the piston

8D.69 Invert the input shaft/housing assembly on the bench and remove the retaining ring

8D.70 Remove the 3-4 clutch pack and take-up springs (if equipped) from the housing

Note

Many different 3-4 clutch packs are used, depending on model. Make careful notes of the stack-up in the 3-4 clutch so it can be reassembled in the same order

8D.71 Pry the forward clutch retaining ring from the lugs and remove the ring

8D.72 Invert the input housing and remove the forward clutches and sprag assembly from the housing

8D.73 Remove the input sun gear thrust bearing assembly from the overrun clutch hub

8D.74 Remove the forward clutch plates and steel plates . . .

8D.75 . . . and the forward sprag assembly and the overrun clutch plates

8D.76 Remove the stator shaft thrust bearing and selective thrust washer from the input shaft

8D.77 Place the input housing in a spring compressor or press, depress the spring retainer and remove the snap-ring

8D.78 Invert the housing, tap the housing squarely on the bench and the pistons, retainers and apply rings will all come out together

8D.79 Remove the overrun clutch spring assembly

8D.80 Remove the overrun clutch piston . . .

8D.81 . . . and remove the inner and outer lip seals

8D.82 Remove the forward clutch piston from the
3-4 apply ring . . .

8D.83 . . . and remove the inner and outer lip seals

8D.84 Remove the forward clutch housing . . .

Component inspection and subassembly overhaul

Using an approved cleaning solvent, clean and dry all the components thoroughly, including the case. Do not use rags to wipe the components dry, as lint from the rag may lodge in the oil passages, causing a valve to stick.

Inspect the following transmission components and repair or replace as necessary:

a) **Case:** *Inspect the exterior of the case for damage, cracks and porosity (a porous casting will cause fluid leaks). Check the valve body mating surfaces on the case and valve body for damage and flatness (use a precision straightedge to check for flatness - any warpage means the valve body or case will have to be machined or replaced). Check all the oil passages, the servo bore, the speedometer bore and the governor bore for damage. Check all threaded holes for damage (repair thread damage as described in Chapter 2). Check the oil cooler line fittings for damage. Check the interior of the case for damaged retaining ring grooves, which will mean the case will have to be replaced. Check the low-reverse lugs for excessive wear. Check the output shaft bushing for wear (if necessary, replace the bushing, as described in Chapter 2). Inspect the manual linkage and the park-lock linkage for damage.*

b) **Reaction gear set:** *Inspect the low-reverse piston for damage; check the seal grooves for damage. Check the low-reverse spring*
assembly for damage. Inspect the reaction internal gear, support and carrier for damage. Check for stripped splines, cracked or broken teeth, damaged or worn thrust bearings and bushings. Check the reaction carrier pinion gears for damaged bearings or worn washers. Check the pinion endplay with a feeler gauge; it should be between 0.008 and 0.024-inch. Check the captive thrust bearing in the carrier for wear by turning it with the output shaft sleeve. Inspect the low-reverse roller clutch for damaged rollers or broken springs. Check the finish of the inner and outer race and check the support for damaged lugs. Inspect the reaction sun gear and shell for spline or tooth damage. Check the thrust washers and bushings for wear or damage.*

c) **Input gear set:** *Inspect the reaction carrier shaft/input internal gear and output shaft for damaged splines, broken teeth, and worn bushings. Check the thrust bearing for wear or damage. Check the input carrier assembly for broken teeth, worn washers and a damaged or worn thrust bearing. Check the pinion endplay with a feeler gauge; it should be between 0.008 and 0.024-inch. Check the input sun gear for damaged splines, broken teeth or a worn bushing.*

d) **Input and reverse input clutch assemblies:** *Inspect the input shaft for damaged splines. Inspect the check balls for looseness and the seal rings for damage. Check the clutch housings, pistons, springs, spring retainers, clutch plates, backing plates and retainer rings for wear or damage. Check for nicks or burrs in the lip seal areas. Check the forward clutch sprag assembly for wear, broken springs, spline damage and race finish wear. Check*

8D.85 . . . and the 3-4 clutch spring assembly

8D.86 Remove the 3-4 clutch piston . . .

8D.87 . . . and remove the inner and outer lip seals

8D.88 Remove the input housing-to-input shaft seal from inside the housing

the housing and drum for worn bushings. Check the reverse input housing band apply surface for damage. Lay a steel ruler or straightedge across the surface and inspect for dishing. Inspect the 2-4 band assembly and servo for damage or wear. If the band is extremely damaged or burned, check the band apply pin length during reassembly with the special Band Apply Pin Tool (Kent-Moore J-33037, or equivalent).

Oil pump assembly

Disassemble the oil pump as shown in the accompanying photos. Remove the pressure regulator valve train, the converter clutch valve train, the pressure relief ball and spring (if necessary) and the oil pump cover screen. Lay the valves and springs out on a clean, lint-free towel in the exact order of removal to prevent confusion on assembly. Clean and dry the cover, body and all internal components. Inspect the valves and remove any burrs with a fine lapping compound; inspect the springs for damage or distortion; inspect the valve bores for damage; inspect the capsulated check balls for freedom of movement. Replace any damage components. Inspect the pump rotor, vanes and slider very carefully. Replace the parts with a rotor and vane kit if there are any doubts about their condition.

8D.90 Remove the bolts retaining the pump cover to the pump body

8D.91 Remove the input drum-to-pump thrust washer

8D.92 Separate the pump cover from the body

8D.93 Remove the vane ring . . .

8D.94 . . . and all of the pump vanes

8D.95 Remove the pump rotor and guide . . .

8D.96 . . . and the other vane ring

8D.97 Carefully pry the pump slide spring out of the body . . .

8D.98 . . . and remove the pump slide

8D.99 Remove the pump slide seal and seal support

8D.100 Remove the pump slide pivot pin . . .

8D.101 . . . and the pivot pin spring from the pump body

8D.102 Remove the front seal and O-ring from the pump body with a hammer and chisel

8D.103 Remove the pump body bushing, using the appropriate size driver to knock it out

8D.104 Inspect the pump cover for damage or scoring, replacing it if scoring is deep enough to catch your fingernail - this cover is in good condition

8D.105 Inspect the pump body for damage or scoring in the pump pocket (arrow)

8D.106 Inspect the oil drain-back passage for a restriction (arrow)

Note

On 1982 and early 1983 models the oil pump body may require a modification to prevent oil pressure build-up behind the seal, forcing oil past the lip of the seal or pushing the seal completely out of the pump body. If the passage does not connect with a slot in the pump body casting, enlarge the oil drain-back passage with a 1/4-inch drill bit. Be very careful not to nick the oil seal bore surface and do not drill any further than necessary. Clean the pump body of all metal chips

8D.107 Inspect the stator shaft front bushing and rear bushings for wear or damage. If necessary, remove the bushings with a hammer and bushing removal tool . . .

8D.108 . . . and install new bushings using the appropriate size drivers (see Chapter 2 for more information on removing and installing bushings)

8D.109 Place the stator shaft over the input shaft, spin the pump cover and check the new bushings for freedom of movement. If any binding is noticed, the bushings may be cocked in the bore

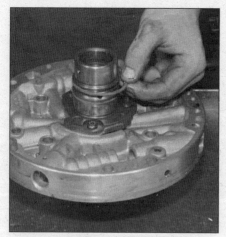

8D.110 Remove the stator shaft sealing rings and inspect the rings grooves for damage. Slight damage to a ring groove can be repaired with a small file

8D.111 Install the pressure relief ball . . .

8D.112 . . . the pressure relief spring . . .

8D.113 . . . and the pressure relief spring retaining pin

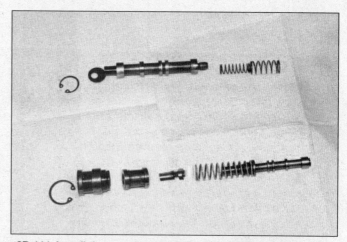

8D.114 Install the pressure regulator and converter clutch valve train components into the pump cover. Retain the boost valves in their sleeves with petroleum jelly

8D.115 Install the retaining rings and check each valve for freedom of movement

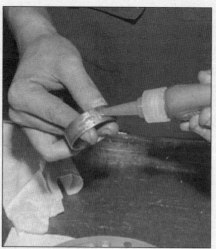

8D.116 Apply a locking compound such as Loctite 609, or equivalent, to the outer diameter of the pump body bushing

8D.117 Drive the bushing into the pump body using an appropriate size driver

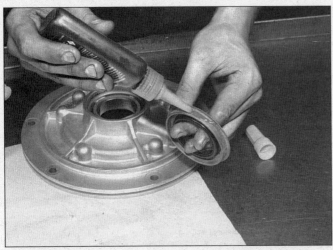

8D.118 Apply a locking compound such as Loctite 609, or equivalent, to the outer diameter of the pump body seal

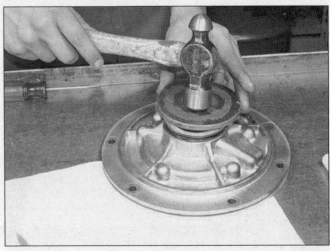

8D.119 Drive the seal into the pump body using an appropriately sized driver

8D.120 Install the pivot pin spring into the pump body

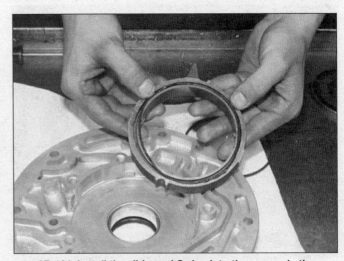

8D.121 Install the slide seal O-ring into the groove in the pump slide

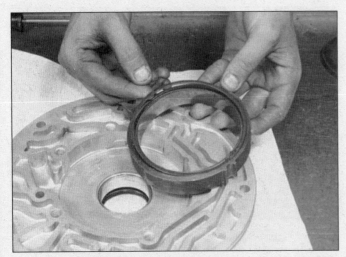

8D.122 Install the oil seal ring into the groove over the O-ring. Use petroleum jelly to retain the seal and ring in the groove

8D.123 Install the slide into the pump body with the oil seal and ring facing down into the cavity. Align the cut-out with the pivot pin groove and install the Teflon slide seal and support

8D.124 Install the pivot pin

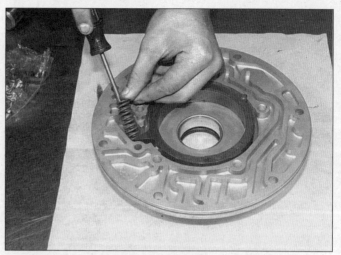

8D.125 Using a screwdriver, wedge the pump slide spring into the pump body (some models use an inner and outer slide spring)

8D.126 Place one of the vane guide rings into the pump cavity

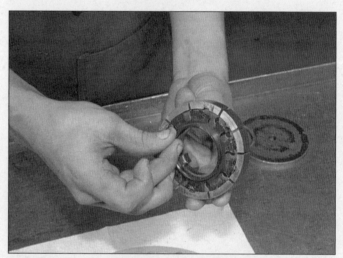

8D.127 Use petroleum jelly to retain the rotor guide to the rotor and install the guide and rotor into the pump body with the guide facing down into the cavity

8D.128 Install a pump vane into each slot in the pump rotor. DO NOT use petroleum jelly to retain the vanes

8D.129 Install the remaining pump vane ring and lubricate the pump rotor, vanes and slide with automatic transmission fluid (ATF)

8D.130 Align the pump cover over the pump body

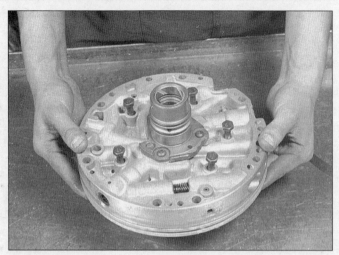

8D.131 Mate the pump halves together and install the bolts, finger tight

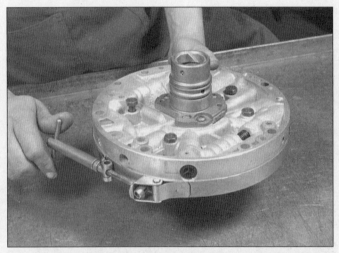

8D.132 Install the special oil pump alignment band . . .

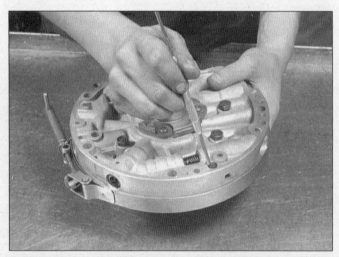

8D.133 . . . make sure the pump bolt holes are aligned . . .

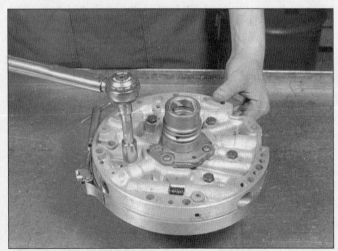

8D.134 . . . and tighten the pump bolts to 18 ft-lbs (if an alignment band is not available, the pump can be aligned by temporarily installing the pump into the transmission case with the stator shaft facing into the case)

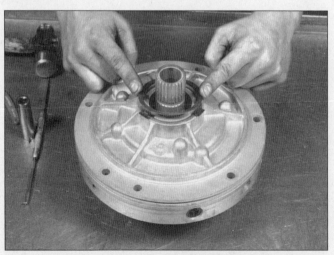

8D.135 Install the front seal retaining ring. Align the tab on the ring at the 5 O'clock position (when the transmission is sitting upright) and tap the ring securely into place

8D.137 Using a small screwdriver or pick, pry each valve against spring pressure - the valve should snap back when pressure is released. Check each valve for sticking

8D.138 Check the TV valve train for freedom of movement

8D.139 If necessary, remove the roll pin retaining the valve train

Control valve assembly

Complete disassembly of the valve body is not necessary unless the valve body has been contaminated. Clean the valve body using an approved solvent and air dry (DO NOT use rags to dry the valve body, as lint from the rag may cause a valve to stick). Check each valve for freedom of movement in its bore. If a stuck valve is encountered, remove the individual valve and components for further cleaning and inspection. Nicks and burrs may be removed by lapping the valve with a fine lapping compound.

If complete disassembly of the valve body is required, lay the valve body on a clean work bench, use clean tools to disassemble and wash the valve body with clean solvent. Remove the valves from the valve body, one at a time. Lay out the valves, springs and bushings in their proper order on a clean lint-free towel. Cleanliness and meticulous care in keeping the valves in order cannot be over-stressed. A tapered number 49 drill bit is helpful in removing any stubborn roll-pins you may encounter.

8D.140 Remove the valve assembly and springs, inspect and clean the valves, bushings and springs, then reassemble the valve train. If the roll pin does not fit tightly, replace it with a new one

Auxiliary valve body assembly

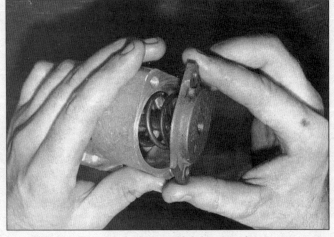

8D.141 Remove the bolts and the accumulator cover

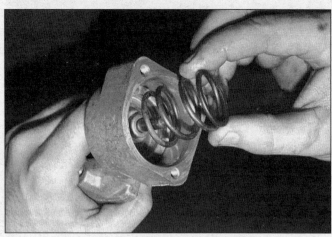

8D.142 Remove the accumulator spring . . .

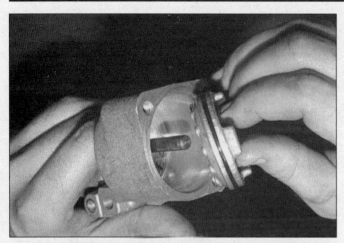

8D.143 . . . and the piston. Inspect the accumulator bore, piston and piston seal. Replace the piston seal and reassemble with the piston legs facing the spring

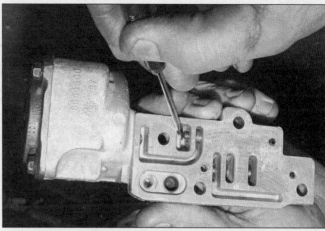

8D.144 Using a small screwdriver or pick, pry each valve against spring pressure and check for sticking. If a valve sticks, disassemble and clean its valve train

Governor

Governor disassembly is only necessary if the governor does not operate smoothly or appears contaminated.

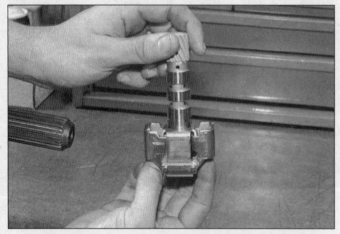

8D.145 Inspect the governor weights and valve for freedom of operation. Inspect the springs for damage or distortion. Check for nicks, scoring or damage to the sleeve

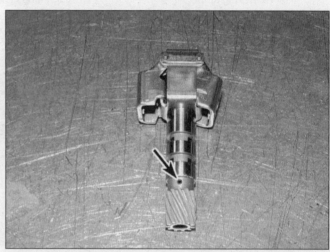

8D.146 Inspect the governor gear for damage. If necessary, drive out the roll pin (arrow) and remove the gear. A holding fixture is necessary to drill the new gear and install the roll pin (see Chapter 8C). Stake the roll pin after assembly

Transmission assembly

An automatic transmission is a precision piece of equipment. Install each component as shown, and do not force any component into place. If it doesn't fit properly, find out why and rectify the situation. Maintain a clean workplace and lubricate all moving parts as they are installed. Lubricate thrust washers and bearings with automatic transmission fluid (ATF) or petroleum jelly. Use petroleum jelly to retain thrust washers and check balls in their proper location as the component is installed. Dip all friction plates in ATF before installation.

8D.147 Inspect the retaining ring groove in the case lugs for wear or damage. If wear is excessive, a new case will be required

8D.148 Install the inner, center and outer seals on the low-reverse piston with the seal lips facing into the case bore. Lubricate the seal lips with ATF, then install the piston in the case using a rocking motion

8D.149 Align the lug on the piston with the notch in the bottom of the case and press the piston in until it's fully seated. When the piston is properly installed, the notch in the piston will align with the opening in the case (arrow)

8D.150 Install the low-reverse clutch spring assembly

8D.151 Install a special low-reverse spring compressor, locking the tool into the case lugs

8D.152 Compress the spring retainer and install the retaining ring

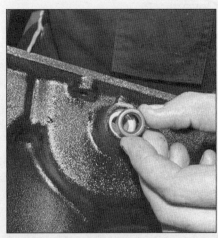

8D.153 Install a new manual shaft seal. Tap the seal in with a seal driver or a deep socket slightly smaller in diameter than the outside diameter of the seal

8D.154 Lubricate the seal lip with ATF and install the manual shaft

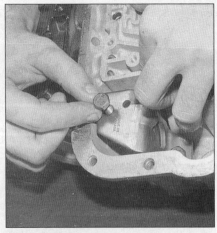

8D.155 Install the park-lock bracket and tighten the bolts securely

8D.156 Insert the end of the actuator rod in the park-lock bracket, slide the manual shaft through the slot in the detent lever and install the nut

8D.157 Slide the manual shaft into the case and install the retainer. Tighten the nut securely

8D.158 Install a new O-ring on the case electrical connector. Lubricate the O-ring with ATF and install the connector, pressing it in until the locking tabs release

8D.159 Apply locking compound such as Loctite 609, or equivalent, to the splines on the output shaft

8D.160 Install the internal reaction gear/support over the output shaft, onto the splines

8D.161 Install the reaction gear-to-case thrust bearing on the support, retaining it in place with petroleum jelly. The race with the outer diameter flange goes against the case

8D.162 Install the reaction carrier-to-support thrust bearing on the reaction carrier, retaining it in place with petroleum jelly. The race with the outer diameter flange goes against the support

8D.163 Lubricate the pinion gears with ATF and install the reaction carrier into the internal gear

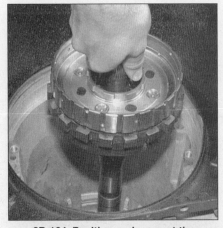

8D.164 Position and support the transmission case in the vertical position for installation of the internal components. Also support the output shaft or it may fall out of the case. Install the output shaft/reaction carrier assembly into the case

8D.165 On 1987 and later models, install the waved plate followed by the thicker selective steel plate. On 1986 and earlier models, install a low-reverse clutch steel plate, indexing the plate with the case lugs (the small notch in the steel plates will face the bottom of the transmission)

Note

On 1987 and later models, stack up the low-reverse clutch pack on the bench and measure the clutch pack overall thickness. Apply light pressure (about 5 lbs.) to the backing plate (do not flatten the wave plate) and measure from the bench surface to the top edge of the backing plate lug - it should be 1.20 to 1.24-inch. If the thickness is not in this range, use a thicker or thinner selective plate. Selective plates are available at a dealership parts department

8D.166 Next install a low-reverse clutch friction plate, indexing the plates with the reaction carrier splines. Dip the friction plates in ATF before installing

8D.167 Alternate steel and friction plates until the remainder of the low-reverse plates are installed

8D.168 Install the low-reverse clutch support retainer spring into the case . . .

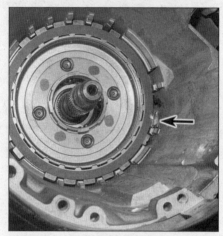

8D.169 . . . in this location (arrow); retain the spring with petroleum jelly

8D.170 Install the low-reverse roller clutch into the low-reverse clutch support . . .

8D.171 . . . and install the retaining ring

8D.172 Install the inner race into the low-reverse clutch assembly (lubricate the race with ATF). If installing from the backside of the support as shown, rotate the inner race in a counterclockwise direction and push in

8D.173 The top of the inner race should be flush with the top of the roller clutch and the inner race should ONLY rotate in a clockwise direction (as viewed from the top)

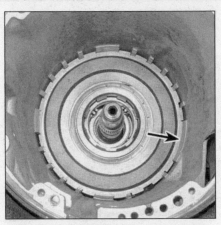

8D.174 Install the low-reverse support assembly into the case, aligning the wide notch in the support with the wide lug in the case (arrow). Press down on the support assembly until its fully seated. Lubricate the roller clutch completely with ATF

8D.175 Install the low-reverse support retainer ring into the groove in the case. Position the ends of the retainer ring as shown (arrows). Make sure the clutch support retainer spring is installed properly and is pressing against the support

8D.176 Install the low-reverse clutch inner race-to-reaction sun shell thrust washer with the tabs down, fitting into the slots in the inner race. Retain and lubricate the thrust washer with petroleum jelly

8D.177 Install the reaction sun gear, meshing the gear with the reaction carrier. Make sure the ring is installed (you shouldn't remove the ring except to replace it)

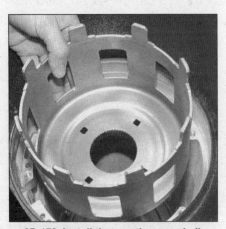

8D.178 Install the reaction sun shell, meshing the splines with the sun gear

8D.179 Install the reaction shell thrust washer, engaging the tabs with the slots in the shell. Retain and lubricate the thrust washer with petroleum jelly

8D.180 Install the input internal gear/reaction shaft assembly, seating it on the thrust washer

8D.181 Install the input carrier-to-reaction shaft thrust washer onto the input carrier, retaining it with petroleum jelly. Lubricate the planetary pinion gears with ATF

8D.182 Install the input carrier assembly, meshing the pinion gears with the internal gear and meshing the splines with the output shaft

8D.183 Install the output shaft-to-input carrier retaining ring, seating it in the groove in the output shaft

8D.184 Install the input sun gear, meshing the sun gear with the input carrier pinion gears and seating it on the thrust washer. Lubricate the gears completely with ATF

Forward clutch sprag assembly

8D.185 Using a small screwdriver, pry off the overrun hub retaining ring

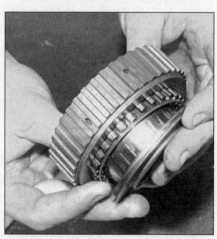

8D.186 Remove the clutch hub and separate the forward sprag clutch and inner race assembly from the outer race

8D.187 Remove the retainer ring from the inner race and inspect the forward sprag clutch assembly for wear or damaged components. Replacing the forward sprag with a new heavy-duty unit is highly recommended

8D.188 Install the new forward sprag into the outer race. When installed properly, the notches in the sprag retainer should point up (arrow)

8D.189 Install the inner race and retainer, turning the inner race counterclockwise as you push it in

8D.190 Install the other sprag retainer ring with the lipped edge of the ring facing toward the sprag

8D.191 Install the overrun clutch hub and retaining ring

8D.192 Test the sprag assembly for proper operation by rotating the overrun clutch in a clockwise direction as you hold the outer race stationary. The sprag should NOT rotate counterclockwise. If the sprag does not operate as described, it's installed backwards and must be reversed

Input clutch assembly

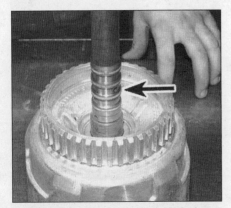

8D.193 Inspect the input shaft O-ring seals for cuts or damage (arrow). Spin the seals - they must fit freely in the grooves. Later models are equipped with a solid ring instead of a scarf-cut ring for better oil control

Note
Solid seals are recommended for replacement on early models and MUST be used on all later models with an auxiliary valve body. The solid seals are not normally replaced unless damaged and WILL be damaged if not installed and sized correctly

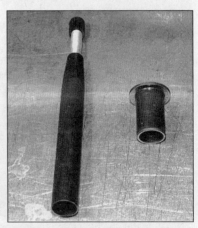

8D.194 Two special tools are needed to replace the solid seals - a seal installer (left) and a seal sizer (right)

8D.195 If the seals are damaged, cut them off with a single-edged razor blade. Place the installer over the input shaft, lubricate the installer with ATF and slide the seal down the shaft until it fits in the groove. Start with the bottom groove and work up, adjusting the installer length with the knob as you go

8D.196 When the seals are installed they will become slightly enlarged. Lubricate the seals with ATF and slide the sizer down the shaft and over the seals. The sizer will force the seals into the grooves. Inspect the new seals for damage

8D.197 Install the forward clutch housing-to-input clutch housing O-ring seal. Lubricate the seal with ATF

8D.198 Install the inner and outer lip seals on the 3-4 clutch piston with the seal lips facing the bottom of the piston bore

8D.199 Lubricate the seals with ATF and install the piston into the input clutch housing. Carefully work the seal lips into the bore with a seal installation tool. Press the piston in until it's fully seated in the bore

8D.200 Install the 3-4 clutch apply ring into the housing. Press in until it's fully seated on the piston

8D.201 Install the 3-4 clutch return spring assembly into the 3-4 clutch apply ring

8D.202 Install the inner and outer lip seals onto the forward clutch piston with the seal lips facing into the bore of the forward clutch housing

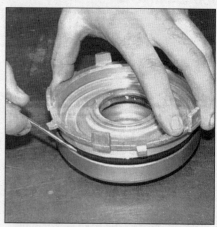

8D.203 Lubricate the seals with ATF and install the piston into the forward clutch housing. Work the seal lips into the housing using a seal installation tool and press the piston in until it's fully seated

8D.204 Two special seal protectors are highly recommended for the next steps - the forward clutch inner seal protector (right) and the overrun clutch inner seal protector (left)

8D.205 Install the forward clutch seal protector over the input housing hub

8D.206 Lubricate the seal protector and the forward clutch piston inner seal with ATF and install the forward clutch piston/housing assembly, indexing the tabs with the slots in the input housing

8D.207 When the forward clutch housing is properly installed, the clutch apply tabs are indexed with the 3-4 apply ring legs (arrow)

8D.208 Install the inner and outer seals onto the overrun clutch piston with the seal lips facing the bottom of the bore

8D.209 Remove the forward clutch inner seal protector and install the overrun clutch inner seal protector. Lubricate the seal protector and seals with ATF and install the overrun clutch piston into the housing

8D.210 Work the outer seal lip into the housing with a seal installation tool. Press the assembly down until it's firmly seated. When properly installed, the overrun clutch piston hub will be approximately 3/16-inch below the input housing retaining ring groove (arrow)

8D.211 Install the overrun clutch return spring assembly, positioning the springs over the projections on the piston

8D.212 Mount the housing in a press, compress the spring retainer and install the retaining ring

8D.213 The overrun clutch plates are the smallest of the three sets of plates installed into the input housing. Install the overrun clutch steel plate, aligning the wide notches with the wide case lugs

8D.214 Dip the friction plates in ATF and install the remaining friction plates and steel plates in alternating order

8D.215 Install the input housing-to-output shaft seal into the input housing. Press the seal into the splines until it's fully seated, then lubricate the seal with ATF

8D.216 Install the input sun gear thrust bearing into the input housing with the flanged inside race against the input housing hub - retain the bearing with petroleum jelly

8D.217 Align the overrun clutch splines with a small screwdriver and install the forward sprag clutch assembly into the input housing. Turn the sprag assembly by hand, indexing the overrun clutch plate splines until the sprag assembly seats on the thrust bearing

8D.218 Install the thick forward clutch apply plate into the input housing

8D.219 Install the forward clutch waved plate next . . .

8D.220 . . . followed by a flat steel plate. Index the wide plate lugs with the wide notches in the housing (arrow)

8D.221 Dip the friction plates in ATF and install the remaining friction plates and steel plates in alternating order

8D.222 Install the forward clutch backing plate with the chamfered side facing up

8D.223 Install the forward clutch retaining ring

8D.224 Snap the retaining ring in the groove and, using a feeler gauge, measure the clearance between the backing plate and the snap ring - it should be between 0.030 and 0.060-inch. If the clearance is not as specified, selective backing plates are available from a dealership parts department

8D.225 Install the 3-4 clutch retainer plate. Index the legs on the retainer over the apply ring legs (arrow)

8D.226 Install the 3-4 clutch apply plate

8D.227 On 1987 through 1992 models, install a flat steel plate next (if one of the steel plates has the same wide lugs as the apply plate, install it next to the apply plate). 1986 and earlier models do not have the extra steel plate; install a friction plate next to the apply plate, then a steel plate

Note
On 1993 and later models, the 3-4 clutch retainer plate, apply plate and wide-lugged steel plate have been replaced with a new single apply plate that takes the place of all three of the previous plates

8D.228 Dip the friction plates in ATF and install the remaining friction plates and steel plates in alternating order

8D.229 On 1988 and later models, install the 3-4 boost springs between the clutch plates and the input housing. A boost spring is placed into each of the five wide slots in the housing and is installed with the captive end down into the housing

8D.230 Install the 3-4 clutch backing plate with the chamfered side facing up

8D.231 Install the 3-4 clutch retaining ring, seating the ring fully in the housing groove

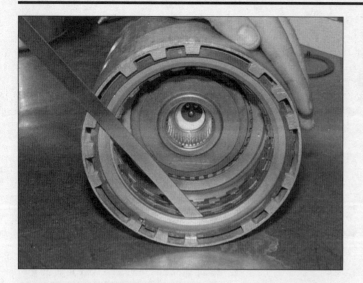

8D.232 Using a feeler gauge, measure the clearance between the backing plate and the first friction plate. Check the gap all the way around the clutch pack to ensure it's uniform. The 3-4 clutch pack clearance should be between 0.060 and 0.090-inch. If the clearance is not as specified, selective backing plates are available from a dealership parts department

Note

The 3-4, forward and overrun clutches can be air-checked by applying air pressure to the feed holes in the input shaft. **Warning:** *Always wear eye protection when using compressed air!*

Reverse input clutch assembly

8D.233 Install the reverse input clutch piston inner and outer seals on the piston with the seal lips facing into the housing

8D.234 Lubricate the seals with ATF and install the piston into the reverse input clutch housing

8D.235 Use a seal installation tool to work the inner and outer seal lips into the housing

8D.236 Install the reverse input clutch spring assembly

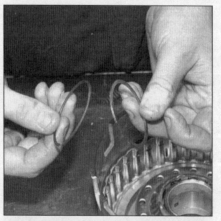

8D.237 The reverse input clutch spring assembly retaining ring is similar in diameter to the low-reverse clutch spring retaining ring. DO NOT mix these retaining rings up - the reverse input spring retaining ring on the right, is thicker (0.063-inch) than the low-reverse clutch spring retaining ring (0.054-inch)

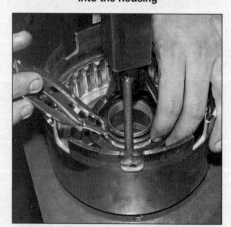

8D.238 Mount the housing in a spring compressor or press, compress the spring retainer and install the retaining ring. Make sure the retaining ring is fully seated in the groove and completely surrounded by the spring retainer when the pressure is released

8D.239 Install the waved steel clutch plate, engaging the tabs with the slots in the housing

Note

1987 and later models use a Belleville-style (semi-cone shaped) plate instead of a waved plate. Install the Belleville plate followed by a steel clutch plate

8D.240 Install a steel clutch plate followed by . . .

8D.241 . . . a friction plate. Alternate steel plates and friction plates until all the reverse input clutch plates are installed. Dip the friction plates in clean ATF before installing

8D.242 Install the reverse input clutch backing plate with the chamfered side out

8D. 243 Install the retaining ring . . .

8D.244 . . . and seat it in the groove in the housing

8D.245 Align the clutch plate splines with a small screwdriver

Note

On 1987 and later models, check the reverse input clutch backing plate travel. Press the backing plate down by hand with your fingers distributed evenly around the circumference of the backing plate. Use medium pressure on the backing plate (about 20 lbs. - excessive pressure will distort the Belleville plate). Using a feeler gauge, measure the clearance between the snap-ring and the backing plate - it should be between 0.040 and 0.075-inch; If not, selective-size backing plates are available at a dealership parts department

Final assembly

8D.246 Install the selective thrust washer over the input shaft

8D.247 Install the input housing-to-pump thrust bearing with the inside flanged race (with black finish) facing up

8D.248 Install the reverse input clutch assembly onto the input housing, indexing the clutch plates with the splines. Rotate the reverse input housing until all the clutch plates are fully engaged

8D.249 Install the reverse input and input clutch assembly into the transmission case, indexing the 3-4 clutch plates with the input internal gear. Rotate the input clutch assembly clockwise, then counterclockwise rapidly as you lower the assembly into place

8D.250 When installed properly, the top of the reverse input housing will be located just below the pump gasket surface (arrow)

8D.251 Install a new 2-4 band assembly into the case

8D.252 Install the 2-4 band anchor into the case and index the pin with the 2-4 band anchor pin lug

8D.253 Use a large screwdriver to seat the 2-4 band tabs in the case. If necessary, push the input shaft toward the top of the case for extra clearance and be careful not to scratch the reverse input housing band apply surface with the screwdriver blade

8D.254 Install two oil pump alignment bolts into the oil pump threaded holes and install the gasket. Make sure the gasket is installed properly and all the holes line up. Alignment bolts can be fabricated by cutting off the heads of two bolts slightly longer than the pump bolts and chamfering the ends of the bolts

8D.255 Install the pump-to-reverse input housing thrust washer onto the pump. Index the tabs in the thrust washer with the holes in the pump hub and retain the washer with petroleum jelly

8D.256 Install new oil seal rings onto the pump hub. Make sure the rings are seated in the groove with the angle-cut ends overlapping. Retain the rings with petroleum jelly

8D.257 Install the pump body-to-case O-ring. Seat it completely in the groove with the yellow stripe facing out. Lubricate the O-ring with ATF

8D.258 Lubricate the case and reverse input housing liberally with ATF. Align the pump properly (the TCC and oil filter bores will face the bottom of the case) (arrows) and install the pump assembly over the alignment bolts. Firmly press the pump assembly into the case until it's fully seated

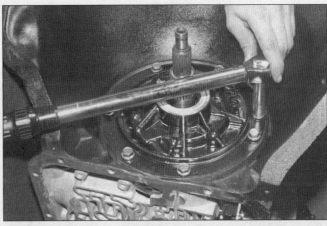

8D.259 Remove the alignment bolts, install new sealing washers on the pump bolts and install the pump bolts. Tighten the pump bolts evenly, working from bolt to bolt in a criss-cross pattern, to 18 ft-lbs.

8D.260 Install a dial indicator to the case and position the needle tip on the end of the input shaft. Zero the indicator and lever the input shaft up-and down to check the endplay. The endplay should be between 0.005 and 0.036-inch; if not, remove the oil pump, 2-4 band and input clutch assembly and change the reverse input housing-to-input housing selective washer with a thicker or thinner washer as required. Selective washers are available at a dealership parts department. If no endplay was indicated, either the selective washer is too thick or the reverse input or input clutches are assembled improperly

8D.261 Position the transmission on the bench or horizontally for the remaining procedures. Install the 2-4 servo return spring in the case

8D.262 Install new oil seal rings on the 2nd apply piston and a new O-ring on the inner housing. Lubricate the seals with ATF

8D.263 Install the inner housing onto the 2nd apply piston and install the assembly onto the case. Press the assembly in and make sure the pin engages the 2-4 band correctly

8D.264 Install a new seal ring onto the 4th apply piston, lubricate the ring with ATF and install the piston into the cover (note that the projection on the piston goes into the cover). Retain the piston in the cover with petroleum jelly

8D.265 Install a new O-ring on the servo cover, lubricate the O-ring with ATF and install the cover into the case, indexing the servo pin into the 4th apply piston

8D.266 Press the cover in and install the retaining ring. Make sure the retaining ring is seated fully in the groove

8D.267 The 2-4 servo can be air-checked for operation by applying air pressure into the fluid passage as shown. Make sure the pin engages the 2-4 band properly. **Warning:** *Always wear eye protection when using compressed air!*

Note

If the original 2-4 band was burnt, check the servo apply pin for the correct length with the special GM intermediate band apply pin gauge (J-33037). Different length apply pins are available from a dealership parts department

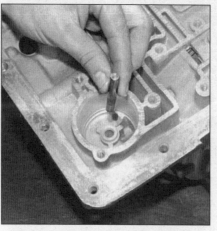

8D.268 Install the accumulator piston pin into the case

8D.269 Install the 3-4 accumulator piston into the bore with the legs facing up

8D.270 Install the 3-4 accumulator spring

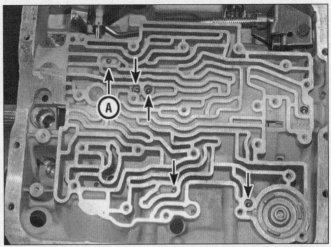

8D.271 Install the case check balls in the locations shown (arrows). On 1988 and later models, DO NOT install check ball A

8D.272 Install the converter clutch screen . . .

8D.273 . . . and the governor screen, pressing them into the case passage

8D.274 Install two valve body alignment bolts into the case and install the case-to-spacer plate gasket. Again, alignment bolts can be fabricated by cutting off the heads of two bolts slightly longer than valve body bolts, then chamfering the bolt ends

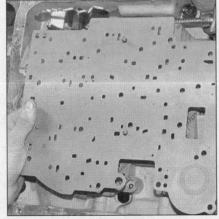

8D.275 Lubricate the spacer plate with a thin film of ATFand install the spacer plate . . .

8D.276 . . . and the spacer plate-to-valve body gasket

8D.277 Install the 1-2 accumulator piston (with the legs facing out of the bore) and the accumulator spring into the accumulator cover

8D.278 Install the 1-2 accumulator assembly and tighten the bolts finger tight

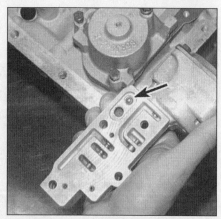

8D.279 Place a check ball into the auxiliary valve body (if equipped) at the location shown (arrow) and retain it with petroleum jelly

8D.280 Install the auxiliary valve body and tighten the bolts finger tight; if not equipped with an auxiliary valve body, install the oil passage cover

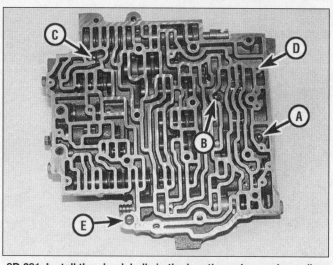

8D.281 Install the check balls in the locations shown, depending on model, and retain them with petroleum jelly - it's easier to retain the E (special copper flash check ball) on the spacer plate
Models WITHOUT an auxiliary valve body - place check balls in locations A, B, C and E (copper flash)

1992 and earlier models equipped with an auxiliary valve body - place check balls in locations A, B and E (copper flash)

1993 and later models - place check balls in locations A, B, D and E (copper flash)

8D.282 Install the manual valve into the valve body bore . . .

8D.283 . . . and install the manual valve link to the manual valve

8D.284 Hold the valve body over the alignment bolts and connect the manual link to the detent lever . . .

8D.285 . . . then lower the valve body over the alignment bolts

8D.286 Install the TV lever and bracket assembly onto the valve body and tighten the bolts to 8 ft-lbs. Check the TV lever and valve operation and make sure the link is installed through the hole in the case correctly

8D.287 Remove the alignment bolts and install all the valve body bolts, placing the wiring harness retainers in the proper locations. Install a new O-ring on the TCC solenoid, lubricate with ATF, install the TCC solenoid and tighten the bolts to 8 ft-lbs

8D.288 Connect the wiring harness connectors to the pressure switches and case plug. Tighten the valve body bolts, working from the center out, to 8 ft-lbs. Tighten the auxiliary valve body bolts (or oil passage bolts) and accumulator cover bolts to 8 ft-lbs.

8D.289 Install the oil pipe (if equipped). Make sure the oil pipe is secured by the retainers (arrows) and is fully seated in the pump

Note
If the oil pump was replaced with a new unit on models without an auxiliary valve body, make sure the oil pipe hole in the pump has a plug in it

8D.290 Install the manual valve detent spring and tighten the bolt to 18 ft-lbs

8D.291 Install a new seal on a new oil filter (on early models, install two O-ring seals). Lubricate the seal with ATF and install the filter

8D.292 Install a new oil pan gasket . . .

8D.293 . . . install the oil pan and tighten the bolts to 12 ft-lbs

8D.294 Lubricate the governor sleeve and gear with ATF and install the governor into the governor bore, meshing the governor gear with the output shaft

8D.295 Install a new O-ring on the governor cover. Apply Loctite 609, or equivalent, to the cover flange and install the cover. Tap the outer ring of the cover in with a hammer and punch until the cover is fully seated

8D.296 Slip the speedometer drive gear over the output shaft. Install the retaining clip tab into the hole in the output shaft and align the slot in the gear with the clip

8D.297 Press the clip down and slide the gear over the clip until the clip-ends catch the rear edge of the gear (arrow)

8D.298 Drive out the extension housing bushing and install a new bushing (for information on removing and installing bushings, see Chapter 2)

8D.299 Tap in a new seal until it's fully seated. Work the seal in evenly, tapping all around the circumference of the seal

8D.300 Install a new extension housing O-ring

8D.301 Install the extension housing and tighten the bolts to 26 ft-lbs

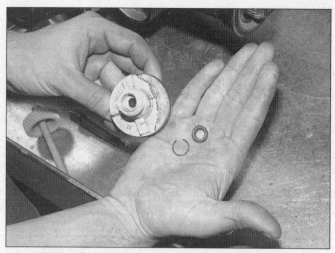

8D.302 Install a new speedometer gear shaft seal into the speedometer gear housing and retain the seal with the small ring. The seal lip faces in

8D.303 Install a new O-ring onto the speedometer gear housing, lubricating it with ATF

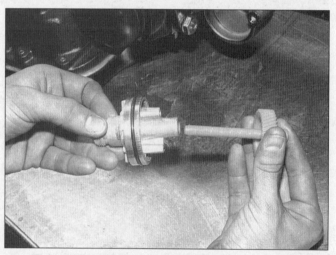

8D.304 Lubricate the gear shaft with ATF and install the shaft into the housing

8D.305 Install the speedometer driven gear assembly into the case, meshing the speedometer gears

8D.306 Install the speedometer housing retainer and bolt, tightening it securely

8D.307 Install new seals into the TV cable and dipstick tube holes. Install the torque converter. The transmission is now ready for installation in the vehicle

Chapter 8 Part E
Disassembly, inspection and assembly
THM125/125-C and 3T40 transaxles

Introduction

The THM125/125-C and 3T40 are three-speed automatic transaxles manufactured for front-wheel drive vehicles. The major components of these transaxles are:

a) *Lock-up torque converter (except the THM125, which uses a conventional converter)*
b) *Sprockets and drive chain assembly*
c) *Vane-type oil pump*
d) *Control valve assembly*
e) *Intermediate band*
f) *Three separate multiple disc clutch packs (direct clutch, forward clutch and low-reverse clutch)*
g) *One roller clutch*
h) *Planetary gear set*
i) *Final drive*

Follow the photographic sequence for disassembly, inspection and assembly. The model shown is a typical transaxle of this type. Differences do exist between models and many changes have been made over the years, so perform each step in order and lay the components out on a clean work bench in the EXACT ORDER of removal to prevent confusion during reassembly. Many snap-rings and clutch plates are similar in size, but must not be interchanged. Keep the individual parts together with the component from which they were removed to avoid mix-ups. Save all old parts and compare them with the new part to ensure they are an exact match before reassembly. Pay particular attention to the stack-up of the various clutch packs. Differences do exist between models and your transaxle may not match the stack-up shown. Note the exact location of the check balls in the case as well as the valve body. Save all the old parts until the overhaul is complete and the transaxle has been thoroughly road tested; old components can be useful in diagnosing any problems that may arise.

The THM125/125-C and 3T40 are metric dimensioned transaxles; use metric tools on the fasteners. Special tools are required for some procedures. Alternate procedures are shown where possible, but some procedures can only be accomplished with special tools. Read through the entire overhaul procedure before beginning work to familiarize yourself with the procedures and identify any special tools that may be needed. Thoroughly clean the exterior of the transaxle before beginning disassembly.

Transaxle disassembly

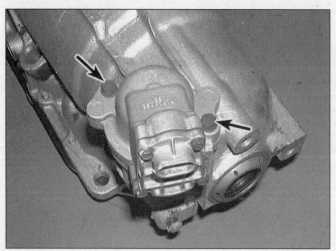

8E.1 Remove the bolts (arrows) and the speed sensor housing

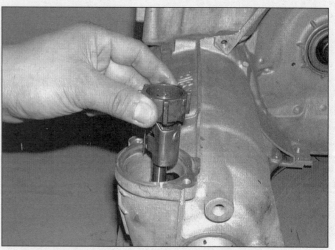

8E.2 Withdraw the governor from the transaxle case

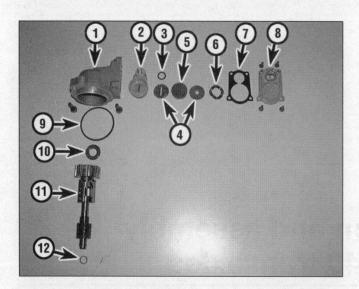

8E.3 Governor and speed sensor exploded view
(with electronic Vehicle Speed Sensor)

1   Speed sensor housing
2   Speed sensor pick-up coil
3   O-ring
4   Washers
5   Magnet
6   Wave spring
7   Gasket
8   Cover
9   O-ring
10   Thrust washer
11   Governor
12   Seal

8E.4 Remove the bottom pan and oil filter, then remove bolts and
the servo cover

8E.5 Withdraw the servo assembly from the transaxle case

8E.6 If necessary, remove the E-clip . . .

8E.7 . . . and separate the intermediate band apply pin from the servo piston

8E.8 Remove the two bolts (arrows) and the park lock bracket and dipstick stop

8E.9 Remove the bolt and clamp . . .

8E.10 . . . and withdraw the oil weir from the transaxle case

8E.11 Remove the accumulator check valve and spring from the transaxle case

8E.12 Remove the reverse oil fluid pipe, back-up rings and O-rings

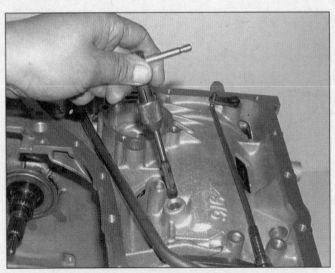

8E.13 Using a 9 mm x 1.0 tap, remove the low-reverse seal from the case

8E.14 Align the legs of the output shaft C-ring up in the access hole and press the clip off the shaft with needle-nose pliers

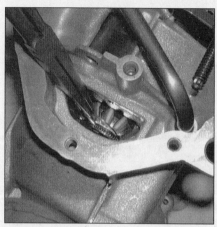

8E.15 Rotate the shaft 180-degrees and remove the clip

8E.16 Remove the output shaft from the transaxle case

8E.17 Remove the valve body cover from the side of the transaxle case and remove the bracket and throttle valve cable link

8E.18 DO NOT remove the bolt marked (A) unless it's necessary to disassemble the auxiliary valve body

8E.19 Disconnect the electrical connectors, remove the valve body bolts, remove the valve body and place it in a safe, clean location with the machined side facing up

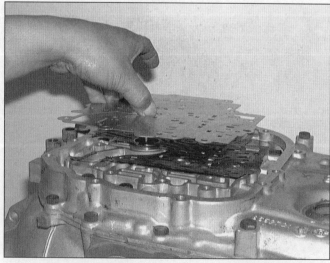

8E.20 Remove the large check ball sitting on the spacer plate, then remove the spacer plate and gasket

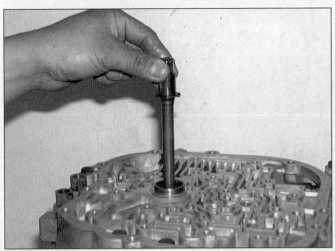

8E.21 Withdraw the oil pump shaft from the transaxle case

8E.22 Remove the five check balls (arrows) from the transaxle case

8E.23 Disconnect the rod from the manual valve

8E.24 Remove the case cover bolts, including the two Torx-head bolts (arrows) (be sure to remove all the bolts; all bolts may not be shown)

8E.25 Thread two self-tapping 12-mm bolts into the dowel pin holes and alternately tighten the bolts to free the case cover from the case - DO NOT attempt to pry the cover off or damage to the cover may result

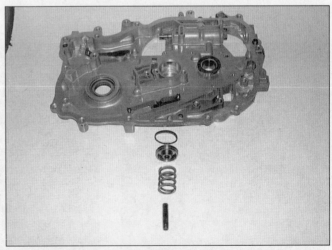

8E.26 Remove the case cover, place it on the bench with the accumulator side up and remove the accumulator spring, piston, pin and seal

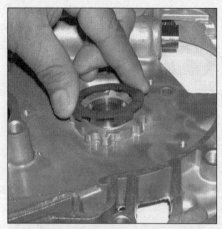

8E.27 Remove the drive sprocket thrust washer from the case cover

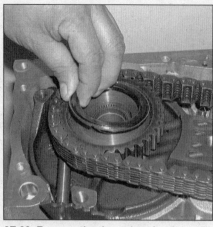

8E.28 Remove the thrust bearing from the driven sprocket

8E.29 Remove the turbine shaft O-ring from the turbine shaft

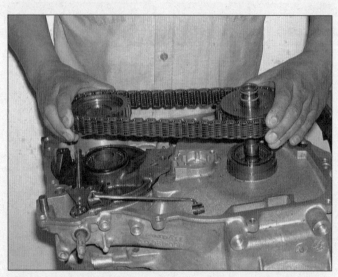

8E.30 Lift the drive chain and sprockets from the transaxle case

8E.31 Remove the drive sprocket support thrust washer . . .

8E.32 . . . and the driven sprocket support thrust washer

8E.33 Using a pin punch, drive the detent lever shaft roll pin out of the hub and shaft and remove it

8E.34 Using a slide-hammer puller, remove the manual shaft-to-case retaining pin

8E.35 Remove the manual shaft and actuator rod assembly

8E.36 Lift the driven sprocket support from the case

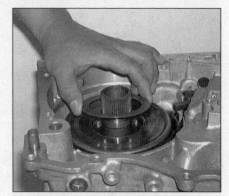

8E.37 Remove the driven sprocket support-to-direct clutch housing thrust washer

8E.38 Remove the band anchor hole plug

8E.39 Remove the intermediate band

8E.40 Remove the direct and forward clutch assembly

8E.41 Remove the input shaft thrust washer

8E.42 Remove the internal gear

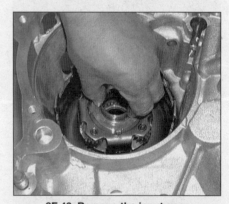

8E.43 Remove the input gear carrier assembly

8E.44 Remove the input sun gear

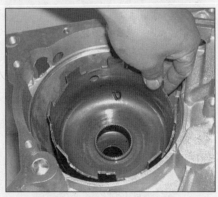

8E.45 Remove the input drum

8E.46 Remove the reaction sun gear

8E.47 Using a screwdriver, pry the low/reverse clutch housing snap-ring out of the grooves in the transaxle case and remove the snap-ring

8E.48 Using the low/reverse clutch remover and installer, pull the low/reverse clutch housing out of the transaxle case

8E.49 Remove the snap-ring . . .

8E.50 . . . and lift the reaction assembly out of the case by the shaft

8E.51 Using a screwdriver, pry the final drive assembly snap ring out of the grooves in the transaxle case and remove the snap-ring

8E.52 Remove the final drive spacer

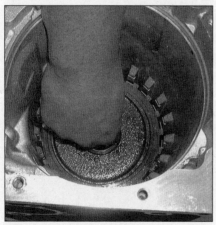

8E.53 Remove the final drive assembly from the transaxle case

8E.54 Remove the torque converter seal . . .

8E.55 . . . and the driveaxle seals

Component inspection and subassembly overhaul

Using an approved cleaning solvent, clean and dry all the components thoroughly, including the case. Do not use rags to wipe the components dry, as lint from the rag may lodge in the oil passages, causing a valve to stick.

Inspect the following transaxle components and repair or replace as necessary:

a) **Case:** Inspect the exterior of the case for damage, cracks and porosity (a porous casting will cause fluid leaks). Check the valve body mating surfaces on the case and valve body for damage and flatness (use a precision straightedge to check for flatness - any warpage means the valve body or case will have to be machined or replaced). Check all the oil passages, the servo bore, the speedometer bore and the governor bore for damage. Check all threaded holes for damage (repair thread damage as described in Chapter 2). Check the oil cooler line fittings for damage. Check the interior of the case for damaged retaining ring grooves, which will mean the case will have to be replaced. Check the low-reverse lugs for excessive wear. Check the drive support bearing for wear and replace it if necessary. Inspect the manual linkage and the park-lock linkage for damage.

b) **Reaction gear set and low-reverse clutch:** Inspect the low-reverse piston for damage; check the seal grooves for damage. Check the low-reverse spring assembly for damage. Inspect the reaction internal gear, support and carrier for damage. Check for stripped splines, cracked or broken teeth, damaged or worn thrust bearings and bushings. Check the reaction carrier pinion gears for damaged bearings or worn washers. Check the pinion endplay with a feeler gauge; it should be between 0.010 and 0.025-inch. Inspect the low-reverse roller clutch for damaged rollers or broken springs. Check the finish of the inner and outer race and check the support for damaged lugs. Inspect the reaction sun gear for spline or tooth damage. Check the thrust washers and bushings for wear or damage.

c) **Input gear set:** Inspect the input carrier, input internal gear, input drum and input sun gear for damaged splines, broken teeth, and worn bushings. Check the thrust bearing for wear or damage. Check the input carrier assembly for broken teeth, worn washers and a damaged or worn thrust bearing. Check the pinion endplay with a feeler gauge; it should be between 0.010 and 0.025-inch. Check the input sun gear for damaged splines, broken teeth or a worn bushing.

d) **Forward and direct clutch assemblies:** Inspect the clutch housings for damaged splines. Inspect the check balls for looseness and the seal rings for damage. Check the clutch housings, pistons, springs, spring retainers, clutch plates, backing plates and retainer rings for wear or damage. Check for nicks or burrs in the lip seal areas. Check the housing and drum for worn bushings. Check the direct clutch housing band apply surface for damage. Lay a steel ruler or straightedge across the surface and inspect for dishing. Inspect the intermediate band assembly and servo for damage or wear. If the band is extremely damaged or burned, check the band apply pin length during reassembly with the special Band Apply Pin Tool (Kent-Moore J-28535, or equivalent).

e) **Differential and final drive assembly:** Inspect the final drive internal gear for damaged teeth and worn bearing surfaces. Check the final drive carrier pinion endplay with a feeler gauge; it should be between 0.010 and 0.025-inch. Check the thrust bearing for damage. Check the governor gear for damage. Check the differential side gears, pinions and shaft for damage and wear. If necessary use a pin punch to remove the roll pin from the shaft and disassemble the differential.

Oil pump assembly

Disassemble the oil pump as shown in the accompanying photos. Remove the converter clutch valve train, solenoid and switches and inspect the components for damage. Lay the valves and springs out on a clean, lint-free towel in the exact order of removal to prevent confusion on assembly. Clean and dry the cover, body and all internal components. Inspect the valves and remove any burrs with a fine lapping compound; inspect the springs for damage or distortion; inspect the valve bores for damage; inspect the pump shaft bearing for wear or damage. Replace any damaged components. Inspect the pump rotor, vanes and slider very carefully. Replace the parts with a rotor and vane kit if there are any doubts about their condition.

8E.56 Remove the bolts and separate the auxiliary valve body cover from the auxiliary valve body

8E.57 Disconnect the electrical connectors and remove the torque converter solenoid and wiring harness from the auxiliary valve body

8E.58 Remove the auxiliary valve body from the main valve body

8E.59 Remove the slide pivot pin and remove the slide and spring; remove the rings, vanes and rotor from the pump body and inspect the components carefully for wear or damage

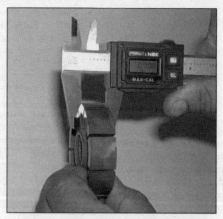

8E.60 If either the rotor, vanes or slide require replacement, measure the thickness of the component and replace it with a new component with a comparable thickness - various sizes are available at a dealership parts department; if the correct components are not used, damage to the transaxle will result

8E.61 If necessary, remove the valves from the auxiliary valve body and inspect them for wear or damage

   1   TCC control valve
   2   Orifice control valve

8E.62 Install the pump slide into the pump body and install the slide seal and support

8E.63 Align the slide, install the pivot pin and the spring

8E.64 Install a vane ring in the pump body cavity, install the rotor and the vanes, then install the second vane ring on top of the rotor - make sure the vane rings are positioned inside the vanes and the vanes are flush with the top of the rotor

8E.65 Install the slide O-ring . . .

8E.66 . . . and oil seal

8E.67 Lubricate the pump with ATF, install the auxiliary valve body and cover with a new gasket and tighten the bolts to 98 in-lbs

8E.68 Using a small screwdriver or pick, pry each valve against spring pressure - the valve should snap back when pressure is released - check each valve for sticking

8E.69 If necessary, remove the clip or roll pin retaining the valve train and remove the valve assembly - clean and inspect the valves, bushings and springs, then reassemble the valve train - if the clip or roll pin does not fit securely, replace it with a new one

8E.70 A small tap may be used to remove roll pins

Control valve assembly

Complete disassembly of the valve body is not necessary unless the valve body has been contaminated. Clean the valve body using an approved solvent and air dry (DO NOT use rags to dry the valve body, as lint from the rag may cause a valve to stick). Check each valve for freedom of movement in its bore. If a stuck valve is encountered, remove the individual valve and components for further cleaning and inspection. Nicks and burrs may be removed by lapping the valve with a fine lapping compound.

If complete disassembly of the valve body is required, lay the valve body on a clean work bench, use clean tools to disassemble and wash the valve body with clean solvent. Remove the valves from the valve body, one at a time. Lay out the valves, springs and bushings in their proper order on a clean lint-free towel. Cleanliness and meticulous care in keeping the valves in order cannot be over-stressed. A tap or a tapered number 49 drill bit is helpful in removing any stubborn roll-pins you may encounter.

Governor

Inspect the governor for damaged springs, seals or gear teeth. Inspect the weights for binding. Inspect the thrust bearing for wear or damage. Inspect the governor screen (in the case bore) for contamination. Replace the governor if it does not operate smoothly or appears contaminated.

Transaxle assembly

An automatic transaxle is a precision piece of equipment. Install each component as shown, and do not force any component into place. If it doesn't fit properly, find out why and rectify the situation. Maintain a clean workplace and lubricate all moving parts as they are installed. Lubricate thrust washers and bearings with automatic transaxle fluid (ATF) or petroleum jelly. Use petroleum jelly to retain thrust washers and check balls in their proper location as the component is installed. Dip all friction plates in ATF before installation.

8E.71 Check the drive sprocket bearing for wear or damage and if necessary, use a bearing puller to pull the bearing from the case

8E.72 Install the new drive sprocket bearing with the appropriate size bearing installation tool

Final drive assembly

8E.73 Check each final drive pinion endplay with a feeler gauge - endplay should be between 0.010 and 0.025-inch

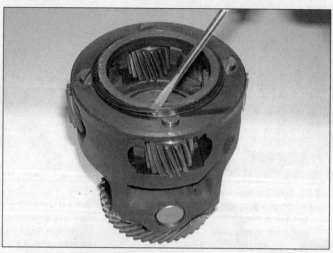

8E.74 If necessary, remove the pinion shaft retaining ring and remove the shafts, pinions, washers and needle bearings for inspection

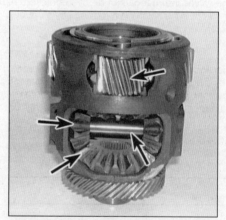

8E.75 Check the differential pinions, side gears and cross shaft for damage or wear - pay special attention to the cross shaft and pinions; they are known to wear

8E.76 Check the governor gear for damage; it can be pulled off and replaced if necessary

8E.77 If necessary, drive out the cross shaft retaining pin, remove the cross shaft and disassemble the differential

8E.78 Install the final drive thrust bearing with the outer race down against the carrier

8E.79 Install the final drive sun gear into the carrier with the stepped side facing up (arrow)

8E.80 Install the differential carrier thrust bearing onto the final drive internal gear with the inner race against the hub - retain the thrust bearing with petroleum jelly

8E.81 Install the internal gear onto the final drive carrier, meshing the internal gear with the final drive pinions

8E.82 Turn the unit over and install the selective thrust washer on the final drive assembly - retain the thrust washer with petroleum jelly

8E.83 Install the differential case thrust bearing with the inner race against the carrier - retain the thrust bearing with petroleum jelly

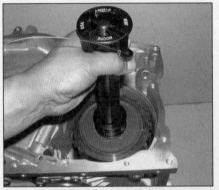

8E.84 Using the special removal/installation tool, install the final drive unit in the case - align the internal gear splines with the case lugs and press the unit down until fully seated

8E.85 Install the final drive spacer and snap-ring, engaging the snap-ring in the case groove (arrow)

8E.86 Make sure the gap in the spacer is positioned to allow proper operation of the parking pawl (arrow)

8E.87 Check the final drive endplay as follows:

1   Position the transaxle with the final drive facing up
2   Insert the loading tool adapter into the final drive
3   Install dial indicator with the stem resting on the adapter, then zero the indicator
4   Pry up on the governor drive gear and note the movement on the dial indicator
5   Final drive endplay should be 0.005 to 0.032 inch - if necessary, adjust the final drive endplay by replacing the final drive-to-case selective thrust washer - washers are available in sizes ranging from 0.055 to 0.095 inch

8E.88 When the final drive endplay is correct, remove the dial indicator, leave the adapter in place and install the final drive loading tool; turn the knob on the loading tool until snug, removing the endplay from the final drive unit

Reaction carrier and roller clutch assembly

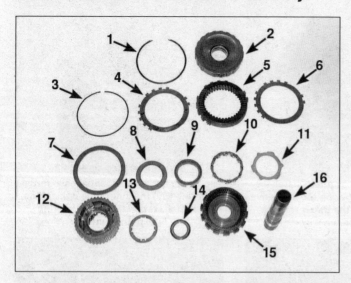

8E.89 Disassemble the reaction gear and inspect the components for wear or damage

1   Snap ring
2   Low/reverse clutch housing
3   Snap ring
4   Low/reverse clutch waved plate
5   Low/reverse clutch plates
6   Low/reverse clutch waved plate
7   Low/reverse clutch backing plate (selective)
8   Low/reverse clutch housing spacer (selective)
9   Low roller clutch race
10 Low roller clutch rollers
11 Low roller clutch thrust washer
12 Reaction carrier assembly
13 Reaction carrier thrust washer
14 Reaction sun gear thrust washer
15 Reaction internal gear
16 Final drive sun gear/shaft

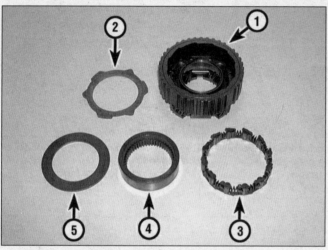

8E.90 Disassemble the low roller clutch and inspect the components for wear or damage

1   Reaction carrier assembly
2   Low roller clutch thrust washer
3   Low roller clutch rollers
4   Low roller clutch race
5   Low/reverse clutch housing spacer (selective)

8E.91 Begin assembly of the reaction carrier and roller clutch assembly by installing the sun gear shaft into the internal gear

8E.92 Install the reaction sun gear thrust bearing with the inner race against the internal gear - retain the thrust bearing with petroleum jelly

8E.93 Install the low roller clutch thrust washer into reaction carrier

8E.94 After insuring the rollers are properly install in the cage, install the low roller clutch rollers and cage assembly into the reaction carrier

8E.95 Install the low roller clutch race with the splined side facing up - rotate the race clockwise and press it in position until fully seated in the carrier

8E.96 Install the reaction carrier thrust washer, engaging the tabs on the thrust washer with the slots in the reaction carrier - retain the thrust washer with petroleum jelly

8E.97 Install the low/reverse clutch housing selective spacer on the roller clutch race

8E.98 Install the reaction carrier/roller clutch assembly into the internal gear

8E.99 Install the reaction carrier/roller clutch assembly into the case

8E.100 Rotate the reaction gear set several revolutions and make sure the splines on the outside of internal gear do not contact the final drive spacer (arrow) - reposition the spacer if they do

8E.101 Install the low-reverse clutch backing plate in the case with the stepped side down

8E.102 Install the low-reverse clutch waved plate

8E.103 Install the low-reverse clutch pack, alternating friction plates and steel plates

8E.104 Install the second waved plate and the thin (0.042-inch) snap-ring

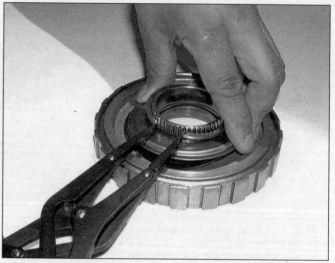

8E.105 Press down on the low-reverse clutch piston spring retainer and remove the snap-ring

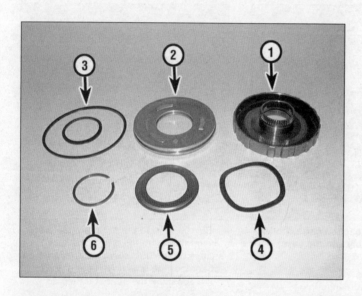

8E.106 Disassemble the low-reverse clutch housing and inspect the components for wear or damage

1   Low-reverse clutch housing
2   Low-reverse clutch piston
3   Low-reverse clutch piston seals
4   Low-reverse clutch piston spring
5   Low-reverse clutch piston spring retainer
6   Snap-ring

8E.107 Install the inner seal on the low-reverse piston . . .

8E.108 . . . and the outer seal - lubricate the seals with ATF and make sure the seal lips face into the housing when the piston is installed

8E.109 Using a seal protector (arrow) on the inner seal, start the piston into the housing

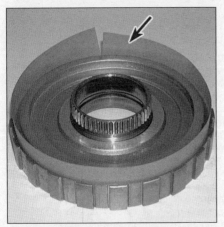

8E.110 Using a seal protector (arrow) on the outer seal, work the piston into the housing until fully seated

8E.111 Install the low-reverse clutch piston spring . . .

8E.112 . . . and the spring retainer with the cupped side down

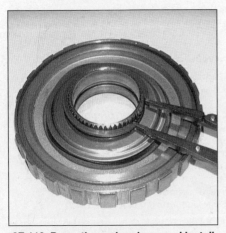

8E.113 Press the spring down and install the snap-ring

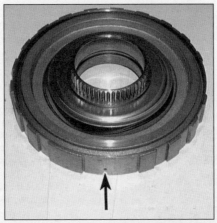

8E.114 Air check the low-reverse clutch piston by applying air pressure (maximum of 90-psi) to the oil feed hole (arrow) - the piston should apply and release as air pressure is applied and removed

8E.115 Using the special removal/installation tool, install the low-reverse clutch housing assembly into the case, aligning the oil feed hole in the clutch housing with the passage in the case

8E.116 Make sure the clutch housing is seated past the snap-ring groove - if it isn't, remove the installation tool and install the sun gear, rotate the sun gear while pressing the clutch housing down

8E.117 When the clutch housing is fully seated, install the sun gear and the thick (0.092-inch) snap-ring in the case groove (arrow)

8E.118 Check the reaction sun gear-to-input drum endplay as follows:

1   *The output shaft loading tool must be in place and the reaction sun gear must be properly seated*
2   *Install the special gauge bar and dial indicator with the dial indicator extension stem resting between the open ends of the sun gear selective snap-ring*
3   *Position the feeler gauge on the gauge bar under the shoulder of the indicator, then zero the indicator*
4   *Rotate the sun gear slightly so the dial indicator extension rests on the snap-ring and remove the feeler gauge from under the indicator shoulder*
5   *Note the movement on the dial indicator; sun gear-to-input drum endplay should be 0.005 to 0.013 inch - if necessary, adjust the sun gear-to-input drum endplay by replacing the sun gear selective snap-ring; snap-rings are available in sizes ranging from 0.089 to 0.140 inch*

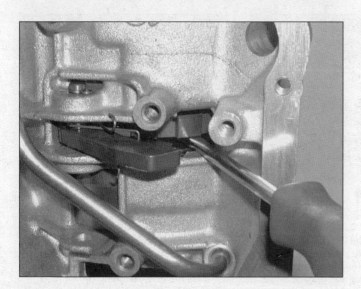

8E.119 Check the low roller clutch endplay as follows:

1   *Install the dial indicator as described in the reaction sun gear-to-input drum endplay check, then zero the indicator*
2   *Working through the parking pawl slot, pry up on the reaction internal gear (do not pry on the spacer) and note the movement on the dial indicator*
3   *Low roller clutch endplay should be 0.003 to 0.046 inch - if necessary, adjust the low roller clutch endplay by replacing the reverse clutch housing-to-low roller clutch race selective spacer; spacers are available in sizes ranging from 0.039 to 0.126 inch*

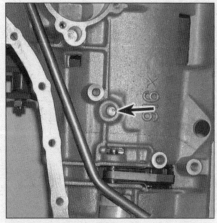

8E.120 Using a 3/8 drift, install a new low-reverse cup plug into the case passage (arrow) - make sure the seal is fitted securely against the low-reverse clutch housing

8E.121 Install the input drum onto the reaction sun gear

8E.122 Install the input sun gear with the groove (arrow) facing up

8E.123 Install the input sun gear thrust washer in the input carrier, engaging the tabs on the thrust washer with the slots in the carrier - retain the thrust washer with petroleum jelly

8E.124 Install the input carrier on to the input sun gear, meshing the pinions with the sun gear teeth and install the input internal gear thrust washer (arrow)

8E.125 Install the input internal gear onto the input carrier

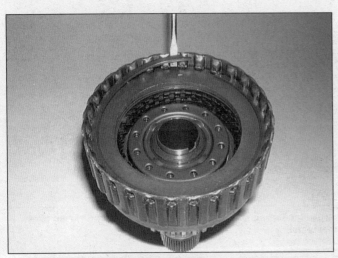

8E.126 Separate the direct clutch from the forward clutch, remove the snap-ring from the forward clutch housing and remove the clutch pack

Forward and direct clutch assembly

When disassembling a clutch pack, keep the clutch components in the exact order as the original stack-up; several updates have been made to the forward and direct clutch plates over the years. Make notes on the number of plates, the installed direction and location of backing plates, apply plates, waved plates, etc. Differences may exist between your model and the model shown. On some models, a second waved plate has been added (one at each end of the clutch pack) to improve shift feel. The correct components for your transaxle should be in the overhaul kit, if you purchased the correct kit.

Before removing a piston seal, note the installed direction of the seal lip. The piston seals must be installed with the seal lip facing the correct direction. If the seal is installed with the lip facing the wrong direction, the piston will not operate properly. If unsure, a common rule-of-thumb is this: the seal lip always faces pressure.

8E.127 Using a clutch spring compressor, compress the clutch spring and remove the snap-ring - remove the clutch spring and piston components from the housing

8E.128 Replace the inner and outer piston seals - make sure the seal lips face into the housing when installed and lubricate the seals with ATF

8E.129 Install the insert into the clutch housing

8E.130 Using a seal protector (arrow), install the clutch piston into the housing - start with the inner seal first then work the outer seal in, be careful not to cut the seals on the snap-ring groove

8E.131 Install the spring guide . . .

8E.132 . . . and the spring assembly - compress the spring and install the snap-ring

8E.133 Install a steel waved plate into the housing

8E.134 Install the clutch pack, alternating friction and steel plates

8E.135 Install the second waved plate . . .

8E.136 . . . and the selective backing plate with the identification mark up

8E.137 Install the snap-ring in the housing groove

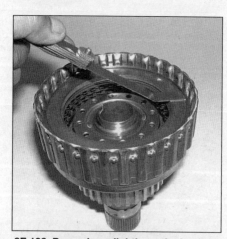

8E.138 Press down lightly on the backing plate and measure the forward clutch pack clearance between the backing plate and the snap-ring - clearance should be 0.040 to 0.060-inch; if it isn't, replace the backing plate. Backing plates are available in sizes ranging from 0.126 to 0.197-inch

8E.139 Replace the oil seal rings (arrow) on the forward clutch housing shaft - make sure the ends properly overlap and coat the seals with petroleum jelly

8E.140 Remove the snap-ring from the direct clutch housing . . .

8E.141 . . . and remove the clutch pack

8E.142 Remove the clutch spring snap-ring . . .

8E.143 . . . and remove the spring retainer . . .

8E.144 . . . and piston from the direct clutch housing

8E.145 Replace the center seal in the direct clutch housing - make sure the seal lip is facing up, out of the housing

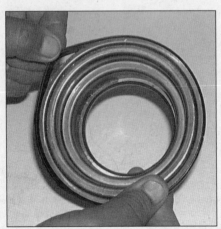

8E.146 Replace the inner and outer seals on the direct clutch piston - make sure the seal lips face into the housing when the piston is installed

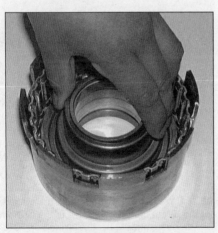

8E.147 Lubricate the seals with ATF and install the direct clutch piston into the housing

8E.148 Install the clutch spring assembly . . .

8E.149 . . . and install the snap-ring in the housing groove

8E.150 Install the direct clutch pack into the housing, steel plate first then alternating friction and steel plates

8E.151 Install the direct clutch backing plate with the chamfered side down . . .

8E.152 . . . and install the snap-ring in the housing groove

8E.153 Install the direct clutch assembly onto the forward clutch assembly - rotate the direct clutch as you slowly lower it into place to ensure all the clutch plates are engaged with the splines

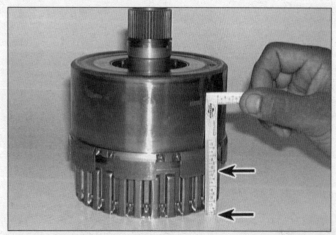

8E.154 When properly installed, the distance between the bottom of the direct clutch housing and the bottom of the forward clutch housing should be 1-7/32 inch on 1986 and earlier model transaxles or 1-13/32 inch on 1987 and later model transaxles; if it isn't the clutch plates may not be properly engaged (be very careful when making this measurement on model years close to the changeover, since earlier model transaxles may be installed in later vehicles)

8E.155 Install the input shaft thrust washer onto the forward clutch housing with the stepped side out - retain the thrust washer with petroleum jelly

8E.156 Install the forward/direct clutch assembly into the case, engaging the forward clutch splines with the input internal gear

8E.157 Place a straightedge across the case and measure the distance from the case to the top of the direct clutch housing - when properly installed the measurement should be 1-11/16 inch

8E.158 Install the intermediate band in the case with the band stops properly located (arrows)

8E.159 Install the band stop plug - if your plug is not equipped with the tab (arrow), it must be staked in place

8e.160 Install the driven sprocket support thrust washer on the direct clutch housing - retain the thrust washer with petroleum jelly

8E.161 Inspect the driven sprocket support bearing and replace it if necessary

8E.162 Inspect the driven sprocket oil seal rings, replacing them if damaged - make sure the seal ends overlap properly and coat the seals with petroleum jelly

8E.163 Install the driven sprocket support - be careful not to cut the seal rings on the direct clutch housing bushing

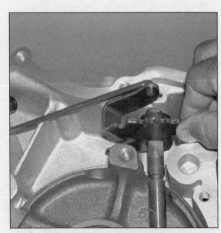

8E.164 Slide the manual shaft into the case and connect it to the detent lever

8E.165 Drive the detent lever roll pin in place . . .

8E.166 . . . and drive a new manual shaft retaining pin in the case

8E.167 Inspect the turbine shaft seal rings for damage - replace these rings only if damaged; they must be cut off, installed and sized with special tools

8E.168 Install the drive sprocket thrust washer on the sprocket - retain the thrust washer on the sprocket with petroleum jelly

8E.169 Install the driven sprocket thrust washer on the driven sprocket support - retain the thrust washer on the support with petroleum jelly

8E.170 Assemble the sprockets and chain (with the colored link on the chain facing up) and install the assembly

8E.171 Install a new O-ring on the turbine shaft

8E.172 Install the driven sprocket-to-case cover thrust bearing on the driven sprocket with the black side facing up

8E.173 Install the manual valve in the case cover (if removed)

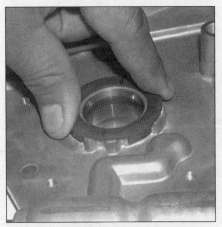

8E.174 Install the case cover-to-drive sprocket thrust washer - retain the thrust washer on the case cover with petroleum jelly

8E.175 Install the 1-2 accumulator pin . . .

8E.176 . . . and 1-2 accumulator piston (with the flat side facing down) into the case cover

8E.177 Install the 1-2 accumulator spring and gasket on the case

8E.178 Install the case-to-case cover gaskets on the case

8E.179 Install the case cover and seat it on the case

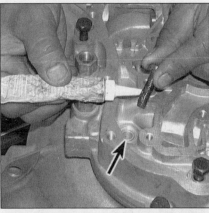

8E.180 Install the case cover bolts; apply thread sealant to the bolt in the location shown (arrow) - tighten all the case cover-to-case bolts to 18 ft-lbs

8E.181 Connect the manual valve link to the manual valve

8E.182 Install the check balls in the case cover at the locations shown (arrows)

8E.183 Install the valve body gaskets and spacer plate, then place one check ball on the spacer plate at the location shown (arrow)

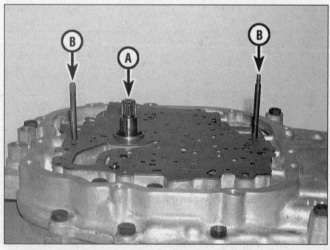

8E.184 Install the oil pump drive shaft (A) - thread two guide pins (B) into the case cover to aid in installing the valve body

8E.185 Install the valve body, oil pipe retainer and the bolts - coat the threads of the one bolt shown (arrow) with thread sealant - tighten the 6 mm bolts to 96 in-lbs and the 8 mm bolts to 18 ft-lbs, working from the center out in a spiral pattern - install the wiring harness and connect it to the solenoid, pressure switch and case connector

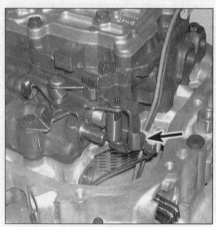

8E.186 Install the throttle valve linkage and bracket and connect the cable link to the lever

8E.187 Install the valve body cover gasket and cover - tighten the valve body cover bolts to 96 in-lbs

8E.188 Install the output shaft into the case . . .

8E.189 . . . and press the output shaft retaining clip onto the groove in the shaft

8E.190 Install the oil weir, retainer bracket and bolt (A), the park lock rod bracket (B) and filter bracket (C) - make sure the park lock actuator is operating properly

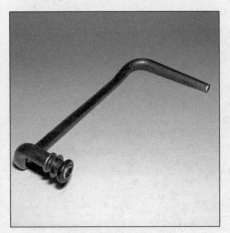

8E.191 Install the washer and a new O-ring on the reverse oil pipe

8E.192 Install the reverse oil pipe and bracket in the case, inserting the oil pipe into the low-reverse cup plug (arrow)

8E.193 Install the accumulator exhaust valve and spring into the case

8E.194 If a problem with the intermediate servo or a burnt band was discovered during disassembly, the intermediate servo band apply pin length may be checked using the special tool as follows:

1   Disassemble the apply pin from the intermediate servo assembly and insert the pin in the case bore
2   Set up the band apply pin gauge and apply 100 in-lbs to the tool
3   If the band apply pin length is correct, the white line will appear in the tool window. If the line is above the window, the pin is too short; if the line is below the window, the pin is too long - band apply pins are available in short, medium and long lengths

8E.195 Install the intermediate servo assembly into the servo bore - DO NOT replace the seal rings unless they are damaged

8E.196 Install the intermediate servo cover with a new gasket . . .

8E.197 . . . and install the bolts and the oil pipe bracket (arrow)

8E.198 Install the oil filter with a new seal - install the transaxle oil pan with a new gasket and tighten the oil pan bolts to 96 in-lbs

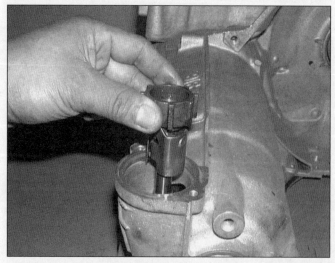

8E.199 Install the governor/speed sensor into the case bore and install the cover with a new O-ring

8E.200 Using the appropriate size seal installer, install new driveaxle seals and a converter seal into the transaxle case - also install any other miscellaneous seals such as the manual valve seal, throttle valve cable seal, dipstick tube seal, etc.

Chapter 8 Part F
Disassembly, inspection and assembly THM440-T4 and 4T60 transaxles

Introduction

The THM440-T4 and 4T60 are four-speed automatic transaxles manufactured for front-wheel drive vehicles. The major components of these transaxles are:

a) Lock-up torque converter
b) Sprockets and drive chain assembly
c) Vane-type oil pump
d) Control valve assembly
e) 1-2 band
f) Reverse band
g) Four separate multiple disc clutch packs (input, second gear, third gear and fourth gear)
h) Input sprag
i) Third gear roller clutch
j) Planetary gear set
k) Final drive

Follow the photographic sequence for disassembly, inspection and assembly. The model shown is a typical transaxle of this type. Differences do exist between models and many changes have been

made over the years, so perform each step in order and lay the components out on a clean work bench in the EXACT ORDER of removal to prevent confusion during reassembly. Many snap-rings and clutch plates are similar in size, but must not be interchanged. Keep the individual parts together with the component from which they were removed to avoid mix-ups. Save all old parts and compare them with the new part to ensure they are an exact match before reassembly. Pay particular attention to the stack-up of the various clutch packs. Differences do exist between models and your transaxle may not match the stack-up shown. Note the exact location of the check balls in the case as well as the valve body. Save all the old parts until the overhaul is complete and the transaxle has been thoroughly road tested; old components can be useful in diagnosing any problems that may arise.

The THM440-T4 and 4T60 are metric dimensioned transaxles, use metric tools on the fasteners. Special tools are required for some procedures. Alternate procedures are shown where possible, but some procedures can only be accomplished with special tools. Read through the entire overhaul procedure before beginning work to familiarize yourself with the procedures and identify any special tools that may be needed. Thoroughly clean the exterior of the transaxle before beginning disassembly.

Transaxle disassembly

8F.1 Begin disassembly by mounting the transaxle on a mounting fixture attached to a sturdy workbench

8F.2 Remove the ancillary components such as the Park/Neutral switch . . .

8F.3 . . . the dipstick tube

8F.4 Remove the throttle valve cable attaching bolt . . .

8F.5 . . . pull the cable housing up and unhook the cable from the link

8F.6 Remove the governor/speed sensor housing bolts and remove housing

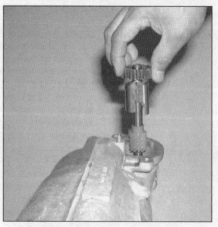

8F.7 Withdraw the governor from the transaxle

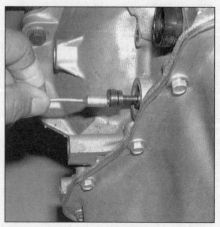

8F.8 Remove the vacuum modulator and using a magnet, withdraw the modulator valve from the transaxle case

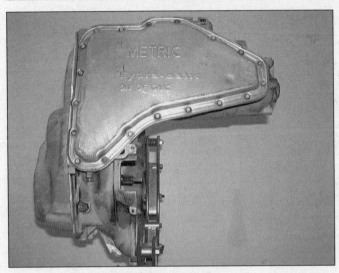

8F.9 Remove the oil pan

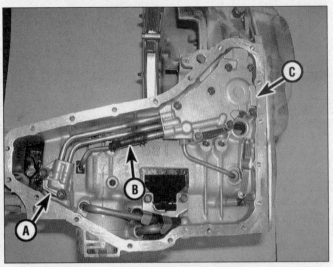

8F.10 Remove the bolts from the governor pipe retainer (A), disconnect the hose (B) from the lube pipe, remove the accumulator cover bolts and remove the accumulator cover (C) and pipes as an assembly

8F.11 Remove the accumulator gaskets and spacer plate

8F.12 Remove the lube pipe retainer and lube pipe - using a magnet, withdraw the spring (under the retainer) from the case

8F.13 Remove the scavenging scoop

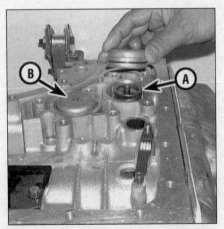

8F.14 a Remove the 1-2 (A) and 3-4 (B) accumulator assemblies - remove the springs and pins and keep the parts together

8F.14b Using a lever, press down on the reverse servo cover and remove the snap ring

8F.15 It may be necessary to twist the cover to free it from the case

8F.16 Remove the reverse servo assembly - label the servos if necessary (rev and 1-2); although they look similar the parts are NOT interchangeable

8F.17 Remove the 1-2 servo in the same manner

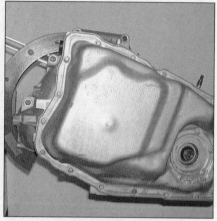

8F.18 Remove the side cover

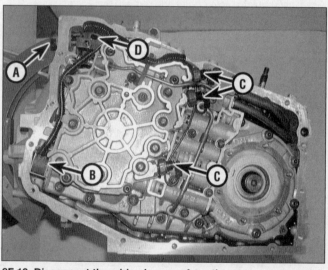

8F.19 Disconnect the wiring harness from the case connector (A), TCC solenoid (B), pressure switches (C), and remove the wiring harness - remove the throttle valve lever, bracket and link assembly (D)

8F.20 Remove the bolts and carefully lift the pump assembly from the control valve assembly - DO NOT remove the three bolts (arrows) retaining the pump cover to the pump body

8F.21 Remove the servo pipe retainer and disconnect the servo pipes from the valve body

8F.22 Remove the valve body attaching bolts and carefully lift the valve body from the channel plate

8F.23 Remove the four check balls from the spacer plate, then remove the spacer plate and gaskets

8F.24 Remove the oil pump driveshaft

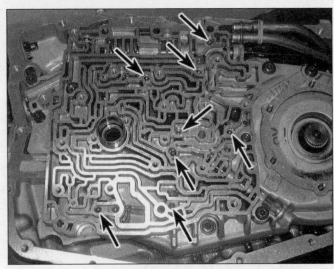

8F.25 Remove the check balls from the channel plate

8F.26 Disconnect the manual valve linkage from the manual valve

8F.27 Remove the channel plate attaching bolts and carefully remove the channel plate from the case

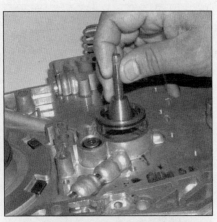

8F.28 Remove the input and TCC accumulator pistons from the channel plate and retrieve the springs from the case - also remove the fourth clutch thrust bearing from the channel plate (on some models, the input clutch accumulator has been eliminated)

8F.29 Remove the fourth clutch plates

8F.30 Remove the fourth clutch hub and shaft

8F.31 Remove the drive and driven sprocket thrust washers

8F.32 Rotate the output shaft until the output shaft/final drive C-clip opening is visible at the final drive unit, using a suitable tool, push the C-clip partially off the shaft . . .

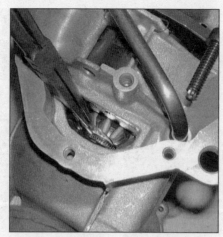

8F.33 . . . rotate the shaft 180-degrees and remove the C-clip

8F.34 Withdraw the output shaft from the transaxle

8F.35 Remove the O-ring from the turbine shaft

8F.36 Remove the drive sprockets and chain assembly - if the chain is separated from the sprockets, note that one colored link on the chain should be facing up

8F.37 Remove the sprocket support thrust washers

8F.38 Remove the oil scoop

8F.39 Remove the driven sprocket support . . .

8F.40 . . . and the thrust washer

8F.41 Using the special removal tool, remove the second/input clutch assembly

8F.42 Remove the reverse band

8F.43 Remove the reverse reaction drum

8F.44 Remove the input carrier assembly . . .

8F.45 . . . and the reaction carrier assembly

8F.46 Remove the reaction sun gear and drum assembly and the 1-2 band

8F.47 Remove the final drive sun gear shaft

8F.48 Remove the internal gear-to-case snap-ring . . .

8F.49. . . and using the special removal/installation tool, lift the final drive from the case

8F.50 Remove the torque converter seal . . .

8F.51 . . . and the driveaxle seal

Component inspection and subassembly overhaul

Using an approved cleaning solvent, clean and dry all the components thoroughly, including the case. Do not use rags to wipe the components dry, as lint from the rag may lodge in the oil passages, causing a valve to stick.

Inspect the following transaxle components and repair or replace as necessary:

a) *Case:* Inspect the exterior of the case for damage, cracks and porosity (a porous casting will cause fluid leaks). Check the valve body mating surfaces on the case and valve body for damage and flatness (use a precision straightedge to check for flatness - any warpage means the valve body or case will have to be machined or replaced). Check all the oil passages, the servo bore, the speedometer bore and the governor bore for damage. Check all threaded holes for damage (repair thread damage as described in Chapter 2). Check the oil cooler line fittings for damage. Check the interior of the case for damaged retaining ring grooves, which will mean the case will have to be replaced. Check the case lugs for excessive wear. Check the drive support bearing for wear and replace it if necessary. Inspect the manual linkage and the park-lock linkage for damage.

b) *Reaction gear set:* Inspect the reaction drum, internal gear, support and carrier for damage. Check for stripped splines, cracked or broken teeth, damaged or worn thrust bearings and bushings. Check the reaction carrier pinion gears for damaged bearings or worn washers. Check the pinion endplay with a feeler gauge; it should be between 0.010 and 0.025-inch. Inspect the third roller clutch for damaged rollers or broken springs. Check the finish of the inner and outer race and check the support for damaged lugs. Inspect the reaction sun gear for spline or tooth damage. Check the thrust washers and bushings for wear or damage.

c) *Input gear set:* Inspect the input carrier, input internal gear, input drum and input sun gear for damaged splines, broken teeth, and worn bushings. Check the thrust bearing for wear or damage. Check the input carrier assembly for broken teeth, worn washers and a damaged or worn thrust bearing. Check the pinion endplay with a feeler gauge; it should be between 0.010 and 0.025-inch. Inspect the input sprag for a damaged race, sprags or broken cage. Check the input sun gear for damaged splines, broken teeth or a worn bushing.

d) *Input, second, third and fourth clutch assemblies:* Inspect the clutch housings for damaged splines. Inspect the check balls for looseness and the seal rings for damage. Check the clutch housings, pistons, springs, spring retainers, clutch plates, backing plates and retainer rings for wear or damage. Check for nicks or burrs in the lip seal areas. Check the housing and drum for worn bushings. Check the band apply surface for damage. Lay a steel ruler or straightedge across the surface and inspect for dishing. Inspect the 1-2 band assembly and servo for damage or wear. If the band is extremely damaged or burned, check the band apply pin length during reassembly with the special Band Apply Pin Tool (Kent-Moore J-33382, or equivalent). Check the thrust washers and bushings for wear or damage.

e) *Differential and final drive assembly:* Inspect the final drive internal gear for damaged teeth and worn bearing surfaces. Check the final drive carrier pinion endplay with a feeler gauge; it should be between 0.010 and 0.025-inch. Check the thrust bearing for damage. Check the governor gear for damage. Check the differential side gears, pinions and shaft for damage and wear. If necessary use a pin punch to remove the roll pin from the shaft and disassemble the differential.

Oil pump assembly

Disassemble the oil pump as shown in the accompanying photos. Remove the pressure regulator valve train, the converter clutch valve

8F.52 Remove the three bolts and separate the oil pump cover from the body - inspect the cover, body, pressure switches, the 3-2 shift valve and the pressure screen for wear or damage

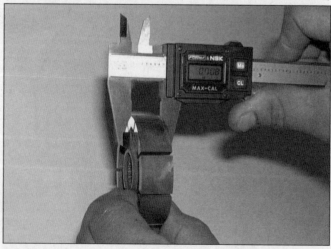

8F.53 Remove the rings, vanes, rotor, slide and spring from the pump body and inspect the components carefully for wear or damage

8F.54 If either the rotor, vanes or slide require replacement, measure the thickness of the component and replace it with a new component with a comparable thickness - various sizes are available at a dealership parts department; if the correct components are not used damage to the transaxle will result

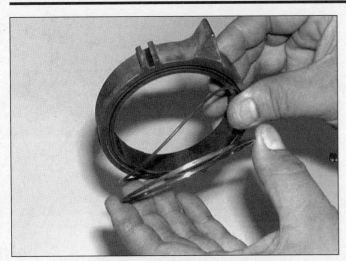

8F.55 Remove the slide seal and O-ring and
inspect them for damage

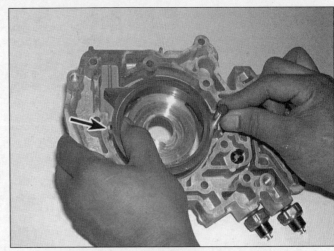

8F.56 Install the pump slide and pivot into the pump body,
push the slide over toward the pivot and install
the slide seal and support (arrow)

train, the pressure relief ball and spring (if necessary) and the oil pump cover screen. Lay the valves and springs out on a clean, lint-free towel in the exact order of removal to prevent confusion on assembly. Clean and dry the cover, body and all internal components. Inspect the valves and remove any burrs with a fine lapping compound; inspect the springs for damage or distortion; inspect the valve bores for damage; inspect the capsulated check balls for freedom of movement. Replace any damaged components. Inspect the pump rotor, vanes and slider very carefully. Replace the parts with a rotor and vane kit if there are any doubts about their condition.

8F.57 Install a vane ring in the
pump body cavity

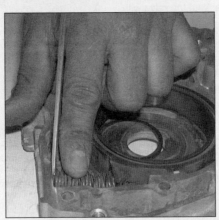

8F.58 Install the slide springs

8F.59 Install the rotor . . .

8F.60 . . . and the vanes - make sure the
vanes are flush with the top of the rotor

8F.61 Install a vane ring on top of the
rotor - make sure both vane rings
are positioned inside the vanes

8F.62 Install the slide O-ring . . .

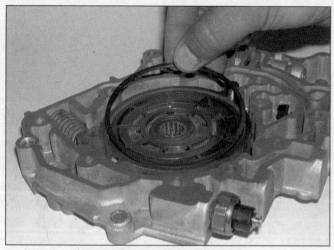

8F.63 . . . and oil seal

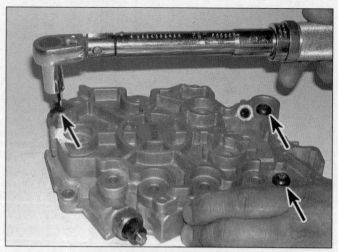

8F.64 Lubricate the pump with ATF, install the cover and tighten the bolts to 20-ft-lbs

Control valve assembly

Complete disassembly of the valve body is not necessary unless the valve body has been contaminated. Clean the valve body using an approved solvent and air dry (DO NOT use rags to dry the valve body, as lint from the rag may cause a valve to stick). Check each valve for freedom of movement in its bore. If a stuck valve is encountered, remove the individual valve and components for further cleaning and inspection. Nicks and burrs may be removed by lapping the valve with a fine lapping compound.

If complete disassembly of the valve body is required, lay the valve body on a clean work bench, use clean tools to disassemble and wash the valve body with clean solvent. Remove the valves from the valve body, one at a time. Lay out the valves, springs and bushings in their proper order on a clean lint-free towel. Cleanliness and meticulous care in keeping the valves in order cannot be over-stressed. A small tap is helpful in removing any stubborn roll-pins you may encounter.

Governor

Inspect the governor for damaged springs, seals or gear teeth. Inspect the weights for binding. Inspect the thrust bearing for wear or damage. Inspect the governor screen (in the case bore) for contamination. Replace the governor if it does not operate smoothly or appears contaminated.

8F.65 Using a small screwdriver or pick, pry each valve against spring pressure - the valve should snap back when pressure is released - check each valve for sticking

8F.66 If necessary, remove the clip or roll pin retaining the valve train . . .

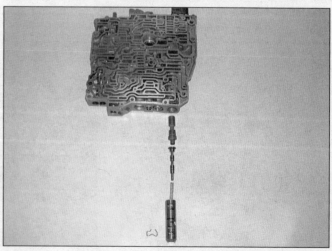

8F.67 . . . remove the valve assembly - clean and inspect the valves, bushings and springs, then reassemble the valve train - if the clip or roll pin does not fit securely, replace it with a new one

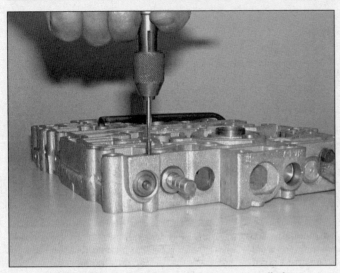

8F.68 A small tap may be used to remove roll pins

8F.69 If necessary, remove the torque converter clutch solenoid, valve and spring from the valve body

Transaxle assembly

An automatic transaxle is a precision piece of equipment. Install each component as shown, and do not force any component into place. If it doesn't fit properly, find out why and rectify the situation. Maintain a clean workplace and lubricate all moving parts as they are installed. Lubricate thrust washers and bearings with automatic transaxle fluid (ATF) or petroleum jelly. Use petroleum jelly to retain thrust washers and check balls in their proper location as the component is installed. Dip all friction plates in ATF before installation.

8F.71 Final drive assembly

1 Final drive internal gear
2 Thrust bearing
3 Parking gear
4 Final drive sun gear
5 Final drive carrier
6 Final drive carrier-to-case washer (selective)
7 Final drive carrier-to-case bearing

8F.70 Check the drive sprocket bearing for wear or damage - if necessary, remove the bolts and replace the bearing support - tighten the bolts to 20 ft-lbs

8F.72 Check each final drive pinion endplay with a feeler gauge - endplay should be between 0.010 and 0.025-inch

8F.73 Check the differential pinions, side gear and cross shaft for damage or wear - pay special attention to the cross shaft and pinions, they are know to wear - also check the governor gear for damage, it can be pulled off and replaced

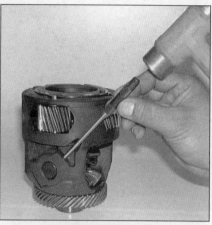

8F.74 If necessary drive out the cross shaft retaining pin and disassemble the differential

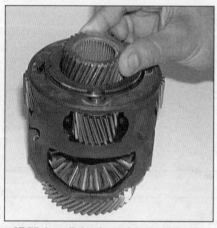

8F.75 Install the thrust bearing into the final drive carrier with the shiny side facing up, then install the final drive sun gear into the final drive carrier with the stepped side facing up

8F.76 Install the parking gear

8F.77 Install the internal gear thrust bearing with the tabs facing out - retain the bearing with petroleum jelly

8F.78 Install the internal gear onto the final drive carrier

8F.79 Install the carrier-to-case washer, then the bearing with the black side against the washer - retain the washer and bearing with petroleum jelly

8F.80 Using the special removal/installation tool, install the final drive assembly into the case - install the snap-ring with the ends in an open case lug

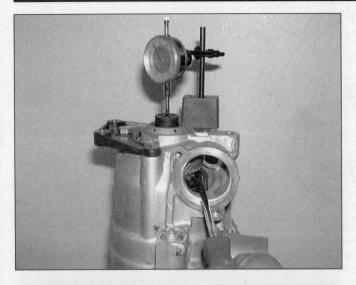

8F.81 Check the final drive endplay as follows:

1   Position the transaxle with the final drive facing up
2   Insert the loading tool adapter into the final drive
3   Install a dial indicator with the stem resting on the adapter, then zero the indicator
4   Pry up on the governor drive gear and note the movement on the dial indicator
5   Final drive endplay should be 0.005 to 0.025 inch - if necessary, adjust the final drive endplay by replacing the final drive-to-case selective thrust washer - washers are available in sizes ranging from 0.059 to 0.082 inch

8F.82 Install the final drive sun gear shaft, long splines first - make sure the splines engage both the parking gear and the sun gear

8F.83 Install the 1-2 band - make sure the band is properly engaged on the anchor pins (arrow) - if a new style band is used (see the following Note) make sure you remove the band stop from hole (A)

Note:

Beginning in late 1990, a new 1-2 band design has been incorporated into the TMH 440-T4 transaxle. The new band is superior in design and material and should be used in all rebuild units. When using the new style band, the correct band apply pin must also be used. The correct pin will be identified by two rings on the tip. The band stop must also be removed from the transaxle case when using a new style band. Band apply pin length need not be checked when using the updated parts. The new style band may be included in your overhaul kit, if not, parts are available at a dealership parts department.

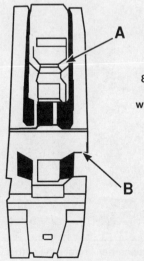

8F.84 The new style band can be identified by the wide band apply pin area (A) and the machined area where the anchor pins contact the band (B)

8F.85 Install the thrust bearing onto the final drive internal gear with the black side facing up

8F.86 Install the reaction sun gear/drum - rotate the drum into the band and check the band alignment

8F.87 Install the reaction sun gear thrust bearing onto the reaction carrier with the inside race on the carrier - retain the bearing with petroleum jelly

8F.88 Install the reaction carrier dam (if equipped) - if this part was broken, the final drive sun gear shaft is too long and it will most likely break again

8F.89 Install the reaction carrier - make sure the pinions are engaged with the sun gear

8F.90 Install the input carrier thrust bearing onto the input carrier with the inside race on the carrier - retain the bearing with petroleum jelly

8F.91 Install the input carrier - rotate the carrier until properly engaged

8F.92 Install the reverse reaction drum - make sure the splines are properly engaged with the input carrier

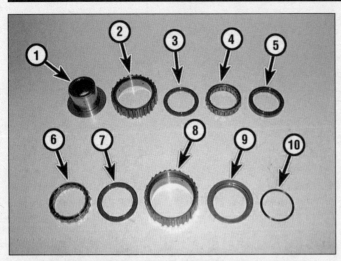

8F.93 Disassemble the sprag and roller clutch assembly and inspect for wear or damage

1	Inner race assembly	6	Third roller clutch assembly
2	Input sprag outer race	7	Wear plate
3	Wear plate	8	Roller clutch outer race
4	Input sprag assembly	9	Oil dam
5	Wear plate	10	Snap-ring

Sprag and roller clutch assembly

Reassembly of the sprag and roller clutch is a very tedious procedure requiring experience and some special skills. Keep all the components in the exact order of removal. If desired, leave the roller clutch in the outer race for cleaning and inspection. If the rollers fall out of the cage, the roller clutch must be replaced.

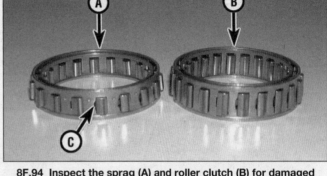

8F.94 Inspect the sprag (A) and roller clutch (B) for damaged sprags, rollers and cages - when installing the sprag into the input sprag outer race make sure the oil groove in the top of the outer race is facing up and the notches on the sprag cage are positioned as shown (C)

8F.95 Install the input sun gear (with spacer installed) into the sprag and roller clutch assembly

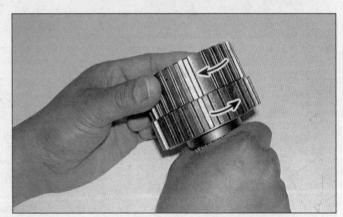

8F.96 While holding the sun gear stationary, the sprag and roller clutch should hold in the direction of the arrows and freewheel in the opposite directions

8F.97 Remove the input clutch backing plate snap-ring

Input/third clutch assembly

When disassembling a clutch pack, keep the clutch components in the exact order as the original stack-up; several updates have been made to the third clutch plates over the years. Make notes on the number of plates, the installed direction and location of backing plates, apply plates, waved plates, etc. Differences may exist between your model and the model shown. On some models, note the groove on the input clutch apply plate; it faces the clutch pack. Some models are equipped with double-sided clutch plates, some are single-sided. The correct components for your transaxle should be in the overhaul kit, if you purchased the correct kit.

Before removing a piston seal, note the installed direction of the seal lip. The piston seals must be installed with the seal lip facing the correct direction. If the seal is installed with the lip facing the wrong direction, the piston will not operate properly. If unsure, a common rule-of-thumb is this: the seal lip always faces pressure.

8F.98 Remove the input clutch backing plate . . .

8F.99 . . . input clutch pack . . .

8F.100 . . . and input clutch apply plate

8F.101 Remove the third clutch snap-ring

8F.102 Remove the third clutch backing plate . . .

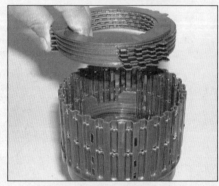

8F.103 . . . third clutch pack . . .

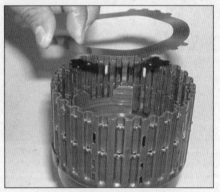

8F.104 . . . and third clutch apply plate (may or may not be a waved plate)

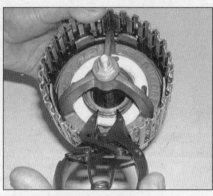

8F.105 Using a clutch spring compressor, compress the third clutch spring retainer and remove the snap-ring

8F.106 Remove the spring compressor and the third clutch spring assembly

8F.107 Remove the third clutch piston

8F.108 Remove the third clutch inner seal

8F.109 Using a clutch spring compressor, compress the third clutch piston housing and remove the snap-ring

8F.110 Remove the third clutch piston housing . . .

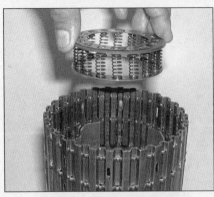

8F.111 . . . and input clutch spring assembly

8F.112 Remove the third clutch housing O-ring

8F.113 Remove the input clutch piston from the housing and remove the seals

8F.114 Remove the input clutch inner seal

8F.115 Remove the solid seal rings from the input housing shaft and install new seals (special seal installation tools are required)

8F.116 Install the input clutch piston outer seal - lubricate the seal with ATF

8F.117 Install the input clutch inner seal on the housing - lubricate the seal with ATF

8F.118 Install the input clutch piston in the housing

8F.119 Install the O-ring - lubricate the O-ring with petroleum jelly

8F.120 Install the spring retainer . . .

8F.121 . . .and the third clutch piston housing

8F.122 Compress the piston and install the snap-ring

8F.123 Install the third clutch inner seal - lubricate the seal with ATF

8F.124 Install the third clutch piston . . .

8F.125 . . . and the spring retainer

8F.126 Compress the spring retainer and install the snap-ring

8F.127 Install the third clutch apply plate, then install a steel plate followed by a friction plate, alternating steel and friction plates (on single-sided friction plates, the friction side faces up; some models will be equipped with four steel and friction plates, others with five). Dip the friction plates in ATF before installation

8F.128 Install the third clutch backing plate with the stepped side facing up

8F.129 Install the third clutch snap-ring

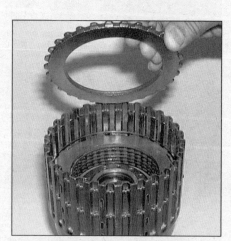

8F.130 Install the input clutch apply plate with the notched side down (against the snap-ring)

8F.131 Install the input clutch pack - dip the friction plates in ATF before installation

8F.132 Install the input clutch backing plate with the beveled edged against the clutch plate

8F.133 Install the input clutch snap-ring

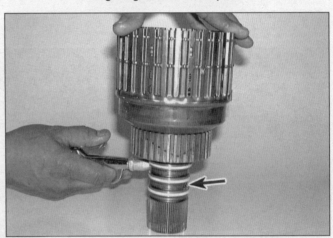

8F.134 Air check the operation of the clutch pistons by applying air pressure to the holes of the input shaft - use an air nozzle with a rubber tip to seal the hole and DO NOT apply more then 85 psi - the clutch pistons should apply fully and hold air pressure

Second clutch assembly

On some models, the second clutch backing plate has been redesigned, incorporating the support ring, backing plate and snap-ring into one assembly.

The second clutch steel plates are coated with a special black coating. DO NOT clean the plates in solvent or remove the coating. If the coating is worn, the plates must be replaced.

8F.135 Remove the second clutch snap-ring . . .

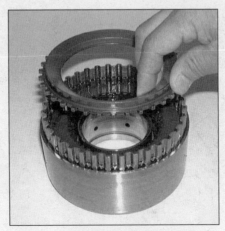

8F.136 . . . and remove the second clutch backing plate

8F.137 Remove the second clutch plates and waved plate

8F.138 Remove the snap-ring . . .

8F.139 . . . and remove the second clutch spring retainer and the apply ring

8F.140 Remove the second clutch piston

8F.141 Install new seals (inner and outer) on the second clutch piston - make sure the seal lips are facing the correct direction and lubricate the seals with ATF

8F.142 Install the second clutch piston in the housing, install the apply ring (with the inside lip facing up) and install the spring retainer and snap-ring

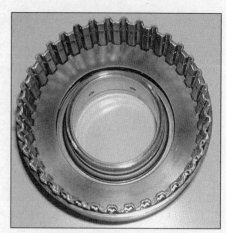

8F.143 Install the waved plate

8F.144 Install a steel plate first, then alternate friction and steel plates - dip the friction plates in ATF before installation

8F.145 Install the second clutch backing plate and the snap-ring

Note:

Air check the operation of the clutch piston by applying air pressure to the housing check ball - use an air nozzle with a rubber tip to seal the hole and DO NOT apply more then 85 psi - the clutch piston should apply fully and hold air pressure.

8F.146 Install the thrust washer on the input housing - engage the tangs on the thrust washer with the locking sleeve and retain the thrust washer with petroleum jelly

8F.147 With the input housing on its side, install the sprag and roller clutch assembly - make sure the sprag and roller clutch is fully seated and engaging all the clutch plates

8F.148 With the housing standing on end, install the input sun gear

8F.149 Using the special installation tool, install the assembly into the case - remove the tool and rotate the input shaft several times to make sure the sun gear is properly engaged in the carrier

8F.150 Install the second clutch housing thrust washer . . .

8F.151 . . . and thrust bearing with the large race facing down

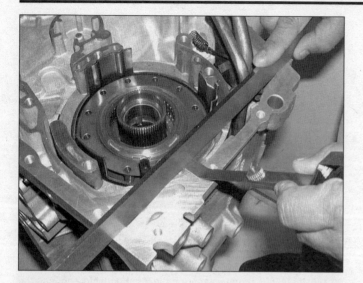

8F.152 Check the input endplay as follows:

1 Install the final drive loading tool and remove all endplay from the final drive unit
2 Temporarily install the driven sprocket support
3 Place a precision straight edge across the case flange and measure the clearance between the straightedge and the top of the driven sprocket support
4 The measured clearance should be 0.006 to 0.12-inch. If it isn't, replace the second clutch housing thrust washer - washers are available in sizes ranging from 0.110 to 0.200-inch

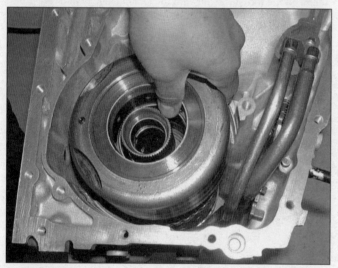

8F.153 When the input endplay is correct, install the second clutch drum - rotate the drum to engage all the clutch plates

8F.154 Install the reverse band - make sure the band is located properly on the anchor pins (arrow)

8F.155 Compress the driven sprocket support spring retainer and remove the snap-ring (an arbor press may be used, if available)

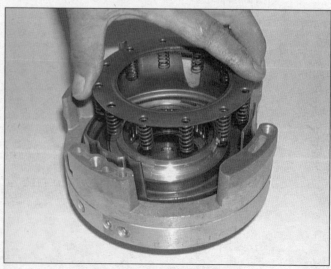

8F.156 Remove the spring retainer . . .

8F.157 . . . and the fourth clutch piston

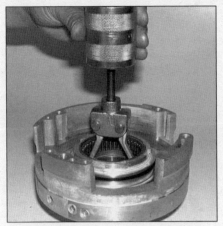

8F.158 Inspect the driven sprocket support bearing for wear or damage; if necessary remove and install a new bearing

8F.159 Replace the driven sprocket support oil seal rings - lubricate the seal rings with petroleum jelly

8F.160 Replace the fourth clutch piston inner and outer seals (the inner seal is on the support) - lubricate the seals with ATF

8F.161 Install the fourth clutch piston and spring retainer, compress the springs and install the snap-ring

8F.162 Install the driven sprocket support thrust washer - retain the thrust washer with petroleum jelly

8F.163 Install the driven sprocket support in the case . . .

8F.164 . . . and install the oil scoop

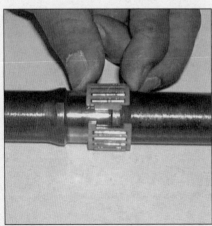

8F.165 Inspect the output shaft bearing and replace it if necessary - lubricate the bearing with ATF

8F.166 Install the output shaft . . .

8F.167 . . . and the output shaft C-clip

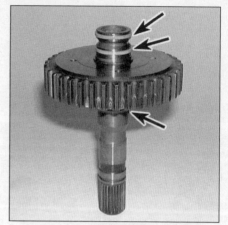

8F.168 Install new seals on the drive sprocket shaft (cut the old seals with a razor knife to remove them; special installation and sizing tools are required for installation) - lubricate the seals with ATF

8F.169 Install the drive sprocket thrust washer - retain the thrust washer with petroleum jelly

8F.170 Install the driven sprocket thrust washer - retain the thrust washer with petroleum jelly

8F.171 Assemble the chain and sprockets (colored link on chain facing up) and install the assembly

8F.172 Install the fourth clutch shaft

8F.173 Install the fourth clutch apply plate with the identification mark (DN) down

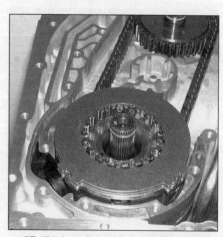

8F.174 Install the fourth clutch pack

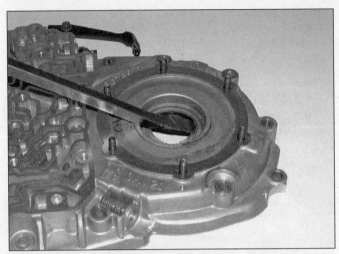

8F.175 Pry the axle seal from the channel plate and install a new seal

8F.176 Install new seal rings on the accumulator pistons and install the pistons and guide pins in the channel plate - retain the pistons and pins in the channel plate with petroleum jelly

A   Input clutch accumulator piston (not all models are equipped with this component)
B   Torque converter clutch accumulator piston

8F.177 Install the accumulator springs in the case

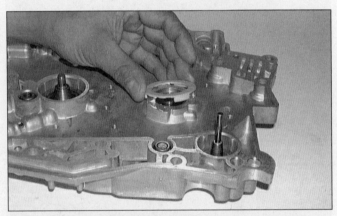

8F.178 Install the drive sprocket thrust washer on the channel plate - retain the thrust washer with petroleum jelly

8F.179 Place the new channel plate gaskets in position and install the channel plate on the case - make sure the fourth clutch plate tabs are properly aligned with the lugs in the channel plate and the lubrication passage on the driven sprocket support is properly aligned with the passage on the channel plate

8F.180 Install the channel plate fasteners - tighten bolt (A) to 10 ft-lbs, tighten the remainder of the bolts to 20 ft-lbs

8F.181 Install the valve body alignment pin in the channel plate

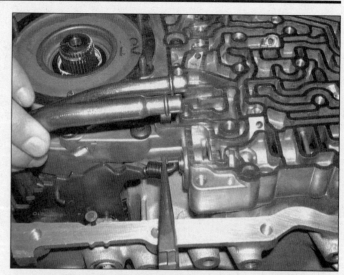

8F.182 Connect the shift linkage to the manual valve and install the detent spring and roller

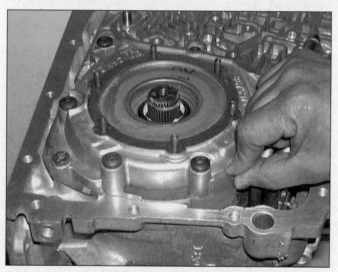

8F.183 Install the lubricating oil dam

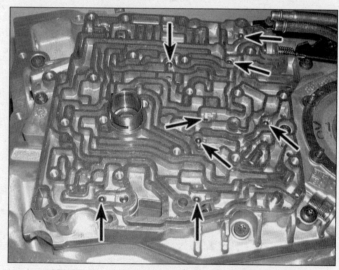

8F.184 Place the check balls in the channel plate at the locations shown

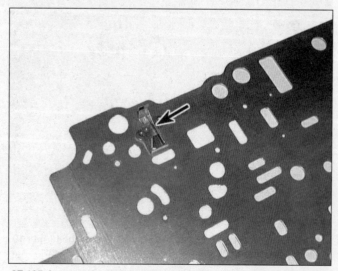

8F.185 Inspect the thermo element on the spacer plate - at room temperature, the thermo element should be straight

8F.186 Install the spacer plate and valve body gaskets

8F.187 Install the torque converter clutch screen at (A) and the valve body alignment pin at (B)

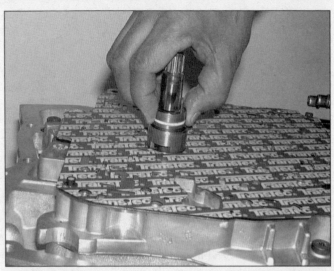

8F.188 Install new seal rings on the oil pump drive shaft, lubricate them with petroleum jelly and install the oil pump drive shaft

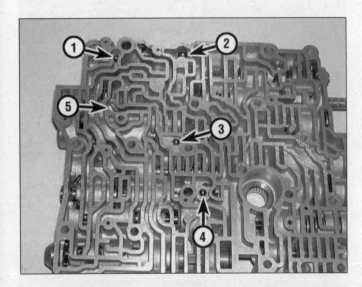

8F.189 Place the check balls in the valve body in the locations shown and retain them with petroleum jelly - note the different location for the 2-3 accumulator check ball on 1985 models (with the original transaxle) and 1986 and later models

1   Reverse servo check ball
2   2-3 accumulator check ball (large) - 1986 and later
3   Fourth clutch check ball
4   Third clutch check ball
5   2-3 accumulator check ball - 1985 only

8F.190 Install the valve body onto the channel plate. Tighten the two bolts (arrows) to 10 ft-lbs, tighten the remainder of the bolts hand-tight only at this time

8F.191 Install new O-rings on the servo pipes, lubricate them with ATF and connect the servo pipes to the valve body

8F.192 Install the oil pump on the valve body - install the bolts, hand-tight only at this time

8F.193 Install the throttle valve linkage - make sure the cable link is connected and positioned through the hole in the case

8F.194 Install the clamping plate and oil pipe with a new gasket (some models may not be equipped with the oil pipe)

8F.195 Install the TCC solenoid and the wiring harness, positioning the retainers in the proper locations - tighten the bolts starting in the center and working out in a circular pattern - tighten the large bolts (arrows) to 20 ft-lbs, tighten all the others to 10 ft-lbs - rotate the oil pump driveshaft (from the other side of the transaxle) and make sure it turns freely

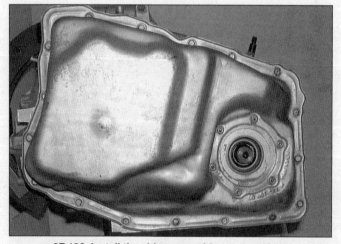

8F.196 Install the side cover with a new gaskets

8F.197 Replace the accumulator piston sealing rings, lubricate them with petroleum jelly and install the accumulator springs, pins and pistons (the 3-4 spring is the larger of the two)

A   1-2 accumulator   B   3-4 accumulator

8F.198 Install the oil pipe spring in the case and install the oil pipe retainer with a new seal (A) - apply Loctite no. 271 sealant, or equivalent, to the oil pipe and press it into the driven sprocket support lubrication passage (B)

8F.199 Assemble the accumulator cover, oil pipes and governor adapter; install the assembly using new gaskets - tighten the bolts to 20 ft-lbs

8F.200 Install the oil filter with a new seal . . .

8F.201 . . . and install the oil pan with a new gasket

8F.202 Assemble the reverse servo piston, pin and spring and install the assembly into the servo bore - DO NOT remove or replace the piston seal unless the seal is damaged

8F.203 Install a new O-ring on the reverse servo cover, press the cover in and install the snap-ring

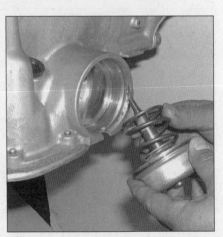

8F.204 Install a new seal on the 1-2 servo piston, assemble the servo piston, pin and spring and install the assembly into the servo bore

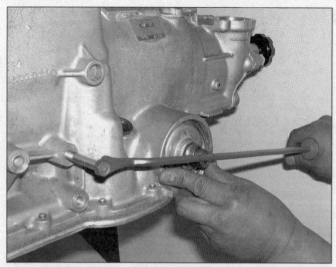

8F.205 Install a new O-ring on the servo cover, press the cover in and install the snap-ring

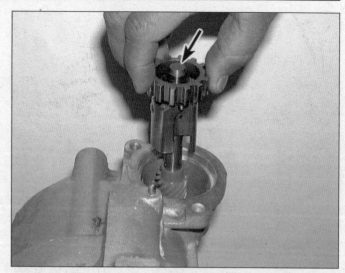

8F.206 Install the governor thrust bearing onto the governor shaft (arrow) and install the governor into the case

8F.207 Install a new O-ring on the governor cover, install the cover and tighten the bolts securely

8F.208 Install the modulator valve and modulator

8F.209 Install the various seals into the transaxle case (dipstick tube seal, throttle valve seal, manual shaft seal, etc.)

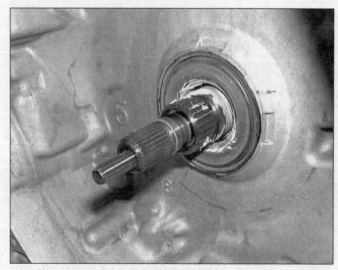

8F.210 Using the appropriate size seal installer, install a new converter seal into the transaxle case

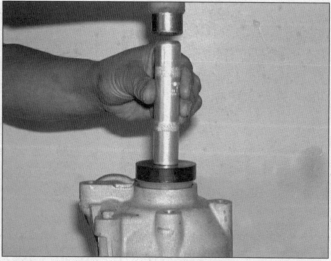

8F.211 Install a new driveaxle seal into the transaxle case

Chapter 9
Improving your automatic transmission

The automatic transmissions covered by this manual are used in all types of vehicles, from medium-duty trucks to compact cars. They are also used for all types of driving, from highway cruising to trailer towing to high-abuse off-road driving - and all drivers expect long life from their vehicle.

When your automatic transmission was designed, engineers had to take into consideration all of these possible types of use and also keep costs low. So the transmission design is actually a compromise of adequate shifting firmness, but smooth engagement; adequate downshifts, but no excessive engine revving; adequate torque multiplication, but good fuel economy . . . and so on.

But you know best what you want from your vehicle, so isn't there a way to undo some of these compromises to get the kind of performance you want out of your automatic transmission? There absolutely is! And automatic transmission modifications are generally easy to make and can make major improvements in the type of performance you want. So read on! There's something for all types of drivers in this Chapter.

Auxiliary transmission coolers

Here's a modification everyone should consider, since it will extend transmission life in almost any application. We consider an auxiliary cooler mandatory for towing, RV's, off-road or street-performance use.

Slippage within an automatic transmission generates heat, and heat is the greatest enemy of any automatic transmission. It is often said that a 10-percent reduction in transmission heat can double the life of an automatic transmission. Heat causes fluid to break down, losing its lubricating and heat-transfer properties, and heat also causes clutch friction material to varnish, causing still more slippage. Since transmission fluid is in contact with virtually all components within an automatic transmission, cooling the fluid will ultimately cool the transmission. Stock transmission fluid coolers circulate pressurized fluid through lines (usually steel tubes) to the radiator. A separate transmission fluid chamber within the radiator bottom or side tank is in constant contact with engine coolant. Since normal engine coolant temperature is lower than normal transmission fluid temperature, the transmission fluid chamber transfers heat to the engine coolant, cooling the transmission fluid.

This "heat exchanger" works well under normal conditions, but if the engine overheats, the transmission will likewise overheat. Also, if the transmission is slipping excessively and building up excessive heat, the engine will also overheat. To overcome these problems and extend transmission life by reducing operating temperature, an auxiliary transmission cooler is called for. Also, if your engine cooling system has a tendency to overheat, installing an auxiliary transmission cooler will relieve the radiator of this additional cooling responsibility and help your engine run cooler when outside temperatures and load-carrying or performance demands on your vehicle increase.

There are two basic types of auxiliary coolers available. The first type is an extra-deep transmission pan **(see illustration)**. The concept behind this modification is that, since a deep pan can hold more transmission fluid, the additional fluid will hold and transfer more heat. Since the pan is deeper, it also exposes more metal surface to the air flowing underneath the chassis. Some deep pans also have longitudinal tubes running the length of the pan that are welded to the front and rear of the pan. This creates holes through the pan that air can flow through and cool the fluid further.

Deep pans have some drawbacks, however. First, they are most effective when the vehicle is moving down the road. When the vehicle is sitting still or moving slowly, they are much less efficient. Second, deep pans reduce ground clearance, so, on off-road vehicles or low-to-the-ground sports cars, they can be more easily damaged by contact with the ground or rocks. Finally, deep pans do not offer nearly the cooling efficiency of a large radiator-type cooler mounted at the front of the vehicle.

The radiator-type cooler, as we'll call it here, is the most popular and most effective type of auxiliary transmission cooler. These types of

9.1 Deep transmission pans are easy to install and can help lower transmission temperature, but they are generally not as effective as radiator-type auxiliary coolers

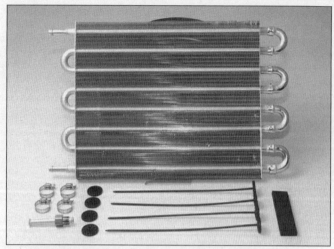

9.2a Here is the auxiliary cooler we'll install in this photo sequence. It is typical of what you'll find in auto parts stores and includes an installation kit and instructions. Before beginning installation, try to park the vehicle so its front end is pointing uphill. This will minimize fluid loss during installation. Read the instructions that come with the kit carefully - they supersede information printed here

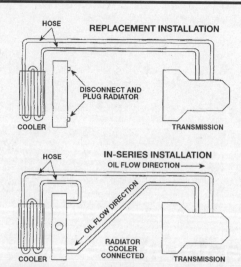

9.2b Decide if you want to use the auxiliary cooler in conjunction with the existing cooler in the radiator (bottom) or use it by itself (top). Generally, if you live in a cold climate, incorporating the existing cooler is a good idea, since it will allow the transmission to reach operating temperature faster. In a warm climate, it's best to use the auxiliary cooler by itself

9.2c If you'll be using the existing cooler, you'll need to establish which line is the outlet from the cooler. With the engine cold, start the engine and shift the transmission into gear for a moment (no more than 10 seconds). Then feel both lines - the warmer line is the inlet, so cut the other line (don't cut the line now, however - it will be cut in a later step)

9.2d Attach the hose provided in the kit to the cooler, but don't cut it (leave it in a loop). The hose clamps should be tightened only to the point where the hose rubber is pressed slightly through the slots in the clamp bands and is level with the clamp band. Do not overtighten to the point where rubber is pressed out above the band slots

coolers are available in an assortment of sizes to suit every need, from trailer towing and RV use to street/strip racing. This type of cooler uses aluminum tubing, running through heat-dissipating fins. The cooler looks somewhat like a small version of a conventional radiator and installs in front of the vehicle's radiator (or condenser, if the vehicle is air conditioned). When installing the auxiliary cooler, you can either eliminate the stock cooler (which will help the engine's cooling system work a little better in warm climates) or install it in-line with the existing cooler (which will speed warm-up in cold climates). If you eliminate the existing cooler, you must make certain the cooler will dissipate enough heat to prevent overheating. Generally, coolers are rated for the Gross Vehicle Weight (GVW) they are capable of cooling for, but bigger is usually better. Get a cooler rated well in excess of the GVW of your vehicle.

Included here is a photographic sequence of installing an auxiliary transmission cooler on a Chevrolet full-size van with a THM350 transmission **(see illustrations)**. This installation is typical of what you'll encounter when installing a cooler - read the captions accompanying each photo for the complete procedure.

Inline transmission filters

The standard transmission filter located inside the transmission oil pan does an adequate job, at best, filtering the automatic transmission fluid. An inline transmission filter can be installed in a transmission cooler line, much like an auxiliary transmission cooler, to double the filtration capacity **(see illustration)**. Metallic debris is a transmission's worst enemy, and any additional filtration capability is likely to prolong the life of your transmission.

Installing an inline filter into an existing metal cooler line is a very simple operation. In fact, if you're installing an auxiliary cooler, it would be very easy to add an inline filter at the same time. Be sure to observe the proper flow direction; the filters are marked with an arrow indicating flow direction, and installing one backwards will cause a no-flow condition and damage your transmission.

Another type of inline transmission filter is the "spin-on" type. This type is also known as a "remote-type" filter because the adapter is

9.2e Find a mounting location for the cooler in front of the radiator or condenser (if you have air conditioning). Make sure you've thought out the routing of the hoses so they won't obstruct anything, then mount the cooler with the nylon straps provided. Be sure to stick the adhesive pads to the cooler so they will be sandwiched between the cooler and radiator when the straps are tightened

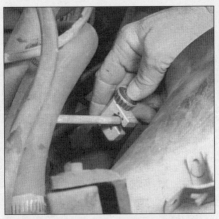

9.2f Find a convenient location to cut off the steel cooler line(s), as close to the cooler as possible. The miniature tubing cutter shown here is very useful in tight spaces. When the lines are cut, fluid will leak out, so place a container underneath to catch the leakage. If you'll be using the existing cooler in conjunction with the auxiliary cooler (recommended in cold climates), only the return line will need to be cut

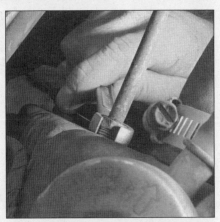

9.2g Using a flare-nut wrench, unscrew the cut-off ends of the line(s) from the radiator fittings. If you'll be using the existing cooler in conjunction with the auxiliary cooler, install the fitting designed for this purpose - it should be included in the kit

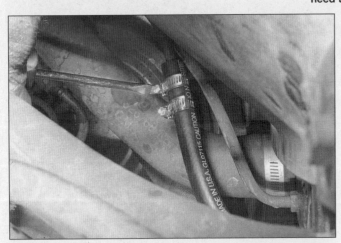

9.2h Carefully route the hose to the cut-off line(s) (and radiator fitting, if you'll be using the existing cooler). Be careful not to kink the hoses or bend them sharply. Make sure the hoses will not be in contact with any sharp surface or near any hot surfaces that could damage them. If possible, secure the hoses to the chassis or other hoses or lines with nylon tie-straps. Attach the hoses with hose clamps, being careful not to overtighten them. Now start the engine and check carefully for leaks. Check the transmission fluid level and add additional fluid, as necessary. After two weeks or so, recheck all hose clamps for tightness

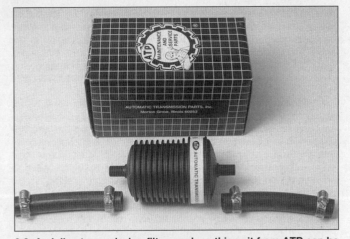

9.3 An inline transmission filter, such as this unit from ATP can be installed in minutes into the transmission cooler lines. This particular filter has dual filtration capabilities that include an internal magnet that attracts loose ferrous particles and a 30 micron paper filter element to trap non-ferrous particles. An internal pressure relief valve assures continuous flow in the event the filter ever becomes clogged

mounted at a remote location, such as a frame rail. A spin-on cartridge filter is threaded on the adapter, much like an oil filter, making this type of filter is very easy to service. Most manufacturers of remote mounted spin-on type transmission filters use a common oil filter for replacement purposes, so parts availability is not a problem.

Shift kits

Since the automatic transmissions covered by this manual are used in luxury cars, engineers have designed in a compromise that's unacceptable to people who tow or drive RV's or high-performance vehicles. This compromise is the stock shifting characteristics. The characteristic of shift softness (hardly being able to tell when a stock transmission shifts) is very desirable for luxury cars so owners can enjoy an imperceptible transition from one gear to another. The main way this softness is achieved is through more *overlap*, which is the time during a shift that both the engaging gear and releasing gear are applied at the same time. Obviously, from a performance and durability standpoint, overlap is quite undesirable. Applying two gears at the same time causes slippage, which leads to wear and excessive heat, so the less overlap, the better it is for transmission life. Also, racers claim the time and energy wasted during a heavily overlapped shift can lead to slower quarter-mile times. So, if you can put up with a shift you can feel, there is transmission life and performance to be gained. Most drivers of high-performance cars say they prefer to feel a good, firm shift than to "slide" into the next gear.

Several aftermarket manufacturers produce quality "shift kits" to

9.4 Shift kits, such as this one from B&M, are a great way to improve the performance of your automatic transmission. Not only will the shifts be firmer and quicker, but transmission life will usually be extended also

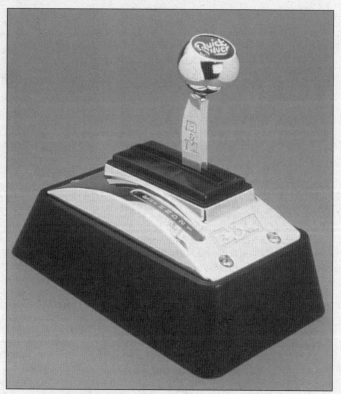

9.5 Aftermarket shifters, such as this one from B&M, add greater precision to manual shifting and can also provide a weight savings

re-program the shifting characteristics of the transmissions covered by this manual **(see illustration)**. Generally, the kits require the installer to replace springs and steel balls in the valve body, as well as do some minor drilling to the valve body separator plate and passages. If done as a part of an overhaul, a shift kit takes very little time to install. Shift kits are a bit more difficult to install with the transmission in place, but can generally be installed in a day. Try to do the installation at the same time you change transmission fluid, so you'll save a little work. Since all shift kits use their own unique methods of changing shift characteristics, we will not detail an installation here - the kit will come with complete installation instructions.

Also keep in mind that shift kits come in different versions for different types of driving. There are RV kits designed to keep very high apply pressures for towing. There are also street/strip kits designed for the performance enthusiast and kits designed for competition racing that are usually not practical for use on the street. Many of the "race only" kits convert the transmission to manual shifting, which is undesirable on the street, since coast-down engine braking is also reduced (this will increase brake wear and can be dangerous on long down-hills). Read all manufacturer's literature carefully to pick the kit best suited to your needs, and be honest - you won't be using the family car for Top-Fuel competition, so don't install components recommended for racing use only - you'll be unhappy with the way the car drives on the street.

High-stall torque converters

In street/strip and racing vehicles, a major disadvantage of the stock torque converter is its low *stall speed*. Basically, stall speed is the engine speed (in rpm) at which the fluid coupling in the torque converter achieves a near lock-up condition that is theoretically so efficient that it can stall the engine when the vehicle is at a stop in gear with the brakes applied and the engine is accelerated. In practice, on most high-performance engines, the brakes fail to hold the engine torque during this test and the rear wheels spin, so a better test is to accelerate the car from a stop at full-throttle (on a race track or similar safe area) and note the engine rpm during the launch.

Stock converters have a stall speed of about 1200 to 1500 rpm, which provides good fuel efficiency, since converter slippage is reduced overall. Basically, on a high-performance engine, a higher stall speed will allow the engine to rev higher before the car must move, which improves initial acceleration (launch).

Since you'll usually be replacing your torque converter at overhaul time, it's a good idea to consider a higher stall converter if you have a

high-performance vehicle. When choosing a torque converter, try to pick one that has an advertised stall speed about 500 to 750 rpm under the rpm at which peak torque occurs. This will allow the vehicle to launch during maximum torque output. But be very careful not to overestimate the rpm where torque occurs on your engine. Too high a stall speed is just as bad (if not worse) than too low a stall speed, since efficiency will be lost during peak torque output, when you want it most. Also keep in mind that torque converter slippage leads to more heat, so a higher stall speed may mean the transmission will have more of a tendency to overheat.

Most street-driven high-performance vehicles will benefit from a torque converter with a stall speed of about 2000 to 2500 rpm. Converters in this range still retain enough efficiency at low speeds that fuel economy will not be significantly affected, if at all.

Some manufacturers also produce torque converters specifically designed for motorhome and RV applications that provide a bit higher-than-stock stall speed (about 1800 rpm) for better torque delivery during hauling and towing. These converters are especially helpful on engines that have an RV-type camshaft in them, since these camshafts will slightly raise the rpm where maximum torque is delivered.

Aftermarket shifters

Quality aftermarket shifters, from companies such as B&M, provide greater shifting precision than stock shifters **(see illustration)**. If you have a racing vehicle that has been converted to fully manual shifting operation, such a rugged and exacting shifter is essential. Even for high-performance street use, if you ever select gears manually, such a shifter can prevent over-shifting into the next higher gear or accidentally shifting into Neutral or Reverse (which could cause major damage). Aftermarket shifters are relatively inexpensive and are generally easy to install. Many of them also offer a weight savings, since they have a lightweight cable that replaces the heavier rod-type linkage often installed at the factory.

Source list

Alto Products Corp.
832 Ridgewood Ave.
North Brunswick, NJ 08902
732-249-3633
Specialty products for automatic transmissions

Automatic Transmission Parts, Inc.
5940 Oakton St.
Morton Grove, IL 60053
847-967-6790
Automatic transmission components and repair kits

B & M Racing and Performance Products
9142 Independence Ave.
Chatsworth, CA 91311
818-882-6422
Automatic transmission repair kits, accessories and complete transmissions

BRYCO
7495 NW 48th St.
Miami, FL 33166
305-592-2760
Automatic transmission components and repair kits

Hayden, Inc.
1531 Pomona Rd.
Corona, CA 91720
800-621-3233
Automatic transmission accessories

A-Tech Trans-Tool
110 Connelly
San Antonio, TX 78203
800-531-5978
Automatic transmission repair tools and equipment

Kent-Moore
29784 Little Mack
Roseville, MI 48066
800-345-2233
GM automatic transmission repair tools and equipment

Notes

Glossary

Accumulator - A device that dampens pressure fluctuations within a hydraulic system. Accumulators allow gradual pressure build-up on application of an apply device, preventing fluid shock and resultant vibration.

Apply device - The term used for devices that hold or drive the planetary gearset. Apply devices include bands, multiple-disc clutch packs and one-way clutches.

Band - A thin steel band lined with friction material that is placed around a circular drum, anchored to the case on one side and held by an apply device on the other side. When applied it holds a drum from turning.

Belleville spring - A tapered spring used in clutch pack assemblies to aid in the control of the disc clutch.

Bevel gear - A gear with tapered or angle-cut ends.

Booster valve - A valve that raises hydraulic pressure when loads are high to prevent apply devices from slipping.

Clutch plates - Steel plates or steel plates with friction material attached. Clutch plates are used in multiple-disc clutch packs.

Control valving - Any devices that reduce, govern or manage the flow of fluid in a hydraulic system.

Compound planetary gearset - A planetary gearset that has two sets of planet gears shared by a single sun gear.

Clutch pack - The assembled group of steel and friction plates in a drum that are used to apply a particular gear range.

Coupling phase - The time at which the turbine and the impeller in the torque converter spin at the same speed and no torque multiplication is present.

Direct drive - When the engine, transmission and driveshaft all turn at the same speed (the gear ratio is 1:1).

Downshift valve - A kickdown valve or detent valve that increases throttle pressure to force a downshift under high driveline loads.

Driveplate - See "Flexplate."

Endplay - A measure of axial movement encountered or allowed in an automatic transmission. Endplay is usually measured at the input shaft.

Filter - A filter traps particles of dirt and other contaminants as fluid is drawn across its surface. Screen and paper filters are usually used in automatic transmissions.

Final drive - The final geared assembly in the transmission.

Flexplate - The thin metal plate that attaches the engine crankshaft to the torque converter of a automatic transmission.

Friction modifiers - Additives that help lubricants maintain their properties over a wide range of temperatures.

Gear pump - A pump that uses an inner drive gear and an outer driven gear, separated on one side by a crescent-shaped boss, to produce oil flow.

Gear ratio - The number of revolutions made by a driving gear as compared to the number of revolutions made by a driven gear of a different size. For example, if one gear makes three revolutions while the other gear makes one revolution, the gear ratio is 3:1.

Gear reduction - Is when the drive gear turns faster than the driven gear. The output speed of the driven gear is then reduced, while output torque is increased.

Geartrain - A series of two or more gears. Meshing of the teeth of two gears enables one to drive the other, thus transmitting power.

Governor pressure - A pressure which varies in relation to speed, usually that of the transmission output shaft.

Governor valve - This valve is driven off of the transmission output shaft and varies hydraulic pressure for upshifts and downshifts in relation to vehicle road speed.

Helical gear - A gear on which the teeth are cut at an angle to the center of the gear.

Hydraulic circuit - A series of fluid passages, control valves and an output device that is used to transmit motion from hydraulic pressure which produces movement or work.

Hydraulics - The physical science and technology of the static and dynamic behavior of fluids and their use to transmit force and motion.

Impeller - A component of the torque converter. Its angled fins produce fluid flow inside the torque converter. Also known as the pump.

Internal ring gear - A spur gear in the form of an internally toothed ring.

Land - The stepped outer circumference of a valve that contacts the valve bore.

Manifold vacuum - The difference in air pressure, or pressure drop, between atmospheric pressure and the air pressure in the intake manifold that occurs just below the throttle plate(s); usually expressed in inches of Mercury (in-Hg).

Manual valve - This valve is manually operated by the shift linkage and used to select the drive range in an automatic transmission.

Multiple-disc clutch - A clutch pack, consisting of alternating steel plates and driven friction plates. When hydraulically applied through a servo piston, the plates lock together and apply a gear range.

One-way check valve - A style of valve that allows fluid to flow in one direction only, and only when the pressure is sufficient to unseat the valve.

One-way clutch - A mechanical holding device that locks up when rotated in one direction and free-wheels when rotated in the opposite direction.

Orifice - A small opening or restriction to flow in a line, pipe, passage or valve.

Overdrive - Any arrangement of gearing which produces more revolutions of the driven shaft than the drive shaft.

Pinion gear - A smaller gear which engages a larger geared wheel or toothed rack.

Planetary gearset - A system of gearing named after the solar system because of similarities between its function and the way the planets revolve around the sun. The sun gear is surrounded by an internal ring gear with planet gears in mesh between the ring gear and the sun gear.

Planetary carrier assembly - Carrier or bracket in a planetary system which contains shafts upon which pinions or planet gears turn. The carrier assembly keeps the planet gears evenly spaced.

Planetary pinions - The gears mounted on the planetary carrier assembly in a planetary gearset. The planetary pinions mesh with and revolve around the sun gear. They also mesh with an internal ring gear.

Ported vacuum - A slot-type port located right at the throttle plates, used for controlling various devices that must work in proportion to the throttle opening. When the throttle plates are closed at idle, there's virtually no vacuum signal at this slot. But as the throttle plates open during acceleration, they expose the slot to increasing amounts of manifold vacuum.

Pressure - Force applied over a surface, measured as force per unit of area. Pressure is usually measured in pounds per square inch or kilopascals. Pressure = Force X Area.

Pressure regulator valve - The valve that regulates line pressure by creating a variable restriction.

Pressure-relief valve - A one-way valve that opens above a preset pressure to relieve excessive internal pressure build up.

Reaction member - The part of a planetary gearset that is held so that output motion can be produced. Other members react against the stationary, held member.

Roller clutch - A type of one-way clutch utilizing spring-loaded rollers to lock on an inner cam-type race.

Rotor pump - A mechanical pump that uses an inner drive rotor and an outer driven rotor to produce oil flow. Lobes on the rotors create fluid chambers of varying volumes and eliminate the need

for a crescent, as used in a gear pump.

Servo - A piston-and-cylinder assembly that uses hydraulic system pressure to operate a transmission band.

Shift valve - A valve moved by throttle pressure and governor pressure to allow a shift at a precise point based on vehicle speed and throttle position.

Speed ratio - Designates the output speed divided by the input speed. Turbine (output) speed is divided by impeller (input) speed and indicated as a percentage.

Spool valve - A valve that has raised lands. Spool valves are used in the valve body to control fluid flow and pressure.

Sprag - A figure-eight-shaped locking element of a one-way sprag clutch.

Spur gear - A gear in which the teeth parallel the center line of the gear.

Stall speed - The engine speed in rpm at which the torque converter becomes efficient enough to stall the engine if the rear wheels are held stationary.

Stator - A component of the torque converter. It redirects fluid flow from the turbine back to the impeller in the direction of rotation, thus creating torque multiplication.

Sun gear - The center gear in the planetary gearset. This gear meshes with the planetary pinions in the reaction and output carriers.

Throttle pressure - The transmission hydraulic pressure that varies in relation to throttle opening.

Throttle valve - The valve that controls throttle pressure based on the movement of the throttle opening or manifold vacuum.

Torque - A turning or twisting force, such as the force imparted on a fastener by a torque wrench. Measured in terms of the distance times the amount of force applied. Commonly expressed in foot-pounds (Ft-lbs), inch-pounds (In-lbs), or Newton-meters (Nm).

Torque converter - A fluid coupling that transmits power from a driving to a driven member by hydraulic action. And, because of its design, this turbine-like device multiplies the torque between the engine and the transmission. It consists of a rotary pump or impeller, one or more reactors or stators, and a driven circular turbine.

Turbine - A component of the torque converter. It's splined onto the end of the transmission input shaft and is driven by the impeller.

Two-way check valve - A type of valve that manages fluid flow in two separate hydraulic circuits, through one fluid passage.

Vacuum modulator - A small canister mounted on the outside of a transmission that has a spring-loaded plunger and diaphragm inside. The diaphragm and plunger move a valve in relation to changes in manifold vacuum. It is often used to control a throttle valve.

Valve body - The housing containing the transmission's hydraulic control valves. Also known as the control valve assembly.

Index

Haynes Automotive Manuals

NOTE: If you do not see a listing for your vehicle, consult your local Haynes dealer for the latest product information.

ACURA
12020 Integra '86 thru '89 & Legend '86 thru '90
12021 Integra '90 thru '93 & Legend '91 thru '95
Integra '94 thru '00 - see HONDA Civic (42025)
MDX '01 thru '07 - see HONDA Pilot (42037)
12050 Acura TL all models '99 thru '08

AMC
Jeep CJ - see JEEP (50020)
14020 Mid-size models '70 thru '83
14025 (Renault) Alliance & Encore '83 thru '87

AUDI
15020 4000 all models '80 thru '87
15025 5000 all models '77 thru '83
15026 5000 all models '84 thru '88
Audi A4 '96 thru '01 - see VW Passat (96023)
15030 Audi A4 '02 thru '08

AUSTIN-HEALEY
Sprite - see MG Midget (66015)

BMW
18020 3/5 Series '82 thru '92
18021 3-Series incl. Z3 models '92 thru '98
18022 3-Series incl. Z4 models '99 thru '05
18023 3-Series '06 thru '10
18025 320i all 4 cyl models '75 thru '83
18050 1500 thru 2002 except Turbo '59 thru '77

BUICK
19010 Buick Century '97 thru '05
Century (front-wheel drive) - see GM (38005)
19020 Buick, Oldsmobile & Pontiac Full-size (Front-wheel drive) '85 thru '05
Buick Electra, LeSabre and Park Avenue; Oldsmobile Delta 88 Royale, Ninety Eight and Regency; Pontiac Bonneville
19025 Buick, Oldsmobile & Pontiac Full-size (Rear wheel drive) '70 thru '90
Buick Estate, Electra, LeSabre, Limited, Oldsmobile Custom Cruiser, Delta 88, Ninety-eight, Pontiac Bonneville, Catalina, Grandville, Parisienne
19030 Mid-size Regal & Century all rear-drive models with V6, V8 and Turbo '74 thru '87
Regal - see GENERAL MOTORS (38010)
Riviera - see GENERAL MOTORS (38030)
Roadmaster - see CHEVROLET (24046)
Skyhawk - see GENERAL MOTORS (38015)
Skylark - see GM (38020, 38025)
Somerset - see GENERAL MOTORS (38025)

CADILLAC
21015 CTS & CTS-V '03 thru '12
21030 Cadillac Rear Wheel Drive '70 thru '93
Cimarron - see GENERAL MOTORS (38015)
DeVille - see GM (38031 & 38032)
Eldorado - see GM (38030 & 38031)
Fleetwood - see GM (38031)
Seville - see GM (38030, 38031 & 38032)

CHEVROLET
10305 Chevrolet Engine Overhaul Manual
24010 Astro & GMC Safari Mini-vans '85 thru '05
24015 Camaro V8 all models '70 thru '81
24016 Camaro all models '82 thru '92
24017 Camaro & Firebird '93 thru '02
Cavalier - see GENERAL MOTORS (38016)
Celebrity - see GENERAL MOTORS (38005)
24020 Chevelle, Malibu & El Camino '69 thru '87
24024 Chevette & Pontiac T1000 '76 thru '87
Citation - see GENERAL MOTORS (38020)
24027 Colorado & GMC Canyon '04 thru '10
24032 Corsica/Beretta all models '87 thru '96
24040 Corvette all V8 models '68 thru '82
24041 Corvette all models '84 thru '96
24045 Full-size Sedans Caprice, Impala, Biscayne, Bel Air & Wagons '69 thru '90
24046 Impala SS & Caprice and Buick Roadmaster '91 thru '96
Impala '00 thru '05 - see LUMINA (24048)
24047 Impala & Monte Carlo all models '06 thru '11
Lumina '90 thru '94 - see GM (38010)
24048 Lumina & Monte Carlo '95 thru '05
Lumina APV - see GM (38035)
24050 Luv Pick-up all 2WD & 4WD '72 thru '82
Malibu '97 thru '00 - see GM (38026)
24055 Monte Carlo '70 thru '88
Monte Carlo '95 thru '01 - see LUMINA (24048)
24059 Nova all V8 models '69 thru '79
24060 Nova and Geo Prizm '85 thru '92
24064 Pick-ups '67 thru '87 - Chevrolet & GMC
24065 Pick-ups '88 thru '98 - Chevrolet & GMC

24066 Pick-ups '99 thru '06 - Chevrolet & GMC
24067 Chevrolet Silverado & GMC Sierra '07 thru '12
24070 S-10 & S-15 Pick-ups '82 thru '93, Blazer & Jimmy '83 thru '94,
24071 S-10 & Sonoma Pick-ups '94 thru '04, including Blazer, Jimmy & Hombre
24072 Chevrolet TrailBlazer, GMC Envoy & Oldsmobile Bravada '02 thru '09
24075 Sprint '85 thru '88 & Geo Metro '89 thru '01
24080 Vans - Chevrolet & GMC '68 thru '96
24081 Chevrolet Express & GMC Savana Full-size Vans '96 thru '10

CHRYSLER
10310 Chrysler Engine Overhaul Manual
25015 Chrysler Cirrus, Dodge Stratus, Plymouth Breeze '95 thru '00
25020 Full-size Front-Wheel Drive '88 thru '93
K-Cars - see DODGE Aries (30008)
Laser - see DODGE Daytona (30030)
25025 Chrysler LHS, Concorde, New Yorker, Dodge Intrepid, Eagle Vision, '93 thru '97
25026 Chrysler LHS, Concorde, 300M, Dodge Intrepid, '98 thru '04
25027 Chrysler 300, Dodge Charger & Magnum '05 thru '09
25030 Chrysler & Plymouth Mid-size front wheel drive '82 thru '95
Rear-wheel drive - see Dodge (30050)
25035 PT Cruiser all models '01 thru '10
25040 Chrysler Sebring '95 thru '06, Dodge Stratus '01 thru '06, Dodge Avenger '95 thru '00

DATSUN
28005 200SX all models '80 thru '83
28007 B-210 all models '73 thru '78
28009 210 all models '79 thru '82
28012 240Z, 260Z & 280Z Coupe '70 thru '78
28014 280ZX Coupe & 2+2 '79 thru '83
300ZX - see NISSAN (72010)
28018 510 & PL521 Pick-up '68 thru '73
28020 510 all models '78 thru '81
28022 620 Series Pick-up all models '73 thru '79
720 Series Pick-up - see NISSAN (72030)
28025 810/Maxima all gasoline models '77 thru '84

DODGE
400 & 600 - see CHRYSLER (25030)
30008 Aries & Plymouth Reliant '81 thru '89
30010 Caravan & Plymouth Voyager '84 thru '95
30011 Caravan & Plymouth Voyager '96 thru '02
30012 Challenger/Plymouth Saporro '78 thru '83
30013 Caravan, Chrysler Voyager, Town & Country '03 thru '07
30016 Colt & Plymouth Champ '78 thru '87
30020 Dakota Pick-ups all models '87 thru '96
30021 Durango '98 & '99, Dakota '97 thru '99
30022 Durango '00 thru '03 Dakota '00 thru '04
30023 Durango '04 thru '09, Dakota '05 thru '11
30025 Dart, Demon, Plymouth Barracuda, Duster & Valiant 6 cyl models '67 thru '76
30030 Daytona & Chrysler Laser '84 thru '89
Intrepid - see CHRYSLER (25025, 25026)
30034 Neon all models '95 thru '99
30035 Omni & Plymouth Horizon '78 thru '90
30036 Dodge and Plymouth Neon '00 thru '05
30040 Pick-ups all full-size models '74 thru '93
30041 Pick-ups all full-size models '94 thru '01
30042 Pick-ups full-size models '72 thru '08
30045 Ram 50/D50 Pick-ups & Raider and Plymouth Arrow Pick-ups '79 thru '93
30050 Dodge/Plymouth/Chrysler RWD '71 thru '89
30055 Shadow & Plymouth Sundance '87 thru '94
30060 Spirit & Plymouth Acclaim '89 thru '95
30065 Vans - Dodge & Plymouth '71 thru '03

EAGLE
Talon - see MITSUBISHI (68030, 68031)
Vision - see CHRYSLER (25025)

FIAT
34010 124 Sport Coupe & Spider '68 thru '78
34025 X1/9 all models '74 thru '80

FORD
10320 Ford Engine Overhaul Manual
10355 Ford Automatic Transmission Overhaul
11500 Mustang '64-1/2 thru '70 Restoration Guide
36004 Aerostar Mini-vans all models '86 thru '97
36006 Contour & Mercury Mystique '95 thru '00
36008 Courier Pick-up all models '72 thru '82
36012 Crown Victoria & Mercury Grand Marquis '88 thru '10
36016 Escort/Mercury Lynx all models '81 thru '90
36020 Escort/Mercury Tracer '91 thru '02

36022 Escape & Mazda Tribute '01 thru '11
36024 Explorer & Mazda Navajo '91 thru '01
36025 Explorer/Mercury Mountaineer '02 thru '10
36028 Fairmont & Mercury Zephyr '78 thru '83
36030 Festiva & Aspire '88 thru '97
36032 Fiesta all models '77 thru '80
36034 Focus all models '00 thru '11
36036 Ford & Mercury Full-size '75 thru '87
36044 Ford & Mercury Mid-size '75 thru '86
36045 Fusion & Mercury Milan '06 thru '10
36048 Mustang V8 all models '64-1/2 thru '73
36049 Mustang II 4 cyl, V6 & V8 models '74 thru '78
36050 Mustang & Mercury Capri '79 thru '93
36051 Mustang all models '94 thru '04
36052 Mustang '05 thru '10
36054 Pick-ups & Bronco '73 thru '79
36058 Pick-ups & Bronco '80 thru '96
36059 F-150 & Expedition '97 thru '09, F-250 '97 thru '99 & Lincoln Navigator '98 thru '09
36060 Super Duty Pick-ups, Excursion '99 thru '10
36061 F-150 full-size '04 thru '10
36062 Pinto & Mercury Bobcat '75 thru '80
36066 Probe all models '89 thru '92
Probe '93 thru '97 - see MAZDA 626 (61042)
36070 Ranger/Bronco II gasoline models '83 thru '92
36071 Ranger '93 thru '10 & Mazda Pick-ups '94 thru '09
36074 Taurus & Mercury Sable '86 thru '95
36075 Taurus & Mercury Sable '96 thru '05
36078 Tempo & Mercury Topaz '84 thru '94
36082 Thunderbird/Mercury Cougar '83 thru '88
36086 Thunderbird/Mercury Cougar '89 thru '97
36090 Vans all V8 Econoline models '69 thru '91
36094 Vans full size '92 thru '10
36097 Windstar Mini-van '95 thru '07

GENERAL MOTORS
10360 GM Automatic Transmission Overhaul
38005 Buick Century, Chevrolet Celebrity, Oldsmobile Cutlass Ciera & Pontiac 6000 all models '82 thru '96
38010 Buick Regal, Chevrolet Lumina, Oldsmobile Cutlass Supreme & Pontiac Grand Prix (FWD) '88 thru '07
38015 Buick Skyhawk, Cadillac Cimarron, Chevrolet Cavalier, Oldsmobile Firenza & Pontiac J-2000 & Sunbird '82 thru '94
38016 Chevrolet Cavalier & Pontiac Sunfire '95 thru '05
38017 Chevrolet Cobalt & Pontiac G5 '05 thru '11
38020 Buick Skylark, Chevrolet Citation, Olds Omega, Pontiac Phoenix '80 thru '85
38025 Buick Skylark & Somerset, Oldsmobile Achieva & Calais and Pontiac Grand Am all models '85 thru '98
38026 Chevrolet Malibu, Olds Alero & Cutlass, Pontiac Grand Am '97 thru '03
38027 Chevrolet Malibu '04 thru '10
38030 Cadillac Eldorado, Seville, Oldsmobile Toronado, Buick Riviera '71 thru '85
38031 Cadillac Eldorado & Seville, DeVille, Fleetwood & Olds Toronado, Buick Riviera '86 thru '93
38032 Cadillac DeVille '94 thru '05 & Seville '92 thru '04 Cadillac DTS '06 thru '10
38035 Chevrolet Lumina APV, Olds Silhouette & Pontiac Trans Sport all models '90 thru '96
38036 Chevrolet Venture, Olds Silhouette, Pontiac Trans Sport & Montana '97 thru '05
General Motors Full-size
Rear-wheel Drive - see BUICK (19025)
38040 Chevrolet Equinox '05 thru '09 Pontiac Torrent '06 thru '09
38070 Chevrolet HHR '06 thru '11

GEO
Metro - see CHEVROLET Sprint (24075)
Prizm - '85 thru '92 see CHEVY (24060), '93 thru '02 see TOYOTA Corolla (92036)
40030 Storm all models '90 thru '93
Tracker - see SUZUKI Samurai (90010)

GMC
Vans & Pick-ups - see CHEVROLET

HONDA
42010 Accord CVCC all models '76 thru '83
42011 Accord all models '84 thru '89
42012 Accord all models '90 thru '93
42013 Accord all models '94 thru '97
42014 Accord all models '98 thru '02
42015 Accord all '03 thru '07
42020 Civic 1200 all models '73 thru '79
42021 Civic 1300 & 1500 CVCC '80 thru '83
42022 Civic 1500 CVCC all models '75 thru '79

(Continued on other side)

Haynes North America, Inc., 859 Lawrence Drive, Newbury Park, CA 91320-1514 • (805) 498-6703 • http://www.haynes.com

Haynes Automotive Manuals (continued)

NOTE: If you do not see a listing for your vehicle, consult your local Haynes dealer for the latest product information.

42023 **Civic** all models '84 thru '91
42024 **Civic & del Sol** '92 thru '95
42025 **Civic** '96 thru '00, **CR-V** '97 thru '01, **Acura Integra** '94 thru '00
42026 **Civic** '01 thru '10, **CR-V** '02 thru '09
42035 **Odyssey** all models '99 thru '10
Passport - see ISUZU Rodeo (47017)
42037 **Honda Pilot** '03 thru '07, **Acura MDX** '01 thru '07
42040 **Prelude CVCC** all models '79 thru '89

HYUNDAI
43010 **Elantra** all models '96 thru '10
43015 **Excel & Accent** all models '86 thru '09
43050 **Santa Fe** all models '01 thru '06
43055 **Sonata** all models '99 thru '08

INFINITI
G35 '03 thru '08 - see NISSAN 350Z (72011)

ISUZU
Hombre - see CHEVROLET S-10 (24071)
47017 **Rodeo, Amigo & Honda Passport** '89 thru '02
47020 **Trooper & Pick-up** '81 thru '93

JAGUAR
49010 **XJ6** all 6 cyl models '68 thru '86
49011 **XJ6** all models '88 thru '94
49015 **XJ12 & XJS** all 12 cyl models '72 thru '85

JEEP
50010 **Cherokee, Comanche & Wagoneer Limited** all models '84 thru '01
50020 **CJ** all models '49 thru '86
50025 **Grand Cherokee** all models '93 thru '04
50026 **Grand Cherokee** '05 thru '09
50029 **Grand Wagoneer & Pick-up** '72 thru '91
Grand Wagoneer '84 thru '91, Cherokee & Wagoneer '72 thru '83, Pick-up '72 thru '88
50030 **Wrangler** all models '87 thru '11
50035 **Liberty** '02 thru '07

KIA
54050 **Optima** '01 thru '10
54070 **Sephia** '94 thru '01, **Spectra** '00 thru '09, **Sportage** '05 thru '10

LEXUS
ES 300/330 - see TOYOTA Camry (92007) (92008)
RX 330 - see TOYOTA Highlander (92095)

LINCOLN
Navigator - see FORD Pick-up (36059)
59010 **Rear-Wheel Drive** all models '70 thru '10

MAZDA
61010 **GLC Hatchback** (rear-wheel drive) '77 thru '83
61011 **GLC** (front-wheel drive) '81 thru '85
61012 **Mazda3** '04 thru '11
61015 **323 & Protegé** '90 thru '03
61016 **MX-5 Miata** '90 thru '09
61020 **MPV** all models '89 thru '98
Navajo - see Ford Explorer (36024)
61030 **Pick-ups** '72 thru '93
Pick-ups '94 thru '00 - see Ford Ranger (36071)
61035 **RX-7** all models '79 thru '85
61036 **RX-7** all models '86 thru '91
61040 **626** (rear-wheel drive) all models '79 thru '82
61041 **626/MX-6** (front-wheel drive) '83 thru '92
61042 **626, MX-6/Ford Probe** '93 thru '02
61043 **Mazda6** '03 thru '11

MERCEDES-BENZ
63012 **123 Series Diesel** '76 thru '85
63015 **190 Series** four-cyl gas models, '84 thru '88
63020 **230/250/280** 6 cyl sohc models '68 thru '72
63025 **280 123 Series** gasoline models '77 thru '81
63030 **350 & 450** all models '71 thru '80
63040 **C-Class:** C230/C240/C280/C320/C350 '01 thru '07

MERCURY
64200 **Villager & Nissan Quest** '93 thru '01
All other titles, see FORD Listing.

MG
66010 **MGB** Roadster & GT Coupe '62 thru '80
66015 **MG Midget, Austin Healey Sprite** '58 thru '80

MINI
67020 **Mini** '02 thru '11

MITSUBISHI
68020 **Cordia, Tredia, Galant, Precis & Mirage** '83 thru '93
68030 **Eclipse, Eagle Talon & Ply. Laser** '90 thru '94
68031 **Eclipse** '95 thru '05, **Eagle Talon** '95 thru '98
68035 **Galant** '94 thru '10
68040 **Pick-up** '83 thru '96 & **Montero** '83 thru '93

NISSAN
72010 **300ZX** all models including Turbo '84 thru '89
72011 **350Z & Infiniti G35** all models '03 thru '08
72015 **Altima** all models '93 thru '06
72016 **Altima** '07 thru '10
72020 **Maxima** all models '85 thru '92
72021 **Maxima** all models '93 thru '04
72025 **Murano** '03 thru '10
72030 **Pick-ups** '80 thru '97 **Pathfinder** '87 thru '95
72031 **Frontier Pick-up, Xterra, Pathfinder** '96 thru '04
72032 **Frontier & Xterra** '05 thru '11
72040 **Pulsar** all models '83 thru '86
Quest - see MERCURY Villager (64200)
72050 **Sentra** all models '82 thru '94
72051 **Sentra & 200SX** all models '95 thru '06
72060 **Stanza** all models '82 thru '90
72070 **Titan pick-ups** '04 thru '10 **Armada** '05 thru '10

OLDSMOBILE
73015 **Cutlass** V6 & V8 gas models '74 thru '88
For other OLDSMOBILE titles, see BUICK, CHEVROLET or GENERAL MOTORS listing.

PLYMOUTH
For PLYMOUTH titles, see DODGE listing.

PONTIAC
79008 **Fiero** all models '84 thru '88
79018 **Firebird** V8 models except Turbo '70 thru '81
79019 **Firebird** all models '82 thru '92
79025 **G6** all models '05 thru '09
79040 **Mid-size Rear-wheel Drive** '70 thru '87
Vibe '03 thru '11 - see TOYOTA Matrix (92060)
For other PONTIAC titles, see BUICK, CHEVROLET or GENERAL MOTORS listing.

PORSCHE
80020 **911** except Turbo & Carrera 4 '65 '89
80025 **914** all 4 cyl models '69 thru '76
80030 **924** all models including Turbo '76 thru '82
80035 **944** all models including Turbo '83 thru '89

RENAULT
Alliance & Encore - see AMC (14020)

SAAB
84010 **900** all models including Turbo '79 thru '88

SATURN
87010 **Saturn** all S-series models '91 thru '02
87011 **Saturn Ion** '03 thru '07
87020 **Saturn** all L-series models '00 thru '04
87040 **Saturn VUE** '02 thru '07

SUBARU
89002 **1100, 1300, 1400 & 1600** '71 thru '79
89003 **1600 & 1800** 2WD & 4WD '80 thru '94
89100 **Legacy** all models '90 thru '99
89101 **Legacy & Forester** '00 thru '06

SUZUKI
90010 **Samurai/Sidekick & Geo Tracker** '86 thru '01

TOYOTA
92005 **Camry** all models '83 thru '91
92006 **Camry** all models '92 thru '96
92007 **Camry, Avalon, Solara, Lexus ES 300** '97 thru '01
92008 **Toyota Camry, Avalon and Solara and Lexus ES 300/330** all models '02 thru '06
92009 **Camry** '07 thru '11
92015 **Celica Rear Wheel Drive** '71 thru '85
92020 **Celica Front Wheel Drive** '86 thru '99
92025 **Celica Supra** all models '79 thru '92
92030 **Corolla** all models '75 thru '79
92032 **Corolla** all rear wheel drive models '80 thru '87
92035 **Corolla** all front wheel drive models '84 thru '92
92036 **Corolla & Geo Prizm** '93 thru '02
92037 **Corolla** models '03 thru '11
92040 **Corolla Tercel** all models '80 thru '82
92045 **Corona** all models '74 thru '82
92050 **Cressida** all models '78 thru '82
92055 **Land Cruiser** FJ40, 43, 45, 55 '68 thru '82
92056 **Land Cruiser** FJ60, 62, 80, FZJ80 '80 thru '96
92060 **Matrix & Pontiac Vibe** '03 thru '11
92065 **MR2** all models '85 thru '87
92070 **Pick-up** all models '69 thru '78
92075 **Pick-up** all models '79 thru '95
92076 **Tacoma, 4Runner, & T100** '93 thru '04
92077 **Tacoma** all models '05 thru '09
92078 **Tundra** '00 thru '06 & **Sequoia** '01 thru '07
92079 **4Runner** all models '03 thru '09
92080 **Previa** all models '91 thru '95
92081 **Prius** all models '01 thru '08
92082 **RAV4** all models '96 thru '10
92085 **Tercel** all models '87 thru '94
92090 **Sienna** all models '98 thru '09
92095 **Highlander & Lexus RX-330** '99 thru '07

TRIUMPH
94007 **Spitfire** all models '62 thru '81
94010 **TR7** all models '75 thru '81

VW
96008 **Beetle & Karmann Ghia** '54 thru '79
96009 **New Beetle** '98 thru '11
96016 **Rabbit, Jetta, Scirocco & Pick-up** gas models '75 thru '92 & Convertible '80 thru '92
96017 **Golf, GTI & Jetta** '93 thru '98, **Cabrio** '95 thru '02
96018 **Golf, GTI, Jetta** '99 thru '05
96019 **Jetta, Rabbit, GTI & Golf** '05 thru '11
96020 **Rabbit, Jetta & Pick-up** diesel '77 thru '84
96023 **Passat** '98 thru '05, **Audi A4** '96 thru '01
96030 **Transporter 1600** all models '68 thru '79
96035 **Transporter 1700, 1800 & 2000** '72 thru '79
96040 **Type 3 1500 & 1600** all models '63 thru '73
96045 **Vanagon** all air-cooled models '80 thru '83

VOLVO
97010 **120, 130 Series & 1800 Sports** '61 thru '73
97015 **140 Series** all models '66 thru '74
97020 **240 Series** all models '76 thru '93
97040 **740 & 760 Series** all models '82 thru '88
97050 **850 Series** all models '93 thru '97

TECHBOOK MANUALS
10205 **Automotive Computer Codes**
10206 **OBD-II & Electronic Engine Management**
10210 **Automotive Emissions Control Manual**
10215 **Fuel Injection Manual** '78 thru '85
10220 **Fuel Injection Manual** '86 thru '99
10225 **Holley Carburetor Manual**
10230 **Rochester Carburetor Manual**
10240 **Weber/Zenith/Stromberg/SU Carburetors**
10305 **Chevrolet Engine Overhaul Manual**
10310 **Chrysler Engine Overhaul Manual**
10320 **Ford Engine Overhaul Manual**
10330 **GM and Ford Diesel Engine Repair Manual**
10333 **Engine Performance Manual**
10340 **Small Engine Repair Manual, 5 HP & Less**
10341 **Small Engine Repair Manual, 5.5 - 20 HP**
10345 **Suspension, Steering & Driveline Manual**
10355 **Ford Automatic Transmission Overhaul**
10360 **GM Automatic Transmission Overhaul**
10405 **Automotive Body Repair & Painting**
10410 **Automotive Brake Manual**
10411 **Automotive Anti-lock Brake (ABS) Systems**
10415 **Automotive Detaiing Manual**
10420 **Automotive Electrical Manual**
10425 **Automotive Heating & Air Conditioning**
10430 **Automotive Reference Manual & Dictionary**
10435 **Automotive Tools Manual**
10440 **Used Car Buying Guide**
10445 **Welding Manual**
10450 **ATV Basics**
10452 **Scooters 50cc to 250cc**

SPANISH MANUALS
98903 **Reparación de Carrocería & Pintura**
98904 **Manual de Carburador Modelos Holley & Rochester**
98905 **Códigos Automotrices de la Computadora**
98906 **OBD-II & Sistemas de Control Electrónico del Motor**
98910 **Frenos Automotriz**
98913 **Electricidad Automotriz**
98915 **Inyección de Combustible** '86 al '99
99040 **Chevrolet & GMC Camionetas** '67 al '87
99041 **Chevrolet & GMC Camionetas** '88 al '98
99042 **Chevrolet & GMC Camionetas Cerradas** '68 al '95
99043 **Chevrolet/GMC Camionetas** '94 al '04
99048 **Chevrolet/GMC Camionetas** '99 al '06
99055 **Dodge Caravan & Plymouth Voyager** '84 al '95
99075 **Ford Camionetas y Bronco** '80 al '94
99076 **Ford F-150** '97 al '09
99077 **Ford Camionetas Cerradas** '69 al '91
99088 **Ford Modelos de Tamaño Mediano** '75 al '86
99089 **Ford Camionetas Ranger** '93 al '10
99091 **Ford Taurus & Mercury Sable** '86 al '95
99095 **GM Modelos de Tamaño Grande** '70 al '90
99100 **GM Modelos de Tamaño Mediano** '70 al '88
99106 **Jeep Cherokee, Wagoneer & Comanche** '84 al '00
99110 **Nissan Camioneta** '80 al '96, **Pathfinder** '87 al '95
99118 **Nissan Sentra** '82 al '94
99125 **Toyota Camionetas y 4Runner** '79 al '95

Over 100 Haynes motorcycle manuals also available

7-12